THE MANAGEMENT OF TIME

THE MANAGEMENT OF TIME

The Art and Science of
Business Management

A. Dale Timpe

Series Editor

Facts On File Publications
New York, New York ● Oxford, England

This is volume two in Facts On File's series "The
Art and Science of Business Management," each
volume of which provides a broad selection of articles
on an important business topic of our time.

THE MANAGEMENT OF TIME

Library of Congress Cataloging-in-Publication Data

The management of time

    (The Art and science of business management)
    Bibliography: p.
    Includes index.
    1. Time management. I. Timpe, Dale. II. Series.
HD69.T54M36 1987   658.4'093   86-11511
ISBN 0-8160-1461-2

Printed in the United States of America

10 9 8 7 6 5 4 3 2 1

Composition by Facts On File/Maxwell Photographics Inc.

CONTENTS

PART III: TIMETABLING: PLANNING AND CONTROL

PART IV: THE PRIORITY PRINCIPLE

PART V: THE DELEGATION DILEMMA

PART VI: PROCRASTINATION: A SERIOUS TRANSGRESSION

PREFACE

Time is a unique commodity that is given equally to everyone regardless of age or station. Time always moves at a predetermined and constant rate, but no one ever seems to have enough time. Since we can't create more time, we must conserve the time allotted us.

All businesses carefully record their financial assets. However, these financial statements never mention one of the company's most vital and irreplaceable assets—time. Since it does not appear as an entry on the company's operating statements, time is taken for granted. Time management attitudes and practices are often casual and lax, almost an afterthought. If time is money, then it should be treated as a precious, nonrenewable resource. Time should receive the same intense monitoring that occurs with other assets.

The subject of time management provides the reader with fascinating insights into human traits and habits. Time management is generally perceived as being synonymous with neatness, organization and a very structured daily routine. These factors are all elements of greater efficiency. However, time management is more complex than that. It is a frame of mind. It is an attitude of personal commitment and, more importantly, a dramatic reordering of priorities and work habits.

Unless time is managed, nothing else can be managed. Most time management ideas are common sense but not common practice. Improved time management does increase productivity and overall performance. It can also improve morale as employees become more effective and more satisfied with the use of their time. Time management focuses on accountability. Many executives believe that their tasks are so varied that time management principles are useless to them. The assumption is that time management practices are more suited to repetitive production line tasks. Certainly the tasks required of the executive are heterogeneous in *content*, but the management *process* is actually quite repetitive. In today's competitive environment, managers who misuse their time are at a distinct disadvantage.

As the executive progresses up the corporate ladder, a transformation must occur: that is, from the process of doing to that of managing. Many find this a difficult challenge. The executive's additional responsibilities require a shift from the utilization of things to the utilization of people and things. Each promotion requires a greater degree of managing if the executive is to use his or her increasingly larger pool of human resources effectively. This process, and the resulting benefits, are generally understood by most executives. However, many resist full delegation, and, as a result, they fail to utilize their own time effectively.

The major objective of time management for the executive is to create more discretionary time, the only part of the day that the executive can control and really call his or her own. Discretionary time is necessary for conceptualizing, planning and creative problem solving. Time management does not provide solutions to management problems. It does, however, provide the discretionary time in which the manager can find those solutions, plan for the future, and assess overall progress.

This compendium is a comprehensive overview of the complexities of time management. The articles present a broad survey of practical knowledge, research and theory on the subject. The diversity of insights, experience and theoretical concepts offers managers a variety of approaches, applicable for both themselves and their subordinates, using their time more effectively. The sources represent a wide range of professional publications, including a number not readily available to most business managers.

For those wanting a more detailed discussion on a particular aspect of the problem, the bibliography provides a valuable resource tool.

A. Dale Timpe
Series Editor

ACKNOWLEDGMENTS

The articles presented in this volume are reprinted with permission of the respective copyright holders and all rights are reserved.

Alessandra, Tony and Jim Cathcart. "A Guide for Managing Time" by permission of *Marketing Communications*, © 1985.

Alexander, Larry D. "Effective Time Management Techniques" by permission of *Personnel Journal*, © 1981.

Baker, H. Kent, and Stevan Holmberg. "Stepping Up to Supervision: Managing Time and Job Pressures" from *Supervisory Management* by permission of AMACOM, a division of American Management Association, © 1981.

Baldwin, Bruce A. "The Art of Procrastination" from *Pace* by permission of Pace Communications, Inc., and Bruce A. Baldwin, © 1984.

Braid, Robert W. "Effective Use of Time" from *Supervisory Management* by permission of Periodicals Division, American Management Association, © 1983.

Burger, Chester. "How to Find Enough Time" from *Nation's Business* by permission of U.S. Chamber of Commerce, © 1974.

Buchanan, Robert D. "How to Effectively Delegate" from *Food Service Marketing* by permission of Robert D. Buchanan, © 1977.

Chambers, Larry G. "Instant Replay: It Works for Management, Too" by permission of the *Public Relations Journal*, © 1979.

Coleman, Linda Jane and Virginia Cavanagh Neri. "Successful Time-Management Techniques for Small Businesses" from *American Journal of Small Business* by permission of the University of Baltimore, © 1982.

Coulter, Borden M. and George E. Hayo. "Executive Time Management: How to Budget Your Time" from SAM *Advanced Management Journal* by permission of the Society for Advancement of Management, © 1978.

Douglass, Merrill E. "How to Conquer Procrastination" from SAM *Advanced Management Journal* by permission of the Society for Advancement of Management, © 1978.

Emanuel, Harold M. "Put Time on Your Side" from *Management World* by permission of the Administrative Management Society, © 1982.

Ferderber, Charles J. "Time: The Executive's Dilemma" from *Healthcare Financial Management* by permission of Hospital Financial Management Association, © 1980.

Forest, Robert B. "Time, Gentlemen, Time..." from *Infosystems* by permission of Hitchcock Publishing Company, © 1979.

Friend, William. "Put a Stop to Procrastination" from *Association Management* by permission of the American Society of Association Executives, © 1984

Gilsdorf, Jeanette W. and Martha H. Rader. "Time Management—But What About Your People?" from *Supervision* by permission of the National Research Bureau, Inc., © 1981.

Gordon, J. and Stephanie Winston. "Organization: The Means to Get You Where You Want to Go" from *Credit & Financial Management* by permission of the National Association of Credit Management, © 1985.

Growney, JoAnne S. "Planning for Interruptions: The Science of Managing Their Effect" from *Interface* by permission of the Institute of Management Science, © 1981.

Hellwig, Karl D. "Ten Steps Toward Successful Work Measurement" from *Management World* by permission of the Administrative Management Society, © 1976.

Hibbard, Janet G. and Robert K. Landrum. "How to Fight Time (and Win)" by permission of *Personnel Journal*, © 1978.

Hoffer, William. "How Do You Perceive Time?" from *Association Management* by permission of the American Society of Association Executives, © 1983.

Hurston, Clifford J., Jr. "How Often Do Executives Delegate Correspondence?" from *Management World* by permission of the Administrative Management Society, © 1978.

Hurston, Clifford J. Jr. "How to Improve Your 'Timing'" from *Management World* by permission of the Administrative Management Society, © 1981.

Jackson, John H. and Roger L. Hayen. "Rationing the Scarcest Resource: A Manager's Time" by permission of *Personnel Journal*, © 1974.

Kirkpatrick, Forrest H. "Have You Got the Time?" by permission of *Personnel Journal*, © 1975.

Klassen, Marlene. "How to Get the Most Out of Your Time" from *Supervision Magazine* by permission of The National Research Bureau, © 1983.

Labovitz, George H. and Lloyd S. Baird. "Managing Time: Positive Clock-Watching" from *SAM Advanced Management Journal* by permission of the Society for the Advancement of Management, © 1981.

Lane, Chris. "Beating Time to Meet Objectives" from *Personnel Management* by permission of Personnel Publications Limited, © 1980.

LeBoeuf, Michael. "Managing Time Means Managing Yourself" from *Business Horizons* by permission of Indiana University School of Business, © 1980.

Lee, John W. and Robert Adcock. "Time, One More Time" from *California Management Review* by permission of the Regents of the University of California, © 1971.

Mackenzie, R. Alec and Gary Richards. "Energy Crisis in the Executive Suite" from *Supervisory Management* by permission of R. Alec Mackenzie, © 1978.

Mackenzie, R. Alec, "Time Management: From Principles to Practice" from *Training and Development Journal* by permission of R. Alec Mackenzie, © 1978.

McCullough, Rose V. "Managing Your Minutes: How to Get a Grip on Your Time" from *Management World* by permission of the Administrative Management Society, © 1979.

McDougle, Larry G. "Time Management: Making Every Minute Count" from *Supervisory Management* by permission of AMACOM, a division of American Management Association, © 1979.

McMurry, Robert N. "What to Do About Executives Who Can't Delegate and Won't Decide" from *Nation's Business* by permission of U.S. Chamber of Commerce, © 1980.

Mead, Charles W. "Put Time on Your Side" from *Computer Decisions* by permission of Hayden Publishing Company, © 1983.

Miller, Dennis E. "Time: A Manager's Most Important Asset" from *Supervisory Management* by permission of the Periodicals Division, American Management Association, © 1983.

Mishra, Jitendra M. and Prabhakra Misra. "Time Management: Getting the Best Out of Your Time" from *Managerial Planning* by permission of Planning Executives Institute, © 1982.

Mitchell, Vance F. "Rx for Improving Staff Effectiveness" by permission of *Canadian Banker and ICB Review*, © 1983.

Office Administration and Automation. "Teleconferencing Systems in Action" from *Office Administration and Automation* by permission of Dalton Communications, Inc., © 1984.

Parker, Susan T. "How the Boys in the Office Mishandle Time" by permission of *Iron Age*, © 1982.

Raudsepp, Eugene. "Delegate Your Way to Success" from *Computer Decisions* by permission of Hayden Publishing Co., © 1981.

Rhodabarge, Dale. "Self-Management: Key to Managing Your Time" from *Computer Decisions* by permission of Hayden Publishing Co., © 1980.

Richards, G.W. and R. Alec Mackenzie. "When You Just Don't Have Time..." from *World Oil* by permission of Gulf Publishing Co. and R. Alec Mackenzie, © 1981.

Say, Jean-Baptiste Leon. "Parkinson's Law Revisited" from *Interface* by permission of the Institute of Management Science, © 1983.

Schilit, Warren. "A Manager's Guide to Efficient Time Management" by permission of *Personnel Journal*, © 1983.

Schilit, Warren. "Thinking About Managing Your Time" from *Managerial Planning* by permission of the Planning Executives Institute, © 1982.

Schilling, Charles W. "Time Planning: How to Divide Up Your Day" from *Supervision* by permission of The National Research Bureau, © 1980.

Sheppard, I. Thomas. "The Art of Delegating" from *Management World* by permission of the Administrative Management Society, © 1984.

Sheridan, John H. "Do More, Work Less" from *Industry Week* by permission of Penton/IPC Inc., © 1978.

Sinclair, J.M. "Evaluating Your Job the IE's Way" by permission of *Public Relations Journal,* © 1979.

Sondak, Arthur. "How Good a Time-Killer Are You?" from *Management Review* by permission of AMA Membership Publications Division, American Management Association, © 1982.

Sondak, Arthur. "The Multiplier Effect of Good Time Management" from *Supervisory Management* by permission of Periodicals Division, American Management Association, © 1985.

Stanton, G.B., Jr. "How to Control the Use of Staff Time" from *Research Management* by permission of G.B. Stanton, Jr., © 1977.

Steffen, R. James. "Time: How to Make a Little a Lot" from *Management World* by permission of the Adminstrative Management Society, © 1982.

Strenski, James B. "Time Management" by permission of *Public Relations Journal,* © 1979.

Tyson, John. "Video Teleconferencing Cuts Costs, Boosts Productivity" from *Management Review* by permission of AMA Publications Division, a division of the American Management Association, © 1986.

Weiss, Henry. "The Computer As Time Manager" from *Personal Computing* by permission of Hayden Publishing Company, © 1984.

Wilkinson, William R. "Don't Spend Time—Invest It" from *Michigan Business Review* by permission of Division of Research, Graduate School of Business Administration, The University of Michigan, © 1974.

Part I
TIME MANAGEMENT: THEORIES AND PERCEPTIONS

1.
DON'T SPEND TIME—INVEST IT

William R. Wilkinson

Stop spending time. Begin to manage and invest it. It could be the best investment you will ever make for yourself and your company.

Few among us in management could stand the glare of a time-study without blushing at the results. We waste time; we fritter away precious hours chasing the wrong things at the wrong time; we do other people's work for them, and we finish up exhausted yet put up a brave front which only strains ourselves, our families and our health.

If you doubt this, let me ask a few questions about yesterday:

1. What were the three outstanding problems you tackled? Were they truly *your* problems at *your* level of business—or should they have been handled by someone else?
2. Take any one of these problems. Did you solve it "for keeps?" Did you put a tracer on it to get to the root of it and establish the real underlying cause of it—or did you merely solve what you saw on the surface?
3. How many pieces of paper did you sign "as a rubber stamp"—and did you ask yourself if your signature truly meant anything or should that signline have been altered to save your time and be more meaningful?
4. Did your secretary act as a business partner or as your servant?
5. Did you react more than act?
6. How much backtracking did you do—tracing (somebody else's mistakes, for instance) versus preventing next year's problems?

To be really efficient as a manager we must get things done—mostly *tomorrow's* things—smoothly, without wear and tear, and with the smallest expenditure of energy. "Work" is *not* an objective in itself; it is usually a psychological malady. An efficient person uses facts, skill, thought and imagination.

He also uses time.

Unlike energy, money and skill, time never returns nor can it be recreated. Once it's gone it's gone. For this reason it is the most relentless and possibly the most precious of all the commodities used in business. Yet for some strange reason it is too often treated like so much trash.

Time is something to be *invested*, not spent. And the manager's time is very valuable indeed. The higher the manager, the higher the investment for his organization. And like most important factors in business, this investment can be made more efficient in small ways day by day because time *is* an hour-by-hour, day-by-day investment.

Managers in business and industry can learn a great deal from people in other professions. For example, doctors learned years ago to maximize the use of their time by organizing duty rotas for night work with other doctors in their area. Policemen in the United Kingdom have learned how to relieve valuable patrolmen from schoolcrossing duties by the allocation of this work to retired men and women called "Lollipop people." Nurses in hospitals save valuable time in countless ways in their strict procedures and practices *before* an operation; not a minute is lost.

Here are a few time-savers and efficiency-starters that will help a manager to get more out of his business day and less out of himself.

LEARN THE *LANGUAGE* OF ON-THE-JOB TRAINING

How many times have you thought, "By the time I've explained what's needed, I could do the job myself in half the time." And, of course, you *know* that's the kiss of death for training, delegation and intelligent planning.

Count up the number of small jobs you do each day, jobs that could really be done by one of your people. Count up the number of assignments you undertake yourself, assignments that would be challenges to some of your subordinates. Count up the number of opportunities there are in your daily function for the training and developing of some of your people—and you will see that "doing it yourself" defeats everything. It defeats the aim of having a balanced workload; it defeats the whole idea of delegated work, and it defeats the essential and constant necessity for training our people. Shoulders never develop if they are given no opportunity for exercise. Learn the *language* of on-the-job training. It will save you *years* of time later.

YOUR SECRETARY IS YOUR BUSINESS PARTNER

Few of us who have the good fortune to have a secretary use her properly. One way or another, good secretaries tend to develop themselves by their own initiative. As one girl put it to me, "Almost every fresh responsibility I've taken on has been done *in the face* of my boss's reluctance to let me handle it."

This is all wrong. We tend to think that secretaries need no training or formal guidance and that they take up their duties as ready-made, competent people who know just what they're supposed to do. The very reverse is often the case.

Have your secretary see visitors, evaluate the importance of their business, give you an assessment. Those visitors who call without an appointment could possibly be handled by the secretary, herself.

Why should you dictate every letter yourself? Let your secretary compose and type some of the letters; she should know a great deal about many of the problems, sufficient to allow her to frame a suitable reply. She may do it better than you.

Your secretary should be gradually trained to be a sort of "deputy" to you. The things she cannot handle in your absence should be countable. Throw her "off the deep end" occasionally. If you don't, you have no complaint if you get only what you ask for, and if you waste your own time as a result.

THE TELEPHONE

The telephone is a funny instrument. It has some peculiarities that few of us think about. For years we have been giving it credit as a time-saving, efficient means of communication. So much credit do we give it that we forget some of its drawbacks.

One of the funny things about the telephone is its tendency to encourage schizophrenia; it can actually cause the psychological disorder of splitting personalities. The man you speak to on the telephone is sometimes a different personality from the man you know is behind the phone. And the reason for this is a simple one: A person's amplified voice and a person's face-to-face communication give two different impressions to the listener.

Now what does this mean in everyday business communication? Nine times out of ten—nothing. But on the tenth occasion—when the conversation runs into the possibility of ruffled tempers, when the subject is a delicate one, when there is a danger of healthy relationships being damaged to the detriment of the company's work—that is the time to think twice about using the telephone. Telephones should seldom be used to discuss sensitive subjects such as work performance problems and personal problems.

There are other occasions, too, when a face-to-face conversation is much better than one by telephone. For instance, if you know beforehand that the subject you are going to discuss may develop heatedly or that the person you are addressing feels strongly because you know he has a habit of bawling aggressively into a telephone—that is the time *not* to use the telephone. Sometimes quiet, timid men become dragons behind the screen of a telephone, giving a totally false tone to the conversation. A bad telephone discussion could cost you hours of time later unscrambling the misunderstanding.

TRAIN TO THE POINT OF NO RETURN

When one of your people makes a mistake or exercises bad judgment or fouls up some assignment, what do you do? Do you belabor it? Ignore it and hope he won't repeat the behavior? Mark it against him? Minimize it?

You would be right, of course, to say, "Well, it all depends on the type of mistake and the type of person."

There is, however, one common opportunity running through all mistakes: the opportunity to learn from them. And learning from mistakes involves action; it involves *saying* something which will help dispatch that type of error "to the point of no return." No mistake large or small should be repeated in a business operation—that is the ideal situation to which all management should strive. And one way of getting along that road is by using mistakes to train people. "Now let's see what we can learn from this, Charlie" is a good prologue to a healthy discussion that trains rather than rebukes. "Inventing the wheel" all over again may be the most time-consuming disease we have in business today.

DON'T RUSH MEETINGS

Be firm about your appointments. Don't take on more than you can cope with reasonably. If you have a meeting scheduled for ten o'clock, don't accept another one for 9:30 in the *vague* hope that the business to be discussed could be disposed of in just half an hour; be sure that it can really be disposed of in that time and won't require time-consuming meetings to wrap up loose ends.

Very often, claimants on your time are very pressing and, in a weak moment, you may imprudently accede to their pressure. Resist it. If a subject is worth discussing, it is worth discussing well, in good order, within proper boundaries of time. Rushing from meeting to meeting produces harassed personalities, grasshopper minds, faulty judgment, hasty decisions—and possibly ruined health.

THE PAPER DAM

Ask yourself this:

1. How many sheets of paper arrive by mail each day into a company or department?
2. How many carbon copies of letters are generated each day in a company or department?
3. How many letters are generated each day for internal reading?
4. How many sheets of these papers ever reach final disposal?

What does this tell us? Doesn't it say that a company is a *dam* for sheets of paper? Ninety percent comes in—ten percent goes out.

Paper uses clerical labor. Paper has to be read, sorted, filed and stored. Paper—the mere handling of paper—is one of the costliest overheads in the operation of business today. Simply storing it involves expensive office furniture that is used for nothing else.

Now ask yourself this: If you went through your own office files to decide what pieces of paper are truly essential and should be retained, what percentage would you find? Without doubt, most of us read pieces of paper every day, initial them and put them out for filing whereas we should be putting them out! We are inclined to use our files as waste-folders. Filing cabinets become refined garbage cans.

There is only one way to remedy this and to reduce the level of the "dam" to reasonable proportions: Destroy those pieces of paper which we know we will not require again. This involves risk, of course, and it also involves judgment. But some risk and some judgment is better than a mountain of paper work that is already out of date and non-functional, doing nothing productive, saying nothing pertinent and recording nothing valid.

A senior manager once estimated that in an eight-hour business day, a piece of paper went across his desk for consideration or signature every three minutes.

One of the peculiar things about the flow of paper on our desks is that it *always* increases. It never decreases.

The whole trick in getting paper cut back to a manageable level is to pounce on a whole batch now and then and analyze it. These are the kinds of things you may find:

1. "Automatic" pieces that don't really require your attention; one of your own people can quite easily deal with them. Delegate it.

2. Bills may appear for your O.K. before one of your people has checked the items. Tell your secretary to reverse this procedure.

3. Carbon copies of other managers' correspondence telling you little, inviting no action and wasting your time. Get off these "automatic" mailing lists.

4. Business journals you never read anyway. Stop your subscription or transfer it to someone who can benefit from it.

5. Appeals for charity, personal or corporate. Get them to the right source of attention permanently. Does your organization have a Contributions Committee?

6. Advertising literature and sales appeals that have been sent to you by another department in the vague hope that you might be interested. Get a closer "sorting out" done of this material before it reaches you. Ask your secretary to use her judgment first, before the paper reaches you.

Stop spending time. Begin to manage and invest it. It could be the best investment you will ever make for yourself and your company.

William R. Wilkinson has established an international reputation in the field of personnel management. His articles and papers on management have appeared in the business periodicals of ten countries; a book on modern management techniques was published in Germany in 1971.

2.
TIME MANAGEMENT: GETTING THE BEST OUT OF YOUR TIME

Jitendra M. Mishra
Prabhakra Misra

You have to be in control of your life if you are to manage your time effectively. The well-organized life leaves time for everything, for planning, doing and following through. Time is not used up in regretting, or in trying to live life retroactively, or in explaining why something needed has not been done.

Time is a unique resource. Time cannot be saved; it can only be spent wisely. Time past is gone forever. Time is irreplaceable and inelastic. Time is the most valuable resource available to a person. Time is also irreversible.

Time is equal for everyone. Everyone has 24 hours a day, seven days a week, and 52 weeks a year available to them. The amount of time is not important but rather how that time is managed. Time can be managed effectively in the future only by planning today. It is a personal choice of how we use our time—to randomly move from one task to another without direction or planning, or to plan our day's activities, which will result in more productive use of time and the ability to accomplish much more in the same amount of time.

The area of time management is rapidly becoming more important in both the private lives of individuals and in the corporate structure, especially pertaining to managers, from top administrators to first-line supervisors. Good management of time is beneficial in terms of both cost savings for projects and also the use of an organization's most valuable resource—people. In the words of Peter F. Drucker, "Time is the scarcest resource and unless it is managed nothing else can be managed."[1]

The purpose of this paper is to examine the human aspects of changing attitudes toward a better managing of the valuable resource of time. *The object of time management is to increase and optimize the use of your discretionary time.*

There is a multitude of "systems" aspects which also can be implemented to improve the quality of time use. Examples of these systems are: what type of

desk you use, how to set up a good filing system, how to set up a good information retrieval system, and a host of other time and work-saving devices. These
systems, however, must be set up according to the purpose and type of organization and the individuals who use them.

But far more important than any gadget or system is the recognition of the
importance of good time management and the goals and objectives that can be
reached by both the individual and the organization.

The authors' research of the topics of time management has resulted in the
conclusion that there exist five major areas which are imperative to improving
the management of time. First, the realization that the way we spend our time
is largely habitual in nature; second, that setting personal goals is crucial to
proper time management; third, priorities must be categorized and evaluated;
fourth, proper communications are essential to good use of time; fifth,
procrastination is probably the largest obstacle to time management. Each of
these five premises will be examined in the article.

THE HABITUAL USE OF TIME

Man is indeed a creature of habit. The way we spend our time is largely
habitual. Most people do not really consciously think about how they are
spending their time. Time management expert Merrill E. Douglass says about
habitual time use:

> The way you spend your time determines how you live your life—and that is who
> you are. Tomorrow is connected to today just the same as today was connected to
> yesterday.[2]

Douglass challenges his readers to think about how they spend their time
now. "Learning to control your time means changing some of your time habits.
But you can't change time habits until you first know what those habits are."
Douglass suggests keeping a record of how you spend your time for a week or
two, or more if necessary. Record whatever you do as you do it so as not to forget
anything. At the end of each week, summarize what you did and check
percentages of time spent on each activity. Next, check how much of this time
was actually spent on goal-oriented, prioritized activity and how much activity
was aimless, repetitive, of low priority.

Another authority on time management is Harry C. Rotenbury, manager of
installation systems with the Insurance Company of North America. Mr.
Rotenbury also prescribes the use of a "time log" to combat the habitual wasting
of time. He recommends, in addition to logging activities, writing down the
specific reason in relationship to corporate or personal objectives.

Summarizing the log will give you a good idea as to whether you are controlling your own time or your time is being controlled by outside influences or
habit.[3]

Writing in another article on time management, Mr. Rotenbury uses a model by Norris/Gottfried to show a breakdown of how a manager should spend an average day:

> Pay-Off Time—50% of average day. This is the time a manager is operating within his own technical expertise. This time includes: decisions of immediate benefit, delegation time, problem solving, correspondence and decision making.
> Investment Time—25% of average day. Determining long-range programs, planning and developing alternate solutions are examples of investment time.
> Organization Time—15% of average day. This time is for the administrative tasks: reports, conferences and executive meetings.
> Wasted Time—10% of average day. This time includes nonproductive activities, unplanned problems and the like.[4]

The value of recording, analyzing and updating a system of keeping track of how time is spent cannot be over-emphasized. According to Merrill Douglass, almost everyone wastes at least two hours of time each day.[5] Analyzing how you spend your time will leave you with more discretionary time, which is the only time you really control. Make a list of things that must be done. What was left on today's list should be transferred to tomorrow's list unless it is too late or so unimportant that it can be delegated from the new list. Don't keep lists for several days; they are made to be rewritten, crossed out and torn up. In short, make lists, a new one every day, and try to group similar tasks.

GOAL SETTING

After making an analysis of how we are presently spending our time, it should be evident as to how our lives are balanced in relationship to the various aspects which comprise our lives. These aspects include career, family, social and personal development, and spiritual goals. Merrill Douglass, on goals, states:

> Most of us don't think about goals very much. We just respond or react to pressures from other people or things. If you want to control your own time and life, then you must decide what your goals will be. No one can do this for you. And since we tend to find what we look for, it is important to be pursuing the right personal goals.[6]

Plan your time by setting goals, goals about what you want to do, divided into long-term and short-term objectives. Determine the time you plan to devote to each of the goals you set. This involves a game plan for your day as well as lifetime goals.

During your day, emphasize two or three major things you would like to accomplish instead of doing bits and pieces of everything. Your goals should be specific, sub-divided into concrete objectives, as well as realistically attainable.

Once your goals are established, you need to set priorities. Rate your goals as to how important they are. After you use a priority system on your goals and objectives, you must concentrate on doing those most important to you. A good rule to remember is Pareto's Principle. "If all items are arranged in order of value, eighty percent of the value would come from only twenty percent of the items, while the remaining twenty percent of the value would come from eighty percent of the items."[7] To become more effective and satisfied with the use of your time, learn to concentrate on the 20 percent activities with the high value. This 20 percent will usually represent the best use of your time.

Goals should become a very integral part of life. Besides being a tool for better time management, goals can have a secondary effect on reducing stress in our daily lives. By setting goals in the areas of our business life and personal life, we can gain a better idea of who we are and where we are going.

PRIORITIES

The process of setting priorities involves planning. Professors Hibbard and Landrum have this to say about planning:

> Even though planning does consume time on the front end, it overcompensates both by bringing in better results and by saving time in actual performance of activities. So take time to plan. Do not engage in crisis management. In order to properly plan and determine priorities, use either end of each day to set daily goals, ranking them by their importance.[8]

The authors feel that priorities should be set on a daily basis. Write down all the things you plan to do tomorrow and then rate them by importance: "A", "B" or "C". Start with the "A" priorities so that you are spending your time on the most important things first. Develop the habit of planning each day. Write out your goals and plans on a *daily list* and then follow it. This is a very quick way to gain more control of your time. Actually, you are analyzing the way you use your time before the act—when you can still change it. Daily planning of sub-goals is essential to good time management. To make the planning of daily goals effective, *priorities must be established.*

By scheduling your time effectively through prioritizing, you learn to avoid over-committing yourself. Learning when and how to say "no" becomes important because your overcommitment dilutes your effectiveness. Inability to concentrate on important goals is often due to devoting a little time to everything rather than committing a great deal of time to a few things. Setting priorities forces you to delegate responsibility to others because you must make best use of prime time. In fact, don't do anything that can be delegated to someone else. Don't work yourself on low-priority items.

More can be done in the time you have by effective scheduling. *The first step is to set aside some time each day for thinking, reflecting and planning.* It should be a quiet time to organize your thoughts. This is most important. A "quiet hour" insures time to think and plan. The quiet hour is not a completely new idea. Effective managers from time to time close their doors and have their secretary or the switchboard operator take calls to provide a period of uninterrupted concentration.[9] All of us have a prime time, that hour or two each day when we can think creatively and work with peak efficiency. For some, this is early morning, while for others it is late at night. This is the time to use for preparing a talk, writing a paper, or catching up quickly if you have fallen behind. The most effective managers are able to make their discretionary time occur during these peak hours. Those who hate sunrise and work better better at night can "sign out." Others can start early, to avoid interruptions. In short, you should use prime time for important tasks, thinking and planning.

By analyzing time use, by setting goals and priorities, you become organized; you overcome a major obstacle to the efficient running of an office, business or home. By being better organized in the office or at home you have clearer insight as to what is the more important job that needs action first. Countless numbers of hours are wasted every day by the disorganization visible in most offices. This is most obviously exemplified by the appearance of a person's desk.

A desk should be a tool for the person who needs it to accomplish his work rather than a storage cabinet for any junk that may collect. Your desk should be functional, not just nice to look at. The drawers of the desk should be used as a temporary storage of things that are constantly needed to perform your work. If you don't need drawers in your desk, don't get them. They can provide places for clutter to build.

After you have found the correct desk, it should be organized. You should be able to see the top of your desk at all times. You can only work on one thing at a time. Everything else should be put in its proper place so it can easily be retrieved when needed. A cluttered desk can distract you and ruin your concentration on the project you should be working on. To be really effective at your desk, clear off all the accumulated material. Don't do this by putting it all in one drawer. This only postpones the problem. Set up a priority system for what goes into the desk drawers. Consider throwing out things if you can't think of anything else to do with them.

The files should also be organized so that they can provide fast retrieval of information instead of becoming obstacle courses. They should be well labeled and organized in a simple arrangement to ensure only a few seconds spent on finding filed material. Files should be arranged into active, inactive and discard categories. Only the active files should be stored near your desk. Get rid of the discards and move the inactives to lower cost spaces. Once this is done, continue to keep the files up to date.

The next step in organizing is the paperwork. There are only three kinds of paper: things requiring action, things to be read and passed on or filed, and things which can be thrown out. Separate your paperwork into these categories and then analyze each. First, don't set aside any item requiring action until some action has been initiated. Do some quick reading in the second category and divide it into items to be passed on and items to be filed. And finally, place the third category in the wastebasket. Continue to follow this pattern each day and keep the paper moving. You only want to handle paper once.

Organizing a desk and the method of handling paperwork is an example of basic priorities in any type of operation. The process of setting priorities insures that such basic necessities for running an office or business are not ignored or discounted.

COMMUNICATION

Once habits have been analyzed, goals identified and priorities decided, this does not mean that an organization or business will then automatically use its working hours in the most efficient way possible. There is still the matter of communicating these goals and objectives to subordinates in such a way that what is planned is actually carried out. In fact, communication becomes management's tool for unifying an organization's activities whereby corporate goals are achieved.[10] It is crucial to determine how effectively this tool is operating before relying on it. In one study 74 percent of the managers sampled from companies in the United States, Great Britain and Japan said that the single greatest barrier to corporate excellence was communication breakdown.[11] It is said that communication is to the organization what blood is to the body—without which both will die.

Effective communication will achieve clarity, understanding, commitment and creativity.[12] For clarity and understanding to take place, the vertical channels of communication must be open. Subordinates have a right to know what is expected of them by their supervisors. They must be given relevant information, promptly, concisely and directly. Not only must there be downward communication, there must also be upward communication, from subordinate to supervisor. This can be encouraged by the supervisor through actively seeking feedback; by requesting, recognizing, and giving credit to ideas presented; by being flexible in accommodating improvements suggested by subordinates. This will lead to commitment and creativity on the part of the subordinate; and where there are committed, creative people, time management is not likely to be a problem.[13]

A constant, efficient communication network is necessary in order for subordinates to understand the organization's needs and goals. A climate of open communication improves the chances for high productivity and job satisfaction, which leads to achievement of individual and organized goals.

PROCRASTINATION

All the planning possible can be done. A statement of goals and priorities can be written. An analysis of how time is presently being spent and a program instituted to correct the deficiencies can be implemented. But all of this is to no avail if it is not put into action. This failure to act is called procrastination. Most time wasted is wasted by us, not by others! So as you try to get control over your time, you must begin to get the distasteful tasks out of the way early.

Procrastination is a major stumbling block for almost everyone seeking to improve his use of time. There are three causes which lead to procrastination: 1) unpleasantness, 2) difficult projects and 3) indecision.

For most people, unpleasantness is the greatest single cause of procrastination. We tend to put things off because they are unpleasant to do. In other words, we don't get any satisfaction in doing this particular activity. Postponing unpleasant tasks which need to be done eventually just makes the job more unpleasant. One solution lies in how the day's activities are scheduled. Those tasks which you find most unpleasant and keep putting off should be scheduled first. That way you can quickly get them out of the way, leaving you free to concentrate on the rest of the day's work. The feeling of satisfaction received from completing a dreaded, unpleasant task will serve as reinforcement for completing the other scheduled assignments. When these tasks are done, your mind is free to move on other topics—you no longer have to worry about doing unpleasant tasks—and very often, if attacked head on, unpleasant tasks are not as bad as you may have feared.

Other ways of dealing with unpleasant tasks are: analyzing the task to see what makes it unpleasant; tackling unpleasant tasks in small pieces, doing the task for five or ten minutes at at time; learning to recognize your few critical activities and focus your attention on doing those things first. Harry Rotenbury recommends: "Set a deadline for every goal. There is no better way to speed performances."[14]

The second cause of procrastination, difficulty, calls for an approach of breaking down the difficult task into smaller units and focusing on one part at a time. This can be accomplished by either breaking down units by content or by time to be spent on each sub-unit. This method will result in making a very complex task into a series of simpler ones. This will give us a better perspective on where to start. Once a task is started it will be easier to fit in the pieces. Quite often we avoid difficult tasks because we simply don't know where to start.

The third cause of procrastination is indecision. Everyone wants to make the right decision so as to avoid unsatisfactory results. The best thing to do is gather all the information available, make the decision, and then move on from there. Above all, don't keep fretting and fussing or rehashing the problem. If something goes wrong with your decision, you can deal with it when the problem arises.

sion, scholars in the field give two ideas on how to keep from
ng. First is to clarify your objectives, make sure that what we think
o is what we really want to do. The second recommendation is to
abit of planning each day. Write down the particulars of what you
want to accomplish each day, then do them beginning with the most important
things first. In the end, procrastination, like any problem, can be overcome by
positive action.

CONCLUSION

You have to be in control of your life if you are to manage your time effectively. "The well-organized life leaves time for everything, for planning, doing
and follow through. Time is not used up in regretting or in trying to live life
retroactively, or in explaining why something needed has not been done."[15]

Learn to use good time management practices to improve your use of time.
"The real point of managing your time effectively is to carve out as satisfying
and rich a life as you possibly can."[16] You can control your time and your life.
You will accomplish more and have more satisfaction from what you are doing.
As your feelings of achievement, satisfaction and fulfillment increase, so does
the quality of your life. Your time is your life. "Time is life, life is time; you
waste your time, you waste your life; you control your time, you are in control of
your life."[17]

TEN HINTS FOR EFFECTIVE TIME MANAGEMENT

- Make lists of things to be done, a new one every day.
- Use "quiet hour/prime time" for thinking, planning and doing important
  tasks.
- Group similar tasks.
- Set goals—long term and short term—and set deadlines for every goal.
- Set priorities on a daily basis. Rank tasks in order of priority and im-
  portance.
- Do the important tasks; delegate the urgent and not so urgent. Avoid
  overcommitting yourself. Don't work yourself on low priority items.
- Organize the paperwork: things requiring action, things to be read and
  passed on or filed, or things that can be thrown out.
- Avoid procrastination.
- Do unpleasant, distasteful or dreaded tasks first.
- Recognize when you are wasting time—and take appropriate
  action.

References

1. Peter F. Drucker, "How to Be an Effective Executive," *Nation's Business* (April 1961), pp. 34-35, 44, 48.
2. Merrill E. Douglass, "Creative Use of Time," *The Personnel Administrator* (October 1975).
3. Harry C. Rotenbury, "The Time Log." *Management World* (July 1979), p. 21.
4. Harry C. Rotenbury, "Time Management and Scheduling," *Management World* (May 1979), p. 24.
5. Douglass, op. cit., p. 63.
6. Douglass, loc. cit., p. 63.
7. Pareto's Principle, or the 80/20 rule.
8. Janet G. Hibbard and Robert K. Landrum, "How to Fight Time and Win," *Personnel Journal* (May 1978), p. 256.
9. R. Alec Mackenzie and Dennis le Kau, "Take a Quiet Hour . . . For Time to Think and Plan," *American Society for Training Directors* (June 1977).
10. Harry C. Rotenbury, "Time Management and Communication," *Management World* (September 1978), p. 28.
11. R.R. Blake and Jane S. Morton, *Corporate Excellence Through Grid Development* (Houston, Tex.: Gulf Publishing Co., 1968), p. 4.
12. Jay Hall, "Communication Revisited," *California Management Review* (Vol. XV, No. 3), pp. 30-48.
13. Larry G. McDougle, "Time Management: Making Every Minute Count," *Supervisory Management* (August 1979), p. 40.
14. Harry C. Rotenbury, "Time Management and Scheduling," *Management World* (May 1979), p. 24.
15. "Why Procrastinate?", *The Royal Bank of Canada Monthly Letter* (Vol. 40, No. 9) p. 52.
16. Bensahel, Jane G., "Getting the Best Out of Your Time," *International Management* (June 1979), p. 60.
17. Porter, W. Thomas, Jr., "Time and Self-Management," *Journal of Accountancy* (June 1978), p. 58.

Jitendra M. Mishra is professor of management, Seidman College of Business and Administration, Grand Valley State College, Allendale, Michigan. He has been widely published and has served as consultant to many organizations. Prabhakra Misra is the dean of the Indian Photo-Interpretation Institute, Dehra Dun, India. He holds a BS and BE from India and an MS and MBA from Ohio State.

3.

ORGANIZATION: THE MEANS TO GET YOU WHERE YOU WANT TO GO:
An Interview with Stephanie Winston

J. Gordon

"Most time management material I've read suggests you keep track of your time each day in a log basis. This would show most people that they are disorganized, which they already know."

The average executive can usually manage to do 40 hours of work in a 50 hour work week. Simple subtraction will tell you that this is no formidable feat. Then why is it that leaving the office at 5:00 p.m. is an occasion to rejoice for so many executives? The greatest complaint of the modern manager may be time privation caused by inefficient time management. And a temporary ailment may cause long-term setbacks. In the following interview, Stephanie Winston gives some remedies for an ailing schedule.

Q: How does a business executive or manager go about becoming organized?
A: That's a very broad question. Maybe I could break it down a little bit. Organizing, as I define it, has three basic areas: management of time, management of paper and management of people.

Your paper you have total control over, even though it does seem like your papers are reproducing on your desk at night. Time management is a little more tricky because there are aspects of time management that you really can't control, while there are other aspects that you really have to manage rather than control. And when you're working with people then you're getting into the most tricky area because if you have direct subordinates it becomes a question of control and it takes on proportionately greater importance. So first of all you have to identify the areas in which you want to get more organized. Then you have to break this down into concrete questions or problems that you want to solve.

Q: Would you describe your system of paper management?

A: There are only four things you can do with a piece of paper. The problem of paper handling is not neatness as many people think it is. Neatness doesn't signify anything. The real problem with paper is a problem of decision-making. What tends to happen is that a piece of paper comes in through the mail or whatever, and a person looks at it and says "I don't know what to do about this," and puts it to the side of his desk in what I call the Scarlett O'Hara syndrome, meaning "I'll think about it tomorrow." And then tomorrow and tomorrow and tomorrow comes and you've got a huge stack of papers and then you really are in trouble.

So your first action with papers is the decision—making process of what to do with them physically, or how to sort them. There are four things you can do: *throw it away; refer* it to somebody else if it falls more in their area of competence and expertise or if you want to delegate it to them (any involvement of a second party constitutes referral); you can take *action* because you have to act on it yourself personally; and you can *file* something to be kept for future reference. These four things create an abbreviation that I call TRAF which stands for Toss, Refer, Act, File.

Your first act in dealing with paper is to physically put papers in their appropriate receptacles. For toss, it's obviously the wastebasket. For a referral, if you have an out box just write a note and put it in the out box where it will be picked up and distributed. Another way is if you have two or three or four people you deal with on a regular basis, your boss, your assistant, colleagues whom you're always in touch with, you might have individual manila folders for them. Then if you think, "Oh yes, I want to speak to Suzy about this," you drop it into Suzy's folder and the next time you see Suzy coming down the road, whether you have a meeting or you pass each other on the fly, you whip out your Suzy folder and say, "Do you have a minute, there are some things I want to talk to you about," and you have an instant agenda.

For action stuff, a person who is "neat by temperament" will have a specific place to put these papers. For example, this fat folder, which is a little beat up, is nonetheless my action folder and I do keep all my stuff there until I actually start working on it. Somebody else might just fling action papers all over the side of the desk, which does give it a messy look, but is still perfectly well organized because there is logic and coherence to it.

Finally filing. People who have a secretary might normally put things into the out box for the secretary to file in the office file, but I recommend that people do their own filing in their personal deskside files.

Q: A major function of the credit department is to produce reports for top management. What is the best way to go about organizing an outgoing report so it gets vital information across to the reader?

A: Well, the type of reports I normally advise on are fairly extensive written reports. Reports like that, for example, in a corporation that wants to analyze monthly sales figures or aging figures and come up with some kind of interpretation of what they mean for future behavior. And these reports can sometimes become very long.

What I would do in that case is recommend that a report be structured in three parts: a top page, one single page that would summarize the body of the report, and the conclusions and recommendations, because some people may not have to read any more than that. Then a mid—portion that would be a more extensive discussion of the different factors. Then if there is raw data that would be in the form of a computer printout, or however the company produces this material, then that would be the third part. But in general, I always recommend that the conclusion of a report be summarized so that it can be viewed without a whole lot of dredging around.

Q: Would a business person interested in gaining better control over his or her time begin to organize time by preparing logs and lists summarizing daily activities?

A: No, actually I'm basically not in favor of logs. Most time management material I've read suggests you keep track of your time each day on a log basis. This would show most people that they are disorganized, which they already know.

Most cases of disorganization are fairly straightforward and it doesn't give you any particular value to log in your time on any regular 15 minute basis while you are in a disorganized state. What you have to assume is that the basic techniques of paper and time management are being put into play.

A lot of people who are disorganized or want to be organized have a tendency to make lists, a lot of lists, using scraps of paper, the back of an envelope or whatever is available. My recommendation on lists is that you establish two. One I call the Master List is kept in a single spiral looseleaf notebook that you carry with you all the time. As every assignment or task or project comes up you write it down. You can have a lot of items on your Master List, hundreds conceivably, but this would be more than most people could deal with; they would find it very intimidating. The way to get around this is that each day you pull a few items out and rewrite them on what I call the Daily List, which is simply a list of some six to ten, depending on what your schedule is, tasks to do that day.

In other words, your Master List serves the function of sort of a reservoir from which you pull out your day-to-day activities. Another important point is that you shouldn't have more than two or three high priority things in one day; it is one thing that leads to executive burnout.

Q: Have you ever had an experience when you recommended that a client make these lists, and had them come back and say, I can't deal with taking the time to keep them?

A: Well, yes and no. By the time a client comes to me, they are usually in fairly bad shape and are really anxious to do what has to be done. There are a lot of different ways you can do it in principle.

For example, I have one client who carries a little personal tape recorder with him all the time, and when he has a thing to do he talks on a tape and has his secretary transcribe it onto a list he keeps on green paper to distinquish it, and that in effect is his Master List. If you are going to be organized, that is an act of will and some kind of list does have to be kept in some manner or means.

Q: Once you've prepared a Daily List and figured out exactly what you want to accomplish that day, how do you avoid interruptions?

A: Well actually, I think a lot of people, in a way, intimidate themselves with interruptions because they think in terms of trying to protect the whole day from interruptions and you really can't do that. Even for people who are really senior who could theoretically do so since they have the authority to do so, I never recommend it. It's a very dangerous thing to do because you're out of touch with what's going on. I would turn it around and say your goal is to protect from interruptions only an hour or two hours of your time during the day, with two hours as a maximum.

There are several interruption techniques you can use. If you do have a secretary or assistant or receptionist, get them to screen more. I think people don't screen enough. If you don't have a secretary, you can switch off with a colleague. You ask your colleague to take your phone calls for an hour or an hour and a half and in exchange you do it for him or her later in the day. Another method some people use is leaving the premises. A person will come in at 8:30 or 9:00, and make their presence known, and slip out again. I know somebody in New York City who goes to a coffee shop between 10:00 and 11:30. I know somebody else who goes to the public library. One thing I'm beginning to hear more about is people working part—time at home. The main point is that the only amount of time you try to really protect from inter-ruptions is this up to two hours. Beyond that I would treat the rest of the day much more flexibly.

Q: What if you're trying to protect your two hours in the office and the person who wants to interrupt you is your boss or a superior who wants to come to you with something?

A: Well, you have to use your judgment. In some cases it depends on who you are and what you do. If you're senior enough so that you don't have to account for your time to your boss, then that's the ideal time to actually not be on the premises. If your boss comes in it's kind of difficult to say, "I don't want to see you now."

There are some diplomatic ways you can do it. "I'm working on a project right now that I know is very high priority for you. Maybe we can postpone this." That is a very delicate situation that needs a lot of diplomacy. Whereas, if you're not there you're not there. So you'll see your boss in an hour. Now if you're not in a very senior position and you have to account to your boss for your time and your boss is saying where are you, why aren't you there and so forth, then I think if diplomacy won't work, you have to accept that there are certain types of interruptions you really can't control.

Q: In "The Organized Executive," you recommend delegating whatever tasks you can to somebody else as a method of saving your own time. In the credit department that might mean delegating handling of X, Y and Z accounts. What about the time you then have to spend supervising?

A: That's an important question. If you are delegating properly, this first of all means finding the right person. If you have a small department then obviously you don't have a vast selection at all; some people are detail oriented, they're very good at keeping track of things that account supervision might require. Other people just aren't. They might be more big picture or people oriented, gregarious, whatever it might be. So if you have any kind of discretion in delegation, then choosing the right person to do the job, matching the right person with the right type of task, is important.

Whether you've done that or not, whether that's possible or not, training the person is extremely important so that he or she really understands what is supposed to be done very very clearly so that all areas of ambiguity and uncertainty have been solved. The person must also have clear—cut goals or requirements. He or she must know, in supervising accounts, for example, there are certain things that are supposed to happen and there are things that are not supposed to happen. These must be defined very clearly. So in this case there will be a very intensive period of time during which the supervisor will have to be keeping a pretty close eye out to make sure things are done right.

But this is a function that should obsolesce itself. If a supervisor must continually keep an eye on staff in this intensive manner then something's wrong. Either the person isn't the right person for the job or hasn't been instructed properly, or else the person does not have a clear enough idea of what he or she is supposed to be doing. But, after a certain training period the supervisor should be able to meet with the person on a periodic basis to exchange data and discuss problems.

Q: In your book you mention people having goals. How can your organizing techniques be used by business people to advance their long-range career or personal goals?

A: The main thing about longer—range goals is that one problem with them is that it's all very well to say five years from now I want to be this, that or the other thing. That's fine; you do have to articulate some kind of desires or long-term plans personally and specifically in terms of your career. But too often, these goals are not resolved because, what are you really acting on day-to-day? You're acting on your Daily List. So what you soon realize is that you have to find some way to incorporate into your daily actions something that leads to your long-term goals.

This is how I suggest you do it. Let's say the credit person who wants to advance within his or her department or move to another, larger one, wants to take the action that will let him or her do that. So what the person would have to do is break this down into steps. What has to be done to get to this point? Now one thing that might have to be done is taking continuing education courses within the association. Another thing one might have to do if he or she works in a large credit department is raise visibility with the powers-that-be. That might mean writing an article for a trade publication that is regularly distributed.

So now we have two large tasks. Now these would be entered on your Master List. Now, still working on your Master List, you break these large tasks down. You say, "Okay, education. What do I need to do? First, I need to get the catalog of the association programs." Fine, that's a task. Write it down. And that goes on your Daily List one day. That day, you call up or write to get the catalog.

All of these very broad, abstract, long-term goals for the future can be broken down into smaller, concrete tasks, like my education example. Then they have to be broken down into even smaller specific actions. And then those specific actions such as writing an article, have to be broken down into day-to-day tasks that get integrated onto your Daily List. It's kind of a funnel, from the broad opening at the top of the big goals, down to the small specific tasks.

Q: You make it all sound so easy.

A: It is easy. It's essentially common sense. And the wonder to me is why people, intelligent, thoughtful, often successful people get so confused. Part of it is simple education. By that I mean that the basic idea of organization in a fundamental sense is the putting together of seemingly random data into patterns. The problem is not your basic capacity to organize. It's what gets in the way of your management of your paper and time and all that.

Q: Have you ever had someone come to you and ask for your help and just been totally unable to get them organized?

A: Never. Again, if the desire is there, if you just go through the steps and procedures which are basically common sense, then there is no one who can't be organized. A person can choose not to be organized. That is a personal choice. But if the choice is there, then no, you can't not be organized. It's simple. It's basic.

Q: Is there anything else you would like to say or stress about organization?

A: I would like to reemphasize the idea that organizing is not an end in itself. Actually, this is a good opportunity to say this. There are three things organizing is *not*, that people often think it is. First of all, as I said earlier, it is not being neat. Second, it is not being perfect. It does not mean having everything at right angles, pencils sharpened and lined up like little soldiers. Third, it's not a moral issue. Being organized does not make you a better human being. A lot of people get very involved in guilt, saying "I'm not organized, I'm a terrible person." That may be, but, be that as it may, it has nothing to do with being organized.

Being organized is simply a set of tools, methods and techniques that will allow you to get where it is you want to go. You say, "I'm here at point A, and I want to get to point B." The methods of organization are the tools or, maybe more aptly, the vehicle to get there. They are a means to an end. They are not an end in themselves. And actually, one of my personal goals is to divest organizing of a lot of this underbrush that surrounds it.

J. Gordon is an editor with Credit and Financial Management *magazine. Stephanie Winston is the president and founder of The Organizing Principle, New York, N.Y., a management consulting firm that promotes management productivity. She is the author of* Getting Organized *and* The Organized Executive.

4.
HOW DO YOU PERCEIVE TIME?

William Hoffer

Benjamin Franklin defined time as the stuff of which life is made. Your individual tempo really reflects the stuff of which you are made. This simple test will help you determine what your individual tempo is.

The common denominator of any business day is time consciousness. Whether you work from 9 a.m. to 5 p.m. or from 7 p.m. to midnight, whether you take a two—hour lunch or brown bag it at your desk while studying reports, whether your daily appointment calendar is jammed or open, you will probably glance at your watch on dozens of occasions throughout the day.

Whenever you do, you will react in a characteristic manner, one that may be quite different from those around you and those individual differences in time perception may play a critical role in your ability or inability to relate to others.

ARE YOU ALWAYS EARLY?

Are you always early for appointments? Or are you chronically late? Do you become agitated by a fellow worker who seems to take forever to make a point? Or do you bristle when you encounter someone who talks at high speed but never seems to have time to listen? Are you a young executive in a hurry? Or an experienced manager who takes pride in pacing yourself?

Few people can satisfactorily define time. Inside, we have an intuitive sense of what time means to us, but we remain largely unaware that others may have a completely different sense of time. It is this variety of individual time perceptions that often sets up needless human confrontations. By understanding your own sense of time and that of your associates, you can become a more effective manager.

Mary Ann Walsh Eells, an associate professor at the University of Maryland, Baltimore, and a private practice family systems therapist, has refined a simple test that clearly depicts one's sense of time. It is from previous studies that indicate that individuals with certain emotional tendencies have specialized concepts of time.

In a few short moments, you can discover how you perceive time. You will better understand your own management style and will be able to gauge your chances for future success as an executive. In addition, certain time perceptions are actually symptomatic of possible health or emotional problems.

TRY IT ON YOUR FRIENDS

You may also wish to try the test on your family, friends, and associates. Once you have correlated your concept of time with those around you, it will be easier to blend your staff into a team that operates with optimum effectiveness.

The test is simply this. Take a sheet of paper and draw three circles that depict your past, your present and your future. Do it right now, before reading further.

Now determine what your circles reveal about your perception of time.

TIME PERCEPTIONS

Almost everyone draws a pattern of circles that falls clearly into one of eight common categories, though a few people blend two patterns together and thus exhibit some of those qualities found in both types. You should be able to match your circles with one or more of the following types:

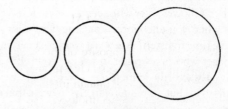

FUTURISTIC

About 65 percent of all people depict a steadily expanding sense of time. Such a person is in the mainstream of life, a solid and capable, if somewhat average, citizen. An executive who draws a futuristic circle pattern probably does not worry unduly about past mistakes and injustices.

He or she is aware that they are living in the present and that today is important, but nevertheless plans carefully for the future. He gets along with almost everyone. He is less spectacular than some of his peers, but likely to compile a normal, if modest, career record. In short, he is probably a competent and conscientious worker, a steady asset to any organization.

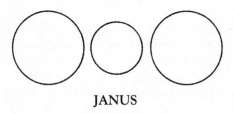

JANUS

To this person, the present is unimportant, perhaps painful. He or she is a busy person but usually involved with things rather than people. An executive who draws this pattern is probably highly successful in organizing a smooth-running office, particularly in this age when technological innovations are omnipresent. He or she should, however, guard against a tendency to treat people with the same mechanical orientations.

He or she is optimistic about the future, intelligent, motivated and decisive. He loves gadgets and typically will wear a digital watch featuring all the latest gimmicks, yet is generally late for appointments. Because of their uneasiness with the present, however, the Janus type has a tendency toward alcohol abuse.

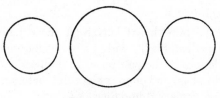

EXISTENTIAL

In many ways this person is the opposite of the Janus type. He or she is oriented toward people rather than objects. He is prompt and punctual. He will do well in all phases of business where human interaction is essential, but he may have difficulty coping with new technology.

The executive who draws the existential pattern lives most of his life in the present and may, therefore, experience difficulty visualizing long-term goals. The present is sometimes so overwhelming that, like the Janus type, he also exhibits a tendency toward alcohol abuse. In almost all other ways, however, Janus and existential types are so opposite that they may have interpersonal difficulties unless they are aware of their opposing ideologies.

EXPLOSIVE

Charismatic and full of energy, this person does all of his living in the here and now. The association executive who draws the explosive pattern is probably a dynamo who is in constant motion, but the very speed of his actions may promote mistakes and difficulties in human relations. He talks incessantly but is often too busy to listen to others. He tends not to respect another person's space or time.

The explosive type may often seem to be successful because of the sheer force of his personality, but he or she is, quite literally, a time bomb. This impulsive, internally angry individual is a prime candidate for high blood pressure.

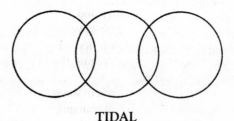

TIDAL

A quietly content person who is relatively pleased with his past, present and future, the tidal type lives his life with a sense of continuity. He or she has learned how the lessons of the past relate to the present. He is steady and deliberate. He works hard and often achieves his ambitious goals. He or she values freedom, autonomy and initiative.

The executive who draws the tidal pattern is probably not a flashy individual, but his chances of success are good.

MEDALLION

A balanced, imaginative individual who always seems to see all sides of the question, the medallion type is the most rare of all patterns to draw in the circle test. He or she may be even more scarce among executives than among the general public because, although they are quite capable of creating a successful career, such achievement may be unimportant to them.

Family and friends are likely to take exaggerated precedence over job considerations. A subordinate job may be perfect, however, because the medallion type is not judgmental and is capable of getting along well with almost anyone.

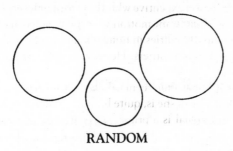

RANDOM

This person has no sense of identity and is not moving his life in any particular direction. In short, he doesn't have it together. He or she lives a chaotic life and probably suffers from a deep inner problem. This pattern should also be rare among executives because the individual who draws it is most assuredly not career oriented.

Be aware, though, that the random pattern sometimes shows up temporarily, drawn by people who are in the process of changing their time orientation from one category to another.

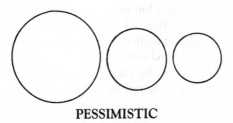

PESSIMISTIC

As is obvious from the drawing, the future holds little promise for this individual. This is the most dangerous of all time perceptions. The executive who draws a pessimistic pattern may be severely depressed and even suicidal. He or she feels as though they have nothing to look forward to.

Anyone who exhibits a pessimistic time pattern should strongly consider getting professional help. They must change their perception of time to one that will give them a more optimistic view of life.

Each second that ticks off the clock denotes the passage of a portion of your allotted time. This realization may cause the explosive personality to crowd each moment with activity in order not to squander his or her personal resources. Yet the same realization may cause the existentialist or medallion personality to slow down and savor time. The Janus type does not want to think about the present and will hustle his or her thoughts into the future. The futurist finds a middle ground, steadily progressing toward ultimate goals.

It is essential for an effective manager to gain an appreciation for others' points of view. You may wish to assign certain tasks on the basis of the time perceptions of others, saving for yourself those assignments that fit your inner metronome. Team assignments can also be planned to mesh the efforts of employees with compatible time perceptions.

ANOTHER MANAGEMENT TOOL

An awareness of the time perceptions of a staff is one more management tool that can increase efficiency and decrease office tension. It can also help you learn more about yourself.

5.
MANAGING TIME MEANS MANAGING YOURSELF

Michael LeBoeuf

Self-discipline is the key to managing time, but has this knowledge changed the way anyone behaves? Read the results of the time management survey, take the quiz yourself, and find out.

Time management seminars, books, pamphlets, articles and films abound, all trying to teach us, not to work harder, but to work smarter. I was recently struck, however, with a sobering thought: Are people out there really listening and applying all this information to their own lives? In order to find out, I made a survey of 40 sales representatives and 50 engineering managers. I gave them identical questionnaires in order to find out how they used their time and whether the differing demands of the two types of jobs would cause them to use their time differently.

THE TOP TIME WASTERS

In the first part of the survey, each subject was given a list of 15 time wasters and asked to choose and rank the ten that hinder him or her the most. The 15 items, chosen and ranked by executives in fourteen countries are as follows:

1. Telephone interruptions
2. Drop-in visitors
3. Meetings (scheduled and unscheduled)
4. Crises
5. Lack of objectives, priorities and deadlines
6. Cluttered desk and personal disorganization
7. Ineffective delegation and involvement in routine and detail
8. Attempting too much at once and estimating time unrealistically

9. Lack of, or unclear, communication or instruction
10. Inadequate, inaccurate or delayed information
11. Indecision and procrastination
13. Confused responsibility and authority
14. Leaving tasks unfinished
15. Lack of self-discipline[1]

Table I shows which items were chosen and how they were ranked by sales representatives and engineering managers.

Despite the differences between the two occupations, members of both chose eight of the same time wasters in their top ten. They differed in order of occurrence, but the telephone, visitors, meetings, crises, lack of self-discipline, procrastination, leaving tasks unfinished, and unclear communications were included by both. Unlike the executives in the other survey, neither group felt that a cluttered desk or the inability to say no was a major problem.

Table I

Top Ten Time Wasters
Ranked by Sales Representatives and Engineering Managers

Sales Representatives	Engineering Managers
1. Telephone interruptions	1. Inadequate, inaccurate or delayed information
2. Drop-in visitors	2. Ineffective delegation
3. Lack of self-discipline	3. Telephone interruptions
4. Crises	4. Meetings
5. Meetings	5. Unclear communication
6. Lack of objectives, priorities and deadlines	6. Crises
7. Indecision and procrastination	7. Leaving tasks unfinished
8. Attempting too much at once	8. Indecision and procrastination
9. Leaving tasks unfinished	9. Drop-in visitors
10. Unclear communication	10. Lack of self-discipline

Among the top five time wasters, both sales representatives and engineering managers listed only one item which could be described as a personal shortcoming. The sales representatives listed lack of self-discipline and the engineers, ineffective delegation. Perhaps this is indicative of the natural human tendency to look first for the source of a problem outside ourselves.

ALLOCATING TIME

In the second part of the survey, each subject was given a list of seven ways that time is commonly spent on the job: meetings, telephone calls, paper work and reading, correspondence and reports, planning, interruptions, visitors and social conversation. Subjects were asked to approximate how much time out of a standard eight-hour day they allocated to each of these activities. Their answers appear in Table II.

Table II

Percentage of Sales Representatives and Engineering Managers Allocating Varying Amounts of Time to Activities at Work

	Percentage of Subjects Spending Less Than 30 Minutes Per Day		Percentage of Subjects Spending 30 Minutes to 1 Hour Per Day	
	Sales Reps	Eng Mngrs	Sales Reps	Eng Mngrs
Meetings	21	50	68	29
Telephone	20	32	20	36
Paperwork	16	8	11	16
Correspondence	42	20	21	40
Planning	50	17	44	38
Interruptions	40	26	40	48
Visitors	71	95	24	5
Social Conversation	32	64	37	36

	Percentage of Subjects Spending 1 to 2 Hours Per Day		Percentage of Subjects Spending More Than 2 Hours Per Day	
	Sales Reps	Eng Mngrs	Sales Reps	Eng Mngrs
Meetings	11	13	0	8
Telephone	40	28	20	4
Paperwork	53	32	20	44
Correspondence	26	28	11	12
Planning	6	13	0	32
Interruptions	15	26	5	0
Visitors	0	0	5	0
Social Conversation	26	0	5	0

Differences in the amount of time allocated to the activities appears to be due to the differing demands of the two jobs. It is not surprising, for example, that a manager in a technical specialty devotes more time to planning than a sales representative. However, as in the first part of the survey, what they have in common seems more interesting; 73 percent of the sales representatives and 76 percent of the engineering managers report spending more than one hour per day on paperwork. Perhaps this is indicative of how the growth of government regulation and the use of computers and copying machines is shaping the way time is spent on the job.

MANAGING YOUR OWN TIME

The purpose of the third (and most important) part of the survey is to compare how the two groups evaluate their own performance in managing time. In order to do this, each subject was given ten statements that reflect generally accepted principles of effective time management. The instructions, statements and scoring are given in the box at the end of this essay. You may wish to take the quiz yourself.

If you feel, after taking the quiz, that there is much room for improvement in your own performance, take comfort from the fact that the mean score of the sales representatives was 17.3 and that of the engineering managers was 14.6. The data suggests that, because they are more able to attribute their job behavior directly to their income, sales representatives have a higher average score than engineering managers. Table III compares the average scores of each group by question.

The sale representatives' average score was higher on nine of the ten questions. Engineering managers scored higher only on the question about eating a light lunch. The data from the survey supports the hypothesis that the "time is money" nature of the sales representatives' jobs results in their being better managers of their time.

Table III

Scores of Respondents, by Question

Question	Average Scores	
	Sales Reps	Eng Mngrs
1	2.35	1.68
2	1.50	1.28
3	1.80	1.24
4	1.25	0.96
5	1.60	1.56
6	1.40	1.28
7	2.30	1.88

8	1.85	2.28
9	1.55	1.12
10	1.70	1.32
Total Score	17.30	14.60

CONCLUSIONS

The number of respondents to my survey, 90 subjects from two businesses, is too small to allow me to make any sweeping generalizations about the population at large. And I suspect that the respondents may not really know how they spend their time. My experience as a time management consultant has convinced me that few, if any, of us know how we spend our time until we make the effort to keep a log. Frequently, there is a considerable disparity between how we think we spend our time and how we actually spend it.

However, the survey did suggest several thoughts. It does appear that sales representatives are more inclined to manage their time better than persons who cannot directly relate their behavior and use of time to their income.

The data suggest that time management is really a misnomer; it should be called self-management. Perhaps thinking of time management gives us an excuse to blame our self-management problems on other people and external factors.

The paperwork problem is a growing impediment to the effective use of time and hence the producitivity of people in industry.

There is plenty of room for improvement. Despite all the books, seminars and training films no one in this survey scored especially well. Perhaps the Achilles' heel of time management is best summarized in what has been called The Harvard Law of Animal Behavior:
Under carefully controlled conditions,
Organisms behave as they damn well please.

Reference

1. R. Alec Mackenzie, *New Time Management Methods for You and Your Staff* (Chicago: Dartnell, 1975), p.75.

HOW WELL DO YOU MANAGE YOUR TIME?

Listed below are ten statements that reflect generally accepted principles of good time management. Answer these items by circling the item most characteristic of how you perform your job. *Please be honest.* No one will know your answers except you.

1. Each day I set aside a small amount of time for planning and thinking about my job.
   0. Almost never. 1. Sometimes. 2. Often. 3. Almost always.
2. I set specific, written goals and put deadlines on them.
   0. Almost never. 1. Sometimes. 2. Often. 3. Almost always.
3. I make a daily "to do" list, arrange items in order of importance, and try to get the important items done as soon as possible.
   0. Almost never. 1. Sometimes. 2. Often. 3. Almost always.
4. I am aware of the 80-20 rule and use it in doing my job. (The 80- 20 rule states that 80 percent of your effectiveness will generally come from achieving only 20 percent of your goals.)
   0. Almost never. 1. Sometimes. 2. Often. 3. Almost always.
5. I keep a loose schedule to allow for crises and the unexpected.
   0. Almost never. 1. Sometimes. 2. Often. 3. Almost always.
6. I delegate everything I can to others.
   0. Almost never. 1. Sometimes. 2. Often. 3. Almost always.
7. I try to handle each piece of paper only once.
   0. Almost never. 1. Sometimes. 2. Often. 3. Almost always.
8. I eat a light lunch so I don't get sleepy in the afternoon.
   0. Almost never. 1. Sometimes. 2. Often. 3. Almost always.
9. I make an active effort to keep common interruptions (visitors, meetings, telephone calls) from continually disrupting my work day.
   0. Almost never. 1. Sometimes. 2. Often. 3. Almost always.
10. I am able to say no to others' requests for my time that would prevent my completing important tasks.
   0. Almost never. 1. Sometimes. 2. Often. 3. Almost always.

To get your score, give yourself:
   3 points for each "almost always"
   2 points for each "often"
   1 point for each "sometimes"
   0 points for each "almost never"
Add up your points to get your total score.
If you scored:
   0-15 Better give some thought to managing your time.
   15-20 You're doing OK but there's room for improvement.
   20-25 Very good
   25-27 Excellent
   28-30 You cheated!

Michael LeBoeuf is an associate professor of management at the University of New Orleans and the author of Working Smart *published by McGraw-Hill.*

6.

TIME:
THE EXECUTIVE'S DILEMMA

Charles J. Ferderber

Using time effectively may mean changing some long-time bad habits. We all recognize the symptoms but changing will be difficult.

It makes little sense to exempt the executive suite from productivity and emphasize only the production worker.

We all need better ways to use our time. Yet time is difficult to manage. Although it's predictable in amount, it eludes control. Although it's irretrievable, we think we can make up time lost. Although it moves at a predetermined rate, it often seems to fly and sometimes to drag. The greatest paradox of all is that, although no one has enough time, everyone has all there is.

Time is allocated as 24 hours every day to all persons—no more, no less. Yet how often we hear, "I don't have enough time." Experts on time management claim that top executives spend 90 percent of their time on trivia and ten percent on creative work. To put it another way, they are too busy to be efficient. If that has a familiar ring, you have already identified a time problem indicator. Time is not the problem, but rather how you use it.

Working overtime is not the answer, nor is taking work home at night—often referred to as "briefcaseitis." The solution, simply stated, is better use of one's time while on the job. Successful persons are successful because they think in terms of objectives. They are goal-oriented and allocate time to realistic goals, set priorities and concentrate on the important things. In order to save time, one must think and plan ahead. Five minutes of thinking can often save hours of work. The best time generator is sound management.

Time can be divided into two categories: uncontrollable and controllable. Uncontrollable time stems from the demands of the boss, which can seldom, if ever, be regulated. Therefore, one must make maximum use of the time that one can control.

There are many myths associated with time management. For example, "managers who are most active are most productive." This in not necessarily true. Perspiration should not be confused with efficiency. They are not synonymous. A politician once said, "Having lost sight of the objective, we redoubled our efforts." Don't spin your wheels unnecessarily—plan ahead and set goals.

It's also generally considered to be a fact that people who are paid the most money make smarter decisions. Not always true. We are indecisive because we either have no solution or we tend to look for the "perfect" solution when realistically a decision is needed now. Good management practice states that decisions should be made at the lowest possible level consistent with good judgment and possession of relevant facts. In fact, a manager is employed to make decisions and is evaluated on the ability to make effective decisions—effective from a superior's point of view. Indeed, some feel that decision making is synonymous with management, that it is the essence of management.

Procrastination is a thief of time. In the 19th century, Pareto, an Italian economist, discovered that the significant items in a given group normally constitute a relatively small portion of the total items in that group. Stated another way, focusing major effort on the significant 20 percent of one's activities will generally provide 80 percent of the results; 20 percent of one's departments produce 80 percent of the revenue. Twenty percent of the personnel for most of the sick time, and 20 percent of one's subordinates demand 80 percent of his/her time. The important thing here is to recognize which is the 20 percent and which is the 80 percent and then concentrate on the 20 percent.

George H. Labowitz, Ph.D. president of Organizational Dynamics, Inc., asked a group of hospital executives, "How much of your day's work could you delegate to a volunteer candy striper, if one was assigned to you?" The consensus was that 50 to 60 percent of their duties could be delegated to the candy striper.

We all need to evaluate how we spend our day. Are we productive? Can we delegate? Delegation is only effective when properly planned and careful consideration is given to selecting the person to whom the project is delegated. Every hour spent in effective planning saves three to four hours in execution. A cursory analysis of the problem frequently leads to a hasty decision. If one can't find the time to do it right, how will he/she ever find the time to do it over? Inadequate planning and disorganization create the illusion of too little time.

The "I'd rather do it myself" syndrome very often assumes that no one else can do the job as well. The boss who does it himself/herself gets much too involved in the work. As a result, his/her subordinates never need to make a decision. At times, we all suffer from the delusion of indispensability or omnipotence. We don't really need to do it ourselves. We don't need to work 60 to 70 hours per week. With good planning, the work can be accomplished in the normal course of the day, or perhaps even less.

Executive stress frequently interferes with productivity. Unless recognized and dealt with, stress can cause an executive to deteriorate and become withdrawn. He/she becomes less effective in accomplishing his/her tasks. Stress and insecurity may make an executive unduly subservient and defensive. As a consequence, he/she may lose his/her creativity.

To correct many of the problems and myths related to time management, it helps to recognize why some leaders are more effective than others. Dr.Charles D. Flory, partner, Rohre, Hibles and Replogle, summarizes the following characteristics of the most efficient managers.

- The ability to do it now. At least 80 percent of the business coming across the executive's desk is handled immediately.
- The ability to delegate. A good executive surrounds himself/herself with competent employees.
- Willingness to take time to support, encourage and show concern for subordinates.
- The ability to separate the "chaff" from the "wheat." The executive who can do that avoids being trapped by trivia.
- Refusal to waste time on the "impossible." An effective executive can admit defeat and move on to bigger things.
- The ability to project himself/herself into the future.
- A sense of timing and a feel for reality.
- Ability to establish reasonable suspense dates on all projects.

What specifically can you, as an executive, do to correct your time dilemma?

Set goals. The president of US Steel told his industrial engineer many years ago that he would pay him $25,000 for a great time-saving idea. His engineer handed him a blank piece of paper and pencil and asked him to write down the five most important things he should do starting the next day. He was to list the least desirable task first, then the next least, down to item five. In the morning, he was to proceed to tackle each problem.

One project might take several days, but at least it starts you on your way to stated objectives. If you do this every day, the result will be gratifying. It will pay off many times over.

Keep an accordion folder on your desk that holds only unfinished projects or parts of projects, filed by priority. Finished projects are removed from the folder and sent to the permanent file. Maintain only an "in" file and no "hold" file. A "hold" file tends to be an expedient way to get rid of projects that are controversial or hard to resolve. Handle most documents only once. Throw out mail that does not contribute to goal tending.

Don't overcommit yourself. Don't be "nice" and volunteer for all tasks and committees. Ask yourself, "Is it my fire to fight?"

Delegate with authority. In other words permit the individual to follow through and give the necessary authority to act for you, including necessary funding, if appropriate. Remember, however, the final responsibility is yours.

Permit your subordinates to do the job delegated. Be there only to direct and expect feedback from time to time as well as progress reports. Above all, set a suspense date (time you would like to see the end product) not only for yourself, but also for your subordinates. This can be flexible, and if it needs to be changed—change it! If you adopt the attitude, "I would rather do it myself," your subordinates may never have a chance to develop, or, even more importantly, never have a chance to make a mistake. Be realistic in your goal setting.

Do not substitute meetings for decision making. Of all the organizational activities which waste the most time, meetings lead the list. Essential meetings need not be long, dull, inefficient, disorganized or (least of all) unproductive. First, identify why you need to meet. Evaluate all the committees that you are assigned to and ask yourself, "Which of these are essential to my operation?" Try scheduling meetings that always seem to run overtime just before lunch or dinner. It is amazing how many problems can be resolved in 45 to 60 minutes; meetings should rarely, if ever, exceed that time span. Following are some ideas for improving the quality and effectiveness of committee meetings.

1. Prepare an agenda well in advance of the meeting and disseminate it so participants understand the parameters of the discussion.
2. Keep discussions on the track, document proceedings, urge all to participate. Committees should not be so large as to preclude involvement of all members (seven to 12 is a good size).
3. Above all, follow through on the committee's recommendations.
4. Select committee members on the basis of expertise and authority to implement decisions.
5. Motivate members to achieve the group task.
6. Do not select members with characteristics (i.e., unequal status) that might hinder full participation.
7. Do not run meetings in the old town meeting style with everyone having a say about what is to be done and how the project is to be carried out.
8. Investigate alternatives to holding meetings, such as memos, a telephone call or discussions with key personnel.

Research by management experts has shown that committee members working on a problem individually are infinitely more effective at reaching certain solutions than working collectively.

Don't allow the telephone to waste your time. For many, it is difficult to know when to cut off a conversation. Have a secretary screen your calls. Never interrupt the boss in a conference for a telephone call unless it is a matter of urgency. (Very important conferences frequently lose their effect when interrupted. More importantly, you may be keeping some very expensive employees waiting unnecessarily.) Be brief in your conversation and eliminate the platitudes. On the other hand, you can gain time by using your telephone instead of dictating long interoffice memorandums.

Handle magazine and junk mail only once. Let the secretary screen and discard unimportant mail. We all get magazines, journals, trade pamphlets, etc. For years, these used to accumulate on my book rack. Now, when I receive a magazine, I scan through the index very quickly, then paper-clip worthwhile articles which my secretary cuts out of the magazine and files in a reference folder. Be extremely selective about these articles, and then pitch the magazine. Now you have excellent reference material for researching projects.

Block interruptions. Set a certain time for appointments. Have your secretary screen all visitors. Meet outside of offices. Confer standing up. Let your secretary monitor calls. Set time limits on visits and set deadlines.

Don't manage by crisis. Do problems manage you or do you manage the problem? The quality of decision making in a crisis is not always the best. Once you make a decision, take a stand; elect one approach and only use alternatives as a last resort. To reduce decision-making time, be systematic: 1. recognize that a problem does exist; 2. identify possible courses; 3. generate alternative solutions; 4. select and implement a solution.

Practice the three "ates." Time management boils down to three basic principles: eliminate, insulate and concentrate. Eliminate the non-essential duties. Insulate yourself to capitalize on your controllable time. By eliminating non-essential workloads, you have carved out an ample slice of controllable time for complete, uninterrupted concentration. A half hour or so of just thinking, or quiet time with your feet propped in a comfortable position, is conducive to creativity.

Using time effectively may mean changing some bad habits of years. We all recognize the symptoms but changing will be difficult. Consider time as money, invest your time for the best of returns as you would financial investments. Time can be your enemy unless you learn to control it. It takes discipline and the ability to say "no."

You might like to know what it is you do in a given day. Try filling out the time-flow chart illustrated in Table 1. It's simple and easy to maintain. Try it on odd or even days for about two to three weeks, then compute the results. You will be amazed at the initial results.

"We seem not to live long enough to take ourselves seriously." wrote George Bernard Shaw. "While we are laughing most of the time, most of us act as if this life were just a practice run for the next."

It's never too late to change. Experiment; you may like it.

Table 1

Time-Flow Chart
Deaconess Hospital
Evansville, Indiana

Name-Person/Document	Position/Description	Date
Harry James	Vice President	8-8-79

1. On the chart, code the major categories of your work, such as F—Filing, T—Typing Form 100. When you change from one task to another, draw a line across the column at the time of the day, enter the proper code for the category of the work performed.
2. Enter the required information on the Time Distribution Summary at the end of the day.
3. When used for a document time-flow study, attach sufficient forms for the estimated number of days to completion. The above instructions also apply to this type of study. In addition, when you finish your work with the document enter under your time-line "To (person or unit)." When receiving the document enter "Received by" under the time line.

TIME DISTRIBUTION SUMMARY

Code	Description	Time	Percent
B	Breaks: coffee, etc.	40	7
D	Dictation	35	6
T	Telephone	70	13
R	Reading	70	13
M	Meetings	70	13
L	Lunch	100	19
C	Conferences	25	5
P	Projects	55	10
V	Visitations	15	3
E	Errands	10	2
NP	Nonproductive	50	9

Hours of the Day

Time	Code	Time	Code	Time	Code	Time	Code
8 00		15		30		45	D
05		20		35		50	
10		25		40		55	
15	R	30	M	45		3 00	V
20		35		50		05	
25		40		55		10	
30		45		1 00	L	15	
35	T	50	NP	05		20	T
40		55		10		25	
45		11 00		15		30	
50		05		20		35	NP
55		10		25		40	
9 00		15		30		45	
05	B	20		35		50	
10		25	P	40		55	E
15		30		45	C	4 00	
20		35		50		05	
25		40		55		10	
30	T	45		2 00		15	
35		50		05		20	R
40		55		10	T	25	
45		12 00		15		30	
50		05		20		35	
55		10	L	25		40	T
10 00	M	15		30	D	45	
05		20		35		50	NP
10		25		40		55	

References

Baker, H. Kent, "How to Make Meaningful Meetings," Amacom, August 1979.

Drucker, Peter F., The Effective Executive (New York: Harper & Row, 1967).

Elicano, R.V., "Learning from Superachievers," Industrial Engineering (October 1978), p. 30.

Lakein, Alan, How to Get Control of Your Time and Your Life (New York: Signet, 1973).

Mackenzie, R. Alec, New Time Management Methods for You and Your Staff (Chicago: Dartnell Corporation, 1975).

Purvis, George P., III, "How Time Management Got Me Under Control," Hospital Financial Management (January 1979), p. 42.

Tosi, Henry T. and Stephen J. Carol, Management: Contingencies, Structures and Process (Chicago: St. Clair Press, 1976).

7.
HOW THE BOYS IN THE OFFICE MISHANDLE TIME

Susan T. Parker

Blue collar workers are blamed for lower productivity. But it's probably the workers in suits and ties who aren't putting in a full day.

Blue collar workers at the manufacturing level are not nearly as responsible for the declining U.S. productivity rate as many political and economic pundits believe.

Quite the contrary. In fact, if any one segment of the workforce is to blame, it is more likely to be the white-collar workers, maintains Fred Pryor, chairman of Fred Pryor Resources Corp. of Shawnee Mission, Kansas. "They are the biggest time wasters." It is "unfair," he says, to automatically associate low productivity with assembly line workers and steel workers, as is often done.

Pryor says blue-collar workers have been faulted simply because their output can be easily measured against that of the Japanese and European workers. But the nature of the white-collar worker's job defies such close scrutinization. He says he is oftentimes told by white-collar workers that their output can't be measured, because "we use our minds."

"But the blue-collar worker doesn't have that luxury and this is why productivity (in the U.S.) is so lousy today," remarks Pryor, whose firm has recently held several seminars on time management throughout the country. It has also been involved in the development of in-house time management programs for various U.S. corporations.

By no means, he says, are all white-collar workers time wasters, but there are enough of them for it to be considered a problem. He feels strongly that U.S. companies could vastly improve their productivity and profits if their white-collar executives were taught to manage their time better. But before that can happen, white-collar workers first must examine the ways in which they waste or mismanage time.

To start, there are the blatant areas in which time is wasted. Pryor says he finds it "amazing" the number of U.S. companies that hold meetings to discuss insignificant business matters and then never really decide on anything. All business meetings, he believes, should end with a decision of some kind. If not, they are just a waste of the company's time and effort.

He further points out how companies are notorious for never starting their business meetings on time; they always seem to be waiting on one or two stragglers. If companies continue to hold up their meetings, Pryor says, it will backfire in their faces, because eventually even those executives—who previously were punctual—will start coming late. The reason: They have become used to the meetings not starting on time. If a company calls a business meeting for 9 a.m., it should start exactly at 9 a.m., he says.

Pryor further assailed those white-collar executives who go on purported business junkets, but in actuality discuss little or no business; and executives who make a habit of long lunch hours, and those who excessively use their business phone for personal matters.

Companies need to identify these time wasters and then put a stop to them. If not, other employees will misinterpret the company's silence as a sign that these are accepted practices and will start mimicking the top executives. "This is why some organizations are so royally screwed up," Pryor adds. "Everyone does what the other is doing."

But, he says, the three-martini lunches and business junkets are only part of the white-collar worker's productivity problem; in fact, they are a very small part. The majority of white-collar workers who waste time do it because they simply do not know how to effectively manage their time. In many cases, they may not even be consciously aware that they are wasting time.

It's not terribly surprising that more white-collar workers aren't better time managers, considering that only about five percent of the world's population are "superior" time managers. "These are the kind of people who can just knock the clock off the wall," says Pryor. They can juggle six or seven different things simultaneously and do them all well. They can do in two hours what normally might take others eight hours to accomplish.

What is it about them? Are they more intelligent and talented than the rest of us? Pryor thinks not. They are simply better organized and are willing to give a little more each day than others are.

Business people who are effective time managers are easy to spot and so too are those who are terrible at time management. The effective time managers are well organized (just look at their desks); they work against the clock even when they aren't under deadline; they know how to handle people and are effective at delegating authority; they set priorities for themselves and they are good problem-solvers and planners.

At the office, a poor time manager sticks out like a sore thumb. These are executives who constantly—night after night—have to take work home with them because they didn't finish it at the office. They are also normally the first ones at the office in the morning and the last ones to leave at night. And despite the long hours, chances are they failed to accomplish a fraction of the work their colleagues did.

The reason they probably didn't achieve much and had to stay late was because they failed to set a deadline for themselves. "Oftentimes people will get more done if they set deadlines. I know I get more done when I have to leave early as opposed to leaving late," says Pryor, who notes that 80 percent of results are produced by 20 percent of the effort.

Staying late at the office each night is a sign of a poor time manager. In fact, Pryor says the executive knows he's in real trouble when he starts muttering things like: "They don't pay me enough to stay this late, (or) I don't care if the entire place burns down, I'm going home."

Probably the most distinguishing feature of the poor time manager is that he or she just doesn't know how to handle people. They don't know how to deal with their colleagues or subordinates who interrupt them; they don't know how to delegate effectively and they let others structure their lives. The most frequent comment Pryor says he hears from executives is: "I feel like a common firefighter. I'm always putting out fires, but I never seem to accomplish anything."

The poor time manager can change, but it will require a lot of time and discipline. The first step for any executive is to identify those areas in which he wastes time and his reasons for doing it.

The ways in which executives mismanage their time and their reasons for doing so are endless, but some of the solutions can be quite simple. For instance, an executive might find that he is wasting a lot of time just by acknowledging the "hello" of his colleagues who pass by his door every morning. Solution: He can either keep the door closed in the morning, or rearrange his desk so that it doesn't face the door.

A large U.S. company recently spent about $1 million to re-position its desks in such a way as to eliminate excessive talking between employees and increase their output, reports Pryor.

Sometimes a simple closing of the door and rearranging of the desk won't do, however. He told of one executive who actually put boxes under his desk to elevate it and then sawed off all the legs to the guest chairs in his office to get his point across. "He had to do all this just to get his privacy."

The other reasons why executives procrastinate are a little bit more complicated. An executive might be lax on the job, says Pryor, because he has lost all "fascination" in his work. Once this is gone, he loses the commitment and drive to achieve.

Or, it could be the executive's own thinking that's getting in the way. He might have convinced himself that he's a procrastinator, and a messy and unproductive worker. If that's the case, says Pryor, "he'll probably live up to his expectations."

Guilt can also be a factor. Instead of feeling good about the things he has accomplished, as he should, the executive constantly feels guilty about the things he hasn't done. To say the least, this can be counterproductive.

Another possibility is that the executive may have mismanaged his personal life to such a point that it's now starting to affect his work. "How you manage your personal time is reflective of how you manage your business time," says Mr. Pryor.

In some instances, executives could be mismanaging their time simply because they have the wrong assumptions about time, explains Pryor. One incorrect notion is: "I just don't ever seem to have enough time." But in reality, he notes, all people have the same amount of time. "Some of us just manage it more effectively than others."

People also tend to incorrectly assume that time can be reinvested, but it can't be saved, says Prior.

Probably the two biggest misconceptions about time are: "the more hours you spend on the job, the more you will accomplish" and "the harder you work, the more you will get done." The later may have been true 20 to 30 years ago, but it's how "smart" a person works that counts now.

Another problem that people have with time is that they fail to realize that it's "accumulative" by nature. While people will get terribly upset if their entire day is wasted, they don't tend to care too much if it's only an hour that's been wasted. But, as Pryor points out, one hour each day spread over a year's period is equivalent to 15 days.

Besides realizing the value of time, executives also need to know their prime times, the best time for them to do work, and their down times, the worst time to tackle work. This could increase their output immensely.

Since most people are adjusted to an 8 a.m. to 5 p.m. workday, their prime time ranges between 8 a.m. and 11 a.m., says Pryor. This suggests that the most important work should be done early in the day before an executive starts to "fizzle out."

For most people, their down time starts at 4:15 p.m.; this is the worst time to make any business decision. It's at about that time that workers start yawning and glancing at the clocks.

There's another type of time that executives ought to know about: quiet time. It's that part of the day when executives need to make an effort to block everyone else in the company out and try to do some serious planning or problem-solving on their own. Pryor tells of one executive who keeps his office door closed between 7 a.m. and 9 a.m. each day, leaving strict orders not to be interrupted.

Executives inarguably would also get more done if they would prioritize more. There's a tendency among white-collar workers to concentrate on work that isn't critical or difficult instead of work that must be done today.

They wait until a job becomes urgent before they tackle it, says Pryor. As a result, it usually takes twice as long to do it.

Executives would probably become much better at setting priorities if they asked themselves one question each day: "Is what I am doing now the most important thing that I ought to be doing now?"

8.
TIME MANAGEMENT: FROM PRINCIPLES TO PRACTICE

R. Alec Mackenzie

At work and in our personal lives it's simply a matter of putting into practice a few basic principles we know so well, but somehow continue to neglect.

When asked by the *Training and Development Journal* editor to address the principles and practice of time management, I was both surprised and pleased. My surprise arose from the continuing neglect of fundamental principles of management on practically all managerial fronts. The pleasure lay in the opportunity presented to expose the problem bluntly to those best positioned to do something about it and to suggest a course of action which could help rectify the situation.

A WASTELAND OF NEGLECT

My interest in principles of management dates back to my first efforts to chart on one graph the entire management process. The results of this effort were published in the *Harvard Business Review* ("The Management Process in 3D") and later in the *Training and Development Journal* under the title, "A Management Process Model for Training and Development Directors."

The American Society for Training and Development's interest then was to point to the great need felt by training and development practitioners for a model or rationale for training programs. The success of that model is due in no small part to its continuing use in management development programs.

Yet, there is a serious tendency for trainers to overlook the importance of management models in providing a rationale for training programs. Equally serious is the tendency to overlook fundamental principles that give meaning to each of the functional areas comprising the management process. It amounts to a virtual wasteland of neglect!

I base this conclusion on a dozen years of full-time effort in research for extensive writing and speaking, in conducting studies in organizations, and in developing programs for foundations, universities, and the largest management development association in the world. I have presented seminars on leadership and time management in 23 countries, offering a continuing laboratory for observation and discussion of management practices and the understanding of management principles.

These discussions occur in seminars with managers and outside seminars with trainers, with program directors and, of course, with program participants ever anxious to explore special problems. In addition, the reading of everything you believe to be important in the field keeps you in touch with new developments and the trends which occasionally bestir the tides of management thought.

A growing conviction has emerged from this continuing involvement in the field of management: That management principles are not only *not* understood by the vast majority of managers at all levels, but also are not understood by the vast majority of trainers! In fact, surprisingly few persons in either category could name a single principle of management correctly. In seminars, I have asked who can name one principle of management. Rarely does a hand go up to volunteer. In one session of 300 chief executives, I asked the question without obtaining a single response. In another with 450 senior executives and trainers, the same question elicited the same response.

Examination of the literature of management is scarcely encouraging. A recent text by a best-known publisher of the subject—principles of management—contains not a single reference to principles either in the table of contents or in the index. The book does deal very effectively with the functions and activities of management, while totally neglecting the principles. The title appears to have been chosen because it would sell.

A recent article in one of the most widely read management periodicals refers to "the principles of addition." The author does not tell us what that principle is, and it is quite clear from the context that he is referring to the principle of consolidation. Thus many authors, encouraged by uncritical publishers, wittingly or unwittingly engage in worsening the wasteland of neglect. The near bankruptcy of knowledge and understanding in this arena should be of paramount concern to trainers. They are surely well-positioned to do something about it, if they would.

RESPONSIBILITY OF TRAINERS

What is the responsibility of trainers in this appalling situation?

- To understand what a principle is and to identify the most important ones in each of the functional areas of management.

- To relate principles to practice and to understand why an understanding of principles is essential to effective managerial performance.

- To understand why, contrary to popular belief, there is nothing more practical than a sound principle.

- Contrary to the approach generally being adopted by trainers today, since time and life are indivisible, to recognize that the management of time essentially is the management of oneself and therefore ought to be approached from a "mastery-of-the-principles" viewpoint.

A "principle," according to Koontz and O'Donnell, is *"a fundamental truth applicable to a given set of circumstances which has value in predicting results."* Principles have also been termed fundamental rules; standards for measurement; guidelines for conduct; and the basis for planning.

The most interesting and helpful definition of a principle is *"the relationship between a cause and its effect."* This definition is most useful since it explains the intensely *practical* nature of sound principles. Let's examine two principles that every trainer will instantly accept, although few will be able to identify the functional area of management in which they fall or state them precisely.

- *Principles of Management Development.* Results will tend to vary directly with development programs aimed at improving abilities of managers in the present position, at making them promotable, and at involving them in the process.

- *Principles of Reinforcement:* One of the most important requisites of effective training and development is reinforcement of lessons learned through review and practice on the job.

These principles clearly fall within the functional category of "staffing." Note that both principles state a cause and an effect. The *causes* respectively are: development programs aimed at improving abilities of managers in the present position, etc., and reinforcement of lessons learned through review and practice on the job. The respective *effects* are results that vary directly and training and development that is effective. The practicality of these principles should be self-evident. Yet trainers who are not familiar with these precise statements will not be able to use them for the most practical of all possible results: the persuasion of managers as to the imperative need of effective training and development and the justification to top management of a training and development program.

NO WONDER BUDGETS ARE CUT!

No wonder training budgets are among the first to be cut. Who wouldn't cut a budget that had never been rationalized or justified to their satisfaction! Yet how many trainers can present a persuasive rationale for their program? How many trainers can list the managerial functions, with confidence that they have not omitted several? How many can identify which functional area of management is being advanced by *each* of their training programs? How many are following the above two principles in their own programs?

Let me relate the very sad experience of two Fortune 500 companies, each of which had spent in the vicinity of six-figure budgets on a time management program consisting solely of a series of seminars mostly conducted for random groups rather than functional groups. I requested of each that we run a follow-up study to determine what results had been obtained with all the money that was spent.

In one company, where reluctance was extreme, I offered to run a one-day follow-up seminar without charge for anyone who had attended a previous seminar in an effort to check results and to provide an opportunity for reinforcement. My offer was refused in both cases but requests for seminars continued. In other words these trainers believed they were getting their points for the *number* of people they ran through my seminar, not for the *results!*

Contrast this reaction with a more recent one of a head trainer who, after a time management seminar, observed:

"There are three things I particularly like about this program. First, it is totally reinforcing of all of our other programs because it identifies time wasters in each functional area and develops solutions, thereby improving performance in all of the functions of management. Second, it can be implemented immediately by the individual without waiting for corporate approval. Third, the individual can measure his or her own progress with regular follow-up assignments which provide extraordinary reinforcement for anyone who is really interested in improvement."

One of the most devastating conversations I've had with regard to the wasteland of neglect problem occurred recently with an experienced trainer who had served with national and multinational companies in the United States and abroad, in a variety of training and development positions. I told him of a new position I had begun to take with trainers inquiring about my program—that I would refuse to accept assignments to present seminars without an agreement in advance for a follow-up program to measure its effectiveness and to validate the guarantee of two hours saved per day per participant. The response of this trainer startled me, but confirmed my worst suspicions. He said: "It's the only way you'll ever get them to do it. Notches on the belt is the name of the game." By "notches on the belt" he meant numbers of attendees at seminars, of course.

The benefits of principles need to be understood and appreciated by trainers before they can hope to become advocates. Koontz and O'Donnell cite the following important benefits of principles:

1. Simplify the practice of management by identifying causal relationships applicable to different situations.
2. Avoid mistakes by utilizing guidelines derived from the experience of others.
3. Improve solutions by transferring lessons learned in terms of fundamental principles to new situations.
4. Improve effectiveness by applying better solutions in less time, saving needless research or trial and error.
5. Improve adaptability to changing conditions by knowing not only what to do—but why.
6. Permit the teaching of others by packaging experience for easy transfer to others.

WHY THE PETER PRINCIPLE IS NOT A PRINCIPLE

The perceptive reader will have no difficulty in determining, on the basis of what's been said above, the reason for rejecting the now famous *Peter Principle* as a principle. It is one of many so-called "principles" which are really a misuse of the term, or so weakly supported as not to merit serious consideration.

Professor Peter's assertion that managers tend to rise to their level of incompetence, and therefore, ultimately, top levels in organizations will be filled by incompetent managers, is partly obvious and partly absurd! It is obvious that managers tend to rise in organizations and that every manager could be said *at a given point in time* to have a certain level of competence. It's absurd to assume that the level of competence of all managers remains static and, therefore, that all positions will ultimately be occupied with incompetent managers.

This conclusion ignores factors which should be particularly sensitive to trainers since they affect competence levels: experience, reading, training and development programs, attrition through retirement, departure for better jobs, promotion to other departments, and the refusal of promotion. The real danger of so-called "principles" is that the obvious aspect of the true portion misleads many people into uncritical acceptance of the absurd portion. The end result may be a serious disservice to the field of management. One obvious result of uncritical acceptance of the Peter Principle has been to encourage readers in the conviction that their bosses were over their levels of competence and therefore readers should be even more critical of bosses.

PUTTING TIME MANAGEMENT PRINCIPLES TO WORK

Over the years I have sought to collect, formulate and catalog by function a list of the fundamental principles of management and time management. By researching the best-known texts in the field, I have accumulated a list of more than 100 such principles. Reducing that list to those directly related to time utilization, and adding a few of my own, I now work in seminars with a list of 59 Principles of Time Management. An example of one principle from each of the functions of management is found in Table 1.

Table 1

Function	Name	Principle
Planning	Priority	For optimum results, time available should be budgeted or allocated to tasks in ordered sequence of priority
Organizing	Consolidation	Similar tasks should be grouped to economize time and effort by eliminating repetitive actions and interruptions.
Staffing	Orientation	The more a person knows about the work and its environment, the more intelligently the work can be done.
Directing	Delegation	A manager's effectiveness will vary directly with his or her ability to delegate effectively.
Controlling	Planned Unavailability	Managers who plan for periods of uninterrupted concentration achieve better results.
Communicating	Brevity	Economy of word and action conserves time while promoting clarity and understanding.
Decision-making	Procrastination	Deferring, postponing or putting off decisions can become a habit which loses time, causes lost opportunities, increases pressure on deadlines and generates crises.

To demonstrate the practical nature of sound principles, participants in time management seminars are given two assignments. The first is a team assignment which requires the initial step in solving the top time waster of a team to be the identification of the principles of time management most applicable to that time waster. Invariably, having identified the most relevant principles, the teams have no difficulty in identifying the most important causes of the time waster because the most serious causes usually result from the violation of one or more fundamental principles. Once the causes are clarified, the solutions are generally self-evident. Like a problem well-stated, it is half solved.

The second assignment in seminars is for each participant to select from the 59 Principles the ten most important to him or her individually, and to identify one action item suggested by that principle. Typical examples of action items selected by participants from England, Canada and the United States for each of the principles named in Table 1 are found in Table 2.

Table 2

Principle	Action Item
Priority	Get priority list approved by boss and use it to say "no" to less-important requests for my time.
Consolidation	Group activities into a "typical" day: dictation, calls, quiet time, meetings, "to do" items. Advise those significantly affected: secretary, boss, staff, peers.
Orientation	Orient organization to district goals and plans. Visit five minutes with three employees per week until entire staff covered.
Delegation	Have C.B. write weekly report from now on instead of doing it myself.
Planned Unavailability	Have secretary take all calls and implement a "quiet hour" for me immediately. When she needs catch-up time arrange "quiet hour" for her using lunchtime replacement or taking calls myself at low traffic time.
Brevity	Describe or report results only, on activity. Avoid temptation to show off verbally.
Procrastination	Schedule difficult and unpleasant tasks first instead of putting them off.

Reactions from participants and trainers to this emphasis on principles and their practical application in terms of "action items" varies from one of interest and surprise to astonishment and excitement. The percentage of attendees who carry out the assignment overnight ranges from 90 percent to 100 percent, suggesting that they tend to take it very seriously and expect that it will have value for them. When asked for their reactions to the assignment, typical responses will be: "Interesting...Provided a reason for a lot of things...Some new insights...Reinforced some actions I've needed to take."

A trainer in Seattle attending an open seminar said she'd stayed up until 3 a.m. working on the assignment. When asked why, she responded that as she got into the assignment she realized she was finding principles to support most of the actions she'd wanted to take in the past year and not been allowed to. She got so excited about it that she couldn't stop.

STEPS TRAINERS CAN TAKE

Since trainers are in an ideal position to do something about the wasteland of neglect of management principles, what courses of action are open to them?

1. Review the Management Process Chart (*Harvard Business Review*, Nov.-Dec. 1969) and develop from it a rationale for your training and development program. Place each course offered in its appropriate functional area (e.g., transactional analysis falls within the communicating function). *Understanding* of the management process at all levels and *mastery* of that process for senior levels should be a categorical imperative. *Career development programs* should be keyed to the functional areas of greatest importance to the individual in his or her present job and in the preparation for promotion.

2. Review principles of management by functional areas. The book by Koontz and O'Donnell is best. Categorize these in appropriate functional areas (planning, organizing, etc.). Discuss these with speakers on various topics to ensure their understanding of and willingness to present them and to discuss practical applications of them in their presentations. Trainers giving courses themselves should base their presentations on the fundamental principles involved, with practical applications being the focus of the entire presentation. Handout materials should be reviewed for applicability to both principles and practices of management.

3. Follow the Principle of Reinforcement in your training programs. Since this principle is universally recognized in the training profession, but practiced very little, take it seriously. Stop counting "notches on the belt" and start reinforcing! Instead of booking five seminars of a subject like time management, book one seminar and require a follow-up program to reinforce

lessons learned. At a given point from three to six months out, test the results, measure the progress. How much changed behavior has occurred? How much of it has persisted? What results can be observed in controlling major time wasters?

4. Take performance auditing seriously by requiring of yourself and speakers criteria for measuring effectiveness. (See "Measuring Managerial Effectiveness," a chapter in *New Time Management Methods for You and Your Team* [Dartnell], for methods of auditing effectiveness in controlling top time wasters.) A speaker should be asked how to measure improvement in his or her subject area three to six months later.

5. Insure that time management programs reinforce your training program by reviewing the functional areas covered by the time management presentation. Avoid the "quickie" approach to saving a few minutes here and there with the cafeteria approach of "hot tips." Remember, we waste time whenever we do anything less effectively than we could. Thus we can instantly identify time wasters in *each* functional area of management.

Analyze the functional areas covered by your time management course. Insure maximum coverage by that course to broaden the reinforcement of your entire program. Be sure the subject is approached from the viewpoint of emphasis on the fundamental principles and practices of management.

Finally, to ensure substantial amounts of time saved aren't wasted, you should require that participants *first* decide how they plan to *use* time saved most productively. By starting with fundamental principles and developing "action items," there is almost no limit to the number of practical applications one can identify.

Indeed, there *is* nothing more practical than a sound principle. Since our time is our life, when we manage our time well, we manage our life well. At work and in our personal lives it's simply a matter of putting into practice a few basic principles we know so well, but somehow continue to neglect. Trainers should be leading the way out of this wasteland.

R. Alec Mackenzie, president of Alec Mackenzie and Associates, Inc., has been actively promoting the management education and professional development of senior executives throughout the world. His publications include: Managing Your Time, The Credibility Gap in Management, The Time Trap *and* New Time Management Methods for You and Your Staff.

Part II
THE DOCTRINE OF TIME MANAGEMENT

9.
TIME, ONE MORE TIME

John W. Lee
Robert Adcock

The only principle which seemingly was followed by a majority of those surveyed was the *Principle of Muddling Through*—little planning, less organization and practically no control.

The time available to executives and managers has become so critical that many companies now consider executive time as the decisive criterion for entering new ventures rather than return on investment, according to Curtis H. Jones.[1] Leo B. Moore has attested to the importance of time to the manager. He contends that the manager's job is so fragmented that his time must be divided between getting today's job done and thinking of tomorrow's activities. It follows that the value of managing an executive's time cannot be underestimated.[2]

Time is a unique resource. Everyone has equal shares. It cannot be bought and everything takes time. The only real solution is better use of available time. Executives and managers must learn to manage the use of their time. Peter Drucker has noted that one of the five habits common to all effective executives is knowing where their time goes and where it should go.[3] The practice of time management is a habit which can be learned.

Learning occurs in many ways. One way is by trial and error. Many successful executives and managers have learned to solve their time problems in this manner, as evidenced by the amount of "how to" literature that has appeared in the past ten years on time conservation. A preferable way of learning is through a methodical, systematic approach to the problem.

NEED FOR TIME MANAGEMENT CONCEPTS

Numerous articles have been written on the subject of time management, many containing similar recommendations for the conservation of this valuable resource. Too many of the time articles focus upon gimmicks, such as how to save time by not having a desk in the office, or how to dictate in your car to save an hour. These tips may be invaluable to a small sector of the business community, but their practicality for the majority of managers is, at best, considered doubtful. The literature did, however, provide usable suggestions. What was needed was unification of these scattered ideas and suggestions into a workable time-management system or process that could be learned and applied by anyone with a time problem.

A review of the literature revealed one reference to time management as it applied to the overall management process. Terry, describing the management process, stated that it consisted of the functions of planning, organizing, actuating and controlling. The management of time was located within the function of controlling.[4] Further reflection on this leads to the conjecture that the management of time, per se, is a process itself, which consists of the functions of planning, organizing and controlling. That is, to manage one's time entails planning and organizing for its efficient use as well as controlling its use.

The benefits to be derived from a conceptual framework of time management are analogous to those derived from management theory. Koontz and O'Donnell state that management theory is a way of organizing experience so that practice can be improved through research, empirical testing of principles, and proper teaching of fundamentals.[5] If this accumulated experience could be distilled into practical principles for general use, a basis for a theory of time management would exist.

The value of principles has been cited in behavioral research. Judd demonstrated that transfer of learning from one situation to another took place more readily in individuals who had been taught principles or generalizations that apply to both situations.[6] Learning how to manage time would seem to be enhanced through development of principles that could be applied according to the situation.

With these considerations in mind, ten principles of time management were developed from an extensive review of the published literature on time management.[7] These principles, while spanning the entire time-management process, are not considered to be all inclusive. They are best looked upon as tentative statements subject to further testing and refinement.

PRINCIPLES APPLICABLE TO PLANNING

Planning is selecting among choices. Planning the use of one's time involves finding out first how it is now used, deciding how it should be used, and scheduling its proper use in the manner desired. But how is the time currently being used? Trickett states that most people are not really aware of what occupies their time.[8] Ruchti suggests two ways to find out where time goes: keep an appointment book or diary, or have someone observe, time and catalogue the work activity.[9]

Until the manager understands how his time is being spent, he cannot choose among alternative ways of using it. Somehow he must find out where his time presently goes. The most commonly accepted procedure is an analysis of an individual's time use from data taken over a typical time period. This is the first planning principle, the Principle of Time Analysis.

The basis of time analysis usually takes the form of a log in which an individual's daily activities are recorded against time. Each 15 minute interval of the manager's workday should be recorded and an attempt made to account for all time used. After sufficient recordings are made to enable the manager to recognize a trend or pattern in his daily activities, an analysis is possible. In performing the analysis, the manager usually finds that considerable time is wasted or is unaccountable for because of procrastination, interruptions, lack of a plan or other reasons.

Principle of Time Analysis. Time analysis is a prerequisite to time management. Keeping a daily log of activities that records increments of 15 to 30 minutes duration over a span of not less than two weeks is essential as the basis of the analysis.

The second planning principle is the Principle of Daily Planning. Inadequate planning has been noted by most authors as a major cause of time mismanagement. Planning effectively will offset this time waste. The recommendations for making plans take on a number of different forms, depending on the author. Most agree that plans should be made daily, and consist of a list of work items and a time schedule for their accomplishment. All seem to agree that the plans should be made before the workday starts.

Principle of Daily Planning. Daily planning, formulated after business hours the previous day or early before business hours on the same day, in consonance with near-term objectives and events, is essential to the effective utilization of personal time.

In constructing a daily plan, priorities must be assigned to the items of work to be accomplished. Drucker said it very well: "Set priorities and abide by your priority decisions."[10]

The method of deciding the priorities has been thoughtfully discussed by Trickett. He has suggested classifying work items three ways to arrive at the priorities. His method is based on the phenomenon that things that are urgent are not always important, and things that are important are not always urgent. He has recommended that the work items be classified according to urgency on a scale ranging from "very urgent" to "not urgent," and then reclassified according to importance on a scale ranging from "very important" to "unimportant." The third recommended classification is of those work items which can or cannot be delegated. Obviously, the highest priorities are assigned to those items which cannot be delegated, are "very urgent," and also "very important."[11]

Listing the work items in the daily plan according to the priorities and budgeting the time available for their accomplishment is the third planning principle, Budgeting by Priority.

Principle of Budgeting by Priority. The time available in the workday should be budgeted for the accomplishment of those items of work that have the highest priorities.

Another important principle that applies to the planning function is the Principle of Flexibility. This is:

Principle of Flexibility. Flexibility should be a major consideration in the selection of plans regarding the use of personal time. Stated simply: Time should not be over- or underscheduled.

In formulating a daily plan, one must be aware of limitations on the amount of time in a workday which can reasonably be scheduled and maintained. The manager who plans every minute of his workday will find that his inflexible schedule cannot be followed. Drucker has stated it aptly:

Any man in an important administrative position who schedules more than half his time is overscheduling. At least half an administrator's time can be expected to be taken up with crises, emergencies and just the pressures of everyday life in a large organization.[12]

Related to this advice, it must be recognized that on the average only 50 percent of a workday can be scheduled, but the jobs selected for accomplishment in the scheduled four hours should be truly worthy of that amount of time. For example, if during a lull period jobs which normally would take less than four hours of an eight-hour day are allowed to expand to fill the time available, poor time-management habits will be acquired. The same strict discipline should be maintained over the use of time when slack periods occur in the workflow. These are safeguards that the planner should implement to preclude the encroachment of work expanding to fill the time available.

PRINCIPLES APPLICABLE TO ORGANIZING

The organization function concerns how the manager organizes his work and his environment to become more efficient in the use of time. The first organization principle is:

Principle of Delegation. Delegation of all possible work items consistent with the limitations of the manager's job is essential to providing the time needed for managerial jobs.

Establishing priorities for the items of work in the daily plan consists also of deciding which of these can be delegated. All items that can be delegated, should be, to free time for those jobs that only the manager can do. To decide whether an item of work can be delegated, the manager should follow the well-established principles of delegation.

A second principle to be used in organizing work is the segmentation of like activities into certain groupings for more efficient accomplishment. This principle is:

Principle of Activity Segmentation. Work items similar in nature and requiring similar environment surroundings and resources for their accomplishment should be grouped within divisions of the workday.

In conjunction with this principle, another principle should be used. This is:

Principle of Control of Interruptions. Adequate controls and/or arrangement of activities to minimize the number and duration of unnecessary interruptions is essential to time management.

The benefits from implementing these two principles are apparent. Interruptions must be minimized, and one way to minimize interruptions is to segment the activities by grouping. If the activities are segmented such that subordinates meet with their manager at a certain time, telephone calls are placed and returned at a certain time, a time for meetings is established, and "quiet" time is built into the day, then the efficiency of time utilization will improve as interruptions are minimized. The number of starts and stops on particular jobs will likewise be greatly reduced. Holding the number of starts and stops to a minimum will materially improve the efficiency of accomplishing the tasks with the resultant saving of time.

Organization of work and staff to reduce the amount of routine work will lead to more effective time use. Probably no manager will ever be able to rid himself of routine work completely, but it should be minimized. Routine work is defined as small, commonly recurring procedures. Estimates of time spent by managers on routine work vary from 30 to 65 percent of the time available. The principle is:

Principle of Minimization of Routine Work. Work items which are routine in nature and which constitute little value to overall objectives should be minimized.

PRINCIPLES APPLICABLE TO CONTROLLING

After planning and organizing the work in line with the applicable principles, there remain only plan implementation and daily follow-up. As Moore states:

The concept of control through plans and schedules is fundamental to sound management and to increasing effectiveness... To gain his objective as planned... he compares the actual expenditure of the resource with the plan and the schedule. The variance permits him to make decisions about the plan, the schedule, and the performance, and to adjust all three in tune with his objectives and the conditions he is facing.[13]

This involves the use of the following principle:

Principle of Plan Implementation and Follow-up. Implementation of the daily plan and daily follow-up is essential to time management.

Plan implementation is essential to the function of controlling. Controlling cannot be accomplished unless there is a plan or standard with which to compare actual with expected results. Following up adjustment of the plan, the schedule, and the performance in consonance with objectives and conditions is controlling.

Drucker recommended repeating the time analysis at least every six months. Moore found that the difficulties involved in implementing a daily plan are such that most managers return to their old practices. To guard against this eventuality, time-usage analysis should be repeated periodically. The principle is:

Principle of Repeated Analysis. Time-usage analysis should be repeated at least semi-annually to preclude reverting to poor time management habits.

RESEARCH RESULTS

The ten principles of time management were developed after conducting an extensive literature review and surveying 64 aerospace management and administrative personnel to determine if the principles were in general use. These individuals, students in Florida State University's master of science in management program, held full-time jobs either in private industry or in a military organization. The average age of the group was 32.8 years, and their managerial experience averaged six years. Their median organizational level was fourth from the top.

The respondents were asked to complete a questionnaire consisting of 43 multiple-choice questions related to the principles of time management. They were not told of the principles beforehand. Each question required them to choose the answer which most nearly described the way in which they perform their jobs.

RESULTS APPLICABLE TO PLANNING FUNCTION

Three of the four planning principles were found not to be in general use. Only the *Principle of Budgeting by Priority* appeared to be used by more than 50 percent of the respondents. Related to the *Principle of Analysis*, it was established that although a majority of the respondents said they had performed a time analysis within the past year, only 15 percent had used a log which accounted for the recommended increments of time or had recorded the log for two weeks or longer. The largest percentage of the group said they had performed a time analysis using some basis other than a log. Many appeared to have performed their analysis as a by-product of some other administrative procedure. Some mentioned they had recorded their activities at the end of the workweek and used this for a time analysis. It was obvious that only a very small portion of the respondents, if any, had performed a time usage analysis of the nature necessary to discern how they spent their time.

The *Principle of Daily Planning* was found not to be in general use. A majority of the respondents did not write their plans, plan before the start of the work day, or plan daily. Fifty-three percent of the respondents stated that their plans consisted of a written list of "to do" items. Only 47 percent disclosed that they did their workday planning either late on the previous day, at home, or before work hours started. The principle recommends planning every day, but only 42 percent stated that they planned with this regularity. It was concluded that a majority of the respondents arrive at the office with some kind of plan—either a written list or a mental list of jobs to be done—but few rarely commit these plans to paper in the form of a schedule.

It was concluded that a majority of the respondents establish priorities for their jobs and budget time accordingly. Evidence indicated that about one-third did not follow their priorities after they were set.

The *Principle of Flexibility* likewise was found not to be in general use. Only 43 percent of the respondents advocated maintenance of strict discipline over the use of their time during slack periods. A mere three percent said that they actually followed this guideline. Fifty-two percent stated that when slack periods in their workflow occurred, they tended to relax and get ready for the next peak period. Only one-fourth of the respondents believed that less than one hour of their eight-hour day could be preplanned and executed. Forty-four percent felt that three to five hours of an eight-hour day could be prescheduled and completed successfully. Since a majority did not believe nor implement strict control of their time use during slack periods, and less than a majority believed that 50 percent of their day could be prescheduled and completed, it was obvious that this principle was not followed.

RESULTS APPLICABLE TO THE ORGANIZING FUNCTION

A majority of the respondents followed the *Principle of Delegation*. This conclusion was reached because of the apparent willingness of the respondents to allow subordinates latitude in their assigned tasks. A willingness to trust subordinates associated with an inclination to assign responsibility and authority was also noted.

The *Principle of Activity Segmentation* was not in general use. The respondents indicated that they did not try to group their telephone calls. Sixty-eight percent scheduled less than one hour of "quiet" time per day, and only 28 percent had some predetermined order in the handling of tasks. The respondents did not confer daily with their subordinates at a regularly scheduled time. Although 58 percent allocated between one and three hours per day for self-improvement, this finding is subject to question because the respondents were part-time students. Little indication of grouping of similar activities within the workday was present.

The number of hours spent in routine work by this group was found to agree with Stewart's empirical research on this subject. Because the group spent an average of 35 percent of an eight-hour day performing routine work, it was concluded that they did not apply the *Principle of Minimization of Routine Work*. This conclusion was backed by other data such as the failure of the respondents to allow their secretaries to absorb more than menial responsibility for such routine items as mail.

The group also did not abide by the *Principle of Control of Interruptions*. They allowed themselves to be interrupted by the telephone. They did not apply the *Principle of Activity Segmentation* with its resulting reduction in interruptions. They neither controlled the access that casual visitors had to them nor did they have a control policy. It was found that many, 47 percent, had to isolate themselves from their regular work area on days when there was a very important item of work which had to be completed.

RESULTS APPLICABLE TO THE CONTROLLING FUNCTIONS

The *Principle of Plan Implementation and Follow-up* probably was not followed by a majority of the respondents. Although 55 percent stated that they compared accomplishments to plans every day, only 42 percent planned daily. It is impossible to implement and follow up a non-existent plan. Since one-third said their day-to-day plans were mental lists of "to do" items, rigorous follow-up to these items cannot be made.

The respondents did not follow the *Principle of Repeated Analysis*. The reasoning behind this conclusion was that they did not analyze their time usage according to the *Principle of Time Analysis*, and although 28 percent of the respondents advocated performing an analysis semi-annually, only 16 percent stated that they actually did so.

CONCLUSION

Ten principles of time management were formulated, were tested on a group of 64 managers, and were found not to be in general use. Further testing of these principles is needed. Expanded testing should lead not only to the validation and refinement of the present principles but also to the formulation of additional principles.

With additional principles, the conceptual framework for time management will crystallize. Time is too important a managerial resource to be used ineffectively. Good intentions, such as those that this study uncovered, without a thorough understanding of the time management process and its principles can lead only to time problems.

In closing, the only principle which seemingly was followed by a majority of those surveyed was the *Principle of Muddling Through*: little planning, less organization and practically no controlling.

References

1. Curtis H. Jones, "The Money Value of Time," *Harvard Business Review* (July-August 1968), p. 95.
2. Leo B. Moore, "Management Time," *Industrial Management Review* (Spring 1968), pp. 77-85.
3. Peter F. Drucker, *The Effective Executive* (New York: Harper and Row, 1967), pp. 26-27.
4. George R. Terry, *Principles of Management*, 4th ed. (Homewood, Ill.: Irwin, 1964), pp. 50-57.
5. Harold Koontz and Cyril O'Donnell, *Principles of Management*, 3rd ed. (New York: McGraw-Hill, 1964), pp. 27-28.
6. Douglas H. Fryer, Edwin R. Henry and Charles P. Sparks, *General Psychology*, 4th ed. (New York: Barnes & Noble, 1954), p. 155.
7. Robert L. Adcock, "The Time Management Process: A Preliminary Statement of Its Functions and Principles and a Survey of Their Use" (unpublished master's thesis, School of Business, Florida State University, 1970).
8. Joseph M. Trickett, "A More Effective Use of Time," *California Management Review* (Summer 1962), p. 5.
9. William Ruchti, "Take Time to Plan Time," *Supervisory Management* (July 1958), p. 3.
10. Peter F. Drucker, "How to Spend Time on Things That Count," *Nation's Schools* (April 1964), p. 75.
11. Trickett, pp. 5-7.
12. Drucker, p. 75.
13. Moore, p. 83.
14. John P. Campbell, Marvin D. Dunnette, Edward E. Lawler, III, and Karl E. Weick, Jr., *Management Behavior, Performance, and Effectiveness* (New York: McGraw-Hill, 1970), p. 89.

John W. Lee is assistant professor of management, The Florida State University. Robert Adcock is manager of NASA studies at the Martin-Marietta Corporation in Florida.

10.
MANAGING TIME: POSITIVE CLOCK-WATCHING

George H. Labovitz
Lloyd S. Baird

It is a paradox of management that those who are responsible for organizing the activities of others often have the most trouble managing themselves.

Perhaps no subject is as popular or of more importance to supervisors than the management of time. A legion of time-management specialists equipped with newly published books, charts, time logs and cartoons is now instructing managers on how to make the most effective use of their time. The difference between *effective* and *efficient* use of time is the key because, as the experts point out, efficiency merely means doing the job right while effectiveness means doing the *right* job right.

Most time-management seminars, which range in length from a few hours to three days, take one of two approaches to teaching time management. One is the gimmick approach, in which hundreds of time-saving tips are tossed out for managers to pick and choose. They suggest, for example: don't face your desk toward an open door because it invites interruptions; don't eat heavy lunches; cut down on the number of meetings you attend; hire a good secretary to screen your mail and answer the phone. These approaches don't depend on a body of knowledge or a theory base. Rather, they are a compilation of handy hints, some of which can be very effective in the organization and utilization of a manager's time.

The other approach is more systematic and is based on developing effective work habits rather than saving a few minutes here and there. For example, it suggests managers learn how to say no to people (including the boss) who want to divert them from the work they are doing and not waste time regretting failures or letting subordinates manipulate them into doing their thinking for them.

In our opinion, time management is nothing more than applying the principles of management to ourselves. So, as a basis for our discussion of managing time, it is probably a good idea to start with a fundamental review of the management process. Whether we're managing a large-scale organization, one secretary, or ourselves, the process of management is composed of four simple steps:

1.   Try to understand what you are trying to accomplish.
2.   Organize your activities.
3.   Achieve results.
4.   Evaluate what has happened.

PARADOXES OF TIME MANAGEMENT

Schwartz and MacKenzie have identified a number of management paradoxes—things that go against our ability to apply these four simple concepts to ourselves. They recognize that by and large most managers don't like to plan. One of the reasons for this is that planning takes time. One paradox is that because managers do not plan their own use of time, they never seem to have time to plan their department's use of time. The less we manage time and allow others to determine what we do, the more likely we are to be working harder and accomplishing less.

Here are some of the other paradoxes that Schwartz and MacKenzie found to be most common in preventing managers from getting on with organizing and managing their own activities:

1.   *Open-door paradox.* By leaving a door open in the hope of improving communication, managers tend to increase the wrong kind of communication, that of the trivial or socializing nature. This multiplies interruptions and distracts them from more important tasks. The open-door approach does not literally mean a physically open door but easy access to management.
2.   *Tyranny-of-the-urgent paradox.* Managers tend to respond to the urgent rather than the important. Thus, long-range priorities are often neglected and thereby become future crises.
3.   *Crisis paradox.* Managers tend to overrespond to crises, thereby making them worse.
4.   *Meeting paradox.* By waiting for latecomers before starting a meeting, we penalize those who come on time and reward those who come late. The frequent result is that the next time, those who were on time come late and those who were late come later.

As we begin to stand back and take a long look not only at what we are managing but also at *how* we are managing what we manage, we should focus on the things that are preventing us from effectively using our time.

The blocks to effective time management are both external and internal. *Externally* generated blocks are generally those things that other people do to us. Two separate studies have found that managers are interrupted on the average of every eight minutes per working day. With that frequency, it is virtually impossible to concentrate on important priorities. Uncontrolled interruptions divert our attention from our objectives, slow down the momentum we've generated, and make it necessary to take yet more time to get back to where we left off.

As we will see, the external timewasters can be controlled. But *internally* generated timewasters are quite different. Henry Mintzberg, in a study of chief executive officers, found that many senior executives *want* to be interrupted. Indeed, Mintzberg found that they actually created interruptions and then complained about them. Psychologically based barriers to managing your time effectively include ego considerations ("Only I can answer a question."); fear of offending ("If no one answers my phone, or someone answers it and tells the caller I am busy, the caller will be offended."); the desire to be available; or the attempt to be a good person.

Regardless of whether or not the blocks are external or internal, you can still overcome them and manage time the way you would any other resource. The first thing that must be done is to define your objectives. The process of managing people by their objectives not only delineates what must be done but also helps set priorities. Without priorities, without objectives, you become enmeshed in what George Odiorne has called the activity trap.

Most managers get caught in the activity trap! They become so enmeshed in activity they lose sight of why they are doing it, and the activity becomes a false goal, an end in itself.

Alan Lakein, in his book, *How To Get Control of Your Time and Your Life*, offers some basic ideas about establishing goals and setting priorities. He recommends that every manager define long-term objectives or goals as *things that have to be done during the next six months*. He recommends ranking both life and job goals according to an a, b, c system: (a) a goal of high value and importance, (b) a goal of lesser importance, such as improving relations with a boss or subordinate, and (c) goals of low value. Lakein then offers six suggestions for more effective management of time:

1. List your goals and set priorities.
2. Make a daily "to do" list. Goals cannot be accomplished without activities and listing those activities that have to be done each day helps to accomplish your objectives.
3. Always start with the "a" and not the "c." Less important activities are seductive because they are usually relatively easy to handle and can be

accomplished in a short time. However, they also provide excellent excuses for not dealing with the more important, difficult and substantive
objectives at hand.

4. Continually ask yourself, "What is the best utilization of my time right
   now?" Take what he calls a "Swiss cheese approach" to overwhelming
   tasks. If there are ten minutes available before lunch, take a bit of an "a"
   and begin the process of dealing with those things that you are trying to
   avoid. Whether preparing a budget or disciplining an employee, begin the
   process and move it forward.
5. Handle each piece of paper only once.
6. Do it now.

THE TIME AUDIT

In order to gain control over your most valuable resources, you must first
obtain an accurate portrait of how you spend your time on the job. Virtually all
time-management experts begin by analyzing how a manager is currently
spending his or her time. The most common way to do this is to establish a time
log kept by you or your secretary. A time log (or a time audit) does not have to
be complicated nor does it have to be kept constantly. Its purpose is to spot-
check how well you're doing. Two basic rules for a time audit are: your activities
have to be written down, and they have to be recorded as you are working.
Recording from memory tends to result in forgetting those times that you were
not being productive and in guaranteeing that your activities will never be
recorded in the log.

The time log can be very simple, as long as it includes a space for listing the
activities that you are engaged in throughout the day and what the purpose of
those activities was. The log may vary according to the type of job being
analyzed; the more standardized the job, the less elaborate the symbols need
be. The log might look like the one that follows.

Time Log

Date
Time

Start	End	Total	Activity	With Whom	Initia-tion	Action/Notes
9:00	10:00	60	C	Data Mgr.	S	Discussed deteriorating market shares. Records due next week.

10:05	10:15	10	TP	Bill Hobber	O	Problems with Q. C. Wants better late access.

Initiation	Activity Codes
O = other	TP = Telephone
S = self	C = conference
	W = writing

For a time-log analysis to work well, the following hints should be kept in mind.

1. Carry your log with you at all times.
2. Note your comments immediately or you'll forget them.
3. Make your entries short but specific.

Record the smallest uses of time, *especially interruptions*. Subdivide long periods. For example, a meeting may cover three or four major areas, such as budgeting, safety or benefits, and each should be noted. Once you have a record of your activities during a typical period, you're ready to analyze how you're spending your time.

ANALYZING YOUR USE OF TIME

Time analysis can be done in several ways. One way is to total the categories and see how much time you spend in various areas such as personal time, telephone calls, conferences and individual discussions. You can then examine how you allocate time to functional areas, and you can also analyze the flow of activities. This includes a study of the time taken up by interruptions. Next, your time can be divided into four categories: creative, preparatory, productive and overhead. *Creative time* is the time devoted to planning future activities. *Preparatory time* is time spent in setting up activities, such as gathering facts. *Productive time* is time actually spent doing the job. *Overhead time* is spent on correspondence and reports.

In analyzing your use of time, William Glueck recommends asking yourself the following questions:

1. Should anybody be doing this activity at all? Does it serve any purpose? (For example, do you really need to meet with your subordinates every morning?)

2. If an activity needs to be done, should I be the one doing it? If a subordinate can do it equally well, why not delegate?
3. If I should do it myself, can it be done in less time? How?
4. Do I keep punctually to my time schedules, or do I waste time with my subordinates?
5. Do I keep my overhead duties handy, so that I can do them while waiting for telephone callers to get on the line or for visitors to show?

HINTS FOR EFFECTIVE TIME MANAGEMENT

In reviewing the literature on time management, one is overwhelmed by the number of "handy hints" provided by experts on the subject. A common element in all of them is recommending confronting those things that are getting in the way of making you productive. Managing that confrontation may be made easier, as follows:

1. Assign long periods of continuous time to major tasks.
2. Control interruptions during critical periods by accepting no visitors and no phone calls.
3. Block out time for creative planning, preparation and overhead activities.
4. Group together related kinds of work to save starting and stopping time.
5. Put all telephone calls together. Get your secretary to dial the next call when you're almost through with the current one.
6. Schedule top-priority projects early in the week.
7. Identify your own "internal prime time"—when you do your clearest thinking—and allocate this time to pursuing top priorities.
8. Reserve an amount of time for unanticipated crises.
9. Schedule your least interesting jobs at your peak energy periods so you'll get more done.
10. Postpone shorter projects until you have started longer ones.
11. Be sensitive to the process of reverse delegation. In other words, how much of your time is being dictated by your subordinates? One executive has a standard response to subordinates who hop into his office with the words, "Boss, we have a problem." His response is, "You sure do."
12. Move fast on reversible decisions and slower on those that are irrevocable.
13. Let subordinates know that there are certain times in the day when you don't wish to be interrupted, and other times when they are welcome to stop by.

14.   Throw out all junk mail. Under the category of mail, other hints include: route mail directly to subordinates, cancel subscriptions to organizations that send you too much mail, and try to get off mailing lists.

Our time and work can be better used and organized if each of us assertively takes charge of those things that are getting in the way of our productivity. But every supervisor is as concerned with effectively managing the time of other people as he or she is with self-management. Since meetings occupy a great deal of everyone's time, it is useful for us to consider them in detail.

MANAGING MEETINGS

After the next meeting that you are responsible for, ask yourself the following questions:

1.   How much of what we discussed was one-way communication that could have been handled with a memo, a letter or a presentation to the people directly involved in the problem?
2.   Was I talking to the whole group, and was the whole group involved? Or was I talking to one or two individuals and expecting the rest just to listen in?
3.   How much of what we did was problem solving or conflict management, and how much was just wasting time? Did the participants come prepared?

Participative-management techniques and the MBO process require face-to-face interaction. But those interactions must be carefully managed so as to ensure that you are wasting neither your time nor the time of your subordinates. Each of us has spent countless hours as a victim of a superior's inability to run and plan a meeting effectively. Because of these negative experiences, many of us who become managers shy away from holding meetings. But meetings can perform many important functions. For example:

• In a simple and most basic way, a meeting defines the essence of the group. Everyone is able to look around and perceive the whole of which he or she forms a part and therefore to get a feeling of collective identity.
• The meeting is a place where the group revises, updates and adds to what it knows collectively. Every group creates its own pool of shared knowledge, experience and judgment.
• A meeting helps every individual understand both the collective aim of the group and the way that his or her own and everybody else's work can contribute to the group's success.
• A meeting creates in its participants a commitment to the group's decisions and objectives.

• In the world of management, a meeting is very often the only occasion for individuals to come together and work as a group and perceive their supervisor as the leader.

A manager must also attend meetings that he or she is not in charge of. What can you do to manage your time in these meetings more effectively? As a participant, you should have the same expectations as if you were the person in charge. You should be informed about the purpose of the meeting so that you can prepare, and you should be involved in whatever is happening and not be expected to sit and idly listen while others carry on conversation.

DELEGATION

Delegation is not only a responsibility of a manager but a prime way for a manager to save time that could be devoted to more important tasks.

There are only a couple of rules to remember when deciding what to delegate. First, you should select for delegation those things that other people have the resources, time and responsibility for working on. Next you should select those things that you could do but others can also do. Third, you should select those things that will help others grow and develop. Remember, delegation is not abdication of responsibility nor is it just passing on those things that you do not want to do. It is a technique for involving others in the work process and giving them the chance to be challenged and to feel a sense of accomplishment.

In conclusion, only by constant attention to what we are personally trying to accomplish can we possibly hope to choose wisely among the numerous activities that we have open to us. Time is a limited resource, and the only option we have is to use what time we have wisely.

George H. Labovitz, PhD, is professor of organizational behavior and management at the Boston University School of Management and president of Organizational Dynamics, Inc. Lloyd S. Baird is associate professor of organizational behavior, also at Boston University, and an authority on human performance in organizations.

11.
HOW TO FIGHT TIME (AND WIN)

Janet G. Hibbard
Robert K. Landrum

Time is the scarcest resource and unless it is managed nothing else can be managed.[1] *You have to mobilize yourself and others in this miniwar.*

Managing your working minutes is a matter of time saving and, specifically, time budgeting, after which work priorities should be established and adhered to. But before budgeting can begin, an audit must be made of what you are currently doing with your time.

AUDIT YOUR UTILIZATION OF TIME

Take inventory of what you do with your time. Do this by keeping a simple dairy or log over a two-week period; you can then determine where your time is being spent.

Many lawyers keep a log of how long the meter runs with each client. You can do the same by recording what transpired in a prior 15 or 30 minute period, or by taking a few minutes in the evening to record briefly the key events of the day and how much time was consumed by each. Be honest about how your time was employed during the two-week survey. Put down time that was wasted, whether by you or others.

A follow-up study will reveal the tasks and activities requiring the bulk of your time. Analysis of the audit will probably also reveal a certain pattern in your schedule. Time-wasting factors will be uncovered, suggesting self-disciplining in possibilities and giving you new insights into your habits and methods.

Utilization of work time should be audited and reevaluated at least twice a year.

77

CONTROL YOUR TIME

After planning and budgeting, you as a manager then practice the control function. So it should be with your time. Establish means of controlling "time wasters"[2] that are either externally imposed or self-generated.

Management of yourself is the very crux of controlling time. Sound habits regarding time usage should be developed and practiced. After you practice good time management and control, the example will also have been set for others in your organization.

Even though planning does consume time on the front end, it overcompensates both by bringing in better results and by saving time in actual performance of activities. So take time to plan. Do not engage in crisis management or stay forever on the defensive. Play the ball; don't let the ball play you.

In order to properly plan and determine priorities, use either end of each day to set goals, ranking them by their importance. At the end of a week, review and summarize your tasks and goal accomplishments, thereby gauging effectiveness. How many of those daily or weekly goals contributed directly to long-range objectives? If only a few, you may have too many conflicts between objectives or between objectives and short-term goals.

Using a checklist and a pocket notebook will also save you time by minimizing oversights.

PATIENCE

The virtue of patience prevents your becoming a slave to the compulsion of the imperative. True, patience consumes time, but it also minimizes false starts and lessens the frequency of crises, both of which are real time wasters. When you hurry into a decision or its implementation, ask yourself if you are being too hasty. Should the passage of time be favorable for your side of a business deal, let time work for you by being patient.

PERFORMING A TASK

Tackle a task the first time an opportunity presents itself; do not waste time thinking and rethinking about how to handle it. When there are many difficult tasks to cope with, concentrate on doing one at a time, just as a baseball game is played an inning at a time.

After you have gathered enough material to make a decision, make it. By deciding promptly, there is more time to alter the decision in the event it needs correction. Procrastination causes not only time-slippage but also delays implementation.

Make the major decisions when you are most alert. You will save time and make the wiser choice of alternatives.

When dealing with an associate who you think might waste time on a decision or its implementation, set a target date. If you set the deadline, there is more likelihood that a project will be completed sooner than if there were no deadline at all. Completion is even more of a certainty if you let the other person set the target date.

MANAGEMENT BY EXCEPTION

There is time to be saved by following the exception principle: Let subordinates monitor the routine, unexceptional matters and make the recurring decisions. You handle only the exceptional problems. Keep away from getting bogged down in details. In short, save your time by getting feedback in summary form and by means of exception reports, those (and only those) relevant to major decision-making activities.

DELEGATION

If you have an office assistant, that person should handle your appointments. This saves you time in arranging each appointment and allows visitors to be screened and eliminated or deferred if they do not meet the cost/benefit criteria for inclusion in your time schedule.

In addition, your office assistant should handle all incoming calls. Consider having your assistant hold all but emergency calls that are made to you during the morning and request a message from each caller. Interruptions will then be minimized and you can return the calls in the sequence you choose and at the hour you select. This will also save you time because fewer minutes will probably be spent on return calls as you will already know what they concern. Should the caller request an appointment, your office assistant can determine from the caller approximately how much of your time the latter will need.

Authorize your assistant to assume responsibility for all correspondence leaving your office, including drafting replies to routine letters. Further authorize the assistant to sign your letters with his/her initials below the signature, except for those letters which may be sensitive or of substantial consequence.

Conserve your office assistant's time by meeting with him/her either mornings or evenings to coordinate both of your schedules. This allows the assistant to plan the day around your activities and priorities, especially when you let that person know if you'll be out of the office, approximately how long, where you can be reached, etc.

Other subordinates can help you save time, too. But in order to assign responsibilities to your subordinates, you must first develop their capabilities. And, of course, this includes helping them to develop effective time management habits themselves.

Consider, however, that the time you save by delegating a project may be disproportionately added to the time of another. You must be aware of whether the tasks will incur more of the subordinate's time than it would of yours. If so, consider doing the job yourself, as it takes up aggregate company time. In fact, the cost of time in possible compensation pay should be used as one of your criteria in time management.

Be certain that you are not programming your time schedule so that you are unavailable to receive requests for assistance from your associates. You may save one of them a great deal of time in giving him/her a few minutes of yours.

Discourage reverse delegation. The monkey that is dropped on your back may consume more caretaking on company time than if the subordinate had never placed it there.

Respect the time of your subordinates. After all, it is usually your priority schedule they are working on. This includes saving your own time by not frequently checking up on subordinates; you may be destroying their priorities, lowering their morale and causing them anxieties that sap their time effectiveness. Give only needed instruction, and avoid attaching more urgency to them than is fully justified. This can interrupt subordinates' priority schedules and cause them to lose time.

Give guidelines to subordinates within which they may work on delegated assignments. Guidelines will save time as well as provide numerous other advantages for the company. So will written policies and other methodologies that aid decision making.

A plausible rule to follow is to delegate those portions of your work that can be developed into a routine. As a consequence, you can recapture this released time for important work.

COMMUNICATIONS

Whether incoming or outgoing, a manager spends a lot of time on communication. To save time, search for a means of keeping communication as concise, brief and yet effective as possible. This means planning all your communications—written or oral. When time is wasted by unnecessary communication, it is multiplied by the number of receivers, since their time is also underutilized. In addition, learn how to terminate conversations or discussions once the subject has been sufficiently covered.

MEETINGS

Discourage unnecessary meetings. Start the necessary ones on time and end them on time, even if it means setting an automatic timer. Let all attendees know the anticipated ending time as well as the starting time.

Carefully prepare and use an agenda for any meetings other than impromptu ones at the water fountain, and include unfinished business from prior meetings. Circulate the agenda before the meeting in order to familiarize attendees in advance with what is scheduled to transpire. Have the meeting routinized where feasible by careful planning and precise execution.

Stick to the subject especially toward the end of a meeting when there is a tendency to begin discussing other problems. Interruptions also take a lot of time. Ask attendees to take written notes of what they want to contribute orally and to make their comments when invited to do so by the chairperson.

Assign follow-through projects to specified associates, noting such assignments in the minutes and on future agendas. Remember also to prepare accurate, concise minutes as soon as possible after adjournment.

Pick your company's least active weekday to hold meetings. Try to have as many standing committee meetings held on that day as can be conveniently scheduled, whether the frequency of a meeting is weekly, biweekly or monthly. Holding meetings during the lunch hour or having stand-up meetings are two additional time savers.

MAIL

Even though you may attempt to keep your fingers on the pulse of your business by seeing and sorting all or a portion of the mail each morning, it can be a time waster. Not only are you dealing with a lot of trivia, but you are using time in that hour of the day when you could be most productive in more important activities. This is for you to decide in your own particular situation. Just be sure that mail sorting, reading and routing is not taking too much of your valuable early morning time and energy.

Whether you, your office assistant or a mail room employee sorts and scans your incoming mail, separate that which does not require immediate attention. It can be read by you at a later time. The Army procedure of answering all mail within 48 hours is a time saver of some merit. At least you do not have to think and rethink about a letter which has needed answering for weeks.

READING TIME

What parts of your on-the-job reading can you defer, condense or have other people do in order to save you time? Determine your answers over a span of time and make appropriate adjustments. For example, your office assistant can route reading materials to your associates on a schedule that will save you time. Your assistant can also put your name last on the routing slip, which allows you to review your associates' comments on articles they felt were worthwhile.

Selective reading[3] is also a form of the exception principle. Scan the table of contents for a rough picture to help you determine how much reading time to spend with an article or book.

Develop standard formats for internally generated memos, policy statements, standard operation procedures, etc., in order to cut down on each reader's reading time.

INTERRUPTIONS

Guard your time against interruptions, whether they are due to bad working conditions, outsiders or your associates. Noise, for instance, makes work take longer to do.

"Can I look it up and let you know?" That question will halt many interruptions dead in their tracks.

TELEPHONE

The telephone can save much time, and conversely, waste a lot of it. First of all, join the ranks of polite callers who start a conversation with, "Do you have a minute?" And when on the receiving end of this question, remember that a simple, "No, may I call you back?" can allow you to get back to more important matters.

Make time the most important factor when you weigh and decide whether to call someone, meet with that person, or write him/her. In numerous instances, conference calls can save time all around.

"Consider the telephone as a message machine and get off the line promptly."[4] Brevity on the telephone can be facilitated by planning for the conversation. Concern yourself only with essentials. Most experienced executives agree that the opening dictates the ending of telephone conversations. "Hi, I need a couple of quick answers if you have a minute"[5] will guarantee a short phone call. You may also want to get a timer to help you keep calls short. It works as a cost saver as well as a time controller.

VISITORS

Allow your office assistant to screen visitors and make tentative appointments when in doubt about whether you wish to spend time with someone. Ask yourself if this visit is really necessary. If so, how could time be saved? Ask yourself also whether this visit should occur in your office or elsewhere. If the encounter is in your office and you want to keep it very brief, there are several means of handling it.

1. Tell a salesperson "no" early in the conversation if you are certain that you will not be a buyer.
2. Meet the visitor outside your office and converse there.
3. Keep the sitting places in your office filled with books or computer print-outs to discourage visitors from sitting down and staying too long.
4. Confer standing up with visitors by not sitting down again after greeting them.
5. Nod to your secretary to accompany the visitor into your office so that he/she can monitor the dialogue.
6. Tell the visitor in advance that you can only allot ten minutes to the meeting, and stick to that time limit.

Once a visitor is in your office, you can use a timepiece to great advantage. With an appropriate comment, you can remove your wristwatch and turn it face up or face down. Face up conveys the message that the interview is specially restricted. Face down lets the visitor know that time is inconsequential and to stay as long as he/she wishes.

An open-door policy sounds great, but it does take your time to deal with whatever and whomever enters. However, a modified open-door policy allows for screening potential visitors. When a visitor does enter, you can keep the meeting short-lived by knowing in advance exactly what it is about. A modified open-door policy also means being unavailable when you do not have time or do not wish to see some visitors.

Try not to keep someone waiting for a long time, or when he/she does get into a discussion with you, the visitor will probably feel entitled to a longer interview than otherwise. You may also feel the same way and spend too much time with that person.

Some internal visits are best handled by going to your associates' workplace.

YOUR DESK

In order to keep down distraction, place your desk so that you sit with either your back to the door or perpendicular to the door. Also keep your desk top as clean and neat as possible. Have a diary pad on your desk, whether you or your secretary makes your appointments.

HIDEOUTS AND DIVERSIONS

You might need a retreat location where you can rest occasionally or think and plan. The Army has learned that a company of infantrymen can march all day if they get a ten-minute break every hour. A rest period revives any person, whether taken each hour, each day or each month. You should take breaks during the day, especially when you feel the need for a change of pace. If feasible, allow your associates to do the same. A diversionary interlude can serve as an escape valve to let off steam and unwind. Also, try to vary the tasks you perform in order to refresh yourself and thereby increase your efficiency.

Planning is a major management function. It requires thorough and forward thinking, so the fewer distractions, the better the results and overall time saving. A hideout can be the best place to do this planning work. Your own private think tank can pay dividends by permitting you to reflect on past happenings and their relevance to company goals and long-range objectives.

In Greece, more than 2,000 years ago, Theophrastus wrote, "Time is the most valuable thing a man can spend." Perhaps one of these suggestions will help determine how best to spend the 1,440 minutes in each of your future days.

References

1. P.F. Drucker, "How To Be An Effective Executive," *Nation's Business* (April 1961), pp.34-5, 44, 48.
2. R.A. Mackenzie, *The Time Trap* (New York: McGraw-Hill, 1975), p.86.
3. J. McCay, *The Management of Time* (Englewood Cliffs, N.J.: Prentice-Hall, 1959), p. 13.
4. Mackenzie, p. 97.
5. *Ibid.*

Janet G. Hibbard is associate professor, College of Business, Eastern Kentucky University, Richmond, Kentucky. Robert K. Landrum is professor and chairman, department of management and industrial relations, Rider College, Lawrenceville, New Jersey.

12.
PUT TIME ON YOUR SIDE

Harold M. Emanuel

Ways to make time work for, not against, you.

There are three simple rules which, if followed, will afford some degree of control over the way we use time, our most precious of resources.

Rule One: Take control of your desk so the work flows naturally to you.

If your desk is like many, you probably haven't seen its surface in weeks, maybe months. It's cluttered with an array of magazines, letters, reports, documents, printouts, memos, advertisements, and scraps of paper that serve as reminders of the myriad of chores you should have done yesterday.

Let's first attack those scraps of paper. Take them and, one by one, list the jobs described on each, neatly, on one sheet of paper. Every time you complete one of these tasks, cross it off the list. Not only does this list give you an orderly and systematic manner of approaching all of those miscellaneous and random assignments, but it's a great feeling to see the lines through the work you've completed.

Next, put all of the magazines and other publications aside. We'll get to them later.

Quickly read through the direct mail advertisements you have and throw away any that don't pertain to your job. Don't be surprised if you discard all of them. Put any that you want to review further with the periodicals.

Now let's get to the heavy stuff, the correspondence. Put all letters and memos that are awaiting responses from others in a folder and file them away. You may need a decision from above or an answer to a question you've posed, but, whatever it is, you can do nothing with this work until someone else acts. So get it out of sight. Every day you'll review this file for items that need follow-up, but until you can get on with the project, keep the paper off your desk.

Take the remaining memos and put them neatly on the side of your desk. You're now organized for action. You have a list of things to do and a stack of paper on the side of your desk, both representing jobs you must tackle. Work waiting for input from others is in a file folder, out of sight.

You've now mastered the first rule, to take control of your desk so work flows naturally to you. You've also discovered the top of your desk is brown. You're ready to go to the next rule.

Rule Two: Make the clock work for you.

Regardless of sex, sect, station or degree, the second hand moves at exactly the same speed for all of us. Those who learn to use the clock to their advantage get more accomplished in the allotted time.

Different times of day lend themselves to different kinds of work. The early morning hours, when people are just starting their workday, are perfect for making telephone calls. According to telephone consultant Harry Newton of Telecom Library, Inc., only 22 percent of business calls are completed because the person being called is usually unavailable. By calling the first thing in the morning, you'll be able to complete most of your calls on the first try, usually catching people while they're still having their first cup of coffee.

You'll find you can get many minor jobs out of the way before your day has really begun. It's a great feeling to know you've already accomplished something and the day is not yet a half-hour old.

The late morning should be used for work that requires heavy concentration and creativity. If you're like most people, your mental abilities are at their peak in the morning. So take advantage of your intellectual clock and do the most demanding activities when you're at your best.

You may find it necessary to get away from your desk to do this work. Find a hiding place in your office, someplace you can go to without being disturbed. When you get to your quiet spot, let only one person know where you are and leave instructions that you are to be called only if the building catches fire, and then only when the temperature reaches 210 degrees Fahrenheit.

Use the early afternoon to attack the many minor assignments you may have that can be disposed of in a few minutes. Your mind and body probably begin to slow down after lunch and, if you're not careful, you'll let the afternoon slip away and accomplish nothing. Even though you're beginning to tire, keep working.

Late afternoon should be used for planning. Put some work that can be taken care of first thing in the morning on top of your pile of paper. (Remember the advice about making telephone calls early every day. Take those memos from the stack that require telephone calls and put them in the middle of your desk. When you get to work the next morning, grab the telephone.)

When you've completed your late afternoon planning, your impulse will be to call it a day. Resist that impulse. Get back to work. Some of you most productive time can be between 4:40 and 6:00 p.m. When everyone has left, the telephone doesn't ring and there's a beautiful quiet throughout the office. You'll be surprised how much you can get done simply by working late one or two nights a week.

It's 6:00 and you're saying goodnight to the guard and the people who do the cleaning. You feel you've used your business time to the fullest. But there's one more ounce of service you can squeeze from the clock.

Take your magazine with you when you leave the office. We live in a business environment that is changing at an ever-quickening pace. Whatever our line of work, we must continually keep up with advances in our field, and business and professional periodicals are the best tool we have for keeping ourselves informed.

But how do we get the time to do all the reading we'd like? Try this. Take these publications with you the next time you have a doctor's appointment, or when you're waiting for the washing machine repairman or while riding the commuter train. These times are often passed in frustrating boredom, so why not use it for professional reading?

You've now mastered the second rule, to make the clock work for you, and you're ready to go on to the third and final rule.

Rule Three: Take control of your job assignment.

Often, it feels as though we have no control over the work we do. We're given assignments and they must be done. To some extent this is true, but we can take some degree of control over our workload by asking ourselves a few simple questions.

First, must the job be done at all? How often has someone called and asked you to do something because it was in your bailiwick (or your province, or area of expertise) and, wanting to be helpful, you took on the job?

Don't be afraid to say no. If you don't have the time, say so.

If it's your boss who's giving you these assignments, you've got to be a little creative when saying no. Every once in a while make a list of all the jobs he or she has given you, along with a brief description of each assignment. Then ask his or her help in prioritizing your work. What should be done first, second...twenty-fifth?

The boss will probably be surprised at how much you have to do and will pick a few of the least important items and tell you not to do them, or wait until you have the time. You have now dumped some of the less important assignments your boss has given you and you've even made him or her think it was his or her idea.

One job that should be universally eliminated from any office is the retyping of memos to make minor changes. If you're a manager who demands perfect copy every time, take counsel from the framers of the Declaration of Independence. When Thomas Jefferson made two errors of omission, rather than redo the entire document, he inserted the missing letters between the lines. If this is acceptable in a document that gave birth to a nation, surely it should be acceptable in a letter that will be briefly glanced at en route to someone's file cabinet or wastebasket.

Once you've determined that a job is important enough to do, ask yourself how well it must be done. Don't get caught in the "paralysis of perfection." Not every job must be done with the utmost precision and accuracy. Some must be done as quickly as possible. Get it done and get on to something else.

Now that you've eliminated some jobs and performed others very quickly, you can spend your productive time on the projects that are of major concern to you and your company.

Once you've mastered these three rules of time management, you must keep on top of them all the time. It won't be easy, but it will be worth it. The importance of time management was probably best stated by Peter Drucker when he said, "Nothing, perhaps, distinguishes the effective manager as the tender, loving care of time."

Harold M. Emanuel is vice president of insurance operations with Insurance Agency Business Systems, Inc., Budd Lake, New Jersey.

13.
STEPPING UP TO SUPERVISION: MANAGING TIME AND JOB PRESSURES

H. Kent Baker
Stevan Holmberg

It may take a while for someone to learn good time management, but the investment made in learning and applying the steps to better time management is worth
the effort.

Don North, a new supervisor, frantically searches through a pile of papers for
information that he urgently needs for an important meeting with his boss.
"Hey, Don, got a minute? We've got a problem on that report you wanted me to
do, and I need your help right away." Trying to explain that now would not be
the best time for the discussion, Don says, "I'd be glad to but..." "Thanks," Ed
interrupts, "I really appreciate it. Now, the way I see the problem..."

Fifteen minutes later, Ed is still talking. The phone rings, and Don's boss
reminds him that he is late for the meeting. He apologizes to Ed and rushes out
of his office without the information that he is supposed to take with him.

Later that day, over lunch, Don admits to a colleague that he is really having
problems dealing with the requirements of his job. Everyday he faces a new
crisis, and the job pressures are really beginning to get to him. He doesn't have
the time to get everything done, which makes him feel frustrated and inadequate.

To an experienced supervisor like his friend, the solution seems simple:
What Don needs is to gain better control over his time.

WHAT IS TIME MANAGEMENT?

Time management is really self-management. The objective is not to become superefficient or superproductive but to use time to achieve one's
objectives—to work smarter, not harder, as the saying goes.

Many stumbling blocks exist in gaining control of time. For example, a manager's job prescribes the tasks or goals he or she needs to perform or achieve while those that the individual wants to perform or achieve are imposed by his or her own value system. They relate to the person's goals.

The value of time management lies in the fact that people have too many tasks they need to do but not enough time for the things that they want to do. Time management helps identify needs and wants in terms of their importance and matches them with time and other resources.

Although time is a valuable resource, many people take a haphazard approach to managing it. They may use a piecemeal approach, trying a new time management technique or gimmick each week. This approach does not work—at least not very well. Changing time habits is a difficult process. A systematic, not a piecemeal, method is required. While the steps to better time management are simple on the surface, they are difficult in practice and require replacing bad time management habits with good ones. Making this change demands effort, patience, commitment and a willingness to change.

BAD TIME HABITS

Everyone has bad time habits. Some are so ingrained that they are difficult to recognize, but these habits must be identified before corrective action can take place. Although some bad time habits are unique, others are quite common among supervisors.

"I don't have time to plan." Supervisors often fall into the trap of not planning because it is too time-consuming. Actually, the time spent planning will save time. Planning is one of the most basic yet essential supervisory functions. Without planning, a supervisor may not have a clear idea of what he or she wants to accomplish or how he or she wants to go about it. For example, a supervisor may discover in the middle of a project that the resources to do the job are lacking. Prior planning might have averted this problem. Lack of planning leads to crash programs, overtime or idle employees, duplication of work, and schedules not being met.

The remedy here is to plan daily. The best time to do this is early in the morning or at the end of the work day. Over time, such planning will become routine. And the few moments devoted to this activity will provide direction and ensure that the supervisor is working on important tasks.

When planning, four questions should be addressed: 1. What are my objectives for the day? 2. What activities are required to accomplish them? 3. What are my priorities? 4. How much time is required to do each task?

"I'm always available." Supervisors frequently make themselves available whenever anyone wants to see them. While an open-door policy can help foster better communication, such a policy when carried to an extreme can also reduce a supervisor's ability to control his or her time. If a supervisor is always available to others, he or she is at their mercy. Interruptions will occur at the worst possible times, such as when Ed interrupted Don with his problem.

The answer here is to practice a modified open-door policy and limit its use to specific times. Some quiet time should exist each day. Employees and others should be notified that the supervisor will not be available during this time unless a real emergency arises. The earlier the quiet time is set, the better. An old proverb states, "As the first hour of the day goes, so goes the whole day." This quiet time can be used to plan, to think, and to work on priority projects—which should contribute to higher accomplishment. Subordinates and others will soon become accustomed to this new habit and will respect it. Setting the same period each day for quiet time will help establish and reinforce this habit.

"Let me do it." Supervisors sometimes willingly accept tasks and responsibilities that belong to others. Knowing that someone respects one's ability may be gratifying but actually doing the job may not be the best use of one's time. Some subordinates are especially skilled in getting their supervisors to do their jobs for them. Supervisors need to learn to resist these employee efforts at upward-delegation. A supervisor has an obligation to coach or train subordinates but not to do the job for them.

A supervisor must learn to say "no" logically, firmly and tactfully, and to delegate. Before a supervisor says "let me do it," she should immediately ask herself, "Is this really the best use of my time?"

"I'll drop everything." Some supervisors suffer from the tyranny of the urgent. When faced with a crisis, they overreact and drop what they are doing to deal with the demands of the moment. They forget that an urgent task may not be the most important thing that they should be doing. The answer is often to separate the urgent from the important.

For example, Don stopped what he was doing to listen to Ed. Unless this problem was a real emergency, he should have insisted that they discuss it after his meeting with his boss. Instead, he became sidetracked on a less important matter. An appropriate response would have been, "No, I don't have a minute now, but I'll come to your office at 11 o'clock."

Don's mistake was in trying to fulfill someone else's priorities at the expense of his own. Daily planning and priority setting can help him by enabling him to identify the high-payoff tasks. If real emergencies arise that are both urgent and important, of course, he should be flexible enough to shift priorities.

"I have it right in front of me, somewhere." A tendency exists to keep too many papers on a desk. Papers pile up, and needed ones cannot be found without shuffling and sorting, a process that gives the impression of disorganization. In addition, stacks of paper distract attention from working on one thing at a time.

The solution is often simpler to say than to do, but a supervisor should try to keep a clean, uncluttered desk.

At the beginning of each day, he or she should sort paperwork into two groups: "action today" and "action tomorrow." Work requiring action today should be placed in a convenient spot on the desk. Paperwork requiring later action can be placed in a desk drawer or a filing cabinet. Putting less important work out of sight reduces the tendency to work on these items at the expense of higher-payoff tasks. "Out of sight, out of mind" is the principle practiced here. A supervisor gains an added benefit—his or her desk is no longer an unsightly mess, and he or she is better organized.

STEPS TO BETTER TIME MANAGEMENT

Overcoming bad habits takes time. A supervisor has to invest time in order to save time. While many of the remedies suggested are simply common sense, uncommon sense is required to combine them into a personalized time management strategy that works. Because time management principles do not apply equally to everyone, the challenge is to implement the rules and principles that best fit a specific situation. The following seven steps to better time management provide a systematic basis for applying time management techniques intelligently.

Gain time-awareness. The first step is to undertake a critical analysis of how time is spent. Without such information, making a determination of which work habits and patterns to change is difficult. A common way of finding out how much time is consumed on various tasks is to keep a time log. This procedure involves maintaining a diary of actual time-use for several days. Each hour is divided into 15- or 20-minute blocks, and a record is made of the activities for each interval. Several days of such recordkeeping can provide a sufficient number of observations for analysis. A supervisor then can summarize the findings from the log and determine what he or she could do to make better use of time.

This procedure for data gathering and analysis takes from one to two hours over a three-day period, but the results provide an accurate picture of time utilization. Estimates of time use can be made but they are notoriously inaccurate because supervisors often perceive themselves as more efficient and effective than they really are.

Identify time robbers. From analysis of the time log, timewasters can be identified. To do this, a supervisor needs to ask himself or herself these questions:

- Which timewasters stem from my own style of management?
- Which timewasters are caused by others?
- Which can be eliminated or controlled?

Supervisors are surprised to discover that they cause many of their own time problems. Such time robbers include procrastination, lack of self-discipline, and the failure to plan and to delegate.

Set goals and list priorities. From his or her list of time robbers, a supervisor should select five or six that he or she wants to correct and prioritize them. Results-oriented goals should be established for each. A supervisor should attempt to deal with these timewasters one at a time. Trying to change too many bad habits at once can lead to frustration and failure.

For example, if a supervisor's greatest timewaster is attendance at meetings, he or she may set as a goal reduction of the time spent in meetings, to an average of no more than five hours per week over the next three months. The goals should be specific and measurable to enable the supervisor to evaluate his or her progress in achieving them. In some instances, a list of subgoals may be needed to clarify broader goals.

Formulate action plans. Next, a supervisor needs to prepare a list of tasks necessary for goal accomplishment. Called an action plan, it acts as a map to the desired results. Action steps should be set, and a deadline for completing each step should be specified that can produce a measurement of progress.

In the case of the supervisor who wants to reduce the time spent in meetings, for example, one action step might be to examine the meetings he or she attends and conducts. The person may discover that he or she can send a subordinate as department representative to some meetings and not go to others at all. The manager may be able to consolidate some of his or her own meetings or reduce the time spent at them by more clearly defining the purpose before calling meetings, by starting and ending on time, and by controlling interruptions and sticking to the agenda.

Develop a time budget. A time budget is a personal planning tool for allocating time for specific tasks. Its function is to make time more productive and profitable through proper scheduling.

In scheduling time in a time budget:

- Always put the schedule in writing;
- Focus on key objectives and priority items;
- Schedule around key events and actions;
- Schedule important or difficult tasks early in the day;
- Block out quiet time;
- Group related items and actions whenever possible;
- Allow sufficient time to do each task;
- Don't overschedule;
- Build in flexibility for unexpected events; and
- Include thinking time.

Apply time management principles. A supervisor may use any of a number of time management techniques to help turn objectives into reality. Selection should be made based on the situation. Here are seven time management principles that have been helpful to supervisors who want to gain control of their time.

Divide and conquer. People often procrastinate because a task seems difficult or overwhelming. Procrastination can be dealt with by dividing a large or difficult task into smaller, more manageable parts and starting on one task right away. By planning the task and doing a small part of it, a supervisor is no longer procrastinating. Doing anything to get started, no matter how small, is the key to eliminating procrastination.

Starting a task is also helpful since an unfinished task is more of a motivator than an unstarted task. As each small part of the job is completed, one's involvement and commitment increase.

Concentrate on priorities. Low priority items are sometimes performed before high-payoff ones because they are easier to do. A supervisor feels that he or she is accomplishing something and justifies doing the trivial items first on the basis that their completion will allow him or her time to concentrate on the high-priority items. Often, though, by the time the low-priority tasks are completed, the supervisor is too tired to focus on the difficult tasks and puts them off another day.

Supervisors who approach their work in this fashion are confusing business with effectiveness. An effective supervisor does the right jobs in the right order. Priority items come first, not trivial items. Even a few minutes spent on a priority task are important.

Tackle tough jobs first. A supervisor should attempt to tackle the tough jobs first and match jobs with his or her body cycles. Difficult jobs should be performed when a person's energy level is high. Doing a difficult task is much easier when a person is fresh than when he or she is tired. During high energy periods, a person can often solve a problem in minutes instead of the hours he or she might labor over the same problem when energy level is down. Low priority items, which usually require less mental effort, are best saved for the supervisor's low-energy periods.

Set realistic deadlines. Deadlines serve as targets or goals. Adherence to deadlines can motivate supervisors who procrastinate or vacillate. But these deadlines must be realistic; otherwise, they cannot be used to appraise performance. Supervisors tend to be overly optimistic in assessing how long a task will take and frustration results when goals are not met.

Hold stand-up meetings. A good technique for controlling the amount of time that visitors stay is to hold stand-up meetings. If the supervisor remains standing, so will the visitor; and the meeting will be much shorter. For instance, a supervisor meets the person at the door and holds the discussion there so the visitor never gets into the office, or he or she might stand up before the other person is seated.

Consolidate similar tasks. This technique minimizes interruptions and economizes on the utilization of resources and effort. For example, instead of making telephone calls sporadically throughout the day, all outgoing calls can be made at one time. Callers can also be asked to call during specific hours. In this way, the supervisor attempts to group incoming calls as well as reduce telephone interruptions.

Use waiting time. A supervisor should always have a reserve of things to do during idle periods. The waiting time before the start of a delayed meeting, for example, can be used to catch up on correspondence or to review a report. Or travel time can be converted into productive planning time. For instance, on the way to work a supervisor can plan his or her day or think about how to resolve a problem.

Monitor progress. This is the final step to better time management. Bad time management habits are hard to break. Frequent monitoring of progress prevents a supervisor from slipping back into bad habits and allows for corrective action.

A FINAL WORD

It may take a while for someone to learn good time management. But, the investment made in learning and applying the steps to better time management is worth the effort. Good time management can reduce job stress and provide greater job satisfaction and accomplishment.

H. Kent Baker, DBA and Stevan Holmberg, DBA, are both associated with Kogod College of Business Administration, The American University.

14.
EFFECTIVE TIME MANAGEMENT TECHNIQUES

Larry D. Alexander

Finding time for complex, long-term tasks is a problem for many managers.

Why is it that most managers and administrators have a hard time making progress on major tasks and special projects? Why is it that managers never even seem to get started on non-pressing projects that are truly important? And why is it that most managers spend such a high percentage of their precious time on the more routine aspects of their jobs?

The answer is that managers avoid ambiguous assignments. Managers tend to prefer to work on concrete tasks over more ambiguous ones. Simple tasks are finished before complex ones are even started. Short-term tasks are emphasized over long-term tasks. And the obvious result is that important long-term projects of a complex nature tend to be postponed, or not even started.

FOUR KINDS OF TASKS

The various tasks and projects that managers, as well as staff administrators, perform can be classified according to the two key dimensions shown in Figure 1. One dimension is degree of difficulty and the second is duration of effort. Degree of difficulty is broken down into simple tasks which are generally clear, understandable and easily completed, and complex tasks which are involved, ambiguous and hard to deal with. Conversely, duration of effort is broken down into short-term tasks which can be completed in less than an hour, and long-term tasks which can take days, weeks or even months to finish. Although these dimensions are shown as distinct subcategories, it might be more appropriate to view each dimension as a continuum between the two extreme points.

Figure 1

Two Dimensional View of Tasks
to Be Completed

Cell 1: simple, short-term tasks	Cell 3: complex, short-term tasks
Cell 2: simple, long-term tasks	Cell 4: complex, long-term tasks

Many of the tasks that are found in *Cell 1* are the routine activities found in any job. These tasks have little ambiguity because they are simple and short-term in nature. Since many of these tasks recur on a frequent basis, routine procedures and unconscious habits are used to handle many of them. *Cell 2* tasks are complex, but they require only a short-term effort for accomplishment. Thus, these tasks have an intermediate amount of ambiguity which is due to their complex nature.

Cell 3 tasks are the opposite of *Cell 2*. These tasks are simple, but unfortunately they require a long-term effort to complete. These tasks may also have an intermediate amount of ambiguity which is due to the long-term effort required to complete them. Finally, *Cell 4* tasks are complex in nature and a long-term effort is required for completion. Obviously, these tasks are of a highly ambiguous nature and are avoided in favor of less ambiguous tasks.

Many approaches used to try to make progress on these high-ambiguity projects do not work very well. One approach is to first complete all of the routine and urgent tasks to get them out of the way. Unfortunately, this usually delays a manager from ever getting started on the more complex, long-term tasks because there is a neverending supply of routine and urgent tasks.

Another approach is to simultaneously try to work on three or four special projects at once. This approach typically fails because the manager is spread so thin that no real progress is made on any of the projects.

Then there is the approach in which the manager promises to get started on some important project when things become less hectic and return to normal. This often doesn't work because the reality facing most managers is a neverending barrage of interruptions, crises and deadlines.

A final approach that some managers use is to continually tell anyone who will listen about the great project they are about to start. Unfortunately, some of these people seem to have a much higher need to impress others with what they are planning to do rather than with what they actually have done.

If the above approaches toward complex, long-term tasks and projects are not very successful, what works? The answer is two-fold. In part, what works depends upon what works for the individual. Thus, it is helpful to experiment with a number of different ideas to determine what works for you. However, to a large extent, it requires using a much more methodical approach to tackling these high-ambiguity, complex tasks.

DEALING WITH COMPLEX TASKS

The following suggestions are specifically aimed at dealing with the complex aspect of high-ambiguity tasks and projects:

Use the five-minute brainstorm. Take five minutes to break the overall project down into as many smaller, double activities as possible.[1] If some of these activities still seem too complex, try to break them down further. Just by putting a complex project down in writing, it can help make it easier to see exactly what needs to be done. The written list should then be used as a plan of action for starting the individual activities.

Work on high payoff activities. The Pareto Principle states that 80 percent of the results can be achieved in 20 percent of the time expended.[2] Thus, identify the few critical elements in the overall project which, when done well, will make a major contribution toward completion of the overall task. Conversely, try to cut down the amount of time consumed with activities that contribute very little to the final outcome.

Focus attention on the smaller, individual activities. By concentrating on the smaller, bite-sized pieces, you can overcome the feeling of being overwhelmed by the entire task. An overwhelmed feeling can easily lead to procrastination.

Block out an adequate length of time. This time might range from 30 minutes to an hour without interruptions. Some complex projects may take ten or 15 minutes merely to get thought processes up to their maximum efficiency. Then it takes additional time to make progress on this aspect of the project. For similar reasons, try to avoid getting started on a complex project just a few minutes before lunch, a meeting or quitting time.

Work when you are at your best. This is what time management expert Alan Lakein refers to as internal prime time.[3] Since we are trying to make progress on a complex task, it makes sense to work on it when one is mentally alert and functioning well. For some people, prime time may be early morning, for others late morning, and still others middle to late afternoon. Avoid wasting this peak period by working on routine tasks. Defer these non-thinking tasks, when possible, to your low energy periods during the day.

Start each session with something easy. Since getting started each day is sometimes the most difficult thing of all, do anything to get going rather than nothing at all. Start a work session with something easy and don't be surprised if your mind starts to think about how to do some other, more complicated aspect of the project. Finish the easy activity and then shift attention to the more involved one.

Redefine the project. Talk with other people in your firm as well as counterparts elsewhere to turn up suggestions for more simplified approaches to accomplishing the same basic purpose. It is important to realize that a less ambitious project actually completed is infinitely better than a more grandiose one that never gets off the drawing board.

Control interruptions. This final suggestion may be the most important of all. Complex projects, by their very nature, require a manager's undivided attention in order to make progress on them. Thus, do everything possible to control incoming telephone calls, drop-in visitors, and incoming mail during work sessions on special projects. If it is impossible to control interruptions, try going to some area away from your department to get some work done. Obviously, tell your secretary where you can be reached, but keep your hideaway a secret.

MAKING PROGRESS ON LONG-TERM TASKS

The following suggestions are offered to help you deal with tasks and projects that require a long-term effort:

Determine a realistic time commitment per week. It is very helpful to specify in advance the amount of time per week you are going to allocate for a special project. Start by being very conservative in your weekly commitment. It is much better to feel satisfied having actually achieved a four-hour objective per week than never to have started. Remember that tremendous progress can be made by spending only a few hours per week, week after week.

Specify tasks in advance. By knowing exactly what aspect of a long-term project you will be working on next, it will be easier to get started on it. It also lets your mind consciously and subconsciously think about what needs to be done before actually sitting down to work. It may be a good idea to end each work session by writing down what activity you will work on next time.

Establish a regular time for working on long-term projects. The advantage of having the same time period each day, or maybe three times per week, is that it helps to develop a habit. It then becomes automatic to begin work on special projects. Efforts should also be made to avoid scheduling other obligations during this reserved time period.

Establish deadlines for intermediate progress points. Try to set self-imposed deadlines for short-term activities which can be completed in a week or less. These intermediate progress points can act as a motivator since they are not too far off in the future. Don't be too discouraged if you experience some date slippage, even for these smaller short-term activities. As each progress point is actually reached, it should provide positive reinforcement that progress is being made on the long-term project.

Switch to other aspects of the overall task. Continuing to work on the same aspect of a long-term task for an extended time might bring about one of several possible adverse situations. You might become bored with the task, frustrated that little progress is being made, or simply give up. To prevent these possibilities, provide variety by switching from one activity to another.

Avoid the activity trap. Although it is helpful to break down the overall project into smaller activities, it is important to avoid what management theorist George Odiorne identified as the activity trap. This idea states that people get so enmeshed in activity they lose sight of the purpose of their work.[4] Thus, make sure that each smaller activity you are working on actually does contribute toward completing the long-term project.

Limit the number of major projects. It is important to realize that the more routine aspects of most jobs take up the majority of time available each week. Thus, there is only a limited number of hours each week to work on complex, long-term projects. It is infinitely better to make real progress on one, or possibly two, major projects, than never to make much progress on a host of different projects. Remember that a large number of projects in progress is not as impressive as several meaningful projects that are actually completed. In selecting which project to work on first, some key criteria to consider are: expected payoff; urgency; relevancy to your job; likelihood of success; and total time commitment.

Record your ongoing progress each week. Some visible method should be used to monitor your day-to-day and week-to-week progress on a long-term project. A calendar or even a blank sheet of paper can work quite effectively. I have used a form which has several blank lines under the seven days of the week. I then enter the specific activity I am planning to work on the next day. The next day, I indicate if I worked on it and also record the amount of time I spent on it. By reviewing the weekly forms or calendar, you can determine if you are allocating enough time for a long-term project.

CONCLUSION

It must be emphasized that time management is a very personal matter. First, try using the various suggestions offered here for dealing with complex, long-term tasks and projects. Then after experimenting with them for a while, don't hesitate to modify some of them to fit the realities of your job situation. In addition, try to come up with some new ideas that work well for you. Please keep in mind that the goal is not using any specific time management suggestion, but rather making progress and completing these high ambiguity projects.

And try not to be discouraged. It may take some time before you will regularly allocate time most days to work on complex, long-term projects. If you have been ignoring this aspect of your job for months on end, don't expect miracles overnight. Changing behavior takes time, and it may involve setbacks along the way; but it can eventually be successful if there is an ongoing commitment.

References

1. Alan Lakein, *How to Get Control of Your Time and Your Life* (New York: Signet, 1973), pp 37-42.
2. R. Alec Mackenzie, *The Time Trap* (New York: McGraw-Hill, 1972), pp. 51-53.
3. Lakein, op. cit., pp 48-50.
4. George Odiorne, *Management and the Activity Trap* (New York: Harper & Row, 1974).

Larry D. Alexander received both an MS in industrial relations and a PhD in management from the University of California, Los Angeles. He is assistant professor of management, College of Business, Virginia Polytechnic Institute and State University, Blacksburg, Virginia.

15.
ENERGY CRISIS IN
THE EXECUTIVE SUITE

R. Alec Mackenzie
Gary Richards

The key to both energy management and time management appears to be the same: management. A manager's time and energy cannot be squandered.

The fossil-fuel energy shortage has affected the way we live, travel and work. More efficient automobiles and lower thermostats are but two examples. There is a genuine concern, for when our fuel sources are consumed, there will be no replacement.

For managers, there is an equally serious energy crisis—the lack of human energy in the office. Managers' energy is being drained away and wasted by duplication of effort, mistakes, unnecessary meetings, and crises that could have been avoided. Executive analysts have long held that the overall average effectiveness of managers is somewhere around 30 percent. This figure represents a reasonable consensus of informed opinion of those in the best position to make intelligent estimates. And the results of surveys of participants in time management seminars further support this figure.

When managers are asked to estimate the length of their average telephone call, they say it ranges from five to six minutes. When they are asked to estimate the "ideal" time for a call (that is, assuming no time is wasted in unnecessary socializing, in trying to answer questions others should have handled, and the like), their answer ranges from one to two minutes. Thus telephone effectiveness (ideal/actual) ranges from 20 percent (one to five minutes) to 33 percent (two to six minutes). Estimates of time spent with drop-in visitors are ten minutes (actual) and two minutes (ideal) for an effectiveness estimate of 20 percent. Estimates of time spent in meetings range from 30 to 60 minutes (actual) and from 15 to 30 minutes (ideal) for an effectiveness of 50 percent.

The average of these four effectiveness estimates is 30.75 percent. If large automobiles guzzle excessive amounts of gasoline, so do large egos in the executive suite "guzzle" excessive amounts of time by taking all calls and admitting all drop-in visitors instead of having them screened by a competent, professional secretary or assistant. High-powered cars burn excessive amounts of gasoline in accomplishing the simple task of transportation. Similarly, high-paid managers waste time and effort making minor decisions that could have been delegated to others with sufficient judgment and knowledge.

INTERRUPTIONS "SIPHON OFF" ENERGY

A study of work habits of American managers by Eric Webster reveals that managers are interrupted on the average of once every eight minutes all day long. Studies in England by Rosemary Stewart, in Sweden by Sune Carlson, and in Holland by Hans Luijk, confirm this finding. But a manager can accomplish nothing of real importance, Peter Drucker has observed, without significant blocks of uninterrupted time. Time is "consumed" faster when fragmented by interruptions, just as coal burns faster when crushed. Kenneth Dunn, a former superintendent of schools in New York, has observed, "Of all the factors bearing on a manager's effectiveness, none has a more devastating impact than interruptions."

A look at the most common managerial interruptions is sobering. They include telephone calls, drop-in visitors, unscheduled meetings, crises and self-interruptions. Managers usually see these interruptions as being caused by others, that is, as being externally generated. But careful analysis reveals the existence of forces at work *within* the managers themselves that cause these interruptions or increase the chances of their occurring.

THE TYRANNY OF THE TELEPHONE

Let's take the case of the telephone. What causes a manager to take his own telephone calls instead of allowing his secretary or assistant to screen them? For many, it is the willingness, even the desire, to be interrupted. Others do it out of curiosity, fear of offending others, and ego.

In answering his own phone, the manager permits the telephone to waste his time, not serve him. Instead of saving time and energy, he wastes both by taking and referring misdirected calls, providing information others could provide more quickly, getting needlessly involved in routine matters, and engaging in nonessential communication. A student in California writes that he spent the summer on a telephone campaign calling companies to sell his product, gift encyclopedias, to the highest executive he could talk to. Of course, he asked for the president and, as he himself put it, "Incredibly I got through ninety percent of the time—often without even being asked the purpose of my call."

Of all people, presidents should be conserving time and energy since presumably theirs is the most valuable to their organizations. Yet surveys of hundreds of presidents have shown that 83 percent complain that they don't have the time to keep up with the reading in their fields and 72 percent say that they don't have the time to think or plan for their business.

THE "HOPELESS DOOR" POLICY

Drop-in visitors are encouraged by the sadly perverted "open door" policy. The open door, of course, invites the passerby to drop in. Yet it was never so intended. The policy was meant to ensure access when needed, not to sanction continuous interruptions. But thousands of organizations are condemning managers to an incessant, hopeless barrage of well-wishers and socializers by mistakenly assuming the policy to mean physically open at all times. Many managers become corridor wanderers looking for an open door and a friendly chat when they are caught up with their own work or want to get away from an unpleasant task.

UNSCHEDULED MEETINGS

The average manager spends ten hours a week in meetings, many of them unscheduled. Nine out of ten managers say 50 percent of this time, or one hour per day, is wasted. What can be done about it? The president of one of the fastest growing airlines in North America decided, after attending a time-management seminar, to reduce the time and energy wasted in his staff meetings. Instead of meeting daily for an average of nearly one and a half hours with his 12 key people, he decided to meet weekly for one hour. Because of the change:

- Meeting agendas are being prepared and followed.
- Only matters of real importance to the whole team are discussed during the meetings.
- Team members come prepared.
- Minutes are distributed immediately to those needing them.
- Action and follow-up assignments are made.

What have been the net results? Ninety man-hours a week spent in meetings has been cut to 12, and better results are being obtained. Because of the president's decision, his top managers have 78 more hours to spend with their own teams and on priority tasks. A great saving of valuable time and energy is being realized for the company.

What really hurts about meetings is that so many are needless. Some are called because of the chairman's need for reassurance that things are going well. Often he wants to know everything his team members know in case his boss asks a question. Occasionally he may be avoiding risk by calling for a committee decision. He may even call a meeting to determine—if you can believe this—whether a meeting ought to be called.

The most common complaint of unscheduled meetings is that they take too long and that they could have been avoided with better planning. Few people know how to hold a meeting—and even fewer know how to let one go.

Waste of energy in meetings alone is perhaps a worse national scandal than waste of energy in excessive lighting, heating and motoring. Consider the average manager who spends ten hours a week in meetings, or two hours a day. Half of that time, or one hour per day, is wasted. Assume conservatively that 500,000 managers attend meetings, that's a waste of 500,000 executive hours daily. At $10 per hour, that's $5 million being wasted each day in meetings.

Figure 1

MATCH YOUR TASKS
TO YOUR
ENERGY LEVEL

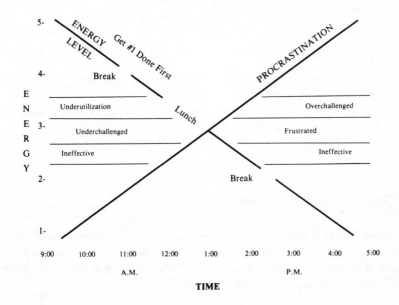

THE CRUNCH OF CRISES

In listing the causes of managerial interruptions, we included crises. Interruptions in the day's work to put out small fires is not unusual. Although the cost is not as easy to calculate as that of meetings (because of the unpredictable quality of crises), they, too, are expensive.

Crises occur for a variety of reasons, but generally they are due to a lack of planning and a failure to anticipate. Whatever their cause, the result is generally the same—wasted time and energy.

SELF-INTERRUPTIONS

The reasons for interruptions are far more extensive than either the list at the beginning of this article suggests or most of us imagine. Visual distractions—perhaps caused by an unfavorable desk or office location—interrupt us continually. Noise is another distraction. It affects plant managers with open offices near assembly lines and personnel with desks near vending machines or other highly traveled areas. But perhaps the most frequent cause of interruptions is the least commonly recognized—self-interruptions. These occur generally when we tire of an unpleasant task and put it aside for almost any available excuse.

The cluttered desk contains piles of potential interruptions. The disorganized manager tends to put things on his desk so he won't forget them. The trouble with this practice is that it works too well. Whenever the manager's gaze wanders from his immediate task to the piles of important matters on his desk, he remembers them and forgets what he is working on. His train of thought is interrupted, and depending on his self-discipline, that interruption may be permanent. He may not get back to the task he allowed to be interrupted.

One test of a manager is his ability to resist interruptions. Another test is his ability to recover from those interruptions he allows.

Observers concluded that it takes three times as long to recover from an interruption as it does to endure it.

SOME POSSIBLE SOLUTIONS

What can be done to solve the energy crisis in the executive suite? First, managers need to ask themselves some hard questions. Then they must follow some time-tested practices. Finally, they should use proven tools to measure and reward effective time use and productivity.

Table 1

Telephone Effectiveness Audit

SAMPLE

Preseminar Telephone Effectiveness
(Indicate Status Prior to Time Management Seminar)

POINTS	NONE	SOME	HALF	MOST	ALL
	(0)	(1)	(2)	(3)	(4)
a. Have calls screened		1			
b. Block times for returning calls	0				
c. Block times for placing calls; secretary/assistant places calls	0				
d. Limit socializing on calls			2		
e. Secy/Asst. has clear policy in handling various calls from routine to VIP	No 0				Yes 4
Add points in each column	0	1	2		

Total Points = 3

Three questions should be asked by managers:

What should not be done at all? The principle of selective neglect is based on the premise that some problems left alone go away and that many low-yield activities are not worth the effort they require. By selectively ignoring such matters, much time and effort can be conserved for more useful pursuits. Effective managers learn to say "no" to such activities. They expect their secretaries or assistants to screen telephone calls and visitors. They realize that half the inquiries that come to their desks can be handled without interrupting them at all.

If the information is not available from the person answering the call, it can be obtained by referring the caller to the appropriate person.

What should be done through others? A fundamental principle of delegation holds that authority for decision making ought to be delegated to the lowest possible level consistent with good judgment and available facts. Effective managers do nothing they can delegate and do those things only they can do. The manager who fails to delegate wastes time and energy on matters that should not have occupied his attention. Refusal to do others' work is a key to the effectiveness of a successful manager.

Unwittingly, some managers find themselves redoing unacceptable work of subordinates rather than sending it back. Others encourage their subordinates to bring all questions to them and, therefore, build overdependence.

By making decisions for subordinates, a manager is working below his level. In effect, the subordinate is delegating upward and can scarcely be held accountable for the results if the boss made the decision.

What should the manager do? Having eliminated those things that should not be done at all and those jobs that can be delegated to others, the manager now faces his remaining tasks—those things that only he can do. The tasks to be done are narrowed down to the essentials, those things that are most important to him.

At this point, many timewasters may affect his performance. How does he get started without procrastinating? How does he stick to the job? How, in the end does he measure his effectiveness? Is he, in fact, achieving the best possible results with the least expenditure of resources, including his time and energy?

THREE PROVEN PRACTICES

Here are three practices for more effective handling of things that you as a manager must do yourself:

Set and keep priorities. A written daily plan, with objectives ranked in order of importance, is mandatory. Tasks should be done as they have been ranked. Then, even if only the first few items actually get accomplished, still the most important ones have been done. Since there is never enough time to get everything done, you have to get the "big tasks" finished first. That's the essence and meaning of the advice, "Work smarter, not harder."

Set deadlines for yourself. Without a deadline, the sense of urgency fades and priorities shift to tasks that do have deadlines. Impose deadlines on yourself and announce them. Enlist the aid of your secretary, assistant, or friend to check your progress. Having someone you must account to—even a friend—makes the deadline seem more real.

Plan to be unavailable. To gain periods of uninterrupted concentration, a manager must arrange to be unavailable to callers and visitors so that he can work on his own priorities. Set up a quiet hour during which you don't permit interruptions except for emergencies. A well-organized hour without interruptions can generate three hours of results and a better quality work. You can save up to two hours per day with this technique alone.

Figure 1 shows the waste of time and energy that results from procrastinating, that is, from putting off more important tasks to the end of the day when energy levels are lowest. It illustrates how ineffective it is to do easy, low-value, trivial tasks first thing in the morning when energy level is highest and to postpone the high priority, important tasks until the end of the day when energy levels are lowest.

TOOLS TO MEASURE EFFECTIVENESS

Reducing managerial energy and time waste may be harder than reducing energy waste. We can't pin a bright orange tag on managers who fail to delegate, like Raytheon Co. energy wardens do to the boss of a secretary who leaves the electric typewriter on overnight. Nor would it be professional to have jingles sung over the intercom to remind managers to set priorities, like Vauxhall Motors, Ltd., does to remind shop employees to turn off machines. Fortunately, however, there are other tools available to help managers pinpoint and eliminate their energy wasters and time wasters!

Time logs. A daily record detailing all activities and interruptions will reveal surprising information on how a manager's time is actually spent. It doesn't go where he thinks it does. An accurate log will reveal true timewasters. It will show the source, importance, duration, and frequency of all needless interruptions, and it will enable each of these timewasters to be rank-ordered. Without such information, effectiveness and improvement in managing time cannot be measured.

In essence, time logs detect the drains on managerial time and energy and permit them to be rank-ordered.

Team timewaster profiles. The rankings of each manager's timewasters can be combined into a team profile, a list of all timewasters of the team in order of their importance. This team profile can be used as the basis for a needs analysis for training programs and for team building.

Team members can jointly develop and implement solutions to their top timewasters. And future team profiles will show whether the effort is working.

Table 2
Managerial Effectiveness Profile and Analysis*
Relative Weight

TIMEWASTERS	10%	20%	30%	40%	50%	60%
1. Interruptions						
- telephone						
2. Crises						
3. Lack of objectives, priorities, and deadlines						
4. Delegation						
5. Meetings						

Jan. 15   Feb. 15   Mar. 15

Monthly Gains in Managerial Effectiveness

	Jan. 15	Feb. 15	Mar. 15
	RATING	RATING	RATING
1. Telephone control	10%	20%	35%
2. Crisis control	10	30	35
3. Objective setting	20	30	50
4. Delegation	15	35	60
5. Meeting control	30	40	60
Average effectiveness	17%	31%	48%

Absolute gain in managerial effectiveness: 48% - 17% = 31%
Relative gain in managerial effectiveness: 31/17 = 182%
*Source: R. Alec Mackenzie, *New Time Management Methods for You and Your Staff* (Chicago: Dartnell, 1975).

TIME MANAGEMENT EFFECTIVENESS AUDIT

Lack of time is one of the major causes of a manager's not applying the principles and practices of management in an effective manner. For this reason, time management should be given attention during performance appraisals.

Criteria exist for assessing how effective a manager is in controlling the most serious timewasters. Table 1 shows the criteria for assessing effectiveness in use of the telephone and a weighting system for evaluating responses.

For each timewaster, an effectiveness rating can be computed by comparing desired practices with actual practices. Then, at successive performance reviews, progress can be measured by comparing the effectiveness ratings. Comparative ratings for five timewasters are shown in Table 2, evaluated three times over a period of several months. Gains in managerial effectiveness, both absolute and relative, are shown in the calculations below the chart.

The key to both energy management and time management appears to be the same—management. A manager's time and energy cannot be squandered.

R. Alec Mackenzie is president, and Gary Richards is an associate, with Alec Mackenzie and Associates, Inc., located in Greenwich, New York.

16.
TIME MANAGEMENT: MAKING EVERY MINUTE COUNT

Larry G. McDougle

Adhering to these "ten commandments" will help you improve your use of time and, as a result, your style of supervision.

Time is one of those words in the English language which everyone is familiar with but often hard put to define. Although the concept of time is universal, each person has his or her own particular definition.

The supervisor sees time as the pivotal factor to be reckoned with in getting done his or her own job and the jobs of his or her subordinates. Good time management is one of the characteristics of good supervision, and there are a number of points that every supervisor should know and remember when trying to make the most of the most valuable resource available to him or her.

These are:

Time is money. This adage is as true as it is old. Supervisors must realize that it is as valid for their time as it is for their employees. Lateness in getting a project completed or a decision made can result in a substantial decline in profits for an organization.

Time is irreversible. The standard dictionary definition of time underscores the fact that it cannot be reclaimed. Hence, lost time represents a major source of waste for any organization.

Time is equal for all. Although people are not born with equal abilities or opportunities, they have the same 24 hours a day, seven days a week, 52 weeks a year, and so on, available to them. The issue then becomes one of how that time is managed.

Time can be maximized. Those who have time to get their work done and who also have time to enjoy non-work-related activities have learned the difference between quality and quantity. They make every minute count.

Time can be wasted. The list of contributing factors is almost endless. Ironically, many of the modern-day technological advances that make our lives much more productive and comfortable are also the major time grabbers. Examples include the computer, copy machine, and the ubiquitous telephone.

TIME WASTERS

As a supervisor, you know how important it is to effectively utilize every minute of your time and your subordinates' time. Nothing undermines this effort at productivity so much as engaging in meaningless activities. You have to develop work habits that eliminate this unnecessary waste of time. Typical time wasters include:

Interruptions. Whether caused by telephone, visitors or employees monopolizing a supervisor's time, interruptions can be devastating to work output if not properly managed.

Meetings. Meetings are an ingenious device for simultaneously wasting the time of more than one person. Make meetings count! Never call a meeting if the same objective can be accomplished by memo, telephone or a personal visit, or if the purpose is nothing more than the dissemination of information.

Inability to say "no." Perhaps the most successful way to prevent yourself from wasting time is by saying "no." There is an old saying that if you want a job done, look for someone who is already busy. Although there is a measure of truth to this, there comes a time when an individual has to protect his or her time from exploitation. There is a limit as to how much any one person can do.

Filing. Particular attention must be paid to what is filed. Thanks (or no thanks) to the copy machine, paper can now be generated in staggering amounts. More than half of it should probably be disposed of immediately. If you are uncertain about the importance of a given piece of correspondence, consider using this technique: Place it on the corner of your desk near the waste basket; if a follow-up doesn't appear within 30 days, throw it away. It obviously wasn't very important.

Unfinished business. A great deal of time is wasted by people who have good intentions when they begin an assignment but never get around to completing it. Managers of baseball teams have become prematurely gray from games lost because a batter failed to score the runner on third base at the end of an inning. The rules in baseball don't allow for partial runs. Neither do the rules of effective management.

Supervisory follow-through can play an important role in making sure a job gets done. As supervisor, you should establish a deadline for the completion of a task, insist on progress reports, and praise an employee for a job well done. The last is a sure-fire guarantee that the next assignment will be performed even better.

Indecisiveness. Effective supervisors are not afraid to make decisions, even those decisions that may bring controversy. Indecision wastes time and money and destroys employee morale. How many times have you heard managers and other supervisors say to one another, "I really don't care what they do as long as they do something."

Perhaps even more counterproductive than the supervisor who can't decide is the one who keeps changing his or her mind. Most people are reluctant to follow someone who can't decide where he or she is going.

TECHNIQUES FOR MANAGING TIME

To help you control your time, consider the use of the following:

The desk calendar. Most supervisors are aware that the calendar can be used for scheduling meetings and appointments, but it can also be used effectively for noting deadlines, due dates for reports, and items requiring supervisory follow-through. It is helpful to schedule tasks and appointments in advance, thus avoiding the unenviable position of needing to be in more than one place or to do more than one thing at the same time.

To-be-done sheets. A very effective approach for managing time is to carry a notebook containing a list of daily or weekly activities that have to be completed. As tasks are accomplished they can be crossed off; others are added as they come to mind. This technique can be especially valuable as a reminder on correspondence to be addressed, phone calls to be made or returned, information to be obtained, and people to see.

Planning sheets. The planning sheet acts as a reference guide to completed activities and those that are pending. It can help the supervisor zero in on how much time is required and should be allocated to complete a given task.

Reflection. Periodically, supervisors should take time out to reflect on how office matters are progressing. Your use of time needs to be continuously reviewed, analyzed and evaluated. Taking time to think can be a profitable exercise for every supervisor. In fact, it may be better than jogging.

THE TEN COMMANDMENTS OF GOOD MANAGEMENT

Now that we've discussed good time management practices and ways you can develop them, let's look at what I consider to be must-dos of good management that relate to good time management. Remember that part of effective supervision is the efficient use of time. Adhering to these "ten commandments" will help you improve your use of time and, as a result, your style of supervision.

Thou shalt have no other clocks before thee. Excessive clock watching may be symptomatic of deep-rooted problems that a supervisor cannot afford to ignore. Chances are that the employee who continually checks the time is not satisfied with his or her job and, as a consequence, is unmotivated and unproductive. A college professor I know had a group of students who spent more time watching the clock than paying attention to what was being said in class. One day they discovered a sign beside the clock. It read, "Time is passing... are you?" Your effectiveness as a supervisor will be challenged when your subordinates fail to perform.

Thou shalt not kill time. Hockey is a sport in which a team's ability to kill time during its opponent's power play is highly valued. Few businesses, however, can survive for long when they possess an overabundance of paid timekillers.

Employees who do this are actually wasting their most valuable resource, and a supervisor who is concerned about the welfare of his or her employees and the organization should not tolerate it for too long.

Honor thy secretary and staff. A good secretary is worth his or her weight in gold. Too many supervisors don't know how to make proper use of one. An informed secretary can eliminate interruptions by screening telephone calls and visitors and sorting correspondence from junk mail. Likewise, a staff that is properly utilized can make a supervisor look good and enhance his or her chances for promotion.

Thou shalt not steal another person's time. Every organization seems to employ people who apparently don't have enough work to keep themselves busy and as a result float from office to office and disturb those who do. They are stealing time not only from the company but also from their co-workers. The economic implications are sobering.

Thou shalt not bear false witness about the use of time. There are many employees who are less than truthful about the use of their time. It is probably one of the reasons time clocks were invented. As individuals progress upward in the management hierarchy, their amount of discretionary time increases and with it an increased requirement for self-accountability.

Thou shalt not eat lunch alone. Taking one hour for lunch each day adds up to more than six full weeks of work per year. There isn't a supervisor in the world who couldn't accomplish a great deal given six weeks.

Lunch hours are necessary but they should not be wasted. This is not to say that all lunch hours have to be business-related. Nor does it deny the importance of private time for meditation and reflection. But lunchtime represents a marvelous opportunity for making contacts, getting to know co-workers better, and making yourself known to higher-level managers. Supervisors who take advantage of this time are bettering their chances of recognition and promotion.

Thou shalt take thy vacation. Every organization has a few workaholic supervisors who think they are so indispensable that they can't afford to take a vacation. Some of them even convince themselves that refusal to take a vacation is a mark of dedication. Nothing could be further from the truth. People need to periodically get away from the job, no matter how satisfying or rewarding it may be.

Thou shalt not procrastinate. Most people are naturally inclined to put off doing anything that is unpleasant, but the simplest advice is the best advice: do it and be done with it.

Thou shalt not be afraid of work. The world is full of supervisors who lack effectiveness because they lack confidence in themselves. They dread the thought of making a presentation before a group because they fear embarrassment or rejection, and they are afraid to take on a new assignment because they "don't know enough about it." People who experience these types of fears should remember one thing: There is no substitute for being prepared. A supervisor who does his or her homework will seldom have cause to be embarrassed or afraid.

Thou shalt not covet another's time. How often are the following expressions heard? "How do they find time to do everything?" "I wish I had time to so some of the things that they are doing. There just aren't enough hours in the day." People who covet someone else's time have not learned how to use their own—and never will unless they are willing to work at it.

SOME IDEAS TO CONSIDER

Most supervisors are familiar with Douglass McGregor's Theory X-Theory Y styles of management. According to these theories, an individual's supervisory style reflects how he or she views human nature. The Theory X manager assumes that people are basically lazy and attempt to avoid work at all costs. The Theory Y supervisor believes that people are willing to do a day's work for a day's pay. No attempt will be made here to debate the relative merits of either approach, but the supervisor should realize that the inherent view he or she has with regard to employee motivation will have direct implications on the effective use of his or her time and that of subordinates. It will be reflected in such areas as the closeness of supervision, degree of delegation, and involvement in decision making.

Subordinates have a right to know what is expected of them. The supervisor must make a conscious effort to establish and communicate goals and objectives to the employee, and those who understand the objectives of the organization stand a better chance of being committed to them. Commitment is the key word. An organization with committed people is not likely to have a time-management problem.

Theories have their rightful place, but there is no substitute for common sense when it comes to management of time and people. Common sense is an expression much like time in that people recognize it but have trouble defining it. There is no doubt that common sense is a highly desirable quality in any supervisor. It will manifest itself in a number of ways. For example, the effective supervisor recognizes that all people do not work continuously at the same speed. Individuals experience fatigue, encounter family problems, suffer unavoidable delays on the job, and have legitmate absences from work. Although a certain measure of uniformity is both desirable and necessary, the supervisor must be prepared to show flexibility when the situation demands it.

Supervisors who manage their time successfully have mastered the art of filtering out the few important from the many trivial on-the-job activities. The good supervisor is one who is not a victim of time but its master and helps his or her subordinates to achieve mastery as well. Remember that your objective is not to get the most out of your subordinates, but rather the best.

Larry G. McDougle is director of the Division of General and Technical Studies, Indiana University, Kokomo, Indiana.

17.
THINKING ABOUT MANAGING YOUR TIME

Warren K. Schilit

Time management is efficiency oriented. It does not provide answers; it only provides time that managers need to solve complex organizational problems.

Although organizations have spent a considerable amount of money in recent years on lectures, seminars, books and workshops on time management, managers are still generally quite lacking in their time management skills. The key to time management—just as the name implies—is to gain control of or manage your time, rather than passively let time happen to you. It involves considerably more than the basic mechanics of following a set of steps or writing down a list of priorities; in essence, it is more concerned with "thinking" than "doing."

IS TIME MANAGEMENT WORTHWHILE?

Managers must first recognize that time is their most precious resource. Time is money and, just like money, one must invest some in order to earn some at a later time. It is a very worthwhile investment because effective time utilization is likely to result in:

- a greater likelihood of an organization meeting its objectives effectively;
- greater devotion to important long-run managerial issues rather than to short-run issues;
- better-developed managers; and
- reduced stress, tension and anxiety.

THINKING VS. DOING

Most people think of time management as an exercise in developing a list of priorities. Although prioritizing one's tasks involves goal setting, which is motivational in itself, it does not enable managers to practice the key aspect of time management—controlling one's time. It is therefore useful to examine time management on two levels: (1) the amount of time that a manager possesses; and (2) the manner in which the manager utilizes his or her discretionary time.

To illustrate this notion, imagine that you have a given amount of time. Your goal is to either expand that amount of time, or at worst, prevent that amount of time from shrinking. This new amount of time is the manager's discretionary time; the manager can then attempt to utilize it as efficiently as possible.

Clearly, the former aspect of time management—expanding one's amount of time—is more indicative of gaining control of one's time and is significantly more important than the latter aspect—utilizing one's discretionary time. If a manager cannot provide himself or herself with more discretionary time, it hardly matters how he or she utilizes that discretionary time. Yet, seminars and writings on time management often stress this latter aspect of time management rather than the former aspect. Perhaps this is because the skills involved in controlling time—developing communication and problem solving capabilities, i.e., "thinking"—are much more difficult to learn than are the skills involved in utilizing a list of activities or following steps mechanically, i.e., "doing."

SUBORDINATE IMPOSED TIME

Managers have difficulty in controlling the amount of their discretionary time because they are constantly faced with both the demands of their bosses—about which they often have little or no say—as well as those of their subordinates. An effective manager must therefore be prepared: to delegate certain assignments to his subordinates in order to free himself of time needed for other activities; and to ensure that his subordinates are not "delegating" their reponsibilities to him. Both of these actions stimulate initiative on the part of the subordinates and enable them to develop their own managerial skills. Managers should therefore emphasize the developmental aspects of these activities.

Delegation clearly entails more than "unloading" work on subordinates. To delegate effectively, the manager should provide goals, feedback, guidelines and support to his or her subordinates. Furthermore, the subordinates should handle the predictable tasks, while the supervisor should tackle the exceptional ones. A manager must be continually informed of the progress of his or her subordinates, regardless of the nature of the task, because it is the manager who is ultimately responsible for the assignment.

A serious error often committed by managers is that they allow their subordinates to take up their time with subordinate-imposed problems (i.e., subordinate-imposed time). In some cases the supervisor is "working" for the subordinate rather than vice versa. For example, a subordinate may greet the supervisor and say, "By the way, we've got a problem," to which the supervisor is likely to respond, "Let me think about it and get back to you on that matter." In this episode, the supervisor has allowed the subordinate to transfer a problem from the subordinate to himself. In essence, the supervisor has taken on the role of the subordinate by: (1) accepting a responsibility from the subordinate; and (2) promising a progress report, i.e., "I'll get back to you." Furthermore, the manager has lost control of his time.

In such a situation, the supervisor should require the subordinate to restate the problem and should encourage the subordinate to prepare and evaluate a set of alternatives with which to solve the problem. This ensures that the subordinate use his or her initiative to solve the problem. The supervisor should provide the subordinate with support and feedback, but the problem should remain that of the subordinate. By ridding himself of the time imposed by the subordinate, the supervisor will provide himself with additional discretionary time in which to accomplish critical organizational tasks. It is only at this time that the manager can take steps to utilize his discretionary time more efficiently.

Some suggestions for utilizing discretionary time more efficiently include:

• Clean up your work space.
• Clarify your objectives.
• Establish priorities.
• Get through your paperwork as quickly as possible.
• Group similar tasks together.
• Break up large tasks into smaller tasks.
• Use tidbits of time efficiently.
• Recognize your productive hours.
• Reduce interruptions and time leaks.
• Avoid perfectionism.
• Learn to say "no."
• Reward yourself.

CONCLUSION

In summary, it should be noted that time management involves getting control of one's time. Before managers attempt to utilize their time more efficiently by prioritizing their tasks, they should take steps to expand the amount of discretionary time, thereby controlling their time. This is achieved by delegating and by reducing the amount of subordinate-imposed time.

Time management efforts are not useful for everyone. Unless the manager has some sense of urgency and demonstrates some basic managerial skills, time management efforts will be virtually worthless.

Finally, the rules noted above do not ensure organization success. There are many successful organizations that employ managers who cannot manage their time; by the same token, there are many successful organizations that employ managers who can manage their time quite well. Time management is efficiency-oriented. It does not provide answers; it only provides time that managers need to solve complex organizational problems.

Warren Schilit founded Catalyst Ventures, a consulting firm specializing in assisting the start-up of business. He is also a professor in the School of Management at Syracuse University.

18.
HOW GOOD A TIME-KILLER ARE YOU?

Arthur Sondak

Anyone can be a time-killer, but managers can waste their subordinates' time as well as their own. Here's a tongue-in-cheek guide to wasting time in the workplace.

Whoever said, "time's a-wasting," didn't know what he or she was talking about. Time doesn't just waste itself; it needs help. Doing nothing is one way to waste time, but it lacks imagination and prevents one from developing a flair for the creative. Indeed, managers have a unique opportunity: They can waste not only their own time, but also that of many others.

Over a period of a year, Personnel Management Services elicited responses from 250 first-line managers (who attended management seminars conducted for the American Management Associations, the American Association of Industrial Management, and the New York Chamber of Commerce and Industry) on how their bosses wasted their time. Our findings confirm that, with a little conscious effort, any manager can become a proficient time-killer. We will review the most common complaints of lower-level management and explore proven time-wasting techniques. Results are guaranteed!

Merely wasting time is easy; multiplying no-accomplishment among your staff is a real challenge. Here's how!

BE A "GOOD JOE/JANE"

It's a well-known fact that employees want their bosses to be down-to-earth, real people. You can demonstrate this by taking a personal interest in your staff—periodically visit with them and socialize a bit.

Remember, timing is all-important. This maneuver is most effective when your visit is a tension-reliever, when they're under the gun to finish some important tasks. Taking their minds off their problems with some small talk is a sure-fire method. Listed in order of effectiveness, these are worth a try:

1. Complain about your heavy workload and how little time you have.
2. Review last night's sporting event, or tonight's sporting event, or tomorrow night's or next week's. Or, if sports is not your target's interest, try movies, sex, politics or whatever is most appropriate.
3. Reminisce about your most recent (or any) out-of-town trip, and either your troubles or joys, or both. Troubles are always well-received, and are recommended as the first choice.
4. Another sure attention-getter is your latest surgery or hospital experience. If you haven't had either, it's okay to talk about how much you dread them, but it's strictly last choice.
5. If none of these work, someone else's medical, marital or in-law problems should raise keen interest. You can even camouflage your own by ascribing them to an unnamed "someone," whose confidence you must respect. That way, you can go into all sorts of endless details, for who knows that "someone" better than you?

PROMOTE TOGETHERNESS...MORE MEETINGS

Meetings present a multitude of delightful time-wasting opportunities. You can get all or a few of your people together almost any time you choose. Assembling as many as possible at one time is always a good idea.

Don't be indiscriminate about meetings; if you're not careful and don't plan, you can neglect real opportunities. Here are six reminders:

Why the meeting? Don't concern yourself with wondering why the meeting is necessary. If you do, you might talk yourself out of it. It's even less important that your people wonder why. If they do, they'll miss the whole idea and the benefit of getting the entire team together.

An even bigger danger is figuring out how much the meeting might cost. (Whoever heard of such a thing?) Some might think that calling together $300 per hour's worth of salaries to resolve a $150 problem isn't worth a meeting. What do they know anyway? After all, money doesn't change hands, so there's no loss.

Stage impromptu meetings. People love surprises; don't disappoint them. It really doesn't matter what else they might be doing, if something comes up that gives you a chance to call them together. For a bigger surprise, don't announce the reason for the meeting until they arrive. Besides, they'd only prepare for it and probably end up dragging the conversation away from what you want to talk about. After all, for meetings to be effective, they must be controlled. They are business get-togethers, not meant to be gripe sessions.

Show your importance—be late. It's essential your people be reminded you're the boss. There's no better way than to keep them waiting a while before you show up. Tell them something came up that required your personal, immediate attention. You haven't deprived them of anything, either, because their own work will be waiting for them when they return.

Discuss items of common interest. Relaxing the atmosphere and making the meeting a pleasant experience is important. This can be done by sliding the conversation into non-business subjects. Almost everyone can get involved, and your participation will make it even better. Some really experienced managers open meetings with non-business matters and save all that other drudgery for later.

If you *must* talk business, keep rehashing what's already been discussed. It will sure make time fly, and fly, and...

Be available to everybody—almost. Accessibility is important; a meeting is no excuse for other people not to be able to reach you. This foresight will really impress your staff. Have a telephone at your finger-tips in case anyone wants to call. It is also helpful for passing along any sudden inspirations that usually occur at a meeting.

Be sure that you are accessible to others who want to see you during the meeting. After all, people always have little things to check with you before finishing a job. They appreciate your continuing help and availability.

(Important: Your secretary should know where you are and be able to direct others to you, with the standing assurance that you want to see them. Doubly important: This accessibility does not apply to your immediate subordinates. See: "Teach Your People to Stand on Their Own Two Feet.")

Look for more meetings—and get your people to them. People love getting together with other people; help them out. Keep posted on other meetings in the organization and be sure to send your people to some of them. They'll be fascinated by the things other people discuss, particularly if it doesn't affect them. The exposure will broaden them and the meeting habit will be reinforced, making your own meetings that much more welcome.

KEEP YOUR PEOPLE BUSY

People usually like to be involved in tasks other than what they're supposed to be doing. That opens up the whole area of delegation.

Here's a usually neglected but highly fruitful possibility. The basic rule still stands: Get rid of as much of your own detail as possible; this is marvelous experience for lower management. But don't stop there.

To make those moves really meaningful, insist that they, and they alone, handle *each and every assignment.* Otherwise, they might re-delegate it to someone lower down who could handle it, and that would defeat your purpose.

Pass along things like placing your phone calls, screening your mail, and locating information you need. Don't overlook the obvious, like checking a column of figures—or, even better, preparing a column of figures.

BE FLEXIBLE WITH PRIORITIES

Jobs always include unexpected things. With luck, if you're a top-notch time-killer, that can be several times a day.

Being flexible is important, and you should develop this desirable trait in your people. The best way is to stamp a "right-now" priority on every little thing that comes up. It's also a great chance to call an impromptu meeting of all your people to announce the priority.

Be careful not to fall for a line some lower managers like to use: If they have some other things prioritized, they may ask you "where the new ones fit." Tell them that's why they're managers—to make decisions and get things done. This ploy also allows you to criticize someone for not doing something.

While you're waiting around for new time wasters to develop, take a look at current activities. If they're in some priority sequence, shift them around, and call a meeting to announce it. Set new timetables, particularly when one project is nearing completion. That way everything else will have a chance to catch up and imagine the splash you'll make when everything gets done at once. (If you're a real pro, though, you won't bother with nonsense like priorities in the first place.)

Give the same assignments to a few people. That way there's a good chance that nothing will be overlooked. To get maximum benefit from this technique, don't let the assignees know what you've done. They'd only combine efforts instead of duplicating them.

TEACH YOUR PEOPLE TO STAND ON THEIR OWN TWO FEET

First, let's examine a good way to assign responsibilities:

- Calculate a tight timetable then shorten it by ten percent.
- Put a "rush" on every assignment.
- Have a few "rushes" conflict with one another.
- Show your people *exactly* how you want each detail handled, and review it with them at least four times.
- Emphasize that if any question comes up, they are to consult with you before proceeding.
- Leave out a few pieces of information they'll need at critical points, to make that consulting need a reality.

And be someplace else when they need you. Some possibilities: out-of town, on vacation, at lunch, or out handling some pressing personal business. You could even be at "an important meeting" (any kind qualifies) with instructions not to be disturbed "under any circumstances."

You will recall that the principle of accessibility while at meetings did not apply to your subordinate managers. (See: "Promote Togetherness—Have Meetings.") Be creative at not being available.

Think of all the other places you could *really* be while at "an important meeting."

STAY IN CONTROL...KEEP ON TOP OF THINGS

There's no point in assigning jobs and responsibilities and then forgetting about them. Recalling the recommended approach for assigning responsibilities ("Teaching Your People...Their Own Two Feet"), you should capitalize on opportunities for control.

1. Stop by frequently to see how they're doing. The best times are when deadlines are approaching.
2. If you can time visits with snags that have been hit, control becomes even better.
3. A supportive comment should accompany your contact. Especially recommended, in order of effectiveness, are:
   "How's it going?"
   "Where does it stand?"
   "What's new on the (name your project)?"
   "Think we'll make it on time?" (Always be sure to use "we", except when timetables are not met. Then it's "you".)
   "Are you done yet?"
4. It's important that your tone of voice convey genuine and supportive concern. As for body language, a worried frown always helps. If your people still refuse to go to pieces, nail-biting is especially effective.

We've detailed the more frequent cries of first-line managers bemoaning time infringement by their bosses. If you didn't recognize your own contribution, maybe you've discovered an approach or two you'd like to try. We hope our hints will help.

To close, a fitting childhood rhyme is recalled:

> Hickory dickory dock
> Mickey's a rotten clock
> Both hands go around
> But he don't make a sound
> Trying to save time is a crock!

Arthur Sondak heads Personnel Management Services, an Edison, New Jersey-based consulting firm which specializes in employee-management relations and management training and development.

19.
EVALUATING YOUR
JOB THE IE'S WAY

J.M. Sinclair

How to analyze your job the way an industrial engineer would to find the best available methods, set realistic goals, and make the best use of your time.

No matter what your job title or function, you know the frustration of never having enough time. Your days are ruled by a series of small crises, telephone calls and interminable meetings. You watch in dismay as the immediate deadlines of some projects push aside important programs.

You belong to the legion of harried public relations practitioners. I know because I'm one of you.

I recently found help from an unexpected source: the field of industrial engineering, whose basic principles were well formulated by the 1920s and have been used in industry since the 1930s.

Industrial engineers work on the premise that if a procedure is repeated frequently, even slight improvements in methods can result in substantial improvements in productivity. Consequently, they analyze integrated systems of people, machines and materials in order to design and install the best systems. They may eliminate a slight hand movement in a process, or redesign an entire plant—all in the cause of increased efficiency.

Because of the emphasis on repeated procedures, industrial engineering principles have been applied primarily to mass production situations. As I became interested in the field, however, I wondered whether those principles could not also be applied to a public relations manager's job, such as my own. The consensus of my associates was that while those principles might help someone else, "they wouldn't work for me because my job is different every day of the week."

You probably would agree, but before you do, ask yourself how often you open mail, answer correspondence, make telephone calls, attend staff meetings, read trade papers or journals, visit a typesetter or printer or photography lab, write news releases, write feature articles, give tours, or represent your organization at community meetings?

When I asked myself this question, it became apparent that while the *content* of my job changed constantly, the *process* remained the same. In addition, after a few weeks of keeping track of how I spent my time, it also became clear that there was a remarkable similarity from day to day in the sequence in which I performed those processes.

Based on the assumption that there was enough repetition in my work to justify the analysis, I tried looking at my job as an industrial engineer would. It doesn't require a stopwatch or a slide rule, but it does require two assumptions.

First, you have to believe there is a better way of doing your job and it can be found. Industrial engineers are optimists. Even when they find a better way to do something, they never refer to it as the best method. They are more likely to call it the best available method or the best method yet devised. They assume that further improvements can always be found.

The second requirement is a questioning attitude. Set aside smugness. It's natural to feel you're doing the best that can be done under the circumstances but an industrial engineer questions everything, including the circumstances.

If you're with me so far, you probably already meet these two requirements for thinking like an industrial engineer.

ANALYZING THE PROCESS

Before an industrial engineer suggests improvements in a process, he studies it. So I kept a daily log of my activities in as much detail as possible, along with the amount of time each activity took.

Before you toss aside this idea as impractical, try it. It takes less time than you might think, and it's an easy routine to sustain. It doesn't take elaborate charts. I set an empty note pad on my desk, wrote down the date, and at intervals during the day wrote down what had happened up to that point.

Keeping a log of your activities forces you to use a technique of industrial engineering: breaking a method into its smallest units of work. Some early pioneers in the field, Frank and Lillian Gilbreth, used motion photography as a way of analyzing those steps. They developed units of work according to categories such as reach, grasp, move, reposition, release.

To see how this principle can be applied to public relations, take the unspectacular but ever-present promotion press release. On your list of things to do during a day, you might just indicate "write promotion release." A close look at your log, however, will reveal that this is a set of many separate operations. (See Table 1.)

Table 1

Promotion Press Release Components

1. You are notified of a promotion.
2. Collect background information. *
3. Draft the release.
4. Have release typed.
5. Proof the release.
6. Transport the draft to whoever approves it. **
7. Check changes in draft when returned to you **
8. Give corrected copy to secretary to retype. **
9. Proof the retyped release. **
10. Return proofed copy to secretary to have it printed, mailed to appropriate publication, delivered by cab to local newspaper.

   If photographs are needed:

11. Locate prints or take a photograph. *
12. Have negatives delivered to photo developing shop. *
13. Select negative to have printed.
14. Pick up finished prints and label them. *

* Delegate
** Eliminate

After breaking a method into its units, the industrial engineer looks at each component to see if it is: unnecessary and can be eliminated, can be delegated, or can be combined with another step. In the case of the promotion release, you might want to ask if copy approval by anyone other than yourself is necessary, or has it just always been done that way? Unfortunately, when asked to review a release, an individual often doesn't feel he or she has done justice to your request unless they make a change, whether it is needed or not. Consequently, eliminating copy approval also eliminates the need to have the release retyped and reproofed.

Many of the steps in a pro forma release such as this can be delegated by using a basic information sheet on which you check what information is needed, if photos are required and how many, and when you could take the photo if one is not available. The next time someone calls to say a promotion needs to be announced, fill in the name, check the appropriate categories, and ask yourassistant to follow through. (See Table 2.)

Table 2

Revised Method for Promotion Press Release

1. You are notified of a promotion.

2. Check boxes on information sheet, give to secretary or assistant.
3. Draft release.
4. Have release typed.
5. Proof release.
6. Select negative or photo.
7. Return proofed release to secretary to have it printed, mailed by cab to local newspaper.

Through this analysis, you've done exactly what an industrial engineer would. You have subdivided the process and rebuilt it to establish the best available method. While the amount of time saved may seem insignificant, an industrial engineer would point out that when any activity is frequently repeated, small improvements in methods result in substantial savings in time and energy.

COMING TO GRIPS WITH REALITY

Only after an industrial engineer has determined the best available method does he figure out how long it will take. You might ask why he cares how long it takes if he already knows it's the best method he can devise.

The answer lies at the heart of the value of industrial engineering: it enables you to *predict* in advance how much can be produced in a given period of time so you can set realistic goals. These predictions are valuable because they are based on observations of how long it takes to complete a task, as opposed to how long you would like it to take.

For example, after several weeks of keeping a log, I had developed some concrete data on how long it took me to accomplish certain tasks. When I made up a list in the morning of what had to be completed that day, I would include a time estimate for each task. When I added up the time estimates one morning, I discovered that I had nine hours in which to accomplish 15 hours of work.

The advantage of recognizing your plight at 8:00 a.m. instead of at 5:00 p.m. is that it forces you to make decisions about your priorities early in the day and to make realistic predictions about what can be accomplished. For example, on the day in question, I started back over my list to figure out how to cut out six hours of activities.

I had three hours blocked out in the middle of the day for lunch and a presentation from a new public relations agency. I was interested in seeing some films they had developed, but this was a low priority item. I canceled the meeting and rescheduled it for next week. Net gain 2.5 hours.

I kept that extra half-hour for lunch. Based on what I knew about myself, as well as what an industrial engineer would say, I knew rest throughout the day was one of the best ways of combating fatigue and its companion, disorganization.

While I usually warmed up to each day by reading *The Wall Street Journal* and skimming some trade publications, I resigned myself to just skimming the *Journal* headlines. Net gain: .5 hour.

There was some copy at the typesetter which I had planned on picking up on my way back from lunch. I called the typesetter and explained I was on a tight schedule. Would he deliver it? He agreed. Net gain: .5 hour.

A routine staff meeting was scheduled at 9:00 a.m. Those meetings usually ran an hour and a half. I asked my boss if he could postpone it or hold a streamlined version. He promised to keep it to 30 minutes. Net gain: one hour.

That gave me 4.5 of the six hours I needed to eliminate. Now came the hard part—picking out what wasn't going to get done. The 2.5 hours set aside for the three-year plan due tomorrow were sacrosanct. Also, the copy for the monthly publication had to be finished.

The article I had promised another department was almost done, and I was anxious to finish it, but it could wait. I called the other department manager, explained the problem, and promised to try to get to it next week. He wasn't pleased, but he knew I was right in giving priority to the three-year plan. He also respected the fact that I took a disciplined approach to my work.

THE 88 PERCENT SOLUTION

When an industrial engineer projects how much an operator can complete in a day, he doesn't assume 100 percent efficiency. He figures in lost time due to personal needs and fatigue. The percentage of time allowed for fatigue varies according to the type of job and the conditions under which it is performed.

When I plan my days now, my goal is seven hours of concentrated work. If you're working efficiently, it's amazing how much can be accomplished in that time, as well as how tired you feel when you're finished.

I also try to take into account what an industrial engineer would call the curve of productivity, the result of fatigue on production during the day. For most people it takes a little while to warm up to the job in the morning, but they quickly pick up speed. There's a slight slowdown before lunch. The starting level after lunch is a little slower than the steady pace of the morning, and productivity declines more rapidly than in the morning until it hits a low point at the end of the day.

If you think about your own curve of productivity, you can match your schedule for a day to your own changing energy level. I try to skip reading *The Wall Street Journal* now until right before lunch or late in the afternoon because that's when I'm likely to slack off anyway.

I've discovered, ruefully, that it is difficult to be this disciplined every day. It requires patience and emotional stamina. In fact, what seems to help me most is simply a good night's sleep.

I keep trying, however, because of the enormous reward. Being conscious of how you organize your work and use your time decreases the likelihood that you'll waste it. As you gain control over time, you increase the odds that you'll be able to make the significant contributions to your organization that you would like to make—if you only had time.

J.M. Sinclair is manager, employee communications and community relations, Genesco, Inc., Nashville, Tennessee.

Part III
TIMETABLING: PLANNING AND CONTROL

20.
RATIONING THE SCARCEST RESOURCE: A MANAGER'S TIME

John H. Jackson
Roger L. Hayen

Time waits for no one, and even those who don't realize—or won't admit—that they waste it should analyze just how efficiently they use this valuable commodity. One key to managerial effectiveness lies in the elimination or at least the reduction to a minimum of all non-essential activities. How do you rate in the "management of time?"

At the present time, when scarcity of resources is a much discussed topic, consideration should be given to rationing the nation's scarcest resource, the time of its most competent managers.

The efficiency of production workers can be rather accurately measured by checking the utilization of their time during production. Frederick W. Taylor pioneered this methodology for improving the efficiency and effectiveness of labor that is directly applied to the production effort. The efficiency of clerical workers and skilled trades personnel can be measured by work sampling techniques. Although this lacks the precision of a stop-watch time study, efficiency can be satisfactorily evaluated this way.

Work sampling can be further utilized in a self-initiated mode by professional employees such as engineers and teachers. For this type of study, an electronic device is usually utilized, which "beeps" at random times. The person then stops what he is doing and records his activity. Of course, for the individual engaging in numerous short duration activities, a large number of observations may be required to obtain accuracy.

The typical manager is engaged in many different tasks during a typical day. Peter Drucker[1] feels the best way to increase such an individual's effectiveness is to improve the utilization of his time. However, work sampling and time study do not provide a really workable methodology for quickly assessing the effectiveness of high-level managers. For example, visualize a managerial meeting in which the participants are engaged in self-initiated work sampling. As a buzzer sounds randomly for each individual, the meeting is interrupted so that

135

he can record his activity. In addition to such unpalatable interruptions, there is a high cost associated with such machines and the "analysis" of the data by outside "consultants."[2]

Nonetheless, concern with the effective use of management time has mounted, judging by the emerging literature, studies and management training sessions on the subject. Most of these studies have shown that very few managers know exactly how they actually spend their time, and consequently, do not know how efficiently they use it.

Managers are usually concerned about time utilization from the perspective of "how to do it." Time management in this context is viewed as a series of "principles" to be faithfully followed. Such principles are important rules of thumb and can be used where applicable. However, an additional dimension is required for a manager to be completely effective in the utilization of his time. This dimension is the comprehension of the value of time. Without a conscious realization of the value of managerial time, effective time utilization will not necessarily follow from adherence to principles of time efficiency.

Implementation of this time consciousness requires the awareness and consideration of the hourly value of a manager's time. In fact, the hourly value should be employed in evaluating an investment in management time in terms of an opportunity cost among competing alternatives.[3] This perspective allows the organization to allocate an executive's time to those projects promising the greatest return to the organization.

An executive's busy schedule does not allow sufficient time to do all the things that are worth doing, interesting or demanded. His conscience and the organizational pressures may dictate many tasks that aren't really necessary for effective management. One authoritative study, for example, found a large portion of managerial time consumed by activities such as telephone calls, meetings, reports, visitors, procrastination, special requests, delays and reading.[4] Although many of these activities are positive contributions to managerial effectiveness, they may prevent the manager from achieving his maximum efficiency potential.

The key to increased managerial efficiency and effectiveness is the elimination of non-essential, time-consuming activities. This can be accomplished through time analysis, which helps an individual define the non-essentials.

Time analysis and the utilization of management time are disciplines still in their infancy. Consider, for example, an executive's amazement when he learns from time accounting that he spends 25 percent of his day on the telephone, one-third of which is waiting. No wonder it may seem to him that he can never get anything done.

Formal time analysis is usually accomplished through recording one's activities, times and accomplishments in a daily log. Once this is done on a continuing basis, principles of work simplification can be applied to make time expenditure more effective. It may be difficult to admit that one has been wasting time or not using it to the maximum, but acceptance of the fact is necessary before any change can be made. Therefore, the list of questions in Table 1 should be answered honestly.

Table 1
Time Management Self Analysis

Listed below is a series of statements about various ways of approaching a job. Answer these items in terms of your characteristic habit patterns. No one except you will see the results. Be honest. See how you rate in "the management of time" compared to others.

	Almost Never	Sometimes	Often	Almost Always
1. I keep a written log of how I spend the major portions of my working day.				
2. I schedule my least interesting tasks at a time when my energy is at its peak.				
3. I review my job and delegate activities that someone else could do just as well.				
4. I have time to do what I want to do and what I should do in performing my job.				
5. I analyze my job to determine how I can combine or eliminate activities.				
6. Actions that lead to short-run objectives take preference over those that might be more important over the long pull.				
7. My boss assigns more work than he thinks I can handle.				
8. I attack short-time tasks (answering phone calls, reading correspondence, etc.) before projects taking a long time.				
9. I review the sequence of my job activities and make necessary improvements.				
10. I arrange task priorities based on the importance of task goals.				
Personal Score	_____	_____	_____	_____

It should be recognized that there will be deviations between the actual use of time and the "best" use, because principles of time management, as any management "principle," aren't universally applicable.

Furthermore, some jobs or occupations may require a response different from the "suggested best answer" because of differing needs. For example, in Item 1 reference is made to keeping a written daily log. This will seldom be answered "correctly" by an accountant or auditor because he probably keeps a log in order to accurately bill his clients. But development of the requisite "time consciousness" and an understanding of the logic behind the "best" answers will enable managers to more effectively utilize their time.

After answering the questions in Table 1, the manager should then compare his answers with the suggested "best" answers in Table 2 assigning the score to each response as indicated in the table. If his total score is above 25, he is using available time well. For a score below 15, time is being ineffectively managed and corrective actions should be taken immediately. Let's look at the logic behind the "best" answers.

Table 2

Suggested Best Use of Managerial Time

Item	Almost Never	Sometimes	Often	Almost Always
1.	2	3	2	1
2.	0	1	2	3
3.	0	1	2	3
4.	0	1	2	3
5.	2	3	2	1
6.	2	3	2	1
7.	3	2	1	0
8.	3	2	1	0
9.	1	2	3	2
10.	0	1	2	3

EXPLANATION OF "BEST" TIME UTILIZATION

Item 1. The suggested best answer to keeping a written log on activities is "sometimes." The successful manager will recognize that this activity has merit when it comes to eliminating redundant or useless effort, but he should realize that he may not need to record every day. Besides, a time consciousness developed through formal analysis will encourage an informal continuing review.

It is entirely possible to become preoccupied with accounting for how each minute is spent and lose sight of the original purpose of time analysis—to become a more efficient manager. One could be in the position of spending more time looking for wasted time than he can justify.

Item 2. The suggested best answer to scheduling least interesting tasks when energy is highest is "almost always."[5] Professor Lee Danielson suggests that managers spend most of their time on activities which interest them, followed by those which they do well, which are pleasurable, and which are forced upon them, and tend to put off until last those activities which are least interesting. The more pleasurable tasks should be handled at the end of the day when energy is at lowest ebb. The effective manager will attack those uninteresting (and probably more difficult) tasks when his personal energies are at their peak during his working day. Self-imposed deadlines can help him to do this.

Item 3. The suggested best answer for delegating activities is "almost always." The logic in this reasoning is found in the words, "someone else could do it just as well." The effective manager is not normally concerned with doing a job perfectly. Rather, he is interested in an optimal quality level which is arrived at by trading off quality with cost. He is interested in doing the job "well enough."

Many "professionals-turned-manager" are victimized in this regard by their own inquisitive minds. They tend to feel they must do the highest-quality work possible; that tolerances must be extremely close, even though this is not required and is very expensive to attain. This has been termed the "Rolls Royce Syndrome." Most professionals-turned-manager do not drive Rolls Royces even if they can afford them, because they are "too good." The cost of obtaining such quality is too great. In the same vein, the manager who insists on doing all the work himself, because he is the only one who can do it to perfection, is wasting his time and needlessly increasing the cost to his organization.

Item 4. "Almost always" is the suggested best answer to having sufficient time to do what is needed. If the manager is complying with the principles in Items 2 and 3, the time should be available as needed.

Item 5. The suggested best answer is "sometimes" to managerial job analysis and combining of activities. As in the answer to Item 1, a real time consciousness will dictate that this activity be performed occasionally, but it is not necessary for formal analysis on a constant basis.

Item 6. The suggested best answer regarding the relative preference of short-run objectives over long-run goals is "sometimes." It must be recognized that although many people feel the long haul is the important objective, and more immediate objectives should be subservient to the long-run, this is not always true. The most desirable situation is the attainment of short-run objectives concomitant with long-run objectives. Economist John Maynard Keynes has been quoted as saying, "In the long run we'll all be dead." It's important to realize that while long-run goals must be served (sometimes at the expense of short-run objectives), if the short-run is NOT attended to, the long-run will never transpire.

Item 7. The suggested best answer to the assigning of an excessive work load by the boss is "almost never." The assumption of such behavior on the part of a superior is to assume personality quirks of some sort. However, given a normal superior and a higher frequency alternative as a response to this question, it may be an indication that the manager's boss believes he's wasting time doing unnecessary tasks.

Item 8. "Almost never" is also the suggested best answer to attacking short-time duration tasks before long-time duration projects. As Moore found, the ten most common time problems are essentially of a short-time nature. It is entirely possible for the manager to spend his entire day handling little details, while trying to lay out blocks of time to do the big jobs. The catch is that the little jobs are recurrent. The phone will always ring, the mail will always come in. These things simply do not go away unless made to go away, and blocks of time are essential for completing large projects.

The principle behind successfully handling this problem is that little jobs tend to evaporate if unattended. Unread advertisements and unrewarded interruptions by subordinates tend to vanish without a trace if left alone. However, when confronted, they take time and have the debilitative effect of encouraging subordinates, correspondents, etc., to engage in future interruptions. There are obviously limits to how far a manager can go in ignoring these interruptions, but the limit is much further out than most realize.

The manager should "wade right in" on the big jobs at the start of his day and try to pursue them to completion. At least the job will have been started, setting up the psychological aversion to unfinished work present in most humans (the so-called Zeigarnik Effect). The manager is more likely to return to the unfinished job after an unavoidable interruption than to start a completely new task.

Item 9. In reviewing the sequence of job activities, the proposed best answer is "often." The proper sequencing of job activities is all-important to the success of long-run goals. Without frequent review of this nature, the timing of long-run projects may be affected. The common use of the PERT/CPM method in industry today reflects this need. PERT/CPM is nothing more than a method for requiring the manager to properly sequence his activities. This kind of Critical Path Analysis is useful in many instances and can be used quickly and easily with little practice.

Item 10. The suggested best answer to arranging task priorities based on task goals is "almost always." If one doesn't know where he is going, almost any path will take him there. A manager might be inclined to pursue those tasks which are of less than top priority unless he knows the goals of those that are not the most important.

PRINCIPLES OF TIME UTILIZATION

The foregoing analysis is designed to call attention to the most commonly made time use errors. More importantly, however, it is designed to help in developing a manager's time consciousness. This awareness and concern with time efficiency must be present for the following principles or suggestions (collected from many sources) to be of any use. The principles are presented here to summarize and amplify the above.

1. At times, the manager should review the tasks which have been completed, to see if they can be done in less time.

2. The manager should use all shortcuts available to him, keeping in mind that "good enough" or satisfaction is all that is needed in terms of quality performance of most aspects of most jobs.

3. The manager should be willing to tackle the "tough" jobs first.

4. The manager should never have others do something which he can do more quickly himself. (While the effective manager should always delegate jobs, there are some jobs which take more time to delegate than is required by the manager to do the job himself. The key is how much of the manager's time is involved in each alternative.)

5. The manager should be leery of getting "wrapped up" in things which other people can do (or are doing). This is especially relevant to such professionals as engineers or scientists-turned-managers, because their inquisitive minds tend to interest them in research or development which involve other people.

6. The manager must be careful to clarify instructions and orders which are given to subordinates. If he must explain again or correct mistakes, savings from delegation may be lost.

7. The manager must remember to rely on the fact that unfinished business will be a stimulus which will motivate him to continue performance, while unstarted business will not hold such a compulsion.

8. The manager must be decisive and must not procrastinate. If an immediate solution is not available, the manager should go on to something else, returning to the problem at a later time.

9. The manager must plan ahead for his absence and what others should be doing while he is gone. Planning ahead can save large amounts of time.

10. The manager should assign work which will stretch subordinates' capabilities. If the manager feels he has no one to whom he can safely delegate tasks, he had better develop someone. Delegation is a key to getting more work out of the hours available.

11. A manager must learn to relax occasionally, to recharge his mind and body. This means that he must be willing to deliberately "goof off" at times in an effort to be more effective. This involves knowing your capacities, best work times, and, to some extent, your emotional make-up.

12. A manager must be punctual. Not only the effective utilization of his time, but the time of other members of the organization is impaired by being late.

13. The manager should keep trivial details on hand for "idle time" performance. He should do such things as read his mail and return telephone calls, while waiting for a subordinate to report, etc. Such things usually don't require "blocks" of time.

14. The manager should have a plan for the work which he must do "first thing in the morning," and ideas for what must be accomplished before quitting time each day.

The above principles are obviously contradictory in some instances. But "principles of management," by their situational nature, often seem to be contradictory. Nevertheless, the points behind the principles are valid and should be kept in mind by the manager who intends to effectively utilize his time. The significant point to remember is that a continued efficiency awareness through time consciousness is more important than compliance with all the principles that can be delineated.

References

1. F.D. Barrett, "The Management of Time," *The Business Quarterly* (Spring 1969), p. 56.
2. *Business Week*, "Are Executives Efficient?" (December 1, 1973), pp. 52-57.
3. Curtis H. Jones, "The Money Value of Time," *Harvard Business Review* (July-August 1968), p. 98.
4. Leo B. Moore, "Managerial Time," *Industrial Management Review* (Spring 1968), p. 87.
5. Lee Danielson, "Management of Time," *Management of Personnel Quarterly* (Spring 1963), pp. 14-18.

John H. Jackson has held various management positions in industry and served both government and business organizations as a management consultant before joining the management faculty at the University of Wyoming. He is the author of numerous articles in the area of applied management. Roger L. Hayen received his doctorate in management science from the University of Colorado. Hayen is currently assistant director of business and economic research at the University of Wyoming. He has published a number of articles in the areas of applied system and management science.

21.
EXECUTIVE TIME MANAGEMENT: HOW TO BUDGET YOUR TIME

Borden M. Coulter
George E. Hayo

High-level executives need to spend an ever-increasing amount of their day on planning and thinking; only 5.7% of their time is devoted to this function.

As executives advance in their careers, they find themselves working more hours but using their time less efficiently. A survey of top managers shows that 36 percent of their time is consumed by telephone calls, unscheduled meetings, and interruptions. While high-level executives need to spend an ever-increasing amount of their day on planning and thinking, only 5.7 percent of their time is devoted to this function. How can executives make better use of time? How can executives measure the way they allocate time? What are the effective ways of handling phone calls, meetings, interruptions, reading and writing tasks, dictation, and work at home? Let's see.

Executives everywhere have become increasingly conscious of the need to manage their time better. Many find themselves working 50 to 60 hours a week, and even then there doesn't seem to be enough time. Moreover, they find that as the time they spend at work increases, the ROI for time invested decreases.

As an executive moves up the organizational ladder from middle management to senior management positions and then to a top management position, he should be allocating less time for day-to-day details and more time for planning and thinking.

There has been a drive for greater performance and productivity at all levels of the organization, except at the top. What about the boss? What steps can he take to make better use of his time? Can executives at the senior and middle management levels learn to improve the use of their time?

The Emerson Consultants have worked with a number of top executives over the past several years to collect and analyze data about how these executives spend their time.

Table 1
Distribution of Time

Inside the office	Time (minutes)	Percent
Telephone	108.0	18.0
Scheduled meetings	88.8	14.8
Unscheduled meetings	64.8	10.8
Interruptions	44.4	7.4
Reading and writing	40.8	6.8
Dictation-machine or secretary	27.6	4.6
Planning and thinking— working alone	34.2	5.7
	408.6 (6.8 hours)	68.1%

Away from the office		
Conferences and business meetings	84.0	14.0
Luncheon meetings	57.6	9.6
Work at home	49.8	8.3
	191.4 (3.2 hours)	31.9%

Total time:	10.0 hours	

Note: *Travel time to and from the office was not included in the above analysis. It ranged from 20 minutes per day to four hours.*

As Table 1 shows, the biggest consumer of time is the telephone, representing 18 percent. Of this time, nearly two-thirds is spent on incoming calls. In all, telephone calls, unscheduled meetings and interruptions take up over 36 percent of the typical executive's time; but planning and thinking consume only 5.7 percent.

Each executive must decide for himself how he will allocate his time each day. He should so schedule and budget his time that he will be able to work on his immediate problems, short-range goals and long-term objectives. But a good part of his day should be reserved for planning and thinking.

Planning and thinking includes preplanning for tomorrow's activities, for accomplishing short-range goals, and for developing strategies to achieve long-term objectives. It includes setting goals for subordinates as well as providing for their business and personal development within the overall objectives of the company.

MEASURING HOW YOU SPEND YOUR TIME

As an executive, how are you using your time each day? Does your allocation of time contribute to reaching your goals and objectives? To find out, you can measure how you allocate your time by using electric recording equipment or by keeping a manual record. (The raw data for this article was obtained by using electric recording equipment.)

If recording equipment is used, it can best be handled by the executive himself, with his secretary compiling the results. If a manual record is preferred, the executive's secretary should handle both the recording of time on various activities and the compiling of results.

First, activities need to be established for measurement. A start can be made with those listed in Table 1, and a day of testing will determine if others should be included.

FIGURE 2

DAILY TIME LOG

	8-9	9-10	10-11	11-12	12-1	1-2	2-3	3-4	4-5	Totals
At the office										
Telephone	//		/	/		/	/	//	/	9
Scheduled meetings	/	///				///			/	8
Unscheduled meetings			///	/		/			//	7
Interruptions	//			/			//	//		7
Reading and writing		/	/				/	/		4
Dictation	/	//	/	/		/		/		7
Planning and thinking				//			//			4
TOTALS	6	6	6	6		6	6	6	4	46
Away from the Office										
Conferences and business meetings	1½ hours									
Luncheon meetings	3/4 hours									90
Work at home	40 minutes									45
TOTALS (minutes)										40
TOTAL TIME										175

For manual recording, a time log like the one in Figure 2 can be set up for each day. Activities of the executive are marked on the log as they occur throughout the day. At the end of two weeks, enough observations will be recorded to give a reasonable estimate of how the executive spends his time. Time away from the office in job-related activities can be estimated by the executive and added to data kept by the secretary.

After obtaining results, the time spent on listed activities should be analyzed in terms of your responsibilities, goals and objectives. You may then want to improve your use of time by ranking the categories of work that contribute to accomplishing your objectives. You can designate your most important work an "A" priority, your medium important work as "B" priority, and your least important work as "C" priority.

MANAGING YOUR TIME

What other actions can the executive take to improve his use of time? Here are some of the situations confronted by executives and the steps they have taken to improve their time management.

Telephone. Most executives like to answer their own telephone. However, this actually interferes with their concentration, and some effort is usually required to return their attention to what they were doing.

One executive plagued with constant incoming calls had an outside line installed and gave the number to only selected business associates and acquaintances. All other calls were handled through the switchboard and his secretary. To reduce the frequency of returning calls, this same executive had his secretary group these calls and place them at convenient times twice each day.

Many executives like to place their own calls. But looking for telephone numbers, dialing, waiting for the secretary at the other end to get the called party, and not reaching the called party all waste an executive's time. By having your secretary place the call, your time will be spent only in talking to the called party.

Scheduled meetings. These are meetings called or attended by executives for discussion of routine and priority business. Many of these meetings may be with the same people.

Delegating the responsibility for attendance at these repetitive meetings can save you time as well as contribute to the development of your subordinates. You needn't worry about being kept informed. Important conclusions and recommendations from the meetings can be reported to you.

When meetings are necessary, there should be agendas, the agendas should be adhered to, the duration of the meetings should be fixed in advance, and the meetings should start and end on schedule. Few meetings require more than an hour. The loosely run half-day or all-day meeting can probably be reduced by at least half.

An effective way to start on time and have everyone present is to discuss the most important items first. After just one or two times being late and having topics discussed or decisions made about his area, the perennially late executive will be on time.

Unscheduled meetings. These are in-company meetings called without prior notice, usually in response to an immediate problem, with people from outside the company who are just dropping by or with others, to discuss financial, union, safety or other matters.

Again, some of these meetings can be delegated. One executive chose to stand and remain standing with a visitor to shorten the visitor's stay. Other devices to shorten meetings include insisting that discussion be limited to the subject at hand and adjourning at the earliest opportunity. One executive always tried to hold meetings with small groups in another executive's office. This way the executive was free to get up and leave whenever an opportune moment presented itself.

Interruptions. Drop-in interruptions of short duration to ask questions; to obtain instructions, approvals and signatures; to request donations and so forth, are usually the biggest time wasters for executives. Although they represent only 7.4 percent of the executive's time, the impact of the interruptions can be two to three times the recorded amount.

If you are visible from outside your office, you are a prime candidate for interruptions.

One executive was tired of being constantly interrupted and decided it was time to so something about it. He completely rearranged his office area, including having a second door installed for leaving his office. Anyone wanting to see him had to see his secretary first. The secretary would announce the visitor over the intercom. If the executive didn't want to see the visitor, he could be on his way to another appointment.

Subordinates will sometimes need to see the boss. A scheduled time can be set aside each day for these meetings, with other times reserved for emergencies only. The "open door" policy is good in theory but can be an executive time waster if not controlled.

Reading and writing. Reading periodicals, newspapers and business communications, including reports, letters and memos, can take up a good part of any executive's time. Conversely, the writing of memos, speeches, letters and other communications usually consumes only a small part of the the executive's time.

One way to reduce the amount of general reading is to route material through subordinates first with a request for them to mark articles of interest to other executives and you. A second way, but one requiring more effort, is to arrange for a course or seminar in effective reading. This will teach you techniques to improve your reading skills as well as increase your reading speed.

With the small amount of writing most executives do, the only timesavers suggested to reduce writing time are to mark comments directly on incoming letters for replies by your secretary, to train her to answer letters in your style of writing, and to use dictation or dictating equipment whenever possible.

Dictation. Few executives will preplan their dictation. Usually they will call in their secretaries when they have finished reading the mail, completed a telephone call, or after meeting with another executive. Jotting down a few notes and grouping items for later dictation or using dictating equipment will save you time. Your secretary will also be able to schedule her work better and be a greater asset to you.

Follow-up reports, memos and so forth pertaining to work done outside the office, with rare exception, should be recorded on dictating equipment.

There are certain activities over which executives have very little control but which are a very important part of doing business:

- Conferences and business meetings. Conferences and meetings away from the office with bankers, lawyers, stockbrokers, financial counselors, radio and television executives, members of the local Chamber of Commerce, and the like are considered necessary by most executives. It is likely little effort will be expended to reduce these outside commitments.
- Luncheon meetings. These are meetings away from the office with associates, other industry and business leaders, and representatives of local service organizations. Executives we have talked to on the question of time management considered luncheons excellent for creating a relaxed atmosphere and for developing objective thinking on the part of a busy executive normally engrossed in his own business problems.
- Work at home. This includes reading periodicals and business communications, occasionally telephoning to confirm business arrangements or preparing for special meetings and trips. Because of the interruptions and the short periods of time for concentration on any single subject at the office, some of the executives in the study took home any dictation that required real concentration.

THE NEXT STEP

After analyzing the factors involved in managing executive time, the next step is to implement the findings. In its work with top executives over the past several years, The Emerson Consultants found that once executives realized how they were spending their time, they made many changes.

By measuring how you allocate your time, you will be able to assess how effectively you are in control and whether you use time as if it were an asset. Next, by applying some of the successful methods listed here, plus others gleaned from your own experience, you will be in a position to manage your time better.

After you have made changes to improve you own time management, you may want to go back and periodically remeasure how you now manage time against your earlier benchmark. You will be surprised at how much progress you have made. Perhaps you will not be taking home as much work as you now do. You may even want to start a program for your own subordinates to improve their executive time management.

Borden M. Coulter is a vice president and director of The Emerson Consultants, Inc., New York City, and is headquartered in Houston. He has BS degrees in mechanical engineering and business administration and an MBA from UCLA. George E. Hayo is a senior consultant of The Emerson Consultants, Inc. He has a BS degree in applied mathematics from California State Polytechnic and an MBA from the University of Denver.

22.
HOW TO FIND ENOUGH TIME

Chester Burger

Don't forget: In a Research Institute of America survey, managers were asked: "What is your biggest timesaver on the job? The single most important factor, they answered, is "planning."

Pressed for time? Who isn't, in the business world? You're caught in the executive's time squeeze. How do you ease the pressure, without letting important things slide or fall apart?

Others, including many top corporate figures, successfully use tools that you, too, can employ.

The key to time mastery is no mystery. It's planning. Yet a manager will say sincerely: "I just haven't time to plan. I come in, the phone rings, things happen. The day's shot before I know it."

If so, perhaps it's because he doesn't have something that's a must for systematic planning—a foundation.

A record book, believe it or not, is about the most universally useful tool for building that foundation. Such a notebook can and should be a simple one, if it has certain key features.

The name of the game is convenience. The book will be a tool for you to use personally. Nobody can do an executive's personal planning for him, so it should be at your fingertips anytime you need it. Pocket-size is convenient for managers who are frequently out of the office; a larger size is fine for desk use. Some people, including myself, employ both in combination.

ALL IN ONE

Make the book multipurpose, to serve you best. Unify all daily functions and records, even expenses, in a roomy one- or two-page spread for each day of the year. And keep supplementary material—address/phone list, credit cards, calendar and such—in the same memo and planning book.

That's where many managers miss out.

Their records are scattered, difficult to find and use.

Orderly arrangement, a functionalized format, is crucial. You can buy a blank notebook and lay in a format, or buy one ready-printed for personal executive use.

I use a ready-made one. My pocket edition includes 12 separate booklets, one for each month, and a wallet to carry the current monthly booklet and supplementary materials. The desk version is a single loose-leaf volume.

The format comprises a two-page spread for each day, divided into separate sections for appointments and things to do at a certain hour; other things to do that day; expenses; and a page for diary notes of services performed. On this page you can record when you undertook any action and the length of time you gave it, by virtue of a time-scale down the side of the page.

Such a unified personal planning aid gives you virtually a portable office.

A daily expense section lets the manager make on-the-spot records of travel, entertainment and other out-of-pocket costs easily mislaid or forgotten. I even put credit card charge receipts in my traveling notebook. Back at the office they're stapled to the desk book pages for the days on which each expenditure occurred. It takes just seconds and the record is permanent. On the sole occasion I was audited by the Internal Revenue Service, my accountant merely showed the federal man the record books. It convinced him on the spot.

Henry A. Barnes, late New Your City traffic commissioner, kept a daily record book. As reported by one national magazine, Mr. Barnes was accused of being improperly influenced by a traffic meter manufacturer. The supposed evidence was a photostat of a bill showing the manufacturer had paid for a Beverly Hills hotel room for a Henry Barnes—nearly two years previously.

Mr. Barnes coolly produced a business diary showing he'd been in Baltimore that day and had dined at a friend's home. Apologies. Wrong Barnes. Case closed.

Compact calendar pages for coming months permit you, no matter where you are, to confirm an appointment for a week, a month or even several months ahead. No wheel-spinning in checking later. Such pages, and a slim phone/address book, should be the standard components of your portable office. The containing wallet can also house ready-reference data. I've known the latter to include a table of wine vintage years, family clothing sizes, machine tool tolerances, weight-watcher data, subordinates' vacation times, and stocks' price/earning ratio tables.

SECRETS OF SCHEDULING

Clever scheduling frees far more time than it absorbs. Crawford I. Greenewalt, when he was Du Pont board chairman, said he found that every hour spent planning saved three to four in execution. With a planner book, you can write your schedule down. One marketing manager I know estimates he saves more than 100 hours yearly just by keeping weekly schedules in front of him.

Ace managers advise: Schedule similar tasks together. In tackling kindred jobs one after another, most people hit a pace that knocks off chores in amazingly short order.

Dictating letters all in one session is one example. Here's a tip from a steel company vice president: He reads all mail in one sitting, and acts on each letter immediately. No to-be-answered file. He almost never has to reread and collect his thoughts all over again.

Phone calls can be clustered for hours in which you're likely to get your parties. Patterns vary by city and profession. What are the best telephoning times in your situation? It could pay to take ten minutes and think it out.

Incoming phone calls can similarly be handled at your convenience. A secretary can take all calls, jot down the name of each caller and, when tactful, the subject, and hand you the log for action. Are gobs of your time sponged up by talks in your office? Conferring by phone can eliminate many visits.

As to the rest, scheduling can be very helpful indeed. Witness the way President Eisenhower handled it.

Ike "organizes his time so that he has as many appointments as possible in the morning, thereby leaving an uninterrupted afternoon," disclosed his press secretary. "The President makes every minute count."

You can minimize time spent with each visitor—and maximize results—if you estimate the time each visit should take, and schedule one visit to terminate another. Diplomatically, let each person know the time the next visitor is due. It's a tactful way to set a deadline.

Almost invariably, your guest will get just as much ground covered with fewer words. You will, too. Time is saved for both. Communications experts assert that nearly any subject, on any scale of importance, can be thoroughly covered in a one-hour maximum. So set tight talk time limits. You may be pleasantly surprised.

Your plan should make allowance for the hours of the day when you work at your best. Many people work best in late morning, decline in efficiency after lunch, pick up again for a final spurt from three to four, and then taper off.

Such patterns, perhaps, are formed in early childhood. By the time you become a corporate executive, yours are strongly set. Don't fight them. When you plan your day's activities, consider your personal cycle. Schedule your most important activities for the hours when you're at your peak.

And here's a tip from the chief of one of the nation's leading fashion firms: Start the day with requests for action by others. Then their services will be under way while you tackle other things.

Many things needn't be done at a certain appointed hour—but they surely need doing. For such tasks the canny time-master uses his to-be-done-today notebook heading and applies the golden rule of managing: Decide what's really most important, list work in that order, start at the top of the list, and—short of dire emergency—stick with each task until it's finished.

Simple, yes. But it takes mental discipline and firmly built habit, and you'd be surprised how many executives just can't handle it.

In one case, a prestigious public relations agency was nearly torpedoed by absence of this ability.

The firm was losing accounts but didn't know why. In confidential interviews, its clients repeatedly told me the same story. The outfit's work was top-drawer, but almost always late. When publicity campaigns are breaking, you can't be late, even sometimes.

The trail led to the agency's principal. Always super-busy but always disorganized, he just couldn't handle time. He missed deadlines. Subordinates (in part unconsciously) took their cues from him and low-rated deadlines, too. In addition, his delays impeded their deadlines.

His problem was rooted in personality traits. Faced with business collapse, he fought back. For him, it was tough. He began to use a time-planner book for self-reminders of every deadline, flagged two weeks ahead of schedule. He slated a once-a-week personal contact with every client. He stuck with it. He saved his business.

To whip time, you have to really want to do it.

PLUGGING OTHER LEAKS

To help spot time leaks, keep notes in your daybook occasionally to show where your time goes. Reading and writing reports, for example, is a common clock-killer. Both can be streamlined by an improved report-writing method. (You might want your report-writing subordinates to try this, too.)

Don't wrestle to start your first draft with the "main idea." Relax. Dictate or write things as they come to mind. Then, after your draft is typed, choose the leading idea (often, it turns out to be near the beginning after all). Organize, be sure to condense, and lastly write a brief foreword outline for those readers who will need only the gist of the report.

Some years ago, Edwin A. Locke, Jr., when he was president of Union Tank Car Co., said "verbal incompetence" probably cost corporations more than thefts and embezzlements. Terse report-writing can save much management time.

There's a wealth of other ways to help master the time squeeze. A book on fast-reading techniques, for example, can save you almost unnumbered hours.

Don't forget: In a Research Institute of America survey, managers were asked: "What is your biggest time-saver on the job?"

The single most important factor, they answered, is "planning."

Chester Burger heads the New York management consulting firm, Chester Burger & Co., Inc. He has written several books on management subjects and is a director of a number of corporations.

23.
TIME PLANNING: HOW TO DIVIDE UP YOUR DAY

Charles W. Schilling

Time is cyclical, in which events start, change and stop. The inability to start an event is called reluctance. The inability to change events within time is inflexibility. The unwillingness to stop an event in time is being compulsive.

Time planning is one of the most talked about and yet neglected elements in supervision. "I don't have time..." "I wanted to, but I didn't have enough time..." How often do you hear these words—or how often have you said them yourself? A proverb has stated, "Every scrap of a wise person's time is worth saving." The question is often asked, "How can supervisors organize themselves and the time at their disposal so that they can fulfill their responsibilities and achieve their objectives?"

Sometimes you may feel you have too much to do and wonder how you can control and accomplish it all. Stress, tension and frustrations result, making you much less efficient. Time is as much a resource to the supervisor as machines, material, capital and manpower. The successful use of time requires self-management, work planning, setting priorities, handling interruptions, and time scheduling of people and activities.

The ability to supervise is only the starting point; effective time planning allows that ability to reflect itself in meaningful achievement. Too many supervisors, however, have permitted their talents to lie buried under cluttered desks, confusion, interruptions and busyness without accomplishment.

One way to point up the value of careful time planning is to look at the reverse side: What are the costs to your organization when you allow yourself to be the *victim* of time rather than its *master*? For example, what portion of costs of the following can you attribute to poor time planning: un-utilized time, delayed decisions, unscheduled meetings, meetings extended beyond schedule, unhappy customers, and lost profits? How much has poor time planning (by you or others) cost you, your office, your associates, your subordinates and your family?

In a more general nature, take a moment and consider the following: 1. In what ways has poor time planning caused problems or increased costs in your organization? 2. Describe incidents or occasions when the poor time planning of others has adversely affected you and your organizational profits. 3. Describe occasions when your poor time planning has affected others.

As a professional supervisor, you need to know how you're spending your time and how to plan it. Time control is the willingness to take responsibility for the space and events we choose to put in time. Time is cyclical; events start, change and stop. The inability to *start* an event is called reluctance. The inability to *change* events within time is inflexibility or an inability to change. The unwillingness to *stop* an event in time is being compulsive. Time control is the ability to start, change and stop the time cycle. That's when the work is getting completed. Too much random motion produces confusion and indecision. Over the years, indecision has resulted in the loss of large sums of money to organizations.

The first step in planning time, then, is to know what you are doing with your time. This means keeping track of all your daily activities in the form of a daily log. The daily log shown in Figure 1 provides space for the duration of activities, type of action (interruption, telephone, conferences, writing, dictation, analyzing or other action), individuals or subjects involved, purpose of activities, and location. To begin an understanding of time planning, analyze your activities at the end of a five-day period. Then classify activities into three categories: profit-related productive time, unavoidable non-productive time, and avoidable non-productive time. Analyze each category, and then eliminate the latter activities. This procedure should result in more productive results and in effective use of time.

FIGURE 1

DAILY LOG

Name: _____   Date: _____
Department: _____   Day: (Circle one) M   T   W   TH   F   S   S
Position or title: _____

Starting Time of Activity	Location		Type of Action					Individual or Subject Involved	Purpose of Activity	Termination Time of Activity
	Office	Other	Interrupt	Phone	Confer	Write	Analyze			

Instructions: Each day review this sheet. Analyze each activity as:
   A. Productive time, profit related.
   B. Nonproductive time, not avoidable.
   C. Nonproductive time, avoidable.

Dick Gardner, president of the National Association of Sales Education, conducts dozens of sales training and motivation seminars nationwide every year. He believes that documenting and analyzing your time leads to a higher success ratio. If you can find your strengths and weaknesses, you can improve your use of time. All supervisors must use their time with care; keeping time records is one way of planning and analyzing your time effectively.

The types of questions that you need to answer in your time planning are:

1. What are you doing—is your action productive or non-productive?
2. When are you doing it?
3. How much time are you spending doing it?
4. Who are you doing it with?
5. Where are you?

After answering these questions, you will have more information to plan more effectively the next day. Another question you should ask yourself is: What will I do every day for my organization? If you have no definite plans, places to go or someone to see, you are waking up unemployed for that day.

The daily log which has been discussed should prove to be an eyeopener for more effective use of your time. If you are having time problems, this may be a good way to begin. Other considerations for your time analysis are: 1. Are you doing what you *really* want to do with your time? 2. What can you do? 3. What do you hope to do? Are you then making the best use of your time in relation to the way it is being spent today?

When the "cans" and "hopes" are not being realized, job frustration sets in. In the end results, are your goals and objectives really being obtained? Attaining goals and objectives doesn't just happen. The attainment of results comes by carefully planning your time. Perhaps that is why, as Earl Nightingale comments, only five percent of the people in the world are truly successful by their own standards.

Once you know how you are using your time, the next task is to set priorities for what *must* be accomplished. This results in establishing a Daily Work Plan such as the example in Figure 2. Schedule your appointments and work on a half-hour basis. Then establish a priority ("A" for the highest, etc.) and the order under each priority, as 1, 2, 3. Reschedule breaks, recreation, and personal phone calls to allow time for them, otherwise you will find your time eaten away.

Setting priorities depends on two factors: How you *like* to work and what you *must* do. How you set your priorities is not important, the important thing is that you set them. Without priorities and organization, there is no daily work plan. When supervisors arrive at their offices, they immediately become victims by reacting to external events instead of controlling what they do and what they can accomplish.

DAILY WORK PLAN

FIGURE 2

Name: _____

Department: _____

Position or title: _____

Date: _____

Day: (Circle) M   T   W   TH   F   S   S

Appointments & Work Plan	Priority	Order	Things to Do — Today's Action
7:00			
:30			
8:00			
:30			
9:00			
:30			
10:00			
:30			
11:00			
:30			
12:00			
:30			
1:00			
:30			
2:00			
:30			
3:00			
:30			
4:00			
:30			
5:00			
:30			
6:00			
:30			
7:00			
:30			
8:00			
:30			
9:00			
:30			
10:00			

Instructions: Assign each task a letter of priority (A, B, C, etc.) as well as a number (1, 2, 3, etc.) to indicate order. This daily work plan is an orderly way to keep track of "Things to Do Today."

In the use of the telephone, try to make all outside calls, including call-backs, at one time and continuously. Consider scheduling appointments one after another with approximate time allowances for each. Keep the discussion on business and keep to the point.

Drop-ins and unscheduled visitors are inevitable and often unnecessary. They can't be eliminated but they can be controlled. Any secretarial work should be scheduled to fit the load and mail pickups. Consider preparing secretarial work early in the morning or immediately after lunch so that the secretary can get the work out the same day.

If you cannot conquer time, you can at least control it so that it serves you in a more productive manner.

24.
WHEN YOU JUST
DON'T HAVE TIME...

G. W. Richards
R. Alec Mackenzie

You are really living out a paradox: No one has enough time, yet everyone has all there is. So, is time the problem or are you the problem?

The late Vince Lombardi once said that "fatigue makes cowards of us all." Could it also be possible that mismanagement of time makes incompetents of us all? Clearly, to the extent that we waste precious time, our lives—on and off the job—become less productive and therefore less effective.

With this in mind, we have evaluated many of the reasons that cause people to unconsciously waste time. And we have discovered remedies that can literally change your life for the better, if used.

Timewasters are anything that prevent you from achieving your objective effectively. Timewasters can be grouped by seven principal management functions in which the activity occurs:

- Planning
- Organizing
- Staffing
- Directing
- Controlling
- Communicating
- Decision-making

Forty of the more common timewasters are grouped by management function. Scan them and identify the ones in your life.

40 TIMEWASTERS

Planning

—Lack Objectives/Priorities/Planning
—Crisis Management, Shifting Priorities
—Attempting Too Much at Once/Unrealistic Time Estimates
—Waiting for Planes/Appointments
—Travel
—Haste/Impatience

Organizing

—Personal Disorganization/Cluttered Desk
—Confused Responsibility and Authority
—Duplication of Effort
—Multiple Bosses
—Paperwork/Red Tape/Reading
—Poor Filing System
—Inadequate Equipment/Facilities

Staffing

—Untrained/Inadequate Staff
—Under/Over-Staffed
—Absenteeism/Tardiness/Turnover
—Over-Dependent Staff

Directing

—Ineffective Delegation/Involved in Routine Details
—Lack Motivation/Indifference
—Lack Coordination/Teamwork

Controlling

—Telephone Interruptions
—Drop-in Visitors
—Inability to Say "No"
—Incomplete/Delayed Information
—Lack Self-Discipline
—Leaving Tasks Unfinished
—Lack Standards/Control/Progress Reports
—Visual Distractions/Noise

—Overcontrol
—Not Being Informed
—People Not Available for Discussion

Communicating

—Meetings
—Lack/Unclear Communication, Instructions
—Socializing/Idle Conversation
—"Memoitis"/Over-Communication
—Failure to Listen

Decision-making

—Procrastination/Indecision
—Wanting All the Facts
—Snap Decisions

Causes, solutions. Following are some causes and solutions for three timewasters we find to be quite common to oil companies: telephone interruption, ineffective delegation and ineffective meetings.

Causes and solutions for telephone interruptions and ineffective delegation are grouped as being internal (controlled mainly by our behavior) and external (controlled by other people, situations and policies).

TELEPHONE INTERRUPTIONS

Causes	Solutions
Internal	
1. Unaware of seriousness.	Take time log of phone calls. Evaluate origin, extent and causes.
2. No plan for handling.	Develop plan to screen, delegate, consolidate.
3. Ego. Feeling of importance.	Recognize ego factor. Don't overestimate importance to others of your availability.
4. Desire to be available.	Distinguish between being available for business and for socializing.
5. No plans for unavailability.	Quiet hour; screening; set periods for taking calls.

6. Desire to keep informed.	Accomplish on planned, more certain basis. Recognize that your team members will naturally want to keep you informed of everything they are doing, rather than simply the essentials.
7. Desire to be involved.	Recognize danger of involvement in detail. Divorce yourself from routine matters and details.
8. Taking and placing own calls.	Delegate.
9. Lack of delegation.	Delegate more. Plan calls. List points to be discussed.
10. Not listing items to be discussed.	Organize yourself. Plan calls. List points to be discussed.
11. Overdependent staff.	Refuse to make *their* decisions. Encourage initiative. Allow mistakes.
12. Fear of offending.	Don't be oversensitive. Top secretaries never offend unnecessarily. Concentrate on priorities.
13. Inability to terminate conversation.	Learn and practice technique: Preset time limit ("Yes, Tom, I can talk for a few minutes.") Foreshadow ending ("Bill, before we hang up.") Be candid ("Sorry, Joe, I've got to go now.")
14. Unrealistic time estimates.	Secretary interrupts with reminder of urgent item demanding attention. Three-minute egg timer in front of telephone. Time yourself for one day. Recognize how much longer a call can take than is necessary.
15. Lack ability to manage own secretary.	Study. Develop plan. Implement. Train or replace with experienced secretary requiring no training.

External

16. Ineffective screening.	Analyze problem. Develop plan. Discuss with associates to avoid surprise and offense. Discuss with secretary to ensure her understanding and confidence. Implement. Support secretary.
17. No secretary.	If you need one full- or part-time, do feasibility study to demonstrate need. If you have an assistant, use in place of secretary. If not, develop techniques to have messages taken at certain times. Use a hideaway. Cut-off switch.
18. Misdirected calls.	List of persons and numbers. Instruct personnel on directing of calls. Have "frequently called" numbers visible.
19. Confused responsibilities.	Clarify.
20. "Answer your own" policy.	Recognize waste of time and talent. Revise or eliminate policy.
21. Poor telephone system.	Study and update.

Ineffective meetings. Many managers say that more time is wasted in ineffective meetings than in any other aspect of organizational life. And yet meetings are critical to getting things done. These causes of problems, and their proposed remedies, should prove useful.

MEETINGS

Causes	Solutions
Before	
1. Lack of purpose.	No meeting without a purpose; in writing if possible.

2. Lack of agenda.	No meeting without an agenda. Written agenda for scheduled meeting; verbal agenda if unscheduled to ensure that people come prepared and discussion is scheduled.
3. Wrong people/too many/ too few.	Only those needed present.
4. Wrong time.	Ensure opportune timing.
5. Wrong place.	Select location consistent with objectives of meeting, freedom from interruptions, physical equipment necessary, minimum of travel for majority of people.
6. No planning.	Allow for and schedule appropriate planning for most effective meeting.
7. Too many meetings.	Test need for "regular" meetings. Occasionally don't hold it—see what happens. Or cut time allowed in half for those tending to last a long time.
8. Too few meetings.	Assess need for participation, information and coordination. Schedule accordingly.
9. Inadequate notice.	Provide written notice with all essentials including expected contribution and materials necessary for preparation.
10. Not starting on time.	Start on time. (By delaying for late arrivals, the leader penalizes those arriving on time and rewards those who come late!)

During

11. Socializing.	Reserve socializing for better place. Get down to business.

12. Allowing interruptions.	Set policy and let everyone know. Wherever possible allow no interruptions except for clearcut emergency. Hold messages for delivery at coffee breaks and lunch times.
13. Wandering from agenda.	Expect and demand adherence to agenda. Resist "hidden agenda" ploys.
14. Failing to set ending time or time allotments for each subject.	Time-limit the meeting and each item on the agenda to place discussion time in accordance with importance of subject.
15. Keeping people after they are no longer needed.	Leave after expected contribution made.
16. Indecision.	Keep objective in mind and move toward it.
17. Deciding without adequate information.	Ensure requisite information will be available before convening meeting. Use it.
18. Failing to end on time.	End on time. Otherwise no one can plan for the time immediately following.
19. Failing to summarize Conclusions.	Summarize conclusions to ensure agreement and remind participants of assignments.

After

20. No minutes.	Record decisions, assignments and deadlines in concise minutes. Distribute within one day of meeting.
21. Failing to follow-up.	Ensure effective follow-up on all decisions. List uncompleted items under "Unfinished Business" at beginning of next agenda. Request status reports until completed.

22. Failure to abolish committees
    when business or objectives
    accomplished.

Take committee inventory. Abolish.
those whose mission has been
accomplished.

Delegation. Failure to delegate is one of the major dilemmas that lead to ineffective management. There are at least a dozen internal causes of failure to
delegate and four external causes. Proper delegation may well be the manager's
most useful time-saver and is necessary to develop subordinates' potential.

INEFFECTIVE DELEGATION

Causes	Solutions

Internal

1. Insecurity—fear of failure.	Recognize. Accept risk as inherent. Allow mistakes. Learn from them.
2. Lack of confidence in staff.	Train, develop, trust.
3. Involving yourself in detail and routine.	Do nothing you can delegate; divorce yourself from detail.
4. Delegate responsibility without authority.	Always delegate authority commensurate with responsibility.
5. Giving unclear, incomplete or confused instructions.	Ensure clear, complete, unambiguous instructions. Ask subordinate to restate to ensure understanding.
6. Envy of subordinate's ability.	Laugh at yourself. Then give full credit where it is due. Develop your own replacement.
7. Can do job better and faster yourself.	Lower standards to what is "acceptable," not your own level of performance. Avoid perfectionism.
8. More comfortable "doing" than "managing."	Recognize that practice leads to success, which leads to comfort. Control.

9. Expect everyone to "know all the details."	Recognize that this should not be expected of someone who has delegated responsibility for handling.
10. Failure to establish appropriate controls.	Establish plans, schedules with details, progress reports, monitoring of deadlines.
11. Overcontrol.	Relax. Emphasize goal-accomplishment methods and procedures. Measure results, not activity.
12. Failure to follow-up.	Always check progress in time to take corrective action.

External

13. Understaffed/overworked subordinates.	Limit expectations and reduce accepted responsibilities.
14. Inadequate, untrained staff.	Train, reassign; rehire; better selection.
15. Upward delegation.	Refuse to make decisions for subordinates. If they need help, ask the right question.
16. Problem not clear.	Be candid. Ask subordinate to figure out and keep you informed.

Quiet hour. If you follow the above proposed solutions you are well on your way to becoming an effective time user. But you may find it helpful to consider one final tool for your life and career enrichment. We call it the "quiet hour," our name for any bit of time during which you *plan* to be *selectively unavailable* in order to work on a top priority project without interruptions.

If you take a time log, you will no doubt discover that your normal day included many interruptions that were unnecessary or took too long. You will also find necessary interruptions (short ones) on important topics, but which could have waited until you finished the task on which you were then working. The "quiet hour" can help.

Principal arrangements and steps in setting up a "quiet hour" are:

1. Set a starting and ending time and announce it. People are more willing to wait for you if they know when you will be available and that you will get back to them.

2. Have your secretary (or an associate) screen calls and visitors. If you have no secretary, put calls to the switchboard, turn your bell off, or go to another "hideaway" office or conference room. Put a calendar or appointment schedule on the wall outside your door for visitors to write on to set their own appointment times or to leave messages that you will see and respond to at the end of your "unavailable period."

3. Keep all appointments or reschedule. Follow up on all messages left; that way, necessary communication is not lost, but simply deferred and consolidated. Failure to keep appointments, or to return calls, is offensive. Deferring to mutually agreeable times is not.

There is much to an effective screening system for phone calls and visitors and it requires a well trained secretary and a good plan of attack so that the three criteria for an effective "quiet hour" can be met:

1. Defer lower priority topics that come up. This requires tact in finding out the topic and deferring or setting up an appointment.

2. Satisfy every call or let secretary handle it, provide the information, set an appointment or arrange for a call back; and

3. Allow VIP's and true emergencies to be put through. (Being totally unavailable is no better than being totally available.)

If you do not have a secretary or associate to screen for you during your "quiet hour" then at least consider adopting these helpful personal attitudes and practices:

1. When asked "Have you got a moment," it is perfectly all right to ask "What is it about?" or some equivalent question to determine the topic. Then you can compare its importance to what you are doing, and decide whether to interrupt that, or not. You can test the legitimacy of an interruption only if you know its subject.

2. Few interruptions really need your attention "right now," whereas the task you are involved in *does* need undivided attention to prevent loss of concentration, momentum and insights.

3. Your attitude of helpfulness to others is desirable, but be aware that in excess, the "rescuer" can easily become the "victim." If you condition others to expect you to always drop what you are doing to help them, they may learn that it is easier to ask you than to figure it out themselves. Leave some of the burden of solution on those who will benefit by it. They will be better off and feel a greater sense of satisfaction about themselves and their jobs and will do a *better* job in the long run. Meanwhile, you have gained time you otherwise were losing on needless interruptions.

4. Time that you give to unimportant or untimely interruptions cannot be recovered. It only reduces the time remaining for more important tasks, your family and friends and yourself.

5. Associates, bosses and clients generally will accept and agree with your desire and right to work without interruption, at least for a portion of each day. They too feel the need to do the same, and will probably respect your courage

and discipline, especially if put this way: "If I am dealing with our problems, you want my best effort. I can best provide it by having uninterrupted time to concentrate on the problem's resolution. Of course, I will always be ready to respond to your request for dialog if and when its need supersedes the need to concentrate on the problem at hand."

Take the time. The constructive salvation of time will lengthen your life, in a sense. As you redeem precious minutes, you are likely to experience many side benefits—reduced stress and pressure being only one. As you apply the suggestions made here, good luck! Have the time of your life.

G.W. Richards is associated with Pryor Resources in Shawnee Mission, Kansas. R. Alec Mackenzie is president of Alec Mackenzie & Associates, Inc., in Greenwich, Connecticut.

25.
PUT TIME ON YOUR SIDE

Charles W. Mead

One sure way to waste time at work is to let administrative demands—I call them "administrivia"—overwhelm you.

Time is the one commodity you get only so much of. Once it is used up, you don't get any more. You can't retrieve all the hours—nay, days—you've frittered away, but you can take some positive steps to manage what's left of today, this week, this quarter.

One sure way to waste time at work is to let administrative demands—I call them "administrivia"—overwhelm you. Many managers will admit they approach that daily forced dose of paper-shuffling activities only with the greatest reluctance. Their negative emotions undoubtedly result from the subconscious recognition that administration is a reactive, time-consuming process, trivial work to be accomplished at the expense of "meaningful" management.

Departmental administrivia are the obstacles standing squarely between all managers and the time they should be spending doing "the job." No matter how talented a manager you are, if you cannot reduce administrative demands, you won't have time to demonstrate your talents, and you will remain managerially impotent. Yet, because most management positions encompass enough administrivia to consume all of a manager's time, the only way to create time for real managing is to reduce that personal administrative burden.

Much has been written recently about techniques (e.g., in-basket exercises and prioritization schemes) to master administrivia. Indeed, the proper dispatching of in-basket material—the primary renewable resource of the management ecology—certainly ranks with interpersonal skills as one of the least exact sciences known to management. But to ignore that in-basket's daily persistence or to deal with it haphazardly, is counter-productive and ultimately self-destructive.

If you are caught in this reactive dilemma (and if you are in management, you *are* caught in it), there are attitudes that, if you adopt them, will allow you to recover both precious time and energy. Think first about your attitude toward time itself. Do you routinely (and hastily) postpone your second appointment because the first is running long, or got started late? Or do you think of your time as a resource to be controlled and managed?

You can lick that always-running-late problem by maintaining a *written* schedule of all your commitments by day and by time. A written schedule allows you to schedule, space and control that valuable resource, your time. Far too many managers do not utilize the structure offered by this simple discipline.

If having a written schedule strikes you as logical, your next instinct is likely to be to begin setting priorities for your workload: What shall I do first?

Unfortunately, setting priorities merely orders the effort. It certainly does not eliminate it! The most frustrating by-product of prioritizing jobs is knowing that the work will require more time than is available, but you will nevertheless have to complete it on time. Quality must be sacrificed (and overtime will probably be required to sacrifice it). Wouldn't it be nice if someone could give you a hand?

A HELPING HAND

Management courses usually stress the need to delegate tasks. But if delegating is such an integral part of managing, why do the vast majority of managers choose not to delegate? The truth is, most managers delegate only those tasks that they *cannot* handle personally and save all other tasks to do themselves. How many times have you heard (or said):

- "If I want it done right (i.e., my way), I do it myself."
- "I can get it done faster if I do it myself."
- "It would be more accurate if I do it myself."
- "It would take more time to explain it than to do it myself."

Such statements reflect a conscious management aversion to real delegation of tasks. A more successful strategy for delegating work is: A successful manager will perform only those activities that he or she *must* personally handle and will delegate all other work.

While nearly everyone agrees that managers must delegate, many managers, as well as subordinates, are uncomfortable with the idea. "Sure you can get everything done!" I have been told. "You just assign it to a subordinate. That's easy!" When such a comment sounds like an accusation, it's easy for a manager to become reticent about assigning work to others. Actually there are several reasons managers don't delegate. The rationalizations offered above simply mask other, often hidden, explanations.

Most managers refuse to delegate because they do not trust the delegatee, even when there is no proof that the delegatee cannot, or will not, perform. This attitude of prejudging a subordinate's ability could be a subconscious way for the manager to avoid confronting the fact that he or she may have recruited an incompetent. It is difficult to delegate and witness the process of failure, or to invest the time necessary to develop subordinates to obtain success. Nevertheless, avoiding delegation, because of this feeling, certainly precludes all possibility for subordinate development and proves nothing—except that the manager is doomed to do the work forever.

Some managers feel guilty about delegating work. Most of the administrivia you get will have filtered down from your superiors. If your boss has personally requested that you do something, it's easy to conclude, "I should do it personally." This is not what was asked. You were simply requested to get the task accomplished, even though it may not have been presented that way.

Because delegating, and much of management in general, necessitates at least a passive form of domination, many managers feel a somewhat natural aversion toward assigning work. We are culturally conditioned to egalitarian attitudes ("Don't be bossy!") from childhood.

Non-delegating managers sometimes fear that, by delegating, they will lose personal control of the effort. Certainly, you need complementary mechanisms, like follow-up and project-management techniques. If these complementary tools and techniques are not in place, you may indeed lose control of the project.

Other managers doubt their own ability to judge their subordinates' workload and avoid delegating out of fear they will overburden subordinates and delay other projects.

Overcoming these subconscious obstacles is not easy. Once again, an attitude change is called for. Supplant those attitudes—any of which might be appropriate in another context—with this obvious business principle: The manager's time is more expensive and more important to the company than the subordinate's time—and there are more delegatees than delegators.

Once this concept is internalized, it follows logically that delegation to several subordinates produces more (and more important) work at less cost to the company—the very essence of improving productivity.

MAINTAINING CONTROL

Disciplined delegation, however, simply enables managers to gain control of a task, as opposed to doing it personally. Supporting project-management techniques allows for the maintenance of control. If it is difficult for you to delegate, the less seasoned members of your own management team offer an even greater potential for administrative constipation. Only effective project-management and follow-up techniques will help you break through such bottlenecks.

To delegate effectively (i.e., to conquer administrivia), you must make every effort to surround yourself with the best people available. While this is yet another commonsense precept of management, it, like delegation, needs to be rethought. How many people have been hired—have *you* hired—not because they were the "best," but because it was expedient or because they were readily available, even if they weren't everything you had hoped for?

Obviously, delegating will work only if your staff is trained to handle nearly every aspect of your job (except the functions, like personnel appraisals, you absolutely must perform yourself). No matter how comfortable you become with delegating, your staff must be capable of doing the job, or it won't work.

Making your staff capable of handling the work you delegate is your job. The easiest way to accomplish this is to hire "ideal" subordinates, people who are not only fully trained but who operate "on your wave length." Ideal subordinates are not so easy to find, however, and you'll most likely have to train your own subordinates, if not in specific job skills, at least to get them attuned to your management style.

Have you ever told a subordinate, "I can't really explain what I want, but this isn't it. I'll know it when I see it?" This may be the result of your not having the time to explain what you want. More likely, however, you haven't defined your style and your rules.

Several years ago I came across an anonymous author's rules for "completed staff work." I give a copy of these rules to every new hire. These rules explain that the subordinate's job is to present the supervisor with a finished piece of work, which the supervisor will then approve and send on to someone else. The subordinate's job is to present solutions, not problems, say the rules. The final test of the completeness of a job is this: "If you were your superior, would you be willing to approve the work you have prepared and stake your professional reputation on its being complete and correct?"

These rules help me acquaint my staff with my style. Duplicate copies of the rules are attached to documents that do not meet my standards, with the appropriate phrases highlighted. Over time, this yields a common understanding that helps me delegate work and helps my subordinates carry it out successfully.

One test of your confidence in your staff's competence—i.e., your attitude toward your staff—is your own willingness to leave the office. Can you go on vacation or attend an important out-of-town conference and know that your department can function for days without your presence? If not, what changes—in your behavior and theirs—are needed to raise your confidence to this level?

Those attitude changes are important if you really want to conquer the administrative chores that eat up your valuable time. With the right attitudes, you can easily identify those chores and find ways to reduce the time they demand from you.

HIT THE PHONE, JACK

Take travel, for instance. Not only does travel waste your time, but administrivia builds up on your desk during your absence from the office. Substantial savings have been projected by many large corporations, thanks to business-travel alternatives such as teleconferencing and conference-calling. Once you appreciate the value of your own time, you'll make every attempt to avoid travel by exploring and exploiting all the alternatives modern communications technology affords.

Meetings and discussions, because they are such time-wasters in many organizations, represent another golden opportunity to reclaim time you can spend more productively. If you are chairing the meeting, always provide topical background material and an agenda in advance for meeting participants. Because the attendees will have had the benefit of reviewing these materials, they will arrive informed and, therefore, less inclined to ask basic, clarifying questions. Keep the pre-meeting materials brief, however. If you overload your meeting participants with reading material, they won't look at any of it, and then you're in the same predicament as if you'd distributed no advance materials.

YAKKETY YAK

Meetings are by no means the only opportunities by which to waste valuable time talking. Just the normal daily business intercourse with subordinates, superiors and peers is often enormously unproductive and time-consuming. These discussions can foster many side issues, and only infrequently do they produce the benefits that time expended would seem to promise.

Discipline yourself to resist the urge to discuss. Say what you have to say in writing (via memos, short notes, marginal comments on reports, etc.) if at all possible. Many topics can be expeditiously dispatched with a few written words. You will find that you then control the topic while avoiding irrelevant conversations.

Naturally, you can't eliminate all discussion from your work life. Personnel appraisals, subordinate development, interpersonal relationships, and recruiting are all examples of jobs you must handle through discussion. But you can recover the time you need for those jobs and others by limiting your exposure to non-productive discussions.

One other instance where discussion is a productive use of your time is any time you feel tempted to make a "presentation." The presentation has acquired great appeal lately, especially as a format for conveying information to top management. However, presentations require a great deal of preparation time.

Too many managers waste time worrying over the format of their presentation, at the expense of—of all things—content. Spend your time doing homework for a *discussion* of your topic, not developing fancy presentation materials and techniques.

If you're still in doubt, consider how many presentations you've seen crumble into discussion anyway. Add in the number of presentations you've seen canceled or severely curtailed. Opting for discussion, rather than presentation, also gives you the freedom to dictate the format (perhaps you will speak from an informal outline), and the time to concentrate on what you will say, rather than tracking down overhead transparencies.

"Telephone tag" is another big time-waster. Fortunately, the computer industry offers two ways to help you avoid this one. The newer method is "voice messaging" a sort of global phone-answering system that enables users to retrieve recorded messages from any phone, not just from a single machine. (Phone-answering machines and services still have a role to play, however.) Electronic mail, the older automated alternative to telephone tag, requires a display or printing terminal for the user to retrieve his or her messages.

PUT IT IN WRITING

In addition to the short notes and memos you'll be writing to dodge prodigal discussions, you'll still have to write longer documents, of course. To expedite the report-writing process, take advantage of the office-automation tools that may already be at your disposal. Many managers resist using even one of the oldest and most time-saving techniques: mechanized dictation. Some are simply intimidated by any machine more sophisticated than a pencil sharpener. Others are apprehensive about the cost of using such equipment, but, for prolific writers, the cost of modern dictation equipment can be recovered in a matter of weeks by increasing the productivity of both writers and clerical personnel.

While you're improving your writing productivity, don't neglect your reading productivity. There are two main categories of material placed in your in-basket: intra-company documents and mail from outsiders. It's safe to presume that whoever within the company addressed a document to you either knows your needs or desires that you read the material. So you do.

Mail from outsiders, however, can be screened by your secretary or even by you, if you haven't got a secretary or if you still haven't mastered delegating. This mail can be separated into three categories.

Junk—usually some form of solicitation. Unless you have been looking for some specific item, pitch it! Discarding administrivia is also a legitimate option. If you can't bring yourself to do this, set up a junk-mail file that you can browse through at your leisure. But don't read it!

Information only, no action—read this mail and then, if it is not of a sensitive nature, route it to those who report directly to you. They will appreciate the gesture and become better informed—hence, better able to receive delegation from you. Use routing slips with a disposition (e.g., "toss," "file") checked at the bottom. You don't want this mail back. Make every effort to handle any kind of document only once.

Action required—delegate it if at all possible, and then put a copy in your suspense file. Alternatively, if you can dispatch the job quickly with a hand-written note to the author, do so.

The majority of all administrivia is mail. You can save your time if you remember to handle mail only if you alone have the authority or the knowledge to do so—and then only once.

SOME IMPORTANT DON'TS

All the attitude changes you need to make in order to place a higher, more realistic value on your own time—can be summarized in three "don'ts."

Don't...if you can delegate. Explore every opportunity to delegate travel, attending meetings, writing reports. Explore the obvious, too. A subordinate just might be more capable than you are of handling these tasks.

Don't...if you can ignore it. A significant key to reducing the demands made on your time may be the sixth management sense that tells you if the paper inquiry you've just received is rhetorical or intended to elicit action from you. (Too many managers attempt to respond to every inquiry because they do not fully understand the limits of their authority; they are still waiting for their bosses to define these limits. Authority cannot be defined and delegated. Authority is seized! Managers should continually test their bounds. They will usually find those bounds to be much broader than they'd suspected.) It is always a management option to ignore an inquiry. If you sense it is unimportant, it probably is.

Don't ignore it...if it will compromise your position. Separating the meaningful inquiries from the unimportant ones is a skill honed only through experience. Neither this skill, nor the authority to use it, can be given to you. Be sensitive to the reality that your credibility will be damaged if you repeatedly misjudge the need for action, but weigh this reality against the folly of taking action on all inquiries.

What scheduling, delegating and just plain ignoring will do for you is give back the time you've been spending on administrivia, so you can spend your time practicing the more important aspect of your job: constructing an atmosphere for positive and productive subordinate interchanges. We're not talking here about "quick tricks" or "fast and dirty" methods that undermine the quality of work. If you adopt an attitude of conserving your highest quality time, you'll find both the quality and quantity of your department's work will improve.

Charles W. Mead is director of IM evaluation at GTE Service Corp., Tampa, Florida.

26.
HOW TO GET THE MOST OUT OF YOUR TIME

Marlene Klassen

Not all 20 suggestions will apply to you, but if you can apply even five or six of the ideas it will have been time well spent.

This article aims to help you make better use of your time.

Take Time for Planning. Putting out today's fires often seems more important than long-term planning, but every moment spent in planning saves three or four in executing a task. Practice working with a mental picture of the coming week, month and year. Write down your goals: for work, career, personal life, even finances. You won't accomplish the things you want without careful planning. It is the simple, most important step in effective time management.

Set Priorities. At the start of each day, list the jobs you have to do in the order of their importance. When one job is complete, review your priorities to ensure they're still accurate. At the end of the day, compare what you actually accomplished with what you'd hoped to accomplish. Then prepare a list of things to do the next day. A note of caution here: We can derive a false sense of satisfaction from simply crossing items off a list, especially if most of them are low priority.

Set Deadlines. Set realistic deadlines and stick to them. To develop an accurate sense of how long it takes you to complete routing tasks, time yourself (start to finish, including interruptions) on regular tasks for one week. Then calculate average completion times. Know due dates on assignments and anticipate conflicts that may prevent you from meeting your deadline.

Tackle One Thing at a Time. Forget about everything else until you've finished the one project that's on your desk. Constantly jumping from one problem to another will eventually destroy the power to concentrate on anything for more than a few minutes at a time.

179

Use Your Prime Time Effectively. Determine your peak time of the day and devote that time to top-priority work. You can accomplish more in less time when you feel fresh and mentally alert, so use that time effectively to work on those things requiring your greatest concentration. It's surprising how many people spend their most effective working hours doing routine tasks: reading their mail, scanning the newspaper or chatting on the telephone.

"Do Not Disturb". If your job is flexible, set aside a part of your day (every day) when you don't allow interruptions. Don't spend that time on trivial things: Use it for major projects. Remember: The amount of time you spend on a project isn't as important as the length of uninterrupted time.

Learn How to Make Decisions. The kind of decision required depends on the circumstances. Sometimes, a snap decision is needed, while under other conditions, a more democratic approach is more appropriate. In either case, identify the problem and gather only as much information as you really need. Consider the alternatives and their consequences, then make your decision. If you let perfectionism paralyze you, you'll never get anything done.

Handle Only Once. As soon as you've read that memo or letter, reply immediately while the subject is still fresh in your mind. This saves having to reorient yourself with the situation.

Use the Telephone. Use the telephone for local calls instead of letters and memos. This cuts down on typing, filing and delivery through the mail. Communication via the telephone can be much more effective than a memo because it creates two-way communication. The main reasons for sending memos are to clarify, remind or confirm.

Reply on the Original Memo. For routine, in-house correspondence, jot your reply on the top or side of the memo you were sent and reverse the "to" and "from" instructions. That way the receiver has both the question and answer on one piece of paper.

Make All Your Calls at Once. If you have a half-dozen telephone calls to make, place them constructively. In the long run, it will be quicker than disrupting your work flow throughout the day.

Get Out of Circulation. It's vital to keep in touch with what's happening in the company and the industry, but being on too many circulation lists uses too much valuable time. Have your name deleted from those periodicals or magazines that are of no direct value to you. Or, if there are several others in your department on the same circulation list, divide them among yourselves and circulate only the applicable items.

Set Time Limits on Meetings. If you're planning a meeting, provide an agenda and clearly define the purpose and objective of the meeting. Start on time. Set a time limit and stick to it. Don't let one or two members sidetrack the group. Wrap up with a review of the conclusions reached or action to be taken.

Throw Out Something Every Day. Take a look around you every day, and discard the things you don't really need. It's surprising how quickly useless trivia accumulates. Keep your wastebasket well fed.

Keep Your Desk Clear. Do you suffer from the stacked desk syndrome? If so, every time you look up from your work, you think of each pile on your desk as more work to be done, and your train of thought is interrupted. If you can't resist the temptation to stack your work, at least move the piles out of sight, so they won't distract you.

Stop Procrastinating. Procrastination, worrying and preoccupation with personal affairs (or tomorrow's workload) are three of the biggest time-wasters. Sometimes, we put off doing a job because the work entailed seems so massive. But getting started may be less painful than just thinking about it. Fear of failure sometimes leads us to avoid new situations in favor of doing over and over again those tasks we already do well. It's a sure way of limiting ones's capabilities and usually leads to boredom.

Set Your Watch Three Minutes Fast. Achievement-oriented individuals often set their watches a few minutes fast. It creates an extra sense of urgency. But don't become over-concerned about getting a job done quickly. Sloppy results can mean having to do a job over.

Don't Plan to Work Overtime. Studies have shown that productivity declines rapidly after eight hours of work. Sometimes, especially at peak periods of the year, overtime is essential. But it can also become a habit, and an unproductive one. People who count on working overtime regularly to get their work done are not making the most effective use of their time during regular working hours.

Learn How to Delegate. This is one of the most obvious suggestions, but perhaps the most difficult to follow correctly. It's easy to fall into the trap of thinking something won't get done properly unless we do it ourselves.

Reward Yourself. After you've completed an important piece of work, give yourself a pat on the back. Take a few minutes to relax, and clear your mind before you launch the next one. Enjoy a sense of accomplishment. You deserve it.

Now put these ideas into practice. Analyze your current style of operation to find out when and how you waste time. You may be surprised to find that time is generally wasted in the same way every day. It may be useful to keep a time log for a week or two.

The next step is to change poor habits and work at developing new ones. Can small jobs be left until the end of the day when you're feeling tired? Can others be delegated?

One final suggestion: If you're overwhelmed with work and can't see any light at the end of the tunnel, divide your work into smaller units. The sense of accomplishing one thing at a time may help you regain control.

Marlene Klassen is assistant manager, corporate communication, Great-West Life Assurance Co., Winnipeg, Manitoba, Canada.

27.
HOW TO IMPROVE YOUR "TIMING"

Clifford J. Hurston, Jr.

By "minding your minutes" through an activities diary, you can slash time-wasters and boost your productivity.

Using time effectively is one of the greatest skills a manager can possess. Today things change rapidly; obsolescence is always just a few minutes away, and managers who misuse time put themselves at a great disadvantage. Yet many managers allow themselves and their subordinates to work in ways that waste a great deal of this precious resource.

Improved time management increases productivity. Managers realize this, but many believe that the only way to obtain greater effectiveness is through a highly complicated, organized time-and-motion study, conducted by a professional consultant involving stopwatches, charts, graphs and analyses of the manager's physical surroundings, lighting, noise levels and other factors.

Time-and-motion studies do indicate ways and areas in which managers can increase their productivity, but they are usually costly. For this and other reasons, many companies choose not to conduct them, leaving their managers to help themselves. Though many managers think they know where their time goes, many really have no idea at all. Fortunately, there is a way that managers can check their use of time so that they can improve their overall performance and increase productivity.

The method involves a manager's compiling a diary of his or her activities, analyzing those activities and then asking him or herself three diagnostic questions provided by Peter Drucker:

- What am I doing that really does not need to be done at all, by me or anyone else?
- Which of the activities in my time log could be handled just as well, if not better, by someone else?
- What do I do that wastes the time of others?

Before a manager compiles a diary of activities though, he or she should review his or her job description. If he or she had no job description, then the manager should draw up an organization chart indicating his or her position, to whom he or she reports, who else reports to that superior, who reports to him or her, and including any other member of the organization with whom he or she has frequent dealings. He or she must also describe the job in general terms as it relates to what he or she thinks the job is about, what he or she is trying to do, and what things seem to him or her to be important about the job.

This description will ensure that the manager is absolutely clear in his or her own mind about his or her position within the organization and formal relationships with fellow workers. It also helps a manager clearly recognize work objectives and priorities.

RECORDING

After describing the job, a manager should compile a list of daily activities for a period of one week, if possible, in an activity book or job diary. (A plain notebook will do nicely.) Getting started is the most difficult thing about keeping a diary, and once begun, complete honesty is essential. The degree of detail will depend on several factors: number of entries, accuracy and, to a great degree, time available for recording. The following data is critical:

- day and date;
- sequence number of the activity, which should be consecutive throughout the recorded period;
- duration of each activity;
- identity of each person involved (concealed, if necessary, by use of a code);
- the "initiator" of the recorded activity.

This last entry is of considerable importance to a manager concerned with innovation and improvement. It may be impractical to record events that take less than five minutes, but a manager should do so if it is significant. Instead of recording each activity as it happens, managers can also record their daily activities in 15-minute intervals.

ANALYSIS

After completing this diary, a manager can analyze his or her activities to check on the average number of activities performed per day, average duration of each activity, time spent on the telephone (incoming and outgoing calls), traveling and so on. The results can give managers a vivid picture of their job as it really is, help them reorganize their workday and make time for those activities that they consider to be of primary importance.

Managers can also determine the relative frequency of their contacts with superiors, peers and subordinates during the recorded period, together with any contacts with other people, or groups of people, either inside or outside the organization. Other questions managers ask themselves after studying their recorded activities are:

- Am I delegating correctly?
- Am I supervising well?
- Am I paying sufficient attention to the most important items?
- Am I spending too much time with my subordinates?
- Am I spending too much time with my boss?
- Am I holding too many meetings?
- Am I spending too much time on the telephone?

Weaknesses in organization, training, responsibilities, communication, delegating and so forth are often brought to the surface through the use of the activity book or job diary.

TIMESAVERS

According to both formal and informal time management studies, secondary research, interviews and other data, managers waste valuable time because of unexpected visitors, customers, fellow employees, handling mail, telephone conversations, paperwork, lack of organization and planning, and socializing during business hours—to mention only a few causes.

The Telephone. Telephone interruptions are one of the time stealers that trouble managers most. Some studies indicate that as much as 25 percent of some managers' time is spent on the telephone. To keep these hours more productive, some managers have limited their telephone conversations to three minutes. (One manager suggests using an egg timer to indicate when the time is up.) If the subject seems to require more discussion, of course, the time should be taken, though cautiously.

Some managers take calls only during a certain time period each day—from 2:00 to 4:00 p.m., for example. Anyone who calls at other times is asked by a secretary or subordinate to return the call at a specific time. With the proper information obtained from the caller by the secretary or subordinate, managers are better prepared for the return call, thus using their time more wisely.

Because a telephone is so convenient, managers tend to use it unnecessarily for internal matters. Internal telephone calls usually encourage unnecessary conversation, better known as "conversation fat." A memo in a secretary's tray on the manager's desk is a more effective way to get things done.

Memos are more effective than calls because:

- the message is in writing, and the only way the receiver can handle it is either to act on it or destroy it;
- there is usually little or no misunderstanding about the message and what should be done;
- memos do not interrupt the receiver at unexpected times.

Mail. Managers who sort their mail themselves waste quite a lot of time. They should delegate to a secretary the responsibility of opening, sorting, dating, underlining and annotating all business correspondence. Letters and reports that can be written by a responsible subordinate should be delegated to him or her. The mail should be arranged according to the manager's preference, usually from most to least important item. Applicable materials and information should be attached by a secretary or subordinate to all correspondence to assist managers in dictating replies.

Publications, newsletters, articles and other similar materials should be screened, read and if necessary summarized by a subordinate. Only the materials or summaries needed by a manager should be submitted to him for review.

Planning and Scheduling Activities. Planning the day's events and activities is perhaps one of the most important ways to increase productivity. Every hour spent in effectively planning and scheduling tasks saves three to four hours in their execution. The manager's schedule usually includes telephone calls, meetings, visitors, traveling and lunch, among other activities. The following tips can save time.

- The beginning of the morning should be set aside for reading, without interruption, already-sorted and organized mail.
- Time should be set aside for already scheduled appointments, meetings with a prepared agenda, telephone calls and dictation.
- An uninterrupted period for completing daily tasks and planning the next day's activities should be allotted. Many managers can't decide what to do first during this uninterrupted period. One way to resolve this dilemma is to assign to very important or pressing tasks an "A," a "B" to less important, less pressing tasks, and a "C" to the least important, least pressing tasks. This way, managers are not forced to rank items in a strict "one-two- three" fashion, since many times a number of items are equally important.
- Schedule lunch near the office at a restaurant that is free from traffic jams and parking problems. Use dining facilities in the office building if available, and sometimes have lunch in the office.

- Spend travel time wisely. Managers should use this time to catch up on reading, dictate letters and memos and make future business plans and appointments.
- Allow a little flexibility in the schedule to take care of those unexpected activities involving visitors, conferences and telephone calls.
- Set aside ten or 15 minutes each day to stroll through the department or area to get firsthand feedback from employees. This activity itself saves managers hours of listening to employees make suggestions in the manager's office without prior notice.

Really smart managers are able to squeeze 65 or more minutes out of each hour because they plan their activities in advance, use the telephone and mail as an aid and not a hindrance to efficiency, keep track of how long they engage in face-to-face conversation with visitors, peers, superiors, customers and others, and properly delegate activities to subordinates. In short, they master time by first mastering themselves.

Clifford J. Hurston, Jr. is an assistant professor of business communications and business education with the College of Business Administration at Arizona State University, Tempe, Arizona.

28.
TIME MANAGEMENT

James B. Strenski

Time means much more than sixty minutes to the hour. Indeed, making every minute count is important in getting the job done in a timely and economical manner.

Public relations is creative communications craft. It is a service whose product is communications. Its cost is measured in increments of time applied to staff salaries and in the out-of-pocket expenses associated with specific communications vehicles. The effective management of time in the practice of public relations is essential to its success.

In this instance, time means much more than 60 minutes to the hour. Indeed, making every minute count is important in getting the job done in a timely and economical manner. Beyond that, public relations practitioners need to effectively manage the talent reporting to them. Public relations management needs to recruit the appropriate talent to support its activities, to help implement its programs.

Management needs to be innovative and imaginative in its application of communications techniques to the solution of public relations problems. To get ahead in the profession, the public relations manager needs to effectively merchandise public relations accomplishments to those responsible for the public relations manager's future.

Finally, it is vital to establish and sustain an "environment" that will permit the most cost-effective use of talent in an atmosphere of innovative operating efficiency to generate optimum results within the time available.

One of the least-attended-to responsibilities facing senior public relations practitioners is recruiting, training, motivating, stimulating and retaining talent within the public relations department or firm. It demands substantial allocation of a senior manager's time, evaluation of the techniques for recruiting, training and development, and talking to journalism school seniors. It means constantly keeping the word circulating that you're looking for good people, thus ensuring the growth of your own department or agency and providing the challenge of new opportunities to existing staff.

In the important area of innovation, we're talking about doing the job better. You might characterize the premise for innovative public relations as "working smarter, not necessarily harder."

The effective public relations manager can't afford to be led. He or she must do the leading in the area of fulfilling communications needs for clients. As soon as the organization recognizes that it is giving its public relations representative directions most of the time, rather than taking his directions and counsel, the conclusion will be reached quickly that the public relations function can be done better, perhaps, by somebody else. Finding new ways, or even adaptations of old ways, to communicate better is essential to survival, let alone progress in the practice.

IMPORTANCE OF MERCHANDISING

Innovative communication is also essential to the merchandising of one's success. Without innovative, creative public relations accomplishments, there is little about which to toot one's horn. By the same token, perhaps subtly, but effectively, the public relations manager should let senior management know that a good job is being done for them.

The importance of merchandising public relations accomplishments is no less important than effectively merchandising engineering, legal, manufacturing or other departmental successes. Actions speak louder than words, it is true. But, there are good speeches and there are bad speeches. Good actions tactfully but effectively communicated should be a constant objective of the ambitious public relations manager.

The environment in which to work time-effectively to get the job done covers a wide range of possibilities. In the context of this article, it largely refers to office surroundings, support equipment and support staff. Pleasant, comfortable offices (not necessarily ostentatious) can be conducive to operating efficiency. Accessible filing systems aid retrieval of past information in the implementation of current programs. Getting at that kind of information quickly and easily saves time, which permits more of the working day to be devoted to constructive communication for the present and the future. Information retrieval systems can be made accessible to staff through a wide variety of services.

Providing secretaries and writers with word-processing equipment not only speeds work progress by cutting down correction time and retyping time, but also actually saves money in the long haul by reducing the number of secretaries in favor of highly efficient word-processing people. The same equipment can be programmed to help expedite reports to management on the progress of public relations activities.

In the case of public relations firms, word-processing equipment can facilitate time cost-accounting, as well as billing operations and the maintaining of up-to-date records on accounts receivable and payable. Facsimile systems and sophisticated, higher technology telephone systems can improve internal as well as external communications of the spoken as well as written word.

CONTINUING EVALUATION

The public relations manager, to be truly effective, needs to devote adequate time to continually evaluate the office environment and its impact on the public relations functions. This evaluation should extend to the use of hardware and software as well as the kind of people able to operate such equipment effectively.

Time is important! By recognizing what it stands for in managing the clock as well as your people, you will achieve successes in practicing your craft innovatively, within a working milieu that is efficient and cost-effective.

James B. Strenski is chairman, Public Communications, Inc., Chicago, Illinois.

29.
THE MULTIPLIER EFFECT
OF GOOD TIME MANAGEMENT

Arthur Sondak

Don't get lost in a morass of daily pressures; you can multiply the achievements of the people reporting to you. The result is a synergistic effect—two times two can equal five!

It's an inescapable fact: If you're accountable for the accomplishments of the people working for you, you have a batch of problems. But you also have a wonderful opportunity. Provided you don't get lost in a morass of daily pressures, you can multiply the achievements of the people reporting to you.

Many managers have found ways to improve their own time management and have refined their working habits so they function more effectively. They've sharpened their skills and disciplines and can now focus on what counts most. They've learned to cope with interruptions, changing conditions, and the demands placed on them by others. But even more important, some of these managers have shared the techniques with others, particularly the people reporting to them. Active guidance of their people in group meetings and one-on-one counseling sessions has produced mutual understanding of the best methods for effective time use and has led to improved productivity, minimal frustration and increased job satisfaction for all.

This makes so much and obvious sense that it's hard to believe that there are managers who neglect this participatory approach. But some managers are their own worst enemies. They make the incorrect assumption that their time-effective work habits will be clear to all and over time will be adopted by the supervisors reporting to them, the group as a whole, and other people and groups in the organization. But the reality is that such an occurrence is not automatic. Further, these managers' behavior may be misconstrued and these managers may be seen as curt or abrasive. The attendant resentment may adversely affect work routine and productivity.

THE IMPACT OF MANAGERIAL ACTIONS

It's often difficult for a manager to recognize the impact that his or her actions have on others. Managers usually function with positive and constructive intent. But methodology and timing are crucial; if one or the other is inappropriate, a manager's actions can be perceived as and become real obstacles to achievement. Where a manager functions in a counterproductive manner with subordinate management, the subordinate managers not only may be diverted from what's important but also may transmit changed direction to their own subordinates. As a result, a negative multiplication may take place.

The way to avoid the trap is also the way to achieve a positive multiplication. What's needed is a realization that some actions may not be productive, then an inventory of ti⌐ ⌐wasting habits should be taken and ways to overcome them should be identified. Finally, these new time-effective behaviors should be shared with the entire organization.

WHAT ONE STUDY REVEALED

We tackled that problem. Over a period of a year, we surveyed 250 first- and second-line supervisors participating in management development seminars conducted for client companies, the American Management Association, New York Chamber of Commerce and Industry, and the Industrial Management Association. These managers were asked to identify three things higher management did that wasted their time. From the 674 categorized complaints, it was illuminating to see how the actions of higher management, despite positive intentions, were perceived as or became real obstacles to accomplishment. Here is how the complaints stacked up, in order of frequency of response:

1. The boss stops by to socialize, interrupting priority work.
2. Everything that comes up must be done "right now."
3. Meetings are called that are unnecessary, are called for which my presence isn't needed although I am requested to attend, or go off track and take longer than necessary.
4. Priorities are changed in midstream.
5. The boss isn't available when really needed.
6. The boss gives assignments to my people without my knowledge.
7. My boss gives me assignments that are someone else's responsibility.
8. Assignments are unclear; I'm given incomplete instructions, requirements or information.
9. Projects are given unrealistic timetables.

10. I'm not given the authority to make decisions; my boss must O.K. everything.
11. My boss insists that I personally handle work assignments that my subordinates could do without much direction from me.
12. My boss keeps looking over my shoulder to see what I'm doing.
13. My boss wants minute details on minor matters, ignoring or withholding action on more important ones.
14. My boss procrastinates in making decisions; there are continuing discussions, reviews and requests for advice.
15. My boss reverses his or her decisions.

These were the major complaints of first- and second-line supervisors from almost 200 organizations. Imagine the time lost and the accompanying increase in costs involved. Imagine, too, the impact of these actions if practiced by other managers in the same organizations and untold numbers of managers in thousands of other organizations. The negative multiplication effect is enormous.

WASTED TIME

Needless to say, time management problems and poor work habits can be found at all levels, although our survey focused on the higher levels of management. There's no doubt that with awareness and self-discipline most managers at any level could improve their time use effectiveness by 20 percent. For a manager at the $50,000 level, that's $10,000 worth of increased accomplishment. But that's only the tip of the iceberg because that manager affects the time use and productivity of those reporting to him or her, as well as possibly suffering from misdirection himself or herself from above. This misdirection could represent another 20 percent of misused time, or $10,000 in the case of our $50,000 manager.

Let's assume that our $50,000 manager has four lower-level managers under his or her supervision. If that manager's actions have a negative impact on 20 percent of the time use of these managers who average $35,000 a year, that's another $28,000 worth of time wasted that can never be recovered. In addition, these managers misuse 20 percent of their own time, or another $28,000. Further, it's likely the habits of these four managers will influence the productivity of their line employees. Assume they each direct five subordinates averaging $15,000 annually. A 20 percent misdirection means another $60,000. Given an additional 20 percent waste due to their own misuse of time, we are now at $120,000. If we add two secretaries to this hypothetical operation, at $14,000 each year, 20 percent of their time lost represents another $5,600. With their own time waste, the figure grows to $11,200. That makes a total of $207,200. That's the equivalent of almost 14 people, at an average annual salary of $15,000, doing absolutely nothing for a full year!

Sound farfetched? Hardly. Actually, it's probably a conservative picture. Apply that multiplication to your own operation and calculate the cost. The figure will be more than sobering. And that doesn't even calculate the effect on other parts of the organization through things not done or delayed. Multiply the direct cost of our example (or your own) and the expensive, irretrievable loss of time and productivity is staggering, even frightening.

A POSITIVE MULTIPLICATION

How much more productive it would be to take those same time-cost figures, make them positive, and go through the same multiplication. It can be done, but the process isn't just arithmetic. It means setting in motion the machinery to:

- Make each person aware of his or her own time use and provide the skills and techniques for effective time management.
- Have each person share time management techniques with peers and subordinates and, if appropriate, supervisors.
- Institute direct and combined efforts in an operation to identify interactive timewasters and work toward their elimination. In short, team up for effective time use. That's the positive multiplication, and the most important and neglected part of time management.

If these objectives are to be met, the effort must extend beyond an individual reading about good time management, beyond even attendance at some seminar on the subject. The effort must be within the entire organization and among groups of people from all levels within the same operation, interdependent operations, or completely separate operations. Management groups on the same or different levels, as well as superior-subordinate management teams and manager-employee teams, should work together on time problems.

Identifying objectives and priorities, and the best means to reach them, often results in surprises, and the differences in perceptions must be recognized, faced and resolved. Mutual exploration of timewasting activities, their impact on others, and agreement on their reduction are essential steps. Such a concerted attack will make a 20 percent improvement in accomplishment, cost savings, satisfaction, and reduced stress seem conservative.

The positive multiplier effect needs people working together to team up on time. The result is a synergistic effect—two times two equals five.

Arthur Sondak is president of Personnel Management Services of Edison, New Jersey.

30.
HOW TO CONTROL THE
USE OF STAFF TIME

G.B. Stanton, Jr.

Managers and staff professionals seem never to have enough time. Here is a new
method for controlling and allocating time that has proved successful.

Parkinson tells us that work expands to fill the available time.[1] The staff
professional knows this all too well. If only he had more time, what wonders he
would achieve! Time cannot be manufactured nor can it be renewed. However,
control over the use of his time can ensure that this scarcest of all resources is
applied to the most rewarding of the tasks facing the staff professional.

This paper discusses how the staff professional now controls his time. Then it
reviews the literature on methods that other professionals use to control their
time. Next, it describes Pareto's Law and its use in management. This is
followed by the development of a new method, based on Pareto's Law, which
staff professionals and others can use to gain control over their time. Then, a
case study of the application of this new method by a group of safety and health
professionals is presented. The paper closes with a summary and
recommendations to staff professionals and managers and to researchers.

To begin to answer the question, "Can the staff professional gain control
over his time by applying Pareto's Law?" the meaning of three key words must
first be established. They are time, control and professional. In this paper, time
means a prescribed or allotted period of a person's life for completing a task,
paying a debt, etc.[2]; control, the exercise of authority or dominating influence[3]; and professional, "a person engaged in a vocation or occupation in
which a professed knowledge of some department of learning or science is used
in its application to the affairs of others."[4]

Discussions with employed safety specialists and professionals, and personal
experience as a staff professional lead to three assumptions about the staff
professional and his time. The first assumption is that the staff professional
builds his schedule around meetings of task forces and committees, training

sessions, management presentations, and society conferences. Then he parcels out the balance of his time as needed to develop new projects, maintain ongoing programs, and respond to shifting pressures from managers and clients.

The second assumption is that the staff professional's day is packed to overflowing as he responds to emergencies, solves problems, both large and small, answers requests for information, and carries out the myriad routine tasks that afflict all professionals, with limited aid from an assistant or secretary, if one is available at all. The third assumption is that if he attempts to control his time, he does not succeed in doing so and is frustrated by his lack of success. He studies management and uses systems that he hopes will give him control over this time, but finds they fail when he cannot forecast the time required to accomplish his major tasks.

No matter how many hours he works, he feels frustrated because he believes that his specialized knowledge is being inadequately applied to the affairs of his fellow men. This feeling may be a gnawing unexpressed discomfort, or it may be a vivid mental picture of a catastrophe that he could prevent if only there were 26 hours in a day. Thus, it is inferred that the staff professional would accomplish more and larger goals and find greater satisfaction in his work if a method of time control, responsive to his needs, were available to him.

A review of the literature on time control shows that there are two classes of methods for controlling time in use by professionals and managers. The first class is exemplified by the appointment book; the second, by a pair of pruning shears. Almost every physician and dentist in private practice must have an appointment book to function; the productive practitioner controls his days, and his time within each day, by establishing and staying with a time plan, using his appointment book as his control chart.[5] Following the lawyer's maxim, "plan your work and work your plan," attorneys use daybooks or a system such as the Lawyer's Day.[6] Managers and other professionals use calendars or appointment books or systems such as the Day Timer,[7] which provide a procedure for allocating time to major projects as well as to routine activities. Heyel describes a procedure for finding out how one's time is spent, using a sample of activities and a long-term audit.[8] Drucker states that the time record is the first step in managing one's time and becoming an effective executive.[9] All of these methods, in varying degrees, enable the professional to know how he intended to, and how he actually did, spend his time, and so enable him to charge a client accordingly, or to allocate the time to a major project or to a routing activity.

The second class of method for controlling time is to identify the important activities and not waste time on the less important. Almost every one of Shaw's *114 Proved Plans to Save a Busy Man's Time* falls into this class.[10] Drucker tells executives how to shed time-wasting activities.[11] Recently, Mackenzie said that businessmen and others waste time because they fail to set goals, priorities and deadlines.[12] Heyel tells how to identify the main problem areas by using the maldistribution principle, that is, results are the cumulative effects of many causes, but only a minority of the causes contribute a major share of the total effect.[13] This maldistribution principle is in reality an application of Pareto's Law to management.

PARETO'S LAW

Vilfredo Pareto, an Italian engineer turned economist and sociologist, was a pioneer in econometrics, applying the statistical methods of the physical sciences to the social sciences.[14] He discovered an empirical relation describing the distribution of income among the population of a country. He called this relation the curve of the distribution of wealth.[15] He found, using income tax data, that: $\log N = \log A - \alpha \log X^1$ where "N" is the number of taxpayers having the income, X, or greater, α is characteristic of the country, and A is a constant. This equation is of the form of a straight line; see Figure 1. After examining both current and historical data from a broad range of wealthy and poor countries, Pareto determined that α ranges from 1.24 to 1.97.[15] The wealthier the country, the greater the number of taxpayers who enjoy an income above that needed to sustain life and the closer α is to 1. The poorer the country, the greater the number of taxpayers whose income is close to the survival level and the closer α is to 2.

FIGURE 1

PARETO'S LAW[16]

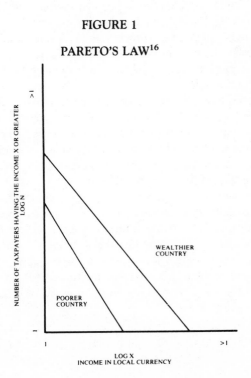

There have been many applications of Pareto's Law to quality control and to management problems. But in none of them have the authors gone back to Pareto's Law and determined the value of A for the particular problem at hand, nor related the value of h to the population under study in the way that α related to the populations of the countries studied by Pareto.

Let us now apply Pareto's Law to time control and consider A and a, instead of neglecting these two variables or assuming an arbitrary maldistribution ratio. In equation 1, let N = number of projects whose time allocation per project is equal to or greater than X, and X = time allocated to a project, as a percentage of total working time. To determine A and α, an analysis based on personal experience, conjecture and assumptions was made. Two cases are analyzed. In the first, A and α are determined for the solo professional; in the second, for a team of staff professionals.

The staff professional, working alone or with minimal assistance, is assumed to be in an organization whose management has little imagination for the possible opportunities in his field and so gives him support for few, perhaps only one, major project in his field. This is thought to be analogous to a poor country. Thus, α is assumed to be 1.7. Experience shows that a major project receiving less than ten percent of a professional's time falls into the *trivial many* and that many experienced solo professionals keep an extra project or two ready in reserve. In this case, A is determined by allocating ten percent of the professional's total working time to one major project, as shown by line I in Figure 2. Following line I shows that the time allocation of all projects is such that there will be a total of two projects, each of which is allocated more than seven percent of the total working time, a total of three projects, each more than five percent, etc. In other words, the *trivial many* soon take hold of the solo professional's time.

Now, let us look at a team of staff professionals. The team of staff professionals is assumed to be in an organization whose management is committed to exploiting advances in their field, and so supports several major projects at the same time. This is thought to be analogous to a wealthy country. Thus, α is assumed to be 1.3. Experience shows that a large percentage of the total working time of the team would be allocated to one major project, that other projects will be given important shares of time, and that the *trivial many* are assigned to support personnel. In this case, A is determined by allocating 25 percent of the team's total working time to one major project. Line II in Figure 2 illustrates this case. Following line II shows that the time allocation of all projects is such that there will be a total of two projects each allocated more than 15 percent of the team's total working time, a total of three, each more than about 11 percent, and so on. In other words, the team's time is concentrated on the *vital few*.

FIGURE 2

PARETO'S LAW APPLIED TO TIME
ALLOCATION FOR PROFESSIONALS.

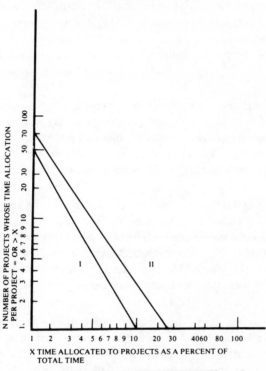

X TIME ALLOCATED TO PROJECTS AS A PERCENT OF
TOTAL TIME

LINE I: PROFESSIONAL, PINCHED FOR RESOURCES $\alpha = 1.7$
LINE II: PROFESSIONAL, COMMITTED RESOURCES $\alpha = 1.3$

CASE STUDY

The application of Pareto's Law to time control originated as a pragmatic
solution to an operating problem. In 1971, a major industrial state reorganized
the regulation of occupational health. The occupational health program was
transferred from the State Department of Health, where it had been, primarily,
an advisory program, to the State Department of Labor, where it became one of
seven sections in the agency which enforced safety and health standards. This
change was made as a response to the Williams-Steiger Occupational Safety
and Health Act of 1970 (OSHA).

The new section was faced with two major tasks. The first was to develop and to implement its part of the state plan for OSHA. The second was to maintain regular field activities. Accomplishing the first major task would extend the reach of the section's occupational health nurses and industrial hygienists by using the agency's safety inspection staff to identify occupational health hazards; would compel corrections in workplaces where excessive exposures had been found, and the recommendations of the advisory program had been ignored; and would provide badly needed equipment, improve the skills and knowledge of the staff, and so increase the quantity and quality of the filed work.

All told, there were over a dozen major projects in the state plan. These projects varied from developing and executing training programs for new and experienced staff members to evaluating new equipment, and then mastering the administrative procedures involved in acquiring the new equipment. The filed activities, the second major task, was the reason for being there and had to be pursued vigorously.

In the course of developing a plan to accomplish these two major tasks, two constraints were identified. One was the lack of the administrative staff necessary to control the time actually spent on so many projects by a staff of nine professionals. The other constraint was the inability to forecast with usable accuracy the time needed to accomplish any of these non-recurring major projects. These two constraints made the use of the usual control charts impractical.

While considering other methods of allocation, the successful use of Pareto's Law and the *vital few, trivial many* distributions to analyze and control the results of organization performance in other management assignments was recalled. (At that time, the analysis to determine A and α had not been developed.)

In this case study, the outputs are the field assignment reports and major project recommendations, and the input is the working time of the professional staff. Field assignments already were being handled as a class. Pressures from the clerical staff and the inspection sections could be relied on, it was believed, to keep the field work current. It was decided to designate the field assignments as the *trivial many*; the major projects then were designated as the *vital few*.

The next step was to allocate the total working time of the staff, the input. If the allocation were made on the basis of conventional wisdom, a large percentage of the total working time ought to be allocated to the *vital few*; however, this does not respond to the real world of the staff specialists. Would it be possible to use Pareto's Law to plan as well as to control? It was decided to apply Pareto's Law using a 20 to 80 distribution, a distribution that had proven itself in personal experience; that is, 80 percent of the outputs come from 20 percent of the input. Each staff member was directed to devote 80 percent of his working time to his field assignments and 20 percent to the major projects. The occupational health section operated this way for about 12 months, accomplishing the state plan as scheduled, while providing an acceptable level of service in field assignments.

In summary, this new method may provide a way to manage the inexorable tide predicted by Parkinson's Law. To staff professionals and managers involved in non-routine projects: Recognize that it is very difficult to eliminate any of the *trivial many* tasks; instead, handle them as a class rather than individually. Develop a very few (perhaps only one) projects which will make a substantial improvement in performance. Assign them to yourself and allocate a block of your time, using Figure 2 to guide you. Be flexible in your time allocations to exploit breakthroughs.

To researchers in management: Test the theory in this paper among professionals and managers in different fields and settings to determine if it helps them to handle their workloads more effectively. Determine if A and a can be used to characterize organizations. Determine if A and α can serve to correlate organization performance in different areas.

References

1. Parkinson, C.N., *Parkinson's Law and Other Studies in Administration* (Boston: Houghton Mifflin, 1957), p.2.
2. Barnhardt, C.L., ed., *The American College Dictionary* (New York: Random House, 1952), p. 1268.
3. Morris, W., ed., *The American Heritage Dictionary of the English Language* (Boston: Houghton Mifflin, 1973), p. 290.
4. Stanton, G. B., Jr., "Managing the Practice of Health Care Services" (Unpublished Master's Thesis, New York University, Graduate School of Business Administration, 1971), p. 4.
5. Stanton, Ibid., pp. 21-4.
6. Day-Timers, *Lawyer's Day* (Allentown, Pa: Day-Timers, 1973).
7. Day-Timers, *Daytimer* (Allentown, Pa.: Day-Timers, 1973).
8. Heyel, C., *Organizing Your Job in Management* (New York: American Management Association, 1960), pp. 26-42.
9. Drucker, P.F., *The Effective Executive* (New York: Harper & Row, 1967), p. 25.
10. Shaw, A. W., *114 Proved Plans to Save a Busy Man's Time* (New York: A.W. Shaw, 1918).
11. Mackenzie, R.A., "How to Make the Most of Your Time," *U.S. News and World Report* (Dec. 3, 1973), pp. 45-48, 53, 54.
12. Heyel, Ibid., p. 77.
13. Tarascio, V.J., *Pareto's Methodological Approach to Economics* (Chapel Hill: University of North Carolina Press, 1966), p. 118.

14. Pareto, V., *Cours d'Economie Politique*, Vol. 2 (Lausanne: F. Rouge, 1897), p. 305, note 1.
15. Pareto, V., Ibid., p. 305, Fig. 47.
16. Pareto, V., Ibid., p. 312.

G.B. Stanton, Jr. presented this paper before an annual meeting of the American Society of Mechanical Engineers. He has been an adjunct professor at New Jersey Institute of Technology and works as a consultant.

Part IV
THE PRIORITY PRINCIPLE

31.
DO MORE, WORK LESS

John H. Sheridan

Some managers haven't stopped to analyze how they should be spending their time. Others know exactly how to spend it—but never get around to it.

Fred Peabody has a problem. He likes to get things done—even if it means doing them himself. And it often does.

He is also a victim of routine. Like a lot of managers, he spends a great deal of his time at the office bogged down in administrivia, including paperwork that seems to pile up faster than he can dig his way through it.

Often, he has trouble just getting to that paperwork because routine office matters—including ceremonial meetings which seem to accomplish little—keep getting in the way. And he is constantly plagued by unexpected interruptions that steal time from the important managerial tasks entrusted to him.

As a result, he frequently works late at night to catch up, pushing himself to the point of fatigue. Or beyond.

When Fred gets home, he's usually too tired to do much of anything except wolf down a few cold leftovers from the dinner he missed and collapse in front of the TV set. During the commercials, he grumbles about how he is overworked.

His family regards him as a grouch. And, despite the long hours he puts in at the office and the physical and psychological price he pays, Fred is probably not doing very well.

Who is Fred Peabody? He is nobody in particular, but he is a lot like many managers who share his dilemma: spinning their wheels while the world passes them by. They are the managers who have to skip important conferences because there is "too much to do" at the office. They are the managers who, on a balmy spring afternoon, find themselves catching up on the paperwork, while their subordinates are out playing tennis or golf.

Perhaps the reason Fred Peabody finds himself in such a fix, suggests Gus Economos, is that he never actually took the time to step back and analyze his job—that is, what his job *ought* to be.

If he did, he might discover it is possible to work less—put in fewer hours behind his desk—and yet accomplish more.

Gus Economos *is* somebody in particular. He is the director of the Graduate School of Business at DePaul University, Chicago. He has served as a consultant to large corporations. And in his wanderings through corporate offices and university complexes he has encountered many Fred Peabodies.

Keep fresh. Mr. Economos, whose areas of academic interest range from marketing strategy and tactics to futurology, has been contemplating the role of the corporate manager for some years—and analyzing how it has changed with the times.

"The job of a manager," he insists, "is not to get tired."

Nonetheless, a lot of managers think that is their job. "When they come home after a tough day, their wives warn the kids to run and hide. And even though he is tired, he often feels pretty good about it, because, he figures, nobody could get that tired without doing some good."

At a conference in New York, sponsored by International Business Machines Corp (IBM), Mr Economos asked an audience of managers: "Do you want to be remembered as someone who was always tired? When you are tired, you are useless to your job and to your family." He suggested that managers should tape-record the conversation that takes place during the first ten or 15 fifteen minutes after they arrive home at night. "And ask yourself: Would you like to meet you in that condition?"

Catalyst or Doer? While reading a chemistry book, Mr. Economos found what he believes is an excellent definition of a good manager: an ingredient that "causes interaction, without itself being used up." It was, of course, the definition of a *catalyst.*

The higher a manager rises in an organization, the DePaul University professor points out, the more important his catalytic role becomes, that of getting things done through others. However, it is often difficult to resist the temptation to continue doing things yourself. "It is a beautiful way to go through life," he notes, "starting something in the morning and finishing it before you go home." And while every managerial position includes tasks that only the manager can and should do, the tendency of many executives is to continue performing some of the functional chores they once did but should now be delegating to others.

Managers continue doing them for a number of reasons. They feel comfortable with those tasks. And they often provide a sense of accomplishment.

"There are two reasons a manager should not do things," Mr. Economos told attendees at the IBM conference. "First, it is not his job. And second, he'll probably screw it up."

Hands off the controls. The progression up the management ranks should force a manager to shift more and more toward being a catalyst. Yet it is not an easy transition to make. Mr. Economos explains why: "When we first start out, we do things ourselves. We are evaluated for having done them. The results are very immediate and very clear. Nobody can take credit away from us, because we've done it.

"Then you get your first promotion, and now your job is to tell somebody else to do it. Then you move up a little higher and you have to tell someone, 'Bill, you tell John to do it.' Then you get a little bit higher and you say, 'Steve, let's do some planning so we can tell Bill to tell John what to do.' Then it becomes, 'Mike, let's check up on Steve's plans.'

"Finally, you really get to the top and you sit there wondering what in the hell is going on down below. Is anybody working?"

Gradually, the manager finds a sense of insecurity creeping in, a feeling that he's lost contact with day-to-day operations.

The upwardly mobile manager never reaches the point where he has "nothing to do," but the nature of what he does changes. He "throws away" the T-square or the computer and becomes increasingly involved in planning, control budgeting and—in perhaps the truest sense of a catalyst—motivating others.

Unless he sheds the tasks he should no longer be doing, either by delegating them or by eliminating unnecessary functions, the manager will fail to fulfill his proper role, Mr. Economos stresses. And he may find himself, like Fred Peabody, working longer and longer hours and often feeling fatigued.

Mr. Economos, who is prone to staying away from his university office when it is not necessary to be there, recalls a time when he had fallen into the trap of working until eight or nine o'clock at night, trying to get "caught up" on his academic paperwork. Then he analyzed what was happening. "I noticed that at about 4:30 I would slow down. Then I'd go get a bite to eat and come back to the office. Then I'd slow down a little more. And by working an extra three or four hours, I was getting perhaps one hour's work done."

He decided that by working less, putting in fewer hours at the office, he could actually get more done. He thinks many managers will find they can too, if they begin analyzing what they are doing—and contrast that to what they *should* be doing.

Motivation. Joseph Redding, executive vice president at the Pittsburgh-based North American Division of H.B. Maynard Co., a consulting firm, observes that two patterns emerge among managers who spend too much time on the job. "Some people feel the need to convey the image of working a lot," he says. "And others let things get in the way; they let things fester, holding decisions in abeyance. They are afraid to make a mistake."

H.B. Maynard, a subsidiary of Planning Research Corp., has done work for large ($100 million-plus) firms in which key executives average about 44 hours a week on the job. "That is on the low side for top executives," Mr. Redding notes, "but it shows that it is clearly possible to do that—and to have more time for yourself."

Mr. Redding also subscribes to the theory that it is possible to do more by working less. "The principal thing is to have priorities and make decisions—and not linger over them."

Researchers, he adds, have found that managers tend to fall into one of two classic "motivation profile" categories. Some are *achievement-motivated*. Others are *power-motivated*.

"The achievement-motivated guy is the most likely to get bogged down in doing work that he should be delegating. He likes to do things himself and have control. He likes personal feedback on how well he is doing. He gets satisfaction in doing things."

The achievement-motivated manager who continues trying to do things he used to do will find himself overworked, and will also have "a devastating impact" on the morale of his organization, Mr. Redding explains. "It emasculates the people who are supposed to be doing the work. They feel it is criticism—that they are being shown up by the boss. And it siphons the manager's time away from the things that he should be doing."

Conversely, the power-motivated executive gets his satisfaction from influencing others. He is more suited to the role of a catalyst. "The power-motivated executive might be able to run a large conglomerate and still take three months vacation each year."

It can be helpful to the achievement-motivated type if he understands what makes him tick, Mr. Redding says. If he recognizes his tendency to be a doer, then when he finds himself in the too-much-to-do predicament, he may be able to chuckle at himself, step back from the work—and delegate it.

A primary safeguard against trying to do too many things is the old managerial bromide: *set priorities*. Some years ago, Mr. Redding recalls, a consultant wrote the president of a large steelmaking firm and advised him on how to better use his time—and save the company money. The advice: At the start of each day, write down the five most important things you must do and concentrate on getting them done. The steel executive liked the advice so much that he paid the consultant $25,000.

Managers' Catch-22. Some managers not only fail to delegate, but also they let their underlings delegate in reverse. In some cases, suggests Herbert A. Cohen, it is a problem of ego. The manager will take on anybody's work, particularly if he regards it as a challenge.

Mr. Cohen, president of performance Management Inc., a Northbrook, Illinois-based consulting firm, says the Catch-22 of management is: "Dumb is better than smart."

A manager, he says, is better able to get things done through others if he trains himself to say. "I dunno. I don't understand. Help me." To illustrate, he cites the egomaniacal manager who thinks he knows everything. "He is a technical expert. A subordinate walks in and says, 'There are a lot of things about this problem that I can't handle. I know you've been away from this technically. I don't know if you can still do it, but do you think you might be able to handle it?' The egomaniacal manager looks at it and says. "Aww, sure, just leave it with me."

"The dumb subordinate walks out and, as he is going through the door, he turns and asks, 'By the way, when do you think you can get that done?' Now, if enough of those guys come in to see that manager, what happens? The egomaniac has got everybody else's problems. And who is getting developed?"

A *master.* A young, semi-competent design engineer for a midwestern high technology company was a master at playing dumb and getting others to do things. Frequently it was the work he should have been doing. When he'd get an assignment he couldn't handle, he would ask one of his drinking buddies in the toolmaking department to design and make the item for him.

On one occasion, however, he was unable to get anyone to design a small tool that was needed. An older, now retired, design engineer who supervised the department recalls that is was a "relatively minor" assignment. But several days went by and the younger man hadn't completed the drawing.

"I got a call from upstairs wanting to know why the design hadn't been sent to the tooling department," the senior engineer explains. "I told them I'd send it through as soon as I received it. Then I went to check up on this young fellow to find out why it was taking so long. I looked at the sheet of paper on his drawing board and noticed that all he had done in three days was to draw a horizontal line. I told him they were in a rush for it."

Two more days went by and again the older engineer went to check on his protege's progress. "He still had nothing on that paper but a horizontal line. So I took the request sheet from him and did the design myself. It took about 15 minutes."

It amazed the senior designer when, some years later, the apparently incompetent younger man was promoted to the job of chief design engineer. "I guess they figured the thing he was best at was getting other people to do the work—so they promoted him."

Know thy job. To be effective in managing other people, a manager must first know how to manage himself, observes DePaul's Mr. Economos. He suggests this approach: First, try to define your job in 30 words or less. Then, determine whether you've included everything you do, or only the things you *ought* to be doing.

For diagnostic purposes, Mr. Economos recommends that managers keep a log of everything they do, morning and afternoon, for two weeks. "Then ask: Should I have done this? Who decided I should?" It is very easy, he points out, "to end up working for your secretary."

The manager who discovers that his secretary is in fact giving the orders should attempt to design the "ideal week": a day-by-day work plan that includes only the tasks a manager should reserve for himself. "If you find you cannot design the ideal week, it means you really haven't thought enough about...what you ought to be doing."

While some managers may have trouble determining how they ought to be spending their time, others know *exactly* how to spend it—"but never get around to it." A manager in the latter category can begin to take corrective action by having a chat with his secretary about all those chores she piles on him. "It is important that your secretary understand how you see your job and what you want done," the DePaul business school director points out. To some degree, her job should be to send people away, sparing the manager unnecessary interruptions, particularly when the visitor *ought* to be talking to someone else, anyway.

In some cases, the overworked manager may need an assistant to handle some of the time-consuming routine work. But often he doesn't want an assistant, either because he isn't sure what to do with one or because the idea "scares" him, Mr. Economos says. "But for relatively little money, a manager can have someone around to take quite a bit of the burden from him—especially if he allows other people to take time away from him."

Who does the work? The idea of delegating work to assistants or nonmanagerial subordinates is not likely to prompt anyone to rewrite a business school textbook. But what about the manager of managers? If he is ensconced in the role of a catalyst—and the subordinate managers are, too—who is actually doing the work? Easy. Each reserves certain tasks for himself. But the more difficult question, says Mr. Economos, is: "How can I get these guys to be better catalysts?"

One approach is to give subordinate managers more work than they can handle, thus forcing them to delegate. Another is to encourage—and, in fact, allow—them to delegate responsibility. If a manager's boss insists that he be able to respond with detailed answers to questions on an instant's notice, he makes it very difficult for that manager to delegate.

"I've seen situations," Mr. Economos says, "where an executive will tell a lower-level manager that he is too wrapped up in details and shouldn't be putting his hands on everything. Then he'll turn around and ask the same manager: 'By the way, how many barrels of oil do we have in the warehouse?' And he expects him to know."

"The answer ought to be, 'I can find out.' But if he says that, the boss may climb all over him and shout, 'Who the hell is running your department anyway?' In a case like that, you can talk all you want about your managers being managers, but it doesn't mean a thing."

Flexibility. While defining the manager's job can be useful exercise, there is a danger that he may view his role in a too rigid framework. As business conditions change and external events intrude, business executives must maintain some flexibility.

"The effective manager tailors his approach," contends H. B. Maynard's Mr. Redding. "It is difficult to simply tell a manager to define his job. That implies you can come up with a formula." He recalls one instance when preconceived notions were discarded—and wisely so. The president of a shipbuilding company discovered that his firm was having difficulty obtaining aluminum plate, a material critical to the scheduling of a project involving huge sums of money. "The company president jumped on a plane to Pittsburgh and helped to expedite procurement of the material. You don't often expect the president to be an expediter for the purchasing department," Mr. Redding notes, "but in that case it was very important. It was a matter of deciding how he could best use his time."

Time-wasters. Frequently, DePaul's Mr. Economos notes, managers waste time on matters of minor significance—rather than concentrating on more crucial affairs, because they fall into the habit of using "the information that is available," rather than getting the information they *need.*

"A good manager will determine what information he needs and where it is. The trouble is, a lot of organizations don't really want to know. They develop myths about what they are and what they can do. Managers have to be myth-destroyers."

Also counterproductive are company "rituals" that do little to move a company toward its goals. Among them are lengthy awards ceremonies and meetings with a department head or division chief on the first Monday of the month, even if there is nothing to meet about. "After a while," Mr. Economos observes, "you learn what to say and what not to say. And the worst thing about it is that, after a while, people realize that it is a ceremony, and they give you what you want. And all the time you're giving them what they want. And there you sit—lying to each other, getting nothing done."

When a manager finds a pattern of repetition, "it may be time to pass it on to someone else, so he can spend his time examining what else can be done—and how it can be done."

Another time-waster, for managers who are reluctant to criticize subordinates, is re-doing their work the right way. The manager who is prone to doing the work over himself may find himself constantly in that position. Even having another subordinate re-do it may not be the wisest approach, Mr. Economos suggests. Often, the best technique is "to acknowledge that a particular job was done poorly, then sit down and point out how it should have been done," and make the person do the job again the right way.

On the rise. Many managers assume that, as they reach higher and higher levels of responsibility, their job becomes "bigger." They're usually wrong, Mr. Economos argues. "The job becomes different, and it requires new skills, but it doesn't get bigger."

The challenge for the upwardly mobile manager, particularly if he is in a company that is growing, is to assess the new skills required. "One reason many executive development programs have failed is that nobody monitored things to determine what new skills and talents a manager needed as he moved up in an organization. So you do all sorts of silly things. You get a course in how to dress right and comb your hair right. And you do pushups so you'll have a flat tummy."

What *is* needed, he asserts, is greater skill in working with, and through, other people, along with increased analytical and planning ability to cope with challenges the company faces.

"Managers today are facing bigger, swifter changes than ever, and they must bring change to their organizations."

Experts on management "control" have devised techniques to give executives a greater sense of security, he notes, "but very often, a manager must realize that he must live with a certain amount of static"—short of chaos.

"The control-people try to give you a better feeling that you have everything under control. But often the best way to do that is to get out of the race," Mr. Economos says.

"It is like taking a racing driver and telling him to slow down and drive more carefully, so he will be safer. The manager is a lot like the race driver; he must go as far as he can as quickly as he can."

Managers who rely too much on the advice of control experts may soon find they have "total control over absolutely nothing."

And the company, as well as the manager, may be spinning its wheels.

32.
TIME: HOW TO MAKE
A LITTLE A LOT

R. James Steffen

Managing time means determining what to do as well as when to do it.

Today's managers are often 20 to 40 percent less productive than they could and should be. The cost of this lower productivity is staggering. But few people know that the individual time-waster suffers as well—from frustration, stress and anxiety. Conversely, managers who have control over their workday are both highly productive and satisfied.

Obviously, there are strong reasons why managers should learn how to use their time efficiently. However, while most of the material aimed at teaching time management is theoretically sound, it falls far short in application. The techniques simply fail to take into account the ordinary, everyday interruptions that strain the typical manager's ability to control his or her time.

Interviews with over 1,000 executives from Fortune 500 companies revealed not only the most common time management tools, but also that time management is learned. Effective managers are made, not born.

ARE YOU A TIME-WASTER?

The most glaring time-wasters arrive at 10 a.m. and leave at 2 p.m., spending the time between at the water cooler or in the washroom. Chances are it won't be long before they're found out and fired.

But when we talk about managerial time-wasters, we're referring to a far more dedicated crew. Many managers sweat at their desks from dawn to dusk, take abbreviated lunch hours and lug home heavy briefcases. Still, they're often terrible time-wasters. This is because time shouldn't be measured in minutes and hours, but in the effort invested in a task and the task's *significance*. Outstanding managers are unique in that they concentrate both on getting the job done right—and doing the right job.

The key to successful time management is *doing the most important job now*. What's more, it means giving the most important job your all now—concentrating on accomplishing this task to the exclusion of all others.

Sound obvious? It obviously isn't, because most managers do just the opposite and waste precious time. See if you recognize yourself making the following common managerial mistakes.

Pitfalls of great expectations. Realistically, all managers realize that it's impossible to get everything done in a single workday. Unfortunately, most managers are unrealistic. They start the day with a list of a thousand-and-one "to-dos." Then, even if they accomplish half that number, they end the day feeling frustrated and overwhelmed. The reason is because frustration is triggered by how much you actually have—or have not—accomplished of what you *expected* to accomplish. Ironically, managers with endless to-do lists concentrate only on getting their tasks done, without thinking about what tasks they're doing. Thus, they expend an inordinate amount of energy on low-priority tasks, leaving little or no time to take care of truly essential ones.

Managers who make good use of their time, on the other hand, understand that they simply can't do it all in one day. They keep their expectations realistic and stave off demoralizing frustration by setting their sights on a select number of goals, arranging them according to priority, and then tackling them one at a time. Having accomplished at the end of a day what they set out to do at its start, these managers are rewarded by feeling satisfied and productive.

The fear of ultimate failure. Some managers compound their problems by trying to do too much too soon. They aim at an ultimate objective and set a tight deadline for its accomplishment. The trouble is, with so much energy aimed at tomorrow's goal, they find it impossible to concentrate on today's task.

By misplacing their energies, these managers are forced to work far below their capacity. Soon it becomes painfully clear that the objective they're reaching for won't be met on time. Though they have not yet failed, they anticipate failure, and the anticipation fills them with fear and frustration. Fear and frustration then combine to form that infamous productivity killer, stress.

TIPS FOR SUCCESS

The lesson to be learned is simple: To get the most out of your workday, focus your attention on the top-priority task of the moment. Get into the habit of accomplishing the "most important now." The question is, of course, how to determine the most important now, and to integrate the practice of focusing on it into your work life. Following are a number of simple steps that will help you do just that.

Establish clear goals. Successful managers share a clear understanding of their individual business goals, and have detailed action plans aimed at achieving them. Make sure that you have a good grasp of your goals by putting them into writing. Pen and paper force you to be clear and precise.

Once you've taken the time and effort to spell out your objectives, don't lose sight of them. To ensure that you don't, review them at regular intervals. Periodic reviews not only help you keep your objectives in mind, they also point out when they've grown obsolete and need updating.

Dissect goals and determine priorities. A goal is too enormous an undertaking to accomplish in one fell swoop. In fact, a goal is the sum of its various tasks. Therefore, to reach your goal, first break it down into its assorted tasks. Again, use pen and paper to help keep things precise and in perspective when you list the tasks.

More often than not, when tasks are set down in black and white, it becomes clear that they can't all be accomplished at once. Therefore, your next step is to arrange tasks according to priority.

Continually update priorities. As every manager knows only too well, it is impossible to predict what will happen in the course of the workday. But you can be sure that something will happen to force the reordering of the day's priorities. Be prepared for these changes in priorities. Each day, have a list of your priority tasks, then constantly update the list as the day progresses.

When you're first getting into the habit of doing the most important now, you may find it helpful to update your priorities list every hour on the hour (initially, some managers update it every 15 minutes). Begin each hour with a clear and reasonable expectation of what you want to accomplish in that hour. Then concentrate on that one task during that hour. (Of course, if something happens and forces another priority to intrude, set aside what you're doing and return to it later.)

Check for success. At the end of the day, find out how well you've managed your time. Look over your most current, and therefore accurate, priorities list. If each task on the list has been successfully completed, you've won the battle, and you should be feeling satisfied and productive.

Get organized. Any manager can use this formula. The only prerequisite is good organization. It stands to reason that only a well-organized and orderly manager will be able to keep the necessary written and mental tabs on his or her objectives and priorities. Therefore, before you begin to attack your time management troubles, be sure to sharpen your organizational skills. Here are a few basic pointers to help you develop these skills.

Memo yourself. Throughout the day, the typical manager is bombarded with an enormous amount of information, too much information for anyone's memory to handle. Therefore, beware not to leave anything that needs to be remembered in the clutches of an unreliable memory. Instead, write it down—immediately. Then once you've got it on paper, store it in a spot where you will be sure to see it. Needless to say, notes that go undiscovered are of questionable use.

Touch it once. Paper, in the form of letters, reports, documents, publications, etc., should not come to rest permanently on your desktop, to be looked at once, then again sometime later, and again, and again. Instead, your desk should be considered a temporary, and brief, stopover that paper makes on its way to wherever you have determined it ought to go.

To accomplish this monumental feat, you must sit down and assign every type of paper a final resting place. For paper you simply don't know what to do with (and there will always be some material that you don't), set up a "maturity table"—a convenient place for those items. When they've sat there too long without being touched, they will have "matured" and be ready for filing in the trash can. The object of assigning every bit and piece of paper a specific spot is to touch everything one time, and one time only.

Expect interruptions. Interruptions are a constant and unavoidable part of managerial life. Learn to live and deal with them. The trick here is to consider each interruption on its own merits. For example, if the interruption is a phone call, you must judge whether or not it takes priority over the task at hand: If the call is from a major client, you may well decide that it does. If it's from your second cousin, Sam, you may decide that it doesn't and cut the call short.

The point is to try and take control of the situation, even when the actual interruption is beyond your control. The only way to do that is to keep uppermost in your mind the word "priorities."

R. James Steffen is president of Steffen, Steffen & Associates, Westport, Connecticut.

33.
BEATING TIME TO
MEET OBJECTIVES

Chris Lane

Keeping diaries and "log books" can help one make more effective use of time but Chris Lane argues that the key to achieving one's long term aims is attitude and commitment.

Most people will readily agree that the most interesting and important subject they could ever spend time considering is their ambitions for the next ten to 20 years, both at work and in private life. Unfortunately a recent survey of 500 key managers in Scandinavia indicated that while the next 20 years' ambitions are interesting, that's about as far as it goes. Only four out of the 500 managers asked had a clear idea in written form of what they wished to get out of their lives during the next few years—less than one percent.

From the point of view of the methods involved, the job of getting more out of life both at work and in private life seems simple: We just need to:

- Decide clearly and in writing what areas of job and private life we need to spend time on;
- Make sure we spend time and energy on these things and on these things only.

The first part—deciding what needs our prime attention—is normally quite easy; struggles tend to arise when we set about putting our intentions into practice. That is when all the interruptions and obstacles appear: People interrupt us, telephones ring, other worries suddenly arrive in our minds. Very soon we have the impression that our whole environment has secretly plotted to ensure our failure and frustration. The fact remains, however, that most managers know what they should be doing, but very few feel they really spend sufficient time doing it. The effective management of time should itself be a key area for most managers, yet how many really feel they have mastered the art? In most cases our potential for results far exceeds our actual performance.

The approach to this problem normally adopted in management courses and in management books is concerned primarily with the methods rather than the attitudes of personal planning and time management. The subject of time management may logically be approached by using a "time log" to identify where time is currently spent; by coming to terms with the major obstacles preventing the effective management of time; and by establishing an im‑ provement program on the basis of the findings of the time log and obstacles analysis, utilizing one of the proprietary planning diaries.

Much scholarly work has been done in this area but one must mention in particular the books of Alec Mackenzie and Alan Lakein in the United States and of Dr. Rosemary Stewart and the recent research done by Bruce Austin in the United Kingdom. John Humble, the well‑known international author and consultant, has also developed a series of seminar programs to enable senior managers to come to grips with the problem of getting better control of their time by making an honest assessment of the obstacles and the problems and by setting up over a period of months a logical improvement program.

In this article I want to put forward an alternative approach to the effective management of time which relies first and foremost on the premise that, if a particular task or goal is important enough, we will make sure it is achieved, irrespective of all the obstacles and difficulties. "You can do almost anything you set your creative mind to do" would be a good motto for this treatment of the subject. One of the main justifications for taking an "attitude related" approach is to overcome one of the biggest problems managers face in looking at their management of time: the pressing feeling they have when they realize as a result of their time log how little of their time they are actually able to control themselves.

We need to rely heavily on the methods and techniques already available, most of which are contained in the literature already mentioned, but if we are to succeed in overcoming the common problem of managers and their control of time we need to grasp three further essential points relative to our attitudes.

WHO OWNS THE PROBLEM?

The first point to be accepted is an honest realization that in relation to all the obstacles and interruptions, the problem is one's own. It is perfectly natural and quite easy for people to identify all the factors limiting the full utilization of their time in important key areas. Colleagues and customers alike telephone at inconvenient moments with seemingly unnecessary queries; meetings overrun, always due to the "other guy."

To leave the matter to rest at this point, however, is less than rewarding. As managers we need to accept that we "own the problem" and can therefore influence the outcome. An example of the boss constantly interrupting his subordinate in the office will illustrate the point. The natural feeling of the subordinate is one of frustration: "Why doesn't he realize?" Or "No wonder I can't get things done." On the other hand, imagine the response if I, the subordinate, accept that the problem is mine: "Bill, you're my boss. Would you kindly help me? I have this problem and I somehow can't find a way out of it. So many calls come through to my phone that..." In our experience in employing this idea in all kinds of organizations we normally find that the boss will be more than happy to "help" with a solution: a daily meeting with his subordinates at 10:30 or better use of the secretary. Very simple, we would all agree; perhaps almost too simple. But are these not the little aggravations which often stand between the manager and his feeling of achievement?

The second factor which needs to be brought into focus concerns the way the human brain works. Although it is well known that we have two distinct sides to the brain, each controlling the opposite side of the body, many managers are not aware of their quite distinct mental functions. Most effective learning is done through our right-side brains; yet many of us, when faced with a new idea or suggestion requiring change, shut down our right side, and proceed to sit in judgment on this idea, evaluating it against our experience. The first question in our minds seems to be, "How does this new idea relate to what we already do?" rather than "What new opportunity will this idea open up for us?" Compare these two reactions against Figure 1 and you will see how very different they are.

FIGURE 1

TWO SIDES OF THE BRAIN

LEFT	RIGHT
Logic	Humor
Reasoning	Creative
Experience	Color, Music
etc.	etc.

The different characteristics of the conscious and subconscious levels in the brain are also vital to effective time management. Modern research assures us that the brain has an almost limitless capacity for information and that we are unlikely ever to utilize more than one percent. The problem is that, although the subconscious part of the brain is at work all the time and can contain limitless information, the conscious brain can really attend to only one thing at a time. Imagine therefore the busy manager working in his office finalizing next year's budget or marketing plan, when suddenly the phone rings or his door opens. What has happened? Yes, his conscious brain has been diverted from the main task in hand. Many managers also realize that they are adept at interrupting themselves, especially when faced with a tricky problem. The eye wanders over the desk until it finds something easier to spend time on, the newspaper or some non-urgent meeting minutes, for instance.

Because of the limitation of the conscious brain, the enormous capacity of the subconscious brain, and our insatiable curiosity, if something is "in sight" it is also "in mind." More relevantly for the manager, "out of sight" also equals "out of mind." Recall for a moment one of those normal days in the office, and make a list of the things which were in sight and therefore in mind: the mail, urgent messages, demands for immediate advice, the bluebottle that was buzzing round the light fitting, and so on.

Is there any wonder we find it difficult to concentrate as much time as we need on the really important things on which the company's future, and therefore our own, depends? The frustration and stress which sometimes result from this situation can be a serious health hazard and totally counterproductive.

If we are to overcome these common obstacles and take advantage of our full mental and physical potential as human beings, then the rewards need to be seen as being well worth the discipline and effort required. Therefore, the third point to make is that, unless a message is seen in terms of "value to me," there is no real reason for changing one's working habits or attitudes; and in the area of time management and personal planning "change" is essential if better results are to be achieved.

So far we have been looking at the philosophy and theory rather than the practice of effective personal planning and time management; and without putting things into practice we can neither get results nor reach the all-important "values level" which alone will motivate us to change habits. Practical down-to-earth methods and techniques are essential and these methods need above all to be capable of encompassing the full spectrum of a manager's interest and responsibilities, both at work and in private life.

The diary, showing either a day, week or month to a page, is the most common planning tool used by managers. Yet how many people were ever taught at school or college to use a diary effectively? To illustrate this point let me ask you to look at your diary now—yes, right now, before reading on. Most diaries are full of appointments with other people, meetings, social engagements and so on. Unfortunately, however essential they may be in the short term, many of these diary entries have very little to do with the plans and ambitions for the next 10-20 years—our own personal development, family relationships, market and product development, for instance. It is a sad fact that the diary, and also much of the instruction available on time management, fails to make anything more than a superficial connection between our long-term goals and day-to-day activities. Without the stimulation of seeing such a connection clearly "in sight and in mind" is there any wonder that many managers unwittingly allow the day to disappear in a mass of interruptions and short term crises?

Imagine for a moment a large funnel (see Figure 2), the neck of which represents the only really important decision we ever have to take relative to our own achievements, i.e., "what to do now?" We take it countless times each

FIGURE 2

THE FUNNEL

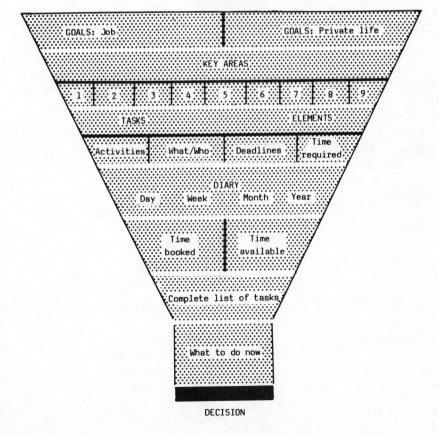

day at work and at home, though sometimes not as consciously as we would wish. At the top end of the funnel we find our long-term goals in both job and private life, our ambitions for the next 20 years, for instance; and for ease of identification these are broken down into "key areas."

Key areas are those parts of our job and private life on which we need to concentrate our time in order to achieve our goals. A sales director might describe some of his key areas as follows:

Job
• Salesman effectiveness
• Optimum sales prices
• Exports
• Cost Center

Private
• Antique collecting
• Personal development
• Family, friends and other personal matters

Note that unlike most job descriptions, key areas are expressed very briefly, and whenever possible they have an "output" orientation. The main advantage of this idea is that, by having his key areas clearly identified in writing in short phrases, the manager can bring the really important area affecting his life "in sight and in mind" whenever he has to make decisions about the use of his time—the decision what to do now.

In order to turn key areas into a practical working state they have to be broken down further into task areas as indicated by the next level in the funnel diagram. Examples of task areas for different key areas might be:

Key area	Salesman's effectiveness
Task area	Bill Smith Joe Thomas Weekly meeting Training plan
Key area	Personal development
Task area	Learn Arabic More time for reading technical literature Be an encourager Golf Better television watching

Each phrase acts as a constant reminder to the brain, so that the decision what to do now may be taken in a goal-related manner.

Apart from having a clear definition of key areas (together with their various subdivisions into task areas and activity plans), the single most important component in a manager's planning kit must surely be a detailed profile of each day. Figure 3 shows a daily plan which schedules time not only for the fixed diary appointments but also for key area work and also for other activities which tend to run away with time if left uncontrolled—telephone work, routine paperwork, etc.

Flexibility is of course vital, but by drawing up a profile of the following day before leaving work, a manager is far more likely to be in a position to write that report, his task of the day, and also to have the all-important satisfaction of seeing himself achieve a majority of the things he sets out to do, especially the things related to his goals and key areas.

APPOINTMENT WITH ME

One very good idea which many managers use to get better control of their time during the day is to make a habit of booking appointments with themselves. "Appointment with me" can be as short as five to ten minutes to take stock of progress, or longer for a specific key area task. If you know you need three hours to write a report, then set a date ahead and book it in the diary just like any other appointment. The effect will be dramatic; first because with no personal effort your subconscious brain will be sifting all the information you need in preparation, and second, you will be sure to succeed so long as you keep your promise with yourself.

Beware that the very simplicity of these ideas does not mask their effectiveness, neither in terms of results achieved nor in the increased sense of achievement and correspondingly reduced feelings of stress and tiredness. Achievement in management is highly stimulating; and while we obviously will feel tired after a good day obtaining results, it will be quite a different feeling from the frustrations we experience when we are continually prevented from turning our plans into action.

Putting logical concepts and techniques into practice during a normal day at the office rather than within the protected surroundings of a management seminar is of course the final acid test to any system. The first day "back at the office" is often the battlefield which witnesses the death of many good intentions and resolutions honestly made during management development programs. It is also vital that these ideas and tools stand this first test.

There is of course no simple solution, only guidelines, and the need for a high degree of individual discipline and commitment. In our experience, however, in working with over 40,000 European managers, the simplest way of

FIGURE 3

DAILY PLAN

Date: *1 JULY*   Day: *MONDAY*

Fixed appointments:		Tasks:
	7	*PREPARE SALES CAMPAIGN*
THOMPSON	8	
	9	
	10	
	11	Speak/write to:
	12	*JOHNSON*
SALES MEETING	1	*STAR LTD.*
LUNCH	2	*MARY*
Tel Calls	3	
Secretary	4	
"MEETING WITH	5	
ME"	6	Don't forget:
DINNER	7	*BUY FLOWERS*
REDLION	8	*FLIGHT TICKETS*

Key areas:	1	2	3	4	5	6	7	8	9
Time spent:									

getting started is, rather than wait until the first day back at the office, get started in detail right there in the seminar while the message is still alive, intentions good and interruptions nil.

To define a comprehensive personal planning system likely to suit all managers' needs is impossible; but we can certainly draw together the main features necessary to enable us to utilize to the full the enormous capacity of the human brain so that we can obtain maximum results in minimum time and with reduced feelings of stress.

Clearly there are no easy answers to the management of time, but two things are quite clear. The individual manager's own commitment is vital and his or her attitude must be positive. Therein lies the clue. Given that the attitude is right and that a proper system is implemented to ensure continuity of effort, the task is simplified. Managers can then work with something which is of value to them. The motivation this provides ensures that they do not work from crisis to crisis, but in a planned and controlled way. Try it and see. It's about time.

Chris Lane is managing director of Time Management International.

34.
"TIME, GENTLEMEN, TIME..."*

Robert B. Forest

In the imperfect world of which we are never in control, it's very difficult to nail down priorities. Too often, we're simply not in charge. We accept someone else's priorities.

Some of us go on diets once in awhile. Others go on the wagon from time to time. Or read books on how to "improve" ourselves, or become "sane." My fits usually involve "getting organized." They don't strike very often or last very long, and I've come to accept them, stoically, like an occasional visit from a relative.

During one of my recent attacks, I started to read a book I had bought several months earlier on managing one's time. But I never got around to finishing it. Couldn't find the time.

Sometimes I think that I would be an ideal candidate for the Procrastinator's Club. This is a group of people who occasionally think about having their first meeting. Procrastination is a mental and emotional disorder caused by the lack of Vitamin P (for Priorities).

Priorities, as Tony Ralston once pointed out to me, are more important than goals. It's usually easy to establish or agree upon a set of general objectives. But it isn't until you set priorities—pinpoint the relative importance of various objectives—that you can get cracking.

In the imperfect world of which we are never in control, it's very difficult to nail down priorities. Too often, we're simply not in charge. We accept someone else's priorities. That can be a cop out. One way to find out is to ask yourself just who or what is in control of your time. Are your activities plan-driven, event-driven or emotion-driven? Let me explain.

Some people work according to a plan. They figure out far in advance just what it is they have to do, what resources they will require, and how they have to manipulate their time—and the time of others—to accomplish their goals. Such people are, perhaps fortunately, rare.

But they are more in control of their time than those of us who are event-driven. When a challenge or a deadline comes up, usually unexpectedly, we tackle it. We throw aside whatever else we are doing and deal with it. Now.

Some things slide, of course. And we have to work hard, fast and long to keep ahead of the alligators. We pride ourselves on our ability to meet "challenges." And we get by. Most of the time, anyway.

Then there are the emotion-driven folks. What motivates them may be pleasing everybody...or pleasing the boss, at least. Mainly, they want to be liked. Or they may be trying to avoid making enemies. A friend of mine used to have on the wall of his office a framed Chinese saying. The translation: "Don't make waves." These people are dangerous...to teamwork and to management. Such people, said another old friend of mine, "pillow you to death." Smother you with goodwill and promises.

Maybe you have a plan. But there are all those interruptions, phone calls mostly, that have to be answered. But do they have to be answered right now? This minute? Probably not—in most cases, at least. Good old Bob Patrick once told me how to handle that problem.

The Sage of Northridge suggested that when I had something to do that required a solid block of uninterrupted time, I could ask my secretary to take messages. I was out. But would return the calls later on. In an hour or two, or whatever. It worked. Exceptions can be made, the secretary given the names of people to let through the blockade. You don't have a secretary? Neither do I, right now. But I have an answering machine.

The Patrick time-blocking technique can be viewed as a subset of a general timing tactic. Besides asking ourselves what we should do, and in what order, we can ask ourselves, "When?" Maybe tasks requiring a high degree of solitude and concentration can be tackled early in the morning. If you can't work at home, you might try getting to work early. Sounds crazy, I know. But you'll find you spend less time in transit (usually). And you'll be amazed at how much you can get done in an office before the phones start jangling, and heads come popping around the door to ask, "Gotta minute?" That "minute" usually lasts a half-hour or more.

Whether we're plan-, event- or emotion-driven, most of us have trouble finding enough time for what could be called creative thinking. Letting our minds drift idly past, or around a problem, consciously or subconsciously. Attacking a problem from another direction. Letting our minds wander. Or wonder.

One way to find such time is to ask the question, "Why?" You would be amazed at the number of meetings that can be avoided. I've learned the hard way—at the expense of thousands of hours—to ask, before I accept an invitation to a meeting, "Just what is the purpose of this meeting?" Lot of times there isn't any...or not one that requires my presence, anyway.

Another technique that I've found useful is to use my subconscious mind to work on a problem while I'm doing other things. Instead of always ramrodding or steamrolling through or over a problem, try pushing it about as far as it will easily go for the moment. Then shove it aside. A day or two later, you may find that you have some ideas about it that had escaped you earlier.

Of course, you have to allow time for that. Which sort of brings us full circle, doesn't it?

* Traditional closing call at English pubs.

Robert B. Forest is associated with Forest & Eyler Computer Communications of Sparta, New Jersey.

35.
INSTANT REPLAY:
IT WORKS FOR MANAGEMENT, TOO

Larry G. Chambers

It sounds more regimented than World War II, but it isn't. It gets things done. It gives me a lot more satisfaction and time in front of the fireplace at night.

Those management manuals—even the good ones—tell you *how to do it,* but they never tell you how to fail so you can succeed later.

All the courses I've spent good money (and better time) on didn't tell me or my staff how to cope with failure—only how to succeed.

Despite all this success, there are days in every public relations manager's life when his or her confidence and satisfaction gets smashed, when he gets hit with *all* the facts. And there are days when the staff believes they are the world's most successful failures.

We're communicators. We're best at it when we're telling someone else how to do it. I'm so much better at consulting for others than I am for myself. It isn't unique to our level of management. A number of former chief executive officers who built reputations on expert communication are back at being experts.

Every practitioner knows that the most untimely, gut-wrenching calls come from the client whose brochure is delayed or wrong, the board of control member whose news story fizzled, or the invited speaker whose sound system quit.

We've had our share, and more, and out of all those ashes in our mouths we've developed a bottom-line, tough-minded, self-management system that gets results. We still fail, but a lot less than we did. We've learned how to concentrate on results management, *to reduce it to writing,* and to use performance evaluation to improve our feedback to each other.

I've learned to combine and apply what may sound like a complicated set of bottom-line tools. After all, any manager knows what to do; he or she just doesn't have the time to do it. What the boss probably understands better than the manager is that the manager doesn't discipline himself well enough to carry out what he knows best.

My approach was to take all of the usual demands on a manager's time—boss calls, client calls, staff calls, performance reviews, monthly objectives, the organization's paper blizzard, future planning, and our own top priority of time management—and run them through the Air Force performance review. The research and testing had already been done, so why not take advantage of it?

I ranked myself and then changed for the better. I said to the staff, "Here's a neat performance evaluation form. It's tough. I don't know if we really want to use it, but I think it's a beautiful way to communicate about production goals, objectives and results."

They bought the idea.

Each staffer now sets his or her own monthly objectives. We review them together. If managers have employees who refuse to set objectives, they eventually ought to get rid of them. If employees have managers of the same mind, they really ought to consider moving on because the entire operation is going nowhere.

The solution for our operation is a combination of management by objective and management by results, neither of which stands alone for us. On crisis days, it quickly turns to management by exception, or dealing with the tough problem only. But we move quickly to pick up the pieces because of good communication through monthly reviews. The next crisis is either prevented or minimized through objectives or results management.

CHECKLIST AND PLANNING

Out of this have come automatic checklists for my phone calls and flexible but detailed events planning. Our methods cope with red carpet VIP treatment, graduations, building dedications, internal communications and community relations. They've helped develop an emergency plan, they help keep us in step with top management, and they get results—on time.

Our system, basically, reduces it all to writing in a plan which has the input and back-checks of all those legitimately concerned with the project. We've printed up "Instant Replay" memos to emphasize that one picks up a phone right away, sets up a detail immediately, lets another know the answer right now, and makes a decision without delay to avoid reshuffling the institution's paper.

To start it all, I closed the door several nights in a row and put most of "that good stuff" from the desk in a garbage bag.

I cried. I prayed. Then I got smart.

I started working at 7 a.m. instead of jogging to win interruption-free time. I switched jogging to 11 a.m. to noon, again to gain interruption-free time. I minimized those friendly, fattening luncheons and turned instead to the friendly, fat-free telephone and cryptic memos.

My secretary, most valuable resource of all, and I meet early. I try to dictate late in the day to give her a fast start the next morning. She arranges time blocks so I can concentrate on one project at a time, behind a closed door. She organizes my meetings, helps with my priorities, worries about me, and keeps me pointed in the right direction.

To keep myself on the results target (nothing matters more), I keep a daily priority sheet. Each member of my staff has adapted a version of it for his or her own system. They can quickly and accurately tell me where they are on tight priority days. My sheet makes me delegate properly, set target dates and evaluate completion. It helps me deal in facts and minimizes emotional and personality conflicts. We use priority sheets on individual projects as well as for whole-day planning.

I also redid my desk. Only three folders remained on top: *mail, to do,* and *urgent.* My secretary insists on only one shuffle per sheet, and that means *instant replay* decision.

My lower left-hand desk drawer is for my VIP file. The lower right-hand desk drawer is the project tickler file. I check them daily. The discipline isn't that easy to start, but it is necessary.

It sounds more regimented than World War II, but it isn't. It gets things done. It gives me a lot more satisfaction and time in front of the fireplace at night—or maybe enough strength to write, consult or go to a concert.

Best test of all: The boss appreciates it. The staff likes the increased participation, the improved forum for ideas, planning and achieving, and the more professional execution of their creativity.

Larry G. Chambers is manager, communications services, Michigan Technological University, Houghton, Michigan.

36.
MANAGING YOUR MINUTES:
HOW TO GET A GRIP
ON YOUR TIME

Rose V. McCullough

You set the working "climate" in the office, so if your office does not seem to be operating at peak efficiency, it may be a good idea to take a look at your own use of time!

Most successful business people have learned to control their time, rather than waste it by occupying themselves with trivialities. They have worked out a system to get the important tasks done, to set their priorities in the right order, and then to adhere to those priorities.

Their thoughts and their work have been so organized that they are able to set short-range and long-range goals, and then see to it that their daily goals contribute directly to the long-range objectives.

Do you have trouble completing important tasks? Are you buried under a load of paperwork on your desk, seeing no way out, and viewing with trepidation the tasks that have to be done to make even a dent in that load?

If so, the key to getting yourself out of this rut is to gain control of your time, and then expand it to fit your needs and goals. Following, are practical ways to do this.

First, find out how and where you are spending your time during your working day. Chart each function you perform, each conversation you hold, and each business luncheon you attend for one or two weeks. Then make appropriate comments by each activity, along with the time spent on each, such as:

- if each telephone call was too long, or perhaps unnecessary in the first place;
- if each discussion held with an employee pertained to work, or was just social chit-chat;

- if the discussion held during the business luncheon was meaningful, either from a business or educational standpoint, or if it really was more important to have skipped the luncheon and attended to a more urgent project in the office.

Next, decide whether or not you want to have some time for yourself—for attending to major projects and for thinking ahead and planning. Or are you going to have a continuous open door policy, being available at all times to those under your supervision? The latter can be lethal in that it has a chain reaction effect.

For example, suppose you have been steadily concentrating upon an important project for a half-hour or an hour, then someone comes into your office, or calls you on the phone, breaking your train of thought. You have to stop thinking about what you are doing and attempt to concentrate on what is being said to you, and on the individual's problem. As a result, not only do you lose your impetus, but you also find it difficult to answer the questions of the other individual satisfactorily. Likely, you do not really comprehend what he/she is talking about, because your mind is still back on the project on which you were concentrating so heavily. This is a time-consuming process, and this type of interruption, which is deadly to the busy and conscientious person, could go on all day if you allowed it to.

What this boils down to is, are you controlling your time, or are you allowing others to monopolize it to your disadvantage? Recognize your priorities, and either ask the receptionist to hold all your calls for an hour or so, and close your office door to visitors for that length of time; or go to a quiet place where you won't be disturbed and can give your project the concentrated attention it deserves.

Another alternative would be to come to work an hour or two early in the morning, before anyone else is about, and complete the task—provided you are a morning person, whose mind is clear and alert early in the day.

You should also analyze the functions you are performing and decide which ones can be delegated. Make a list of your major and minor responsibilities, the steps and approximate time necessary to accomplish each, and any deadlines that have to be met. Then study the list to see if any steps can be combined or eliminated to cut down on time. Next, decide which responsibilities can be delegated to qualified personnel, those whom you can depend on to follow instructions and to see a job through to its completion. Make a list of those tasks which are not management-related, and therefore have no place in your schedule of work. This way you can concentrate on those administrative functions which can only be handled by you.

One way to force yourself to be realistic is to ask yourself how much your time is worth. Assume, for example, that you are earning $500 a week, which is $100 a day, or $13 an hour. Now, is it worth your valuable time to spend it in attending to details that could be handled just as efficiently by a member of your staff who is earning about one-third of your salary?

There is a side benefit of delegation of responsibilities to qualified personnel, in that it creates in them a positive, enthusiastic attitude. Employee attitudes play a major role in any business, either contributing to higher profits or wasting valuable dollars.

The more you bring your personnel into the planning effort by getting them to assist in setting deadlines and to participate in laying out the necessary procedures, the more likely you are to motivate them to adhere to those procedures, to meet those deadlines, and thus to reach your short-range objectives, saving you time.

Also make an analysis of your time-wasting habits, again keeping in mind the $13-an-hour (or similar) figure. Be honest with yourself, and determine how much time you actually take each day for:

- coffee breaks (after subtracting 30 minutes for two each day);
- lunch hours (after subtracting one hour);
- casual conversation around the office;
- reading the paper.

If you will add up the total time spent on these diversions, beyond the usual amount of time spent for lunch and a couple of coffee breaks a day, you may find that quite a large portion of your valuable time has been invested in other-than-business practices.

Everybody needs a break in routine, and it's only natural to discuss sports, politics and other current topics of interest with others in the office. While these discussions may be a pleasant habit to some, they can easily become a distraction to others. Using such conversations to put off inevitable work merely puts you behind schedule. It also slows down your mental processes, so that when you do start to work, it takes awhile to orient your thinking to business matters.

Finally, once you've got your time in order, set a priority on each of your responsibilities. Take the time at the end of each day to set up a working program for the following day: a "Must Do," "Should Do," and "Can Do" list. By checking off each task as it is completed, you will give yourself a feeling of accomplishment.

Progressiveness and foresightedness are two enviable characteristics of the successful businessman. Efficiency starts at the top, with management. You set the working climate in the office, so if your office does not seem to be operating at peak efficiency, it may be a good idea to take a look at your own use of time!

Rose V. McCullough is an assistant editor with Rough Motes Co., Inc., in Indianapolis, Indiana.

Part V
THE DELEGATION DILEMMA

37.
HOW TO EFFECTIVELY DELEGATE

Robert D. Buchanan

Managers need to structure authority, power, responsibility, and accountability in their organizations through the process of delegating and exacting accountability.

Delegation is a means of getting greater results through people. Following are some important principles of delegation, focusing on how a manager must structure the important interrelationships of authority, power, responsibility and accountability within a staff organization.

Delegation is the process by which a manager grants or permits the transfer of authority to subordinates to operate within prescribed limits. It is the key to the achievement of the organization's objectives via a manager's coordination of human and physical elements with an efficient and effective working unit.

In practice, an efficient formal organization is dependent upon the skill with which a manager delegates authority. A manager cannot expect to have a smooth-running organization without delegating both properly and promptly.

A manager has both authority and power. A manager's formal authority, the right to command or to act, flows downward from top management. Whether a manager can enforce his or her rights is a question of power—that is, the ability to influence or cause a subordinate to do what is wished.

Generally, managers can delegate nearly anything that they have a right to do. What is crucial and what complicates directing the actions of others, is whether subordinates willingly obey. Effective authority and power are possible only when there is a two-way endorsement of the relationship.

WHY DELEGATE?

To achieve the most desirable results from a group or organization requires leadership and motivation—as well as the development of cooperation so that subordinates voluntarily and effectively carry out their responsibilities—rather than dependence upon the application of absolute authority. The first prerequisite for building a smoothly operating team is the intelligent handling of delegation. This extends the effectiveness of managers.

There are several advantages resulting from effective delegation:

1. Delegation allows the manager more time for thinking and planning.
2. The person closest to the activity should be better able to make decisions than a distant superior.
3. Delegation tends to encourage initiative in subordinates and to make effective use of their skills. Initiative, in turn, improves morale.
4. Delegation tends to reduce decision time, as it eliminates recommendations going upwards to the superior, where the decision is made, and subsequent downward communication.
5. Delegation develops the skills of subordinates by permitting them to make decisions and apply their knowledge gained from training programs and meetings.

Authority should be delegated to the extent necessary to accomplish results expected. Delegating managers always retain all their responsibilities, however, in the sense of never being freed of ultimate responsibility for the activities of subordinates. Allowing managers to evade their responsibilities simply by getting someone else to assume the duties would break the single chain of command and leave no way of knowing who was accountable for what.

PRIOR TO DELEGATING

Prerequisites to delegation include the development of organization objectives, policies and guidelines; clear definitions of the responsibilities and authority of each job; time schedule, identification of specific results, means of measurement; the specific role of the superior and the subordinate; and provision for control and minimum time between feedback and correction of deviations.

Newman and Warren[1] succinctly point out three inseparable, interrelated aspects of delegation of authority. Change in one will require adjustment of the other two.

Assignment of duties. The person who is delegating indicates what work the subordinate must do in terms of activities and/or results to be achieved.

Granting of permission (authority). The person who is delegating transfers to the subordinate certain rights, such as directing the work of others, using food and supplies, representing the organization to outsiders, or taking other steps necessary to fulfill the duties that create an obligation.

Creating an obligation (responsibility). In accepting an assignment, a subordinate takes on obligations to his boss to complete the job. This is the moral compulsion felt by a subordinate to accomplish his assigned duties.

There are degrees of delegation ranging from fact-finding to decision-making. The degree of delegation is based upon such general factors as atmosphere or setting in the organization, importance of the decision, and management philosophy.

More specific factors include the nature of the task, the ability of the person doing the work, the amount of top management interest, and the time available for task completion. W.H. Nesbitt of Westinghouse Electric Corporation is credited with detailing five degrees of delegation.

1. *Investigate and report back.* Manager makes the decision and takes appropriate action.
2. *Investigate and recommend action.* Manager evaluates the recommendation, makes the decision and takes action.
3. *Investigate and advise of intended action.* Manager evaluates the decision made by a staff member and approves or disapproves.
4. *Investigate and take action; advise of action taken.* Here manager displays faith in the staff's ability but wants to be kept advised of what's going on.
5. *Investigate and take action.* This is full delegation and displays complete faith in your staff's ability.

MAINTAIN COMMUNICATION

Delegation should be as specific as possible and should be made in writing. Clear lines of authority are created by making the scope of authority clear to each subordinate as well as to the manager.

Policies, procedures and statements of the job responsibilities and authority may seem to narrow the range within which a person may make a decision, but tend to provide a greater sense of freedom than if the boundaries were ambiguous or inconsistently maintained.

Effective communication is a very important part of the delegation process and is the means by which delegation is accomplished. There must be clear lines of communication from the top to the lowest level of the organization.

Delegation requires, in addition, certain attitudes on the part of the delegating manager, such as receptiveness to other people's ideas, a willingness to release some decision-making power, a willingness to let others make mistakes, and a willingness to establish and use broad controls, rather than specific, detailed controls. Perhaps the greatest challenge to the delegating manager is the development of a sense of participation in subordinates.

Some managers may be confident that they are truly delegating authority to their subordinates, but in fact subordinates rarely initiate action and invariably clear all questions with the boss. The amount of the suggestions, recommendations and opinions actually initiated by the subordinate provides a clue concerning the extent to which authority is really delegated. Managers may spend so much time with trivial details or reserve so many kinds of problems for personal attention that they are unable to organize, supervise, devote time to forward planning and take advantage of opportunities. Managers will enhance their contribution by concentrating on tasks that contribute most to the organization's objectives and assign to subordinates other tasks.

However, a problem beyond a subordinate's scope of delegation should be referred upward in the organization. That is, managers who have delegated authority and assigned the duties to a subordinate manager should refrain from intervening unless the problem is clearly an exception.

Unfortunately, many subordinates a somewhat apprehensive about the acceptance of authority. It is extremely important for superiors to train and guide subordinates toward independent action. To achieve this, the attitude of mutual confidence between superior and subordinate must exist. Subordinates must understand that, while they must perform satisfactorily, they will not be condemned for every error of judgment. It is particularly important that any error be handled constructively as an education device, rather than as an occasion for destructive criticism.

DETERMINING CONTROL STANDARDS

The assignment of duties is the key to achieving control standards. Assignments should be defined and delegated in terms of results expected and each subordinate's accountability. This implies that objectives have been set and plans made, that these are communicated to and understood by subordinates, and that jobs have been set up to fit plans and objectives.

Although authority, position, responsibility and accountability are seldom equal, it is important for the boss to correlate them thoughtfully. Subordinates should be told to fulfill duties to the best of their ability considering their authority and work conditions.

Once authority and responsibility have been established, a system of accountability by which to monitor actions of each person is needed.

Accountability flows upward through an organization. Managers cannot reduce responsibility by delegating, and also cannot reduce accountability to higher authority by delegating. Managers are still directly accountable to their superiors for the authority they have delegated.

Objective-oriented control permits the subordinate manager to use creative resources in seeking better means to achieve objectives. The evidence suggests that the most effective control system provides direct feedback to the person accountable for the task.

Often the amount of authority delegated is not sufficient for the subordinate to accomplish the assignment effectively. Many managers tend to delegate as little authority as possible because of a fear of undesirable results. However, assuming risks is part of the manager's job. The manager who is unwilling to accept the risk of poor subordinate performance is really not qualified for a managerial position. Most managers are where they are because somebody had faith in them and accepted the calculated risk inherent in delegating authority to subordinates!

Other reasons managers fail to delegate are lack of ability to direct, feelings of insecurity, feelings that they can do it better, incapable subordinates, enjoyment of exercising power, reluctance of subordinates to assume authority, fear of subordinates' personal growth, and lack of feedback.

WHAT TO DELEGATE?

There are certain working rules useful in making good delegations. The trick is in knowing how and when to use them.

Here are some common guidelines in the delegation of authority:

- The superior must understand, and agree with, the theory of delegation.
- Each subordinate should receive orders from and report to only one superior.
- Responsibilities should be assigned as far down the organizational structure as there are sufficient competence and information for effective decision-making and performance.
- Only decisions that cannot be made at a given level should be referred upward.
- Responsibility cannot be delegated, as no superior can escape responsibility for activities, performance and evaluation of subordinates through delegation.
- Accountability, the obligation to report to one's superior, cannot be delegated or assigned.
- A clear definition of the scope, responsibility, authority, objectives, who may provide help, potential consequences and functional relationships must be provided for every position. Delegation of authority for a whole job should be made whenever possible.
- There must be a clear chain of command from the ultimate source of authority to every position. Every subordinate must know who delegates authority and to whom matters must be referred.
- Authority must be commensurate with responsibility.
- Authority and responsibility must be accompanied by accountability for both work and teamwork.

- Jobs must be delegated by the results wanted, the performance standard expected, and how the performance will be evaluated.
- Work should be delegated only to qualified people, or necessary job training should be provided.
- The manager should be accessible when subordinates have problems and should know what kinds of help they need.
- Thinking and goals should be shared with subordinates so they have background for making decisions on their own.
- Controls that indicate early difficulties should be established and necessary corrective action taken. Progress should be checked periodically. Errors must be corrected and successes recognized as the subordinate makes progress.

Dale McConky, in *No-Nonsense Delegation*, suggests the following items be delegated to subordinates:

- Matters that keep repeating themselves
- Minor decisions most frequently made
- Details that take the biggest chunks of time
- Parts of the job the supervisor is least qualified to handle
- Job details the superior most dislikes
- Parts of the job that make the superior overspecialized
- Parts of the job that make the superior underspecialized

McConky also says to "be careful to ensure that the subordinate is given meaningful, challenging assignments and doesn't end up as a dumping ground for unwanted or distasteful tasks of the superior."

IN SUMMARY

Managers need to structure authority, power, responsibility and accountability in their organizations through the process of delegating and exacting accountability. Managers can delegate the work, but can't delegate the accountability for getting it done. Through delegation, managers extend their reach, multiply their talents and increase the scope and the quality of accomplishments.

One of the most important jobs of managers at all levels is to provide their subordinates with enough authority and power to do the things necessary to accomplish assignments. Superiors must provide subordinates with organization objectives; training; understanding of their role in the organization and their relationship to others; clearly defined job responsibilities; and workable controls so that actual results can quickly be compared to desired results.

The principles of delegation for managers are: establish reasonable objectives; offer definite training and instructions; keep yourself accessible;

share thinking and objectives to provide a background for subordinates' decisions, and let them know what is expected of them and how results will be evaluated.

Reference

1. Wiliam H. Newman and E. Kirby Warren, *The Process of Management*, 4th edition (Englewood Cliffs, N.J.: Prentice-Hall, Inc., 1977), pp. 39-40.

Robert D. Buchanan is associate professor and extension specialist, restaurant, hotel and institutional management, Purdue University.

38.
THE ART OF DELEGATING

I. Thomas Sheppard

Striking a subtle balance between delegating too much and too little can make all the difference. The first step to delegating successfully is to realize that it will seldom be easy, perfect or completely to your liking.

Delegation is the best time management tool available to an executive. It is important at every level in the organization, and should be learned thoroughly by everyone who wants to be a successful boss. But over and over again, we hear and see the horror stories of the executive who cannot delegate.

A typical example involved the president and chief executive officer of a medium-sized savings and loan organization in the Southwest. A short time after his appointment to the post, there was not one senior vice president in his organization who could make a decision. Every problem that reached their desks was referred, in various ways, to the chief. They waited for his pronouncements in every area of their responsibilities before they would take any significant action. They became masters of stalling, obfuscation and plain inactivity. They learned to excel at paper shuffling, recordkeeping and points of protocol to keep themselves and their staffs busy. All of this was because it was evident that the boss, while protesting heartily about his own workload, would not allow anyone to take action until all problems were laid before him for his decisions.

Over the years, managers with initiative and drive left this company as they discovered that their attributes were considered liabilities. Promotions were reserved for the ritual-keepers who carefully learned all of the chief's policies and procedures, rules and regulations, and, most important of all, his prerogative in all decision-making situations.

This organization, centered wholly on the energy of one man, became inflexible, ponderous and slow to react. There was no proactive element to its management strategy that sought to anticipate future conditions. Entropy, as it inevitably does, caused the company to slow, then falter, and finally to succumb to the latest economic downturn. It has since been taken over by a larger organization, and the former president is now just that—former.

In another instance, the vice president of a Fortune 500 corporation had a master's degree in business administration and regularly attended various management seminars designed to keep him current with the latest techniques. He started his position as an advocate of decentralization and delegation at every opportunity. His catchphrase to subordinates, "That's your problem, deal with it," was heard often in his department.

At first his people believed him, but it wasn't long before his nonverbal messages bespoke his true feelings. His subordinates eventually began to refer to him as "the helicopter" because, like that aircraft, he could hover in one spot seemingly for hours, always near the subordinate assigned the department's hottest project. In one outrageous hovering incident, he kept tabs on a subordinate even through trips to the men's room.

This executive's propensity to "keep in touch" was really a fear of letting go. He felt he was better qualified to do the job than was the subordinate to whom he delegated it, and that the subordinate lacked the experience of having done a similar job.

This executive is actually robbing himself of further advancement in the corporation. He is not preparing his younger managers to take responsibility. He is not training them in decision making. He has not groomed possible replacements to free himself for promotion. And he is establishing a reputation for saying one thing and meaning another.

The employees with initiative are avoiding assignments to this department, and those in the department are looking for ways out. Our vice president, while reducing his anxiety and tension by keeping a tight rein on everyone, is also unwittingly reducing his own future prospects as well.

THE OTHER EXTREME

The other side of the problem is represented by a young, fresh-out-of-college management intern in a large Texas construction firm. His approach to delegation could be more correctly called "off-loading." He takes every task assigned to him and off-loads it on his subordinates. He gives orders with the assurance of a drill sergeant and uses his position to pass along all of his work to the people in his section. He prides himself on being an expert administrator because his subordinates accomplish all of his responsibilities. The "free" time that he makes for himself in this manner is spent soliciting more projects for his section. "After all," he says, "we're the best, and we can handle anything!"

His youth and inexperience are saving him for the moment because his subordinates are doing his work and hoping that a change will come about as he matures. But since human nature decrees that behavior that is rewarded tends to be repeated with increasing frequency, he will have to have a real incentive to change before their hopes will come true.

DISSECTING DELEGATION

The act of delegating is deceptively simple. There are four basic steps to the process of delegation.

Selecting the subordinate. Who has, or can obtain, all the necessary data to do the job? Does he or she have the capability of dealing with the problem? Can you honestly expect a high probability of success if this person gets the assignment?

Agreeing on the final outcome. Time spent here is well used. There must be a complete understanding of the desired objectives by all parties, and an explanation of how these objectives will be measured. But the specifics of how the task will be accomplished should be left to the subordinate, as long as they fall within company policy and guidelines.

Providing the authority and the means to accomplish the task. The challenge here is to assure that the individual gets enough authority to get the job done, but not so much that it upsets the equilibrium of your department. Define the area in which the subordinate has the freedom to act on his or her own, and provide enough money, human resources and time to get the job done. Define the coordination you expect and be sure all concerned are notified of the project. If disciplinary powers are delegated with the project, be sure they are crystal clear and known by all.

Monitoring the project. Checking the task rather than checking on the person to whom you have delegated the task is a technique a good delegator must learn. This subtle difference goes a long way in developing trust and growth in your subordinates. Use a regular schedule of progress reports and meetings that apply to all your projects. By all means, move about your department with your eyes and ears open, but concentrate on finding strengths and successes, and not on ferreting out small weaknesses and failures. You are in the process of building trust and confidence, and this calls for concentrating on the positive aspects of your human resources.

The relative ease with which we can dissect the act of delegation should not minimize its complexities. This problem has been with us a long time and we are still trying to get it right.

WHY DELEGATE?

The benefits of delegation are twofold. They help the manager who delegates and they are crucial to the development of his or her subordinates. The overall strength and efficiency of the organization is enhanced.

Let's examine the benefits of the delegator first. Successful managers are paid not only for their administrative capability, but also for their innovations and influence. They are expected to handle the routing activities of their departments with aplomb, and to keep the wheels turning smoothly even during unexpected difficulties. But the real measure of their potential value to the organization is in their creativity and their ability to get things done through other people.

Time to hone these two elements can be made through successful delegating. Cutting down on your subordinates' demands on your time, and insisting that they bring you solutions rather than problems, can be a boon to your career. By providing yourself with blocks of subordinate-free time, you can give yourself opportunities to think, ponder and plan. If you want to progress, you must demonstrate that you can do more than you were hired to do, to think beyond the boundaries of your present position.

In conjunction with creativity, you must also display the means of carrying out these innovations smoothly and with as little friction as possible. Your influence, coupled with people skills, is important here. The art of delegation illustrates confidence in your subordinates and your trust that they can do the job. By keeping performance standards high, and letting people know that you truly expect them to be successful in meeting those standards, your influence will grow beyond your domain. Success breeds success, and you will be sought after as a winner who produces winners.

The other aspect of delegation benefits the subordinates. If they learn that you believe in them, that you will provide opportunities for growth and recognition, they will rise to meet your expectations. Your insistence that they face each challenge, that they learn to define problems accurately, search for the root cause, find the best possible solution, and present it to you with their plan of action, is the best managerial training they can have.

The act of delegating can broaden your subordinates' skills and experience. You can make them more valuable to themselves and to your organization. You can provide the climate of mutual trust and growth that nurtures each employee's motivation. Can you imagine the efficiency and productivity of a department wherein each and every member deals with problems as if they were his or her own, strives to meet the highest standards, and feels like a winner?

O'TOOLE'S LAW

Murphy's Law says that if it can go wrong, it will go wrong. O'Toole's Law says that Murphy was an optimist! So what can go wrong when you delegate? Quite a lot, actually, but don't give up hope.

The first step along the road to being a successful delegator is to realize that everything will seldom be easy, perfect and completely to your liking. Remember, someone else is going to do the job and you are going to let him or her take the hurdles by him or herself. Of course, there will be mishaps and disappointments, but they come with the territory, and properly managed they give us growth—in ourselves as well as in our subordinates.

As a manager, your trust is up front when you delegate. Don't be surprised if you have mixed feelings even about your most capable lieutenant. If he or she fails, your judgment is called into question, but if he or she succeeds too well, your own job security might be threatened. These ambivalent feelings are not unusual, and they are simply one more thing you must deal with in a managerial arena that is already filled with doubt, ambiguity and stress.

Your subordinate will also have his or her share of fear: fear of failure, fear of loss of approval, fear of the unknown. But the only way to progress is for both of you to accept these misgivings and begin the process. A helpful analogy can be to remember that kites don't rise with the wind, but against it.

DON'T DELEGATE ALL

In *The Practice of Management*, Peter Drucker sets forth areas of executive action that are management responsibilities that should not be delegated. Described below, they provide a helpful and effective guide for managers who want assistance in this area.

Setting objectives for the department. While subordinates are encouraged to devise their own objectives within the overall plans of the department, the department's objectives are the responsibility of the department head.

Organizing employees into an efficient team. Developing smooth teamwork within the department is an activity crucial to the overall departmental success, and thus must remain a function of the chief.

Motivation and communication. Motivation is intrinsic to the individual, but the manager provides the climate that helps it to blossom. By providing recognition, opportunities for achievement and growth, and designing jobs to foster these conditions, the manager, in essence, is motivating. Communication, which must include listening to employees, is also a necessary activity within the manager's responsibilities.

Checking and analyzing results. This element of the control function is a major managerial activity and can only be accomplished through monitoring the system. This does not imply lack of trust. On the contrary, a good control system allows for even more delegation since corrections can be routinely fed into the ongoing process without shocking the system. The National Aeronautics and Space Administration reports that its manned moon rockets were actually off course more than 80 percent of the journey but constant checking and analysis allowed for the corrections that brought the spacecraft down right on target each and every time.

Developing subordinate job skills in routine decision making. This, of course, is a reference to delegating and reinforces the point that delegating is an exclusive and ultimate responsibility of the manager, and responsibilities cannot be delegated away.

Sometimes an off-the-cuff self-appraisal of your capabilities as a delegator can be misleading. Most managers like to think they are doing well in this vital management function. Here are some exercises you can try to obtain a realistic view of your rating.

Draw up a list of the job responsibilities you would leave behind if you were to suddenly leave your job. Next, list the subordinates qualified to take over each of those responsibilities. If there is no one ready to take over a particular responsibility, leave a blank space. When the list is complete, add up the blank spaces and see what kind of a department you would leave if you were suddenly out of the picture.

Are you happy with what you see? Are those blank spaces representative of the shortcomings of your subordinates, their inexperience, or your own fear of being something less than indispensable? Answer each question honestly.

Draw up a list of duties that could be delegated but have not been. Write down the true reasons you have not delegated these duties, and be sure to burrow down to the root cause.

And, finally, from your position as a subordinate to your own chief, jot down a list of his or her duties. Which of these could be delegated to you, but are not? Devise a plan to make it easier for your boss to delegate these duties to you. What would you have to do? What would you have to change? When are you willing to begin?

These are tough questions indeed, but you'll need the answers often as you move through your career. Good delegators will always have an advantage in the organization because they will always have advocates both below and above them in the hierarchy. Their subordinates will relish the opportunity for experience, growth and recognition, and their superiors will value the people skills, integrity and creativity that delegation helps display. This is an enviable position to be in, so why not start today to become the best delegator you can be?

I. Thomas Sheppard, PhD, is associate professor of management and international business at the University of Texas, El Paso, Texas.

39.
Rx FOR IMPROVING STAFF EFFECTIVENESS

Vance F. Mitchell

Maintaining power over one's operations does not preclude the delegation of duties and responsibilities. It demands one have the time to spend on important departmental issues.

"I just can't please that man! He throws jobs at me with no explanation of what he wants. When I ask him for one, he just looks at me with disgust as if he expects me to have second sight. I try to do the best I know how but when I give him the finished product he'll find fault with it and then more often than not do it over himself. Other times he comes down on me like a ton of bricks because I haven't done something I didn't have a clue I was supposed to do! I tell you, it's driving me up the wall!"

The speaker is a young administration officer who recently completed the bank's training program and was assigned to a medium-sized neighborhood branch seven weeks ago. Now, let's tune in on his boss, the branch manager.

"I just don't know about these young people the bank is hiring these days. The regional training manager keeps bragging about how good their training program is but look at what they've turned out! I have to do over about a third of the work I ask him to do. I keep finding things he hasn't done that he should have and he keeps asking me how to do things that he could figure out if he had any common sense. His attitude is getting worse and it's rubbing off on the tellers. When they transferred my last admin I told them I wanted an experienced replacement, don't have time to train a green kid, but look what they gave me!"

What's up? Plenty! Unless some very positive changes take place soon in the relationship between these two individuals, the frustration both are experiencing is bound to reach the boiling point. The effectiveness of the branch's performance almost certainly will decline, and that won't help the manager's career. It's likely also that the young administration officer will quit; he will join the ranks of others who have become soured on banking as a career, and the bank's training investment will be lost.

Is this scenario exaggerated? No. I have heard variations of these themes repeatedly from managers and their subordinates in every line of business. How can unproductive, frustrating situations such as these be avoided?

The answer lies in training, coaching and delegation; not the inept, sink-or-swim approach used by the branch manager in our scenario, but a carefully thought out approach that is tailored to organizational requirements and to each subordinate's capabilities and experience.

Let's start by reviewing some basics and recognizing that most people want to do well in whatever they set out to do. Of course, "doing well" has a different meaning for different people. For those employees who have no long-term commitment to the job, but only hold on until they can get something better, doing well may mean no more than staying out of trouble. On the other hand, most managers and other longer-term employees aspire to more than merely getting by. In either case it is important to establish a working environment where people will see a direct link between the effort they expend on the job and effective performance, and further, that effective performance will be rewarded in ways that are meaningful to them. Fortunately, meaningful rewards are not limited to salary increases or promotion but include intangibles such as recognition of our competence and dependability, increased responsibility and greater autonomy in what we do. Successful managers skillfully use these intangible rewards to motivate their subordinates and help them develop their capabilities and at the same time make life easier on themselves.

MAINTAINING POWER AND CONTROL

Casual observation, interviews with managers, and common sense suggest that it is reasonable to expect managers to attempt to maintain their own power and discretion as much as possible. Each of us is judged by the results of those operations for which we are responsible, and we want to be able to control the behavior and processes of our subordinates in order to exert some control over the results and, hence, the evaluation others make of our performance.

Consequently, an important factor in the decision to delegate or not to delegate is how to maintain or increase power and control in the face of possible overloading. All managers are constrained by those above and below them and by their own capacity. Most managers, however, keep more power and control in their own hands than is necessary or effective. A good rule of thumb is to delegate those matters involving large amounts of time and small erosions of one's power base. In the banking industry the limits of discretion available to individuals at various levels are largely determined by higher authority. However, these formal limitations do not prevent retention of discretion at a higher level than that at which discretion could be exercised most effectively. Managers who follow this practice invariably find themselves overburdened and surrounded by subordinates who lack the capability to completely perform their own duties.

WHY MANAGERS DON'T DELEGATE

There are a number of reasons why managers are unwilling to give their subordinates the discretion to maintain control over the results of their performance.

Some of the most common reasons are:

1. Preference for operating
2. Demand that everyone "know all the details"
3. "I can do it better myself" fallacy
4. Lack of experience in the job or in delegating
5. Insecurity
6. Fear of being disliked
7. Refusal to allow mistakes
8. Lack of confidence in subordinates
9. Perfectionism leading to overcontrol
10. Lack of organization skill in balancing workloads
11. Failure to delegate authority commensurate with responsibility
12. Uncertainty over tasks and inability to explain
13. Disinclination to develop subordinates
14. Failure to establish effective controls and to follow up

Newly-promoted managers are among the most frequent offenders. There is a natural reluctance to let go of those tasks with which they are most familiar. This tendency is reinforced by initial lack of knowledge of their subordinates' capabilities and the desire that the functioning of their unit be viewed favorably by their superiors. Initial failure to delegate can easily become a habit, particularly if the manager has low self-esteem or feelings of insecurity. As overload builds up, these managers may adopt an erratic pattern of supervisory behavior similar to that illustrated in the opening scenario. These managers have lost sight of the fact that managing is in large part the art of getting things done through others.

TRAINING, COACHING AND DELEGATION

There is a natural tendency on the part of managers, many of whom have had little formal training, to place great emphasis on the value of learning through experience on the job. Training on the job is the most commonly used and can also be the most useful method of training; but it is also the most abused and thus, all too often, turns out to be the most unsuccessful. It is true that people learn best by doing, but the doing needs to be carefully planned and controlled in order to get full learning value from it. Too often, learning comes the hard way, through trial and error.

In theory, one of the great advantages of learning on the job is the avoidance of the transfer problem; learning in the work situation does not involve transfer as is the case with material learned in the classroom. Another advantage is that valid learning is immediately reinforced and rewarded, and invalid learning, quickly corrected. Regrettably, these advantages are not present as often as they ideally should be.

Horticulture provides the best analogy to illustrate the importance of the work setting to train and develop employees. Seeds thrown into a garden haphazardly without attention to the soil, the climate and the provision of food may grow. If they do, they do so accidentally and only the strongest survive totally inappropriate conditions. If, however, they are planted at the right time of the year, to the right depth and are provided with appropriate nutrients, a much higher proportion survive and produce flowers, fruit or vegetables. The task confronting managers therefore, is to be careful in providing the appropriate conditions—environment, climate and food—for their own human plants.

One of the most productive techniques for developing people is coaching. The annual performance review is commonly used to counsel employees as well as to assess them. Unfortunately, coaching is seldom undertaken on a day-to day basis. Any conversation between a manager and a subordinate about the job in general or about a particular task is a potent learning situation for both of them. It is the manager's responsibility to guide the discussion so that the subordinate learns all that the manager expects the employee to know.

MANAGERIAL STYLE

Effective coaching requires a particular managerial style that many managers find difficult to cultivate. The manager as coach must develop a relationship in which inquiry, collaboration and candor are encouraged. It has been found that the consultative managerial style is very effective in this respect. The manager who always tells and never consults learns little from subordinates and teaches even less. The coaching relationship should be that between university tutors and their students rather then that of military commanders. Those who are able to adopt such a style will not only gain the advantage of motivated employees who are eager to improve their skills (and not always aware that they are doing so) but will also benefit through having their own workload reduced by the contributions of their subordinates.

Helping people to help themselves is the essence of coaching. Several managers who successfully use this approach have said to me that the pleasure they get from seeing their subordinates grow has been one of the most satisfying aspects of their business careers.

Certainly, watching my graduate students increase their knowledge and skills is one of the most rewarding aspects of my work.

The major objection to coaching is the time required. Planning coaching sessions or making the most of them when they unexpectedly occur is seen by many managers as an imposition on a busy schedule and as spoon-feeding their subordinates. As previously suggested, part of the answer is that coaching can make a contribution to easing a manager's overloads. In my experience, managers could provide themselves with more time, and become more effective in a number of ways, if they assigned more tasks to their subordinates and delegated more work. Frequently, managers say that they cannot delegate more until their staff becomes more competent. Yet subordinates could effectively perform 90 percent of most tasks in any organization. If these tasks are passed on, the delegating manager has disposed of work which he or she does not need to do and thus gains time to spend on coaching or on other matters. If the extra ten percent really matters and the manager needs to provide that input, time will have been saved and an area identified where the subordinate needs further coaching.

A recurring problem is the "failure to communicate." The manager may not take time to define what is expected and the subordinate may not ask clarifying questions. Both parties should realize that delegation can entail implicit instructions, and each should know what is intended between them. The manager may in effect be issuing any one of the following instructions:

1. Look into this problem. Give me all the facts. I will decide what should be done.
2. Let me know all the alternatives available with the pros and cons of each. I will decide which to select.
3. Recommend a course of action for my approval.
4. Let me know what you intend to do. Don't act until I approve it.
5. Let me know what you intend to do. Do it unless I say not to.
6. Take action. Let me know what you did and the results.
7. Take action. Get back to me only if your action is unsuccessful.
8. Take action. No feedback to me is necessary.

When delegating, managers should be clear about what their expectations are. Clarity in initial instructions will save both time and embarrassment. Experienced managers take extra precautions to ensure that the intended message has been accurately received by asking for feedback to confirm understanding. After the pattern is defined, the supervisor should adhere to it consistently until the delegated task has been completed. Otherwise, subordinates will tend toward instructions 1, 2 and 3 because they will fear taking action for which they might be criticized.

Early experts on delegation recognized the importance of equating authority and responsibility. In addition, they stated that responsibility cannot be delegated. The delegator is always responsible for the actions of subordinates. One may ask: how is it possible to have authority equal responsibility if responsibility cannot be delegated?

The answer is that there are two forms of responsibility: operating responsibility and ultimate responsibility. Managers pass on operating responsibility which, in turn, may be delegated further, but ultimate responsibility cannot be delegated.

A final and crucial component of delegation is acceptance by subordinates of accountability for the tasks entrusted to them. By accountability we mean acceptance by the subordinate of a responsibility to the delegating manager to perform the task satisfactorily. In other words, responsibility is the obligation to do what is assigned, while accountability is the obligation to one's supervisor to do what is assigned in a satisfactory manner.

PROBLEM ANALYSIS

Between coaching and delegation is an area in which managers can both train and test subordinates for future delegation. This is the stage of problem analysis in which the manager presents a subordinate with a problem and asks for proposed solutions. The problem can be presented orally or more formally by asking for comments in writing. The object is both to obtain a solution to the problem and to encourage the subordinate to think on a wider plane and to test the viability of the ideas which emerge. Too often the answer to the complaint that office juniors do not think like managers is that they have never been asked to do so.

For the process to be effective, the manager should insist that the proposed solution be worked out in finished form. This requirement is difficult for inexperienced subordinates to accept initially. The impulse to ask their supervisor what to do recurs more often when the problem is difficult. It is so easy to ask what to do, rather than to study, write, restudy and rewrite until a single proposed solution emerges—the best of all that have been considered. One successful manager who routinely uses this approach summarizes his instructions to subordinates with "Bring me solutions, not problems." Further, a test of their proposals is whether or not the subordinates are prepared to stake their professional reputation on them. This manager has an enviable reputation within his bank for developing people who progress rapidly to positions of greater responsibility.

DEVELOPING PROMOTABILITY

Thus far we have been primarily concerned with the development of fully competent subordinates. However, managers have a further responsibility: to enhance, wherever possible, the promotability of their subordinates. Temporary delegation during a manager's absence provides an excellent opportunity for subordinates to practice the duties of the next higher level position. Coaching for such occasions should be provided as soon as people become competent in their own jobs. Unfortunately, the opportunity to fill supervisor positions during their absence is often not properly conceived and exploited as an opportunity for development. They say the true test of managers' skills is how well things go in their absence. Yet I frequently notice managers at training courses feeling compelled to contact their office two or even three times a day to check what is happening and issue instructions. These individuals should coach their subordinates before they leave and then keep hands off. Moreover, the appropriate question on return is not "What happened?" but "What did you learn?" While this course of action could prompt further coaching, it lessens the likelihood of serious errors being made. Subordinates will certainly have learned something of value from the experience and will have progressed one step closer to promotability.

The chief difference between these methods and those commonly practiced is that systematic development of subordinates is not generally planned. It has been demonstrated repeatedly, however, that managers who cultivate these skills have significantly less overload, more efffectively functioning units, and the satisfaction that comes from watching people remain motivated and grow.

Vance E. Mitchell is professor of organizational behavior and design at the University of British Columbia. His current research interests are the design and management of organizations, and program evaluation.

40.
HOW OFTEN DO EXECUTIVES DELEGATE CORRESPONDENCE?

Clifford J. Hurston, Jr.

What percentage of executives delegate some letterwriting, and what percentage say the time factor is their principal reason for delegating?

In our increasingly technological world, communication, one of the most important functions performed by businesspeople, has become more complex. The effectiveness with which today's businesspeople carry on their basic communication role determines to a great extent the ultimate success of their entire commercial operation.

Typically, the businessperson's basic communications include both written and spoken messages. About 90 percent of modern business transactions are handled by written communications. The written message, or the business letter, is the primary medium of external communication, whereas the memo is the primary medium of internal communication.

As a result of the vast amount of written communications in today's business world, the letter-writing responsibilities of business people have greatly increased. In addition, technology in word processing and dictation equipment has added a new and dynamic dimension to the importance of composing letters and memos.

To assist educators and businesspeople in improving their written communication practices and procedures, a survey was taken of 566 top commercial bank executives employed in 105 state and national banks located in the standard metropolitian areas of Montana, Idaho, Colorado, New Mexico, Arizona, Utah and Nevada. The survey was aimed at determining to what degree business executives (in this case bank executives) delegated letter-writing responsibilities, and asked the following questions:

1. What percentage of executives delegated some letter writing, and what percentage say the time factor is their principal reason for delegating?

2. What do executives identify as their strengths and weaknesses in letter writing?
3. What common characteristics do executives identify in those subordinates who handle most of the delegated writing?
4. What methods do executives use to improve the letter-writing skills of their subordinates?
5. What categories of business letters do executives most often delegate, and what categories do they most often write themselves?
6. What technical matters do executives delegate because they do not have the necessary background to write the letters themselves?
7. How much time, on the average, do executives spend each day in composing and dictating business letters, and what is their attitude toward composing and dictating activities?

Those with titles of president, vice president, junior or senior vice presidents, executive vice president, and chairman of the board (if they serve as either president or a vice president) were included in the list of executives.

Stratification was used to assure that all significant characteristics of the total population were represented in the sample. Four strata were divided according to the total bank deposits of each bank, ranging from $1 million to $1 billion.

The National Education Association random-sampling technique formula was used to determine the size of the random sample needed to draw conclusions. The computation using the NEA random-sampling technique formula indicated that a random sample of 283 bank executives was ideal for a total executive population of 1,068 (using the .05 level of confidence).

To secure the necessary data from the top bank executives, the mail questionnaire was used. Of the 566 who took the survey, 275 responses were used as the base.

Of the 275 respondents, 230, or 84 percent, delegated letter-writing responsibilities. The 45 non-delegating bank executives were affiliated with 30 of the 84 banks surveyed.

Of those delegating bank executives, 47 percent delegated less than a quarter of their letter-writing tasks. Another 21 percent delegated about 25 percent and only 16 percent delegated half or more of their letter-writing tasks.

"Ease workload" and "develop subordinate" were ranked first as reasons for delegating by more than two-thirds of the 230 executives. "Involve subordinate" was ranked second. "Ease workload" was ranked first as the main reason for delegating by the largest group of executives, 42 percent.

The most common reason given by the non-delegating executives for not delegating was "subordinates already overworked." This reason was given by 98 percent of the 45 non-delegators. Fifteen executives mentioned two other reasons for not delegating: "functional department handle letters routinely" and "need to keep on top of the situation myself."

"Knowledge of subject" was the letter-writing strong point listed most frequently, and it ranked first in total responses by both delegating and non-delegating executives. In contrast, "procrastination" was the executive's main letter-writing weakness. "Procrastination" ranked first in total responses, first by delegators and second by non-delegators. The most frequently listed writing weakness of the non-delegating executives was "readability." This was ranked second by delegating executives and in total responses.

The 230 delegating executives are involved in 31 different areas of responsibility. Forty-one percent indicated that their type of work increased opportunities for delegation; 35 percent said such opportunities were limited. Among the latter group, reasons for limitations were "specialized vocabulary" and "lack of technical information."

When not pressured by time, 68 percent of the delegating executives wrote more letters because they like to write. About a fifth delegated a few letters because they do not like to write. Interestingly, no executive delegated many letters because of a dislike for writing.

The largest percent of executives (40 percent of 275) spent a half-hour a day writing and dictating business letters. About a third spent about one hour daily in letter writing. The average time spent in writing and dictating letters was approximately three-fourths of an hour.

To conclude, a majority of executives do allow their subordinates to write their letters, but at different percentage levels.

SUBORDINATES AND LETTER WRITING

Alert executives realize that to carry out their responsibilities successfully, they must often depend upon the assistance of their subordinates.

A total of 34 percent of the executives delegated letter-writing tasks to all or most of their subordinates, and 50 percent of the executives delegated to "a few" of their subordinates.

As to whether the delegators are satisfied, 51 percent and 45 percent were "nearly always" and "usually" satisfied with the letters written by their subordinates. Two percent were "sometimes" satisfied, and 1 percent were "always" satisfied.

When the executives evaluated the letters written by their subordinates, "accomplishment of objective" was ranked first in importance by 76 percent of the respondents. Fifty-one percent mentioned "clear message," and ranked it second as the quality sought when evaluating the delegated letters. "Lack of clarity" was ranked first by half the executives as subordinates most serious letter-writing mistake, and "failure to anticipate the reader's reaction" was ranked second by 34 percent.

Along these lines, approximately one-third of the 230 delegating executives asked their subordinates to enroll in a letter-writing course to help them improve the quality of their assigned letters. And, nearly three-fourths of the delegators stated they studied the delegated letters and discussed the subordinates' letter-writing problems with them.

The main reason why 60 percent of the delegating executives trust their subordinates with their letter writing is because they are "well informed." Ranking second was "trustworthy."

DELEGATING BY TYPES OF LETTERS

The survey included six classifications of delegated business letters: personal-business, good news, bad news, interoffice memorandums, letters involving large sums of money, and confidential.

Personal-business letters were delegated at some time by over half of the executives. Good news or "yes" letters were "always," "nearly always," or "sometimes" delegated by 70 percent of the executives. In contrast, bad news or "no" letters were "nearly always" or "sometimes" delegated by 35 percent. None of the respondents "always" delegated bad news letters as compared with 27 percent who "never" delegated them.

Interoffice memorandums are business letters used primarily within the organization. A hefty 78 percent "always," "nearly always" or "sometimes" delegated them.

Letters involving large sums of money were "sometimes" delegated by almost half; "seldom" by 31 percent; and "never" by 17 percent. Regarding confidential letters, the majority of the executives, 65 percent, "never" delegated them, and 17 percent "sometimes" or "seldom" did.

Looking at the extremes, interoffice memorandums were delegated at some time by 95 percent, the largest percentage group, of the bank executives. In contrast, the smallest percentage group, 34 percent, delegated confidential letters at some time.

As far as writing their own letters, 38 percent of the executives stated their major reason for writing letters in longhand was to save time because of a brief message. The second reason given most frequently was to give letters a personal touch. Perhaps most significant, almost half said they "never" wrote letters in longhand.

"Content" of the letter was generally the main concern of the executives when considering their strong and weak letter-writing qualities, as well as those of their subordinates.

In conclusion, the majority of businesspeople do allow some of their subordinates to compose their letters, but to whom and how many depends upon the following reasons:

- The nature of the message of the letter—good news, bad news, confidential news, etc.
- The writing ability of the subordinates
- The selection procedure for hiring subordinates
- The complexity of the business transaction involved
- The availability of the businessperson's time
- The subordinates' knowledge of the subject

Executives should consider providing more opportunities for delegating letter-writing tasks, even though they may enjoy writing, in order to develop subordinates' letter-writing skill. A subordinate who is well trained in writing letters of all types can easily prove to be one of the greatest assets the businessperson could have.

Clifford J. Hurston, Jr., is professor of business communications of the College of Business Administration at Arizona State University, Tempe, Arizona.

41.
A MANAGER'S GUIDE TO EFFICIENT TIME MANAGEMENT

Warren Schilit

Learn to avoid the manager's dilemma: too little time, too many tasks.

There is one aspect of the manager's job about which most managers agree: There is never enough time to complete all necessary and expected tasks. The typical workday of most managers is hectic. Managers must continually make decisions on a wide range of matters in a minimal amount of time.

How do successful managers develop techniques for effective time management? They learn to prioritize strategically, plan effectively, delegate sufficiently, use discretionary time and avoid procrastination. Successful managers also recognize that management is a time-consuming activity; time is their most precious resource. By managing his or her time wisely, both the manager and the organization will benefit. Specifically, evidence suggests that effective time management may result in:

- a greater likelihood of the organization meeting its objectives efficiently
- greater devotion to important long-run managerial activities, rather than to short-run issues
- improved job-related interpersonal activities
- better developed managers as a result of delegation
- reduced tension, anxiety, and stress, and better physical and mental health

Clearly, effective time management involves much more than developing a simple written list of priorities. Any manager about to embark on a concerted effort at time management must address two key issues:

1. What are the limits of my time and how can I provide myself with more time to accomplish my goals?
2. How can I best use my discretionary time?

VALUABLE ADVICE

I am reminded of the story of Ivy Lee, a consultant, who was dining with Charles Schwab, then chairman of Bethlehem Steel Company.[1] Schwab presented Lee with an unusual challenge: "Show me a way to get more things done with my time, and I'll pay you any fee within reason." Lee suggested that every morning Schwab should write down his six most important tasks for the following day, in order of priority. Then, every morning he should start working on item one and continue until finished with that item; then start on item two, etc. At the end of the day, Schwab was to tear up the list and start again.

Shortly thereafter, Schwab sent Lee a check for $25,000, explaining that Lee's lesson was one of the most profitable he had ever learned. Schwab said this lesson was largely responsible for Bethlehem Steel's transformation into the largest independent steel producer in the world.

On the surface, Mr. Lee's advice seems simple and quite useful. However, there is one major weakness with it: No manager controls all of his time. Managers must deal with interruptions and emergencies. Managers are constantly faced with both the demands of their bosses—about which they often have little or no say—as well as those of their subordinates. An effective manager must therefore delegate certain assignments to subordinates in order to free himself for other activities and ensure that subordinates are not "delegating" their responsibilities to him.

THE DELEGATION BONUS

An important feature of delegation is that it develops managers and opens channels of communication. Managers should emphasize these developmental aspects of delegation. Delegation is most successful when the manager provides a supportive environment and gives subordinates the necessary feedback and directions to accomplish the task. In general, the subordinate should handle predictable tasks, while the manager should tackle exceptional ones. Furthermore, managers should assign relatively important but less urgent matters to more competent subordinates and the less important (but possibly urgent) matters to less competent or less experienced subordinates.[2]

Managers often complain that they are running out of time while their subordinates are running out of work. Actually, this is largely due to subordinates taking up the manager's time with their problems. In some cases the supervisor is "working" for the subordinate, rather than vice-versa.

Managers must recognize when their time is being consumed by subordinates. Oftentimes, this occurs when the subordinate greets the manager and says, "By the way we've got a problem." When a manager tells a subordinate, "Drop me a memo" or "Just let me know how I can help," the manager is placing the burden on himself, rather than on the subordinate, as the manager must ultimately respond. (It is therefore advantageous for managers to meet with subordinates in person or contact them by telephone, instead of communicating with them via mail or memos.) In the above cases, what starts as a joint problem eventually falls on the supervisor alone.[3]

To avoid having his or her time consumed by subordinates, the manager must install certain ground rules:

1. When the manager is helping a subordinate, the problem must remain the subordinate's problem; if it becomes the manager's problem, he or she clearly cannot help the subordinate as the subordinate no longer has a problem.
2. Any subordinate's problem entering the manager's office must leave the office as the subordinate's problem.

Thus, managers must recognize that their time is partly controlled by their superiors and by the organization itself; a manager's own time is, therefore, quite limited. Certainly, managers can uncover some time by delegating. All too often, though, another problem arises: subordinates' demands. This problem can only be prevented or controlled by ensuring that a subordinate's problem always remains his or her own rather than that of the manager.

USE OF DISCRETIONARY TIME

Given the limited amount of time that managers have, how can managers use that time most efficiently? Clearly, managers have significantly more control over the use of time than over the amount of time they possess.

Managers must first recognize that several factors are responsible for wasting their time: office factors—for example, meetings, visitors and telephone interruptions; organizational factors—for example, fuzzy objectives, personal disorganization, and unclear roles; information factors—for example, inadequate information and communication; personal factors—for example, procrastination, indecision and poor self-discipline.

Once he or she realizes that time is often lost due to the four factors noted above the manager can take several steps to utilize time more efficiently. Some of the most useful suggestions include:

Get organized. As a first step, clean up your desk and files in order to reduce the amount of time needed to search for things. File papers away neatly after using them in order to save time later on. Avoid having an in-basket; it just gets in the way. Throw out all unnecessary papers. Ask yourself, "What would be the worst thing to happen if this paper or file were thrown out?"

Clarify objectives. Know what is expected of you in order to avoid duplication and wasted effort. This involves good goal-setting and communication practices, key aspects of time management. Don't attempt too much at once; this often leads to disorganization.

Establish priorities. First, you must know how you are presently spending your time, so establish a time log to record your activities. Then, ask yourself, "What does not have to be done?" and "What can be done by others?" For activities that must be performed by you, prioritize six or seven tasks and allocate time for the two tasks with the highest priorities. If time allows, proceed to items three, four and so on. Realize, however, that you must make trade-offs—for example, work versus pleasure—when establishing priorities.

Shuffle your paperwork. Avoid cluttering your desk with correspondence. If possible, examine a single piece of paper only once, then act on it (if at all possible), forward it or file it in a date file that insures you will act on it on a given date in the future.

Combine tasks. Group similar tasks together whenever possible. For example, respond to all correspondence between 3 p.m. and 4 p.m.; answer all phone calls between 1 p.m. and 2 p.m.

Break up tasks. If you're having trouble getting started—for example, if you are procrastinating—break each task up into smaller tasks. Don't write a book; write chapters or sections.

Use tidbits of time. Make efficient use of tidbits of time, waiting time in offices, etc. One time management consultant suggests that you always carry three kinds of folder: one manila, containing current response items such as letters; one pink, for materials on discretionary projects under way; and one blue, for future activities or new ideas.[4] When in peak form, go through the ideas in the blue folder and decide which ones should be transferred to the pink folder. If the tidbit is brief, just go through the items in the manila folder.

Recognize your productive hours. If you're a morning person, do your most demanding work—perhaps problem-solving—in the morning. Do not spend that time with routine correspondence.

Reduce interruptions and time leaks. Establish a quiet period in the office (preferably during your most productive hours) during which time you will not schedule meetings, accept phone calls, etc. In addition, rearrange your desk so your back is facing the door, in order to avoid interruptions. Cut down on time wasters—lengthy coffee breaks and lunches, chit chat, etc. Recognize that if you're earning $40,000 per year, and if you waste a total of just one-half hour per day, it will cost your company more than $2,500 over the course of the year.

Avoid perfectionism. Become results-oriented, but recognize the trade-off between efficiency and perfection. As suggested by Sir Simon Marks, former chairman of the Marks and Spencer retailing chain, "the price of perfectionism is prohibitive."[5]

Learn to say "no." One management consultant suggests that saying "no" is the most effective and frequent time saving technique.[6] However, avoid using this technique too often with your boss.

Reward yourself. If you've accomplished your objectives, or if you've been successful in using your time more efficiently, reward yourself.

ONLY GUIDELINES

In examining the above rules, keep in mind that personal characteristics of the manager—such as being disorganized or being absentminded—may prevent these suggestions from being carried out. Furthermore, some managers do not sense any urgency to manage their time. In such instances, time management efforts will have only minimal success.

Although the above rules are intended to assist managers to better use their time, they cannot ensure that managers or organizations will be successful. There are many successful organizations which are managed by individuals who use their time very inefficiently. The key to effective organizational success is the organization's ability to adapt and to make proper decisions in the face of uncertainty. Most importantly, therefore, these techniques do not provide managers with solutions, but rather provide them with the sorely needed time to solve complex organizational problems.

References

1. Webber, Ross, *To Be a Manager* (New York: Richard D. Irwin, Inc., 1981).
2. Webber.
3. Oncken, Jr., William and Donald L. Wass, "Management Time: Who's Got the Monkey?" *Harvard Business Review* (November-December 1974), pp. 75-80.
4. Webber.
5. Dubrin, Andrew, *Contemporary Applied Management* (Dallas, Texas: Business Publications, Inc., 1981).
6. Bliss, Edwin, *Getting Things Done: The ABC's of Time Management* (New York: Charles Scribner & Sons, 1977).

Warren K. Schilit is assistant professor of business policy, School of Management, Syracuse University, Syracuse, New York.

42.

DELEGATE YOUR WAY TO SUCCESS

Eugene Raudsepp

Most managers admit, when pressed, that they don't delegate as much as they should. The problem is probably more emotional than procedural.

Most managers accept the premise that the best way to get their work done is to make optimum use of subordinates. Yet most managers admit, when pressed, that they don't delegate as much as they should.

The problem is probably more emotional than procedural. Effective delegation is, admittedly, one of the most difficult managerial tasks. It depends on the finely woven interrelationship among the manager, subordinates and top management. It depends on the type of company and its goals. It also depends heavily on trust and confidence. But the biggest problem is that many managers, as they climb the executive ladder, continue to feel that if they want a job done right, they have to do it themselves.

A manager who delegates with intelligence and consistent follow-up can accomplish far more than the manager who hugs to his (or her) bosom the tasks his subordinates should be doing. The manager should devote most of his time and energy to planning, supervising and delegating. That way, he'll contribute more than he might even if he does a superlative job on tasks that his subordinates really might not do quite as well. Inadequate delegation limits a manager's effectiveness because he gets bogged down in detail. Carried to its logical extreme, nondelegation can bring operations almost to a standstill.

When a manager delegates successfully, he changes his role from a performer to a trainer, motivator and evaluator. Through delegation, he develops initiative and self-starting ability in his subordinates. He broadens them on their jobs, increases production and improves morale. Most employees strive to live up to what is expected of them. They are willing and eager to face challenges, knowing that they are expected to deliver.

WHAT IS DELEGATION?

Delegation is simply the passing on, by one person to another, of responsibility for a given task. But effective delegation involves a great deal more.

267

Delegation is not the abdication of responsibility; it is a continuing process. The manager should always be available to give advice and assistance when needed. He should make sure that needed resources are available, check performance at agreed-upon dates, and generally remain involved as advisor, leader and sharer of responsibility. He should keep checks and controls on every task he delegates. The degree and kind of control varies, of course, with each subordinate. Some subordinates resent overcontrol and do a good job without frequent checking. Others need the security of formalized periodic reports on their assignments. Either way, there's no excuse for suddenly discovering that a subordinate is not handling his assignment properly.

Effective delegation requires patience and an initial investment of time. "I could have done the job myself twice over for all the time I spent explaining the work to him," is a frequently voiced excuse for not delegating. This may be true, especially with new subordinates. But the time expended is bound to pay off in the long run.

Delegation should not be viewed as an opportunity to get rid of unpleasant jobs or jobs in which the manager is not proficient. Also, it's a mistake to delegate too many meaningless or make-work jobs, especially during slack periods. This is a transparent maneuver, one that could lead the subordinate to look on all future delegated tasks as unimportant.

HELPS EMPLOYEES DEVELOP

Ideally, delegation should help a subordinate develop not only his skills but also his judgment. He must understand what kinds of decisions he has the authority to make. If his authority to make decisions is too restricted, he will infer a lack of confidence in his ability to handle responsibility. If a subordinate is to be held accountable, he or she must have responsibility and authority with a minimum of interference. Effective delegation includes the right to make decisions and mistakes.

Delegation requires meticulous planning, particularly if complex or difficult projects are involved. It entails establishing priorities, setting objectives, and deciding how the project should be accomplished and by whom, how long it should take, and how well it should be done. This type of planning isn't easy, and some managers tend to avoid it.

There are dozens of reasons why managers do not delegate. Those given here are the most common, but they can be countered.

Lack of confidence in subordinates. Fearing unsatisfactory results, a manager may reason that a subordinate's judgment might be faulty, or that he will not follow through on his chores. He may feel that the subordinate is too young to command the respect and cooperation of older workers.

Such a manager feels that he must keep track of every detail to get a job done right. He may be a perfectionist who sets high personal standards of performance. He is often tempted to perform a job himself, feeling that he can do the work better and more quickly than his subordinates. Such an attitude must be shunned unless the lack of confidence in a subordinate is based on past experience.

Lack of self-confidence. Many managers, especially those recently promoted or hired, feel insecure in their jobs and in their relationships with their superiors, peers and subordinates. They may feel overwhelmed by their new duties and responsibilities. As a result, they regress to the pleasant and familiar security and routine of the work they did before they became managers.

Poor definition of duties. A manager must have a clear understanding of his responsibilities and authority. Obviously, he can delegate only those responsibilities that have been assigned to him. If he is unsure of the nature of his own job, he can hardly be expected to delegate properly.

Aversion to risk-taking. Delegation involves making calculated risks. Even with clear communication and instructions, proper controls and trained subordinates, something will eventually go wrong.

Fear of subordinates as competitors. This frequently leads to open and excessive criticism of a subordinate's work, thwarting or playing down his achievements, pitting him against another subordinate to put him in a bad light, ignoring or side-tracking his suggestions and ideas, and concealing his talent or misusing it in low-skill jobs.

An inflated self-image. Some managers believe that they are the pivot upon which all their department's operations turn. This type of manager, as a rule, checks on all details himself. He makes all the decisions, and considers his way of doing things the only right one. He goes to great pains to hire people who reinforce his image of himself. To protect his "kingpin" posture, he makes certain, through selective communication, that only he gets the big picture of what is going on.

The effect that the "indispensable" manager has on his subordinates can be devastating. He fosters only dependence. Whatever self-confidence and individuality his subordinates may have had is soon obliterated; they become automatons who follow only directions and never initiate ideas of their own. Eventually, stronger subordinates become restive. They realize that their growth potential is severely stunted and that the only wise course of action is to resign and go on to a place where they can grow.

Equating action with productivity. A manager may be hyperactive. Such a person is often afraid that delegation might leave him with nothing to do. Quite commonly, a hyperactive manager complains constantly about overwork, and subordinates have a difficult time getting to see him.

Fear of appearing lazy. Delegation might be construed, by both superiors and subordinates, as trying to avoid working. This can be a sensitive point. A manager, particularly a new one, or one who is unsure of his own talents, can also feel that it is a sign of weakness to need subordinates' help to keep up with workloads.

Poor example. A common reason a manager does not delegate is that his superior did not delegate. The reasoning is, "If my boss got to where he is with his style of leadership, why shouldn't I copy him?"

Many young or newly promoted managers who have been held back by their own superiors in the past do not delegate because they want to keep the reins in their own hands, as a protective device.

ANALYZING SUBORDINATES

A prime requisite for effective delegation is a comprehensive inventory of subordinates' capabilities, skills, qualifications, experience, special talents, interests, motivations, attitudes, potential and limitations.

Such analyses, which should include meetings with subordinates to get their own estimation of their abilities and aspirations, enables the manager to decide which subordinates he can delegate to immediately, and which need further coaching and experience.

Here are a few ways to make delegation easier for all concerned.

Be sure you and your supervisor agree on what your job is. Take all the initiative you can without encroaching on others' rights. A narrow definition of your job restricts you.

Be sure your subordinates understand what you expect them to do. The simplest way to delegate is to tell your subordinates what authority you reserve for yourself. It may help to list matters you want discussed with you before any action is taken.

Prepare written policies your subordinates can use to guide their decisions. A soundly conceived and clearly understood set of policies lets subordinates make decisions and take action with confidence.

Be humble enough to admit that someone else may be able to do the job as well as you can.

Make as many subordinates as possible directly responsible to you. This will help you communicate, make decisions take action and exercise control.

Make subordinates responsible for accomplishing results rather than activities. Once the expected results are spelled out, the subordinate should be able to choose methods he will use in accomplishing them.

Reward those who get things done. Subordinates will accept responsibility and actively participate in accomplishing objectives only if they feel that rewards go to those who perform. The rewards for being right must always be greater than the penalties for being wrong.

Distinguish between rush jobs and the less immediate but more important things you have to do; spend more time on the important tasks than the trivial ones.

Self-questioning can ease the decision of what and how much to delegate. For example:

- How important is the decision? Are the stakes so high that a mistake cannot be tolerated? If so, the matter probably cannot be delegated successfully.
- Even though you are more competent than your subordinates, are you as close to the problem? Is your decision more apt to be right?
- Does your failure to delegate mean that you are not giving adequate attention to other more important parts of your job?
- Does your failure to delegate mean you are not developing your subordinates? Are they capable of being developed? If not, can they be transferred or replaced?
- What do top managers really expect of you? Are they measuring you principally by results, so that your decisions must be right? Do they really expect you to develop people?

The art of delegation is a difficult one to learn, but it's a vital management skill. If you do it right, you'll improve employees' morale, get more work done, and ease the burden on yourself.

HOW MUCH IS ENOUGH?

You can get a good idea of whether you are delegating as much as you should by answering the following questions. The more "Yes" answers you give, the more likely it is that you're not delegating enough.

- Do you often work overtime?
- Do you take work home evenings and on weekends?
- Is your pile of unfinished work increasing?
- Do you find that daily operations are so time-consuming that you have little time left over for planning and other important matters?
- Do you feel you have to have close control of every detail to get the job done right?
- Do you frequently find yourself bogged down, trying to cope with a morass of small details?
- Do you frequently have to postpone long-range projects?
- Are you harassed by frequent unexpected emergencies in your department?
- Is a good part of your working day spent on tasks your subordinates could do?
- Do you lack confidence and respect for your subordinates' abilities to shoulder more responsibilities?
- Do you understand what your responsibilities and authority are?

- Do you find yourself irritable and complaining when the work of your group doesn't live up to expectations?
- Do you find that your subordinates never show any initiative?
- Are friction and low morale characteristic of your work group?
- Do your subordinates defer all decisions on problems to you?
- Are policies to guide your subordinates in making decisions ambiguous?
- Do you instruct your subordinates to perform certain activities, rather than to accomplish certain results?
- Have subordinates stopped coming to you to present their ideas?
- Do operations slow down considerably when you are away from your job?
- Do you feel that you're abdicating your role as a manager if you have to ask your subordinates' assistance in order to complete your projects?
- After delegating a project, do you breathe down the subordinate's neck?
- Do you believe that your status and the salary you earn automatically mean that you have to be overworked?

Eugene Raudsepp is the president of Princeton Creative Research, Inc., Princeton, New Jersey. Mr. Raudsepp is the author of Creative Growth Games *and* More Creative Growth Games.

43.

TIME: A MANAGER'S MOST IMPORTANT ASSET

Dennis E. Miller

When a subordinate confronts you with a problem, listen, acknowledge the problem, and then ask, "What do you think might be the best solution?" The amount of time this one step will save is unbelievable.

How many times have you heard the following remarks: "I just could not find the time…" "I ran out of time" "If I only had the time to…" "There are just not enough hours in the day to…"

The more I hear a manager complain about his or her lack of time, the more I become concerned about the person's style of management. Time is a manager's most valuable asset, and it worries me that little effort is expended on saving it.

In most firms, all assets, whether they be accounts receivable, inventory, cash or equipment, are carefully checked each month. If errors or discrepancies are found, steps are immediately taken to bring the particular element "up to par." How many managers look as carefully at the way they and their subordinates use time as they look at the other assets under their control? Is the use of time efficient, productive or wasteful? Is unproductive time slowly strangling the department's productivity, or is effective time management practiced so employees' contributions are enhanced? Someone once told me that killing time is only a nice way of saying that time is really killing us. If time management is a weakness with you, or your employees, it's time that you did something about it. There are techniques for managing time that can give you from 20 to 40 percent more time with which to handle your managerial responsibilities.

ENHANCING YOUR TIME

The world of ineffective time management is made up of endless deadlines and surprises, traps and interruptions, sleepless nights and half-done tasks, phone calls not returned, letters not written, promotions and raises not received. But your life doesn't have to be like this. By prioritizing your workload, you can run your work instead of your work running you.

First, list your tasks on a daily basis, and on a weekly basis if possible. By this I mean that you should actually write out what you need to do each day. Spend 15 to 20 minutes at night or in the morning making a daily list. You may have five, ten, or 20 items on it. Keep writing until all the things you should do are covered.

For each item on your completed list, ask the question, "Is this something I must do, or can someone else do it?" If someone can perform a task or do a project, why not let them? Part of a manager's responsibility is to train and develop people. If you constantly do things that staff members could do, you are not only inhibiting your performance as a manager but stifling the creativity of your subordinates. Draw a line through the items that can be delegated. This will leave you with a reduced list of tasks for the next day. (If you have never used this approach, you will be surprised to find out how many items can be delegated.)

Next, prioritize the remaining items. Use a "1" for the most urgent, and "2" for the next, and so on, until all the items are covered. Identify any meetings or other time constraints that may require changing your priorities and adjust the list accordingly. Now you have your completed list.

The next day, act upon it. Start with the first job and stay with it until it is finished, then go to the second, and so on. The self-discipline involved may be hard to find at first, but stick with it. If used daily, this method will work and it will produce results that you won't believe.

At the end of the day, take a few minutes to prepare your list for the next day. On your current list, check off all the items that you have finished. The remaining ones, plus new tasks, will make up your new list. List them, take out any tasks that can be delegated, and prioritize the rest.

Over time, you will notice the low-priority items at the bottom of your list usually stay there continually. You can do one of two things with these items. Delegate them or forget them. Research indicates that ten to 15 percent of the tasks on your list can be eliminated.

You might want to consider keeping a file of your daily lists. Periodically reviewing the lists of the last few weeks can safeguard against forgetting or not completing a required task. This review will also help you determine how you spend most of your time. I know some people who even put the number of hours spent beside each item to help them better manage their time. One's goal should be to make the most effective use of time.

DELEGATION

Delegation, as noted earlier, can play an important role in achieving this objective.

Once you've identified all those tasks on your daily to-do list that can be delegated, write them down on another piece of paper. If you have an assistant with a staff, simply hand over the list and let him or her oversee the process of delegating the tasks to staff members. This, of course, assumes that the individual has been given the proper training. If you personally must delegate the work to staff members, be sure to delegate complete tasks, not just portions. Your objective is to save time while giving your subordinates the chance to develop, and delegating only half-way and/or constantly checking your employees' progress won't accomplish much.

As a means of controlling the work, set time limits, and, when possible, discuss the progress of each task at regular staff meetings preplanned and scheduled for everyone's convenience.

In delegating the work, take into consideration staff members' strengths and weaknesses, likes and dislikes. Tasks that are of an entrepreneurial type or that are non-routine, delegate to employees with judgment and creativity. Tasks that are routine or clear cut, give to the doers. Failure to consider the ability of the delegates to do the tasks can cause you to spend precious time "undoing" something that could have been done right the first time by the right employee.

Needless to say, in delegating work to staff members, you will be showing them you have faith in them. The more trust and confidence you display, the more willing they will be to put forth extra effort when it is needed. Letting employees work independently is also the best way to break down any communication barriers that may exist between you and your employees, and it is an excellent form of on-the-job training. Subordinates should be allowed to make errors as long as they are not of monumental proportions.

HANDLING INTERFERENCE

No matter how well organized you are, there will always be emergency phone calls, rush projects, special assignments, and the like—interferences with your plans. A skillful manager can learn how to handle these interruptions with a minimum of effort and time delay. They do not have to frustrate or create havoc.

Here are some ways to minimize the effect of these interferences.

First, have your secretary screen all incoming phone calls. You should make a sincere effort never to answer the phone yourself. Have your secretary accept calls only from individuals you know, or are expecting to hear from. Surprise calls of any nature, whether by phone or in person, should be put off by asking the caller either to make an appointment or leave some information and a number for a return call.

You can set aside a specific period each day, say 30 to 45 minutes, to return all calls. Stick to this plan. Unless it is an unusual circumstance, have your secretary inform callers that they will hear from you then.

To avoid last-minute surprises, try to maintain good enough communication with your superiors so you are notified well in advance of any special assignments, meetings, or other activities. It is to everyone's advantage that surprises be kept to a minimum.

One trap that managers easily fall into, especially new managers, is spending too much time handling subordinates' problems and questions, leaving little time for the managers' own work.

When a subordinate confronts you with a problem, listen, acknowledge the problem, and then ask, "What do you think might be the best solution? Let me know and we can discuss it then." It is important that your people know that you are there to help, but you shouldn't allow them to lean on you. Teach them problem-solving techniques, and remind them, in a diplomatic manner, that you do not want to hear about any problem unless they have a possible solution or solutions to offer at the same time. They will never learn and develop the necessary skills to move into management if you solve all their problems for them. The amount of time this one step will save is unbelievable.

Dennis E. Miller is district controller for S.I.I. Dyna Drill.

Part VI
PROCRASTINATION: A SERIOUS TRANSGRESSION

44.
HOW TO CONQUER
PROCRASTINATION

Merrill E. Douglass

Procrastination is a costly and draining problem for all of us. The easiest way to deal with procrastination is to never let it get started in the first place.

Procrastination plagues all of us. More plans go astray, more dreams go unfulfilled, more time is wasted by procrastination than by any other single thing. Procrastination is a major stumbling block for almost everyone seeking to improve his use of time. For many, procrastination becomes an insidious habit that can ruin their careers, destroy their happiness, and even shorten their lives.

Procrastination is respectful of no one: All of us suffer from it at one time or another. Procrastination is doing low priority actions or tasks rather than higher priority ones. Procrastination is straightening your desk when you should be working on that report; watching TV when you should be exercising; having another martini when you should get back to the office; calling on the friendly customer who buys very little when you should be preparing a sales presentation for that tough prospect who could buy much more; avoiding a co-worker rather than telling him bad news; staying away from the office to avoid disciplining a subordinate; and postponing activities with your children, because there always seems to be something "more urgent," until suddenly they're grown and you realize it's too late to do any of the things you've always talked about doing together.

Procrastination prevents success. How? Success comes from doing the really important things critical to obtaining results. And these essentials are most subject to procrastination, for we seldom seem to procrastinate about unimportant things. If we could only learn to shift our procrastination from important to unimportant matters, our problem would disappear!

One reason for this habit of postponing what's important is our tendency to confuse the important with the merely urgent, to which we are constantly responding. Important matters are seldom urgent unless they are allowed to reach the crisis state. By responding to the urgent—and postponing the important—we guarantee continual crises in our lives.

HABIT AND INERTIA

To conquer procrastination it is necessary to understand two important elements. The first is habit. Procrastination breeds procrastination. Much of what we do, the way we approach things, even the way we think, is based on habit. This is certainly the case with procrastination. To overcome it will undoubtedly require changing some habits. But which ones? Analyze your habits and make a list of all the things on which you tend to procrastinate, then note patterns and look for revealing symptoms.

The second important element is inertia. From physics we learn that a body at rest tends to remain at rest. It takes greater force, or energy, to start movement than to sustain it. To conquer procrastination you must overcome your inertia; then you will find that, once begun, action is much more likely to continue. It's the beginning that is difficult.

THE THREE CAUSES OF PROCRASTINATION

Much of our procrastination can be traced to three causes. We tend to procrastinate what's unpleasant, difficult, or makes us feel indecisive. Yet these are usually the very things that contribute most to our effectiveness and success.

A variety of techniques can be applied to deal with each of these three areas.

Unpleasantness

Let's first tackle procrastination caused by unpleasant tasks. For most people, this is the greatest single cause of procrastination. But there's a paradox in postponing unpleasant tasks. On the one hand, it's an attempt to make life easier by avoiding unpleasantness. On the other hand, procrastinating the task actually increases unpleasantness, since the job still has to be done.

Some people find that the best way to handle unpleasant tasks is to do them first. Try scheduling your most unpleasant tasks—the ones you tend to procrastinate most often—at the very beginning of your day. Tell your secretary you won't be taking any phone calls from 9 a.m. to 10 a.m. Do the distasteful first and get it behind you, rather than dreading it and continually putting it off.

It also helps to consider the cost of delay. If a task must eventually be done, the actual work may expand with procrastination. Waiting until the last possible minute forces you to work under increased pressure. The longer you wait, the greater the number of things that can go wrong. A typical example is the executive who puts off doing a report until the last minute, then his secretary comes down with the flu.

Procrastination sometimes creates crises for others. Tempers flare. Unkind words are exchanged. Anxiety increases. You become depressed and frustrated with the whole thing. No one works well under these conditions. The quality of your actions is bound to suffer, and you dislike yourself. There are other, long-term costs of delay, which are often more difficult to recognize. Here are some examples:

- Delay answering an inquiry and you may lose a customer.
- Delay servicing a machine and you may have a costly breakdown.
- Delay developing new products and your competitors will have them first.
- Delay going to the dentist and you may learn to live with false teeth.
- Delay exercising and you may shorten your life.
- Delay making a will and your heirs will struggle with difficulties and red tape for years.
- Delay doing the things that are really important to you and you lose out on the richness you might otherwise add to your life.

Considering the costs of delay is sometimes enough to get you moving. When tempted to procrastinate, stop and think for a moment: What problems am I likely to create for myself? If you don't want to live with those problems, don't procrastinate.

Try analyzing each unpleasant task. What exactly makes it unpleasant? Learn to confront the unpleasantness and deal with it directly. For example, many people challenge themselves to do at least one thing they dread every month.

Sometimes it helps to tackle unpleasant tasks in small pieces, doing the task for five or ten minutes with the agreement that you'll quit after that period. You may find once you get moving that it's not so unpleasant after all. And even if you do quit in five minutes, you're still gaining on the task. For example, consider that report you haven't written yet. One way to get started is to begin making notes on the points you need to cover. Or if you've been planning to start that new exercise program the doctor recommended but the thought of all that work is too much, don't focus on an hour at a time. Begin with five minutes. Or if you're still putting off washing all the windows in your home, recognize that in five minutes you can wash one.

A very important precept to bear in mind when you have an unpleasant job to do is Pareto's principle: The majority of the value is accounted for by a minority of the elements. This is also called the 80/20 rule: 80 percent of the value comes from 20 percent of the items, while the remaining 20 percent of the value comes from 80 percent of the items. Some have called this the concept of the important few and the trivial many. Thus, 80 eighty percent of sales come from 20 percent of the product line; 80 percent of employee problems come from 20 percent of the employees; 80 percent of the complaints come from 20 percent of the customers; and 80 percent of your interruptions come from 20 percent of the people.

Learn to recognize your few critical activities and focus your attention on doing those things first. By so doing, you may significantly reduce the urge to procrastinate.

Setting a deadline for the task helps some people get started. The pressure of a deadline, even a self-imposed one, can be sufficient to create action. Make sure your deadline is realistic, and put it in writing. Post the written deadline on the wall, set it on your desk, or put it wherever you will see it frequently.

An even better idea is to let other people know about your deadline. While we frequently break commitments we make to ourselves, we are not so likely to break those we make to others, since it's painful and embarrassing to admit we haven't done the task. So make a commitment to your spouse, secretary, boss, friend or whomever you like. Schedule appointments with this person to discuss results, set deadlines and promise action; then see if you don't find it much harder to fall behind and risk losing face with the other person. A public commitment usually gets honored much quicker than a private one.

Another way to get started and keep going is to promise yourself a reward for completing the task. For instance, you might give yourself an extra-special lunch for finishing that project you've been putting off; or a weekend vacation for painting the house; or maybe take Friday afternoon off if you finish all your assignments by noon. A reward can be anything that appeals to you, large or small. Two main points to remember: If you don't earn the reward, don't give it to yourself; if you do earn it, be sure to take it. Rewards now and then can make life more enjoyable and help you conquer your procrastination.

Some unpleasant tasks will get done much quicker and save you time for more important activities if you can get someone else to do them. Have a subordinate screen the mail in order to give you what's important and to file what's useless in the wastepaper basket. Or ask one of your staff to verify invoices that need your approval rather than doing it yourself. In another context, you won't have to dread painting the living room if you hire a painter to do it. Many times the cost of hiring someone can make sense economically as well as psychologically.

Occasionally you will come across a task that is so unpleasant that nothing seems to get you moving. Try thinking of the task in a larger context. It may not reduce the unpleasantness, but it might make the task a bit more palatable.

Difficult Projects

Procrastination caused by difficult tasks calls for a different set of techniques. Quite often we avoid difficult tasks because we simply don't know where to start. The task may be so complex it simply overwhelms us. The answer lies in finding some way to reduce the apparent complexity so the task no longer appears difficult.

Often it's the difficult, perplexing problems that provide some of our greatest opportunities. Paul Tournier, author of *The Adventure of Living*, describes these problems in terms of adventures.

"There is an astonishing contrast between the heavy perplexity that inhibits before the adventure has begun and the excitement that grips us the moment it begins...As soon as a man makes up his mind to take the plunge into adventure, he is aware of a new strength he did not think he had, which rescues him from all his perplexities."

One excellent approach to begin your adventure is to break the task down into smaller units, the smaller the better, until you can see the first steps.

Breaking things down into subunits is essentially a matter of working backwards. You start with the desired result—the finished task. Then keep asking yourself, "What has to happen for this result to be accomplished?" In this way, you can break the most complex task into units as small as necessary to reduce its overwhelming nature. After breaking the task down, focus only on one part at a time.

For example, you've been putting off doing a feasibility study for a new process that might help your company. No one has ever applied this process in your industry so there are no guidelines to follow. How do you break it down into smaller parts? You might start by outlining the finished report, noting what the key topic areas should be. Next, look at each area and determine what needs to be covered there. What steps are necessary to find the information you need? Who can provide it? Continue in this fashion until you've broken the task into its various elements. The elements never look as difficult as the entire task. Once you've divided a big project into smaller units, you can reserve time every day for working on a unit. This will enable you to gradually complete the time-consuming job without disrupting completion of other important assignments.

Another approach to breaking a task down is to think of all the things that can be done in no more than ten minutes. Let's assume that you need to prepare a forecast of sales for next year. You estimate it will probably take 30 hours to complete the project. Not only is the task difficult, but finding 30 hours is also difficult, and you tend to keep putting it off. How can you break this down into short minijobs? Within a few minutes you might be able to get a copy of last year's forecast, locate the files you will need, determine what information will be required, decide whom you must contact, arrange appointments with other people, request additional information, or assign parts of the project to others. As you begin to think about it, there are many minijobs that can be done in five to ten minutes.

An added benefit of this approach is that these short tasks can be fitted into many odd moments during the day that would otherwise be wasted. And at the same time, all these little things will lead you toward the accomplishment of your task.

To make this approach work best, write down all the short tasks you can find so you won't have to rethink each time you have a few odd moments. Arrange them according to priorities so you can start on the most important ones first. After you have finished several of these short tasks, you may discover the project is no longer so overwhelming or difficult. You may even find a shortcut to make its completion quicker, and then you may want to schedule a large block of time to finish it. The main point is that these short tasks get you started. The more you get done, the easier it is to keep going.

Another technique is to find a leading task. This is especially good for those times when you're procrastinating because you just don't feel up to doing whatever it is that needs to be done.

A leading task should be extremely easy, quick and require no planning. It should demand very little conscious effort on your part. Rolling a sheet of paper into the typewriter can lead to typing that letter. Picking up the telephone can lead to calling on new customers. Buying a paint brush can lead to resuming your art lessons. You certainly can't finish until you first get started.

Sometimes the difficult task we keep postponing calls for creative thought. We keep saying that we're waiting for inspiration or the right mood. Someone once said that inspiration is 90 percent perspiration. If you wait for inspiration, it seldom appears. A little physical action is what's needed. One author had been waiting three years for the right inspiration to begin writing his book. A friend finally convinced him to set aside 30 minutes each day for writing. It made no difference what he wrote, but he had to write for the entire 30 minutes. For the first two weeks the author wrote nonsense phrases, paragraphs about the weather, poetry, notes to himself, and similar nonproductive things. Gradually, though, his writing began to become more serious. He began spelling out ideas for his novel, short descriptions of different characters, various ideas for plots. Before long he was writing his novel. The moral: Don't wait for inspiration; take action now.

Not feeling in the right mood is a common rationalization for putting things off. The trick is to take advantage of your moods rather than have your moods take advantage of you. Occasionally it may be best to wait until your mood is right before starting something. However, there is often some aspect of the task that will fit your current mood. You may not feel like papering the kitchen today, but you might be willing to at least select the wallpaper. When you find yourself procrastinating because your mood is wrong, ask yourself, "Is there anything, no matter how small, that I am willing to do?" Once you find something you're willing to do, and do it, you're beginning to make your moods work for you instead of against you.

It may be that you're not in the right mood because you're busy feeling sorry for yourself. A general lack of motivation or a feeling of depression sets in. What you need is a pep talk. Go find a corner to stand in, and then talk to yourself out loud. Build yourself up, for you can't do anything until you first believe you can. A little positive thinking may be what you need. And a pep talk is one good way to get yourself going in the right direction again.

Things often seem difficult because we don't know enough about them. Non-familiarity also often leads to a lack of interest. The more we know about something the more we want to know and the more likely we are to get involved and excited. So get more information . Read a book, attend a lecture, talk with people who know. A short course in auto mechanics may help you stop postponing needed repairs on your automobile. Finding a photograph of your great grandmother may get you started on developing your family tree. And learning about linear programming may make you eager to solve an inventory-control problem you've been putting off.

Indecision

Indecision is the third greatest cause of procrastination. One cause of indecision is a strong desire to be right.

There is a time to deliberate and a time to act. The time to decide is when further information will probably add very little to the quality of the decision. Make a sincere effort to obtain the best decision and move on. Above all, don't keep fretting and fussing or rehashing the problem.

Desire for perfection is another common cause of indecision. Authors who keep rewriting chapter one, striving for the perfect phrasing, seldom publish books. Managers who keep pushing their subordinates for perfect results seldom achieve them. Perfectionism leads to greater anxiety and tension, strains relationships between people, and accomplishes little. Learn to do your best the first time around, and call it good.

Indecisiveness can also often be traced to vague fears that something will go wrong. Instead of procrastinating by worrying, focus on what you wish to accomplish. Write out all the possible obstacles or problems that could prevent you from achieving your results. Then look over each problem and think of the various ways you might solve it. Write down all the possible solutions and pick the ones most likely to work. You now have the basis for some positive planning and action.

Another technique for overcoming your vague fears is to develop a worry list. Write down all the things you think might go wrong. Keep the list. From time to time read it over and note what has actually happened in each instance. You will probably find that most of the things you worry about never happen. A worry list might help you learn to worry less.

CHANGING YOUR HABITS

Changing your do-it-later urge into a do-it-now habit will require positive action on your part. Answer your mail as soon as you open it. Don't set it aside to be done later. Whenever you say to yourself, "I've got to do something about that," do something about it now, not later. Schedule things, and live by your schedule. And learn to check those unscheduled action impulses that often hide procrastination.

Learning to do this differently won't change the task, but it will change your attitude and perception of it.

You may have to play games with yourself in order to overcome inertia and change the habits that hamper your progress. One manager challenged himself to see how many miscellaneous tasks he could complete and how many odd moments he could find to do them. First he listed all those he avoided doing. Then, in order to finish as many as possible, he grouped together similar ones. Besides doing these during free moments at the office, he found he could complete some on the train to work, on the plane to a business meeting, in the doctor's or dentist's office while waiting for his appointment, and so on.

One woman who frequently procrastinated unpleasant household chores used the same approach. She wrote notes to herself about the various tasks and then taped the notes to the walls of her home. For instance, the note by the bookcase would remind her to dust the books, and the note in the bathroom told her to clean the tile. This kind of game is a variation of setting deadlines for yourself. However, it soon took on the added power of a commitment to others. When she put the notes up, she had forgotten about her friends who frequently stopped by for coffee and conversation. As they began to ask about the notes around the house, she realized that she would have to get the tasks done quickly to avoid embarrassing comments. This led to rescheduling her time and doing at least one unpleasant task first thing each day. Within a few days she had learned the secret of conquering procrastination. She gained new confidence in herself and new respect from her friends.

CONCLUSION

The easiest way to deal with procrastination is to never let it get started in the first place. There are two things you can do. First, clarify your objectives. Procrastination sometimes occurs because what we think we want to do is not what we really want to do. Your subconscious mind may be sending you the message that your priorities are out of focus. If you continually think through your objectives and priorities and focus your efforts on what's most important, you will probably not be bothered too often with procrastination.

Second, develop the habit of planning every day. Ask yourself what you want to accomplish each particular day. Write out a list of things to do and then follow your plan. Do the most important things first. If you develop the habit of planning each day, making a list of things to do, and then doing them, you will probably find that procrastination is something that happens mostly to other people.

One last thought. Perhaps the most valuable thing you can do when you are wasting your time is to admit it. As long as you continue to deny or rationalize it, you are not in a position to solve it. Once you admit that you are indeed procrastinating, examine your situation and try to determine why. Then pick a technique for conquering your procrastination. In the end, procrastination, like any problem, can be overcome by positive action.

Merrill E. Douglass is director of Time Management Center. He is also associate professor of management at Grand Valley State Colleges. Douglass has created and recorded cassette tapes on time management and he has published over 30 articles on various management topics.

45.
PUT A STOP TO PROCRASTINATION

William Friend

> If projects seem too large, procrastinators fill up present moments with trivia, telling themselves: "If I start this now, there's just going to be one interruption after another."

With a report on the new membership program due in a few weeks, Fred Smith made a firm resolution: "This time, I'll get a jump on it early. I'll start pulling the information together right now—tomorrow at the latest—and I'll have the report ready with two or three days to spare."

It didn't work out that way. Fred immediately lapsed into his familiar routine of postponing the project's start. As the days passed, he had to abandon the idea of producing the report well in advance. "No tragedy," he told himself. "Handing it in on the deadline is good enough."

Four days before the report was due, Fred assembled the folders to start the project but then became sidetracked. He answered some letters and telephoned a few friends to line up a retirement luncheon for a co-worker. He also straightened out his desk and cleared out his in-box.

Two days before the report was due, Fred fell into a state of mild panic. He plunged into the project with a frenzy. For the most part, the task went smoothly, but a few hitches did occur. Because he had waited so long, several people were not available or couldn't give him the data.

The report that he submitted—two days late—was not as solid as he thought it would be. "I had trouble prying the information out of some of our people," he told his supervisor. To himself he added: "How could they expect a super job with such a tight deadline?"

Finally, he promised himself: "Next time, I'll get an earlier start."

Do you have any Fred Smiths in your organization? If you do, they may be a heavy drag on your association, heavier than you think.

"It's difficult to estimate what procrastination is costing organizations, but it's very substantial," says William Knaus, a business consultant and clinical psychologist in New York City and Longmeadow, Massachusetts. "Some of our studies indicate that executives may spend as much as 60 percent of their time shuffling papers, making unnecessarily long telephone calls, indulging in busywork, and the like.

For associations, the cost of procrastination may be particularly high.

The necessary review of programs by staff and committees can mean delays and missed opportunities. An energy association in Washington recently submitted a 40 page statement to a congressional committee—five days late. The tardiness so irritated an ally on the committee that he withdrew his support on an important measure.

Another association launched an expensive program to prove to its members in smaller firms that it was working as diligently for them as it was for the major corporations; the effort dogged down and was launched too late to be effective.

And who doesn't know of an association committee that has tabled a promising program for so long that it finally died on the back burner, overtaken by events?

Procrastination also carries a high cost for the individuals who practice it. "We pay a gigantic price for the luxury of indulging in procrastination," says Michael LeBoeuf, a time-management consultant and professor of management at the University of New Orleans, Louisiana. "It's the universal effectiveness killer."

The executive or professional who fails repeatedly to honor commitments quickly loses credibility and is tagged—perhaps fatally from a career standpoint—as unreliable. But aside from the obvious career damage, chronic procrastinators are constantly tormented by problems that have been allowed to grow out of hand. They constantly feel frustrated because they never get around to working toward the goals they consider worthwhile. And often their relationships inside and outside the organization are poor.

ARE YOU A CHRONIC PROCRASTINATOR?

Not everyone who puts tasks off is a procrastinator. All executives change plans and priorities in midstream. It's necessary. The chronic procrastinator, however, repeatedly stalls on projects to the point where the consequences are serious.

True procrastinators often devise desperate strategies for overcoming their handicap. Novelist Victor Hugo repeatedly ordered his servants to keep his clothes until his scheduled writing time was up. And it is said that Demosthenes shaved one side of his head so he would be ashamed to be seen in public—and would stick to his studies.

In more modern times, an economist at one association has found an ingenious way to discourage herself from leaving her desk: She spills a little water on her skirt so she won't want to stand up until it dries. A writer at another organization loops his belt across his chair to discourage himself from leaving his desk.

Psychologists say that such tricks may be useful for some, but they probably won't work very long for most dyed-in-the-wool procrastinators. Before a real cure can take place, the procrastinator needs a full understanding of his or her problem.

One complicating factor is that procrastination surfaces in different areas with different people. For example, a manager may perform efficiently at the office but let personal affairs slide. As a result, he or she may allow bills to pile up and ordinary household chores to accumulate. Or a director may be a terrible procrastinator when it comes to making telephone calls but otherwise be an efficient administrator.

Typical association workaholics also have special areas of procrastination: They may become so immersed in the details of their areas of responsibility that they neglect the long-range planning function, a responsibility superiors may consider the most important part of their jobs.

Procrastinators have a wide range of motives for putting tasks off. Specialists in the field say it simply doesn't make sense for procrastinators to try to reform without understanding why they procrastinate.

Here are several common motives, according to the experts:

Self-doubt. "People often aren't sure of themselves, so they spend lots of time hesitating and second-guessing," says psychologist William Knaus. Procrastinators who have secret doubts about their abilities find innumerable excuses for not doing a task. By avoiding the start of a task, they avoid the risks of anxiety and failure. They also avoid the risks of success and any problems they fear may come from it.

"You can just be your same old wonderful procrastinating self, complete with all the accompanying miseries, misfortunes, and frustrations that you have had in the past," adds Michael LeBoeuf.

Low frustration tolerance. "For many people, the real priority in life is being comfortable," says one psychologist. "As a result, they avoid tasks that seem too large or unpleasant."

If projects seem too large, procrastinators fill up present moments with trivia to avoid starting, telling themselves: "If I start this now, there's just going to be one interruption after another." They delude themselves into believing that they will tackle the project when they don't have to worry about interruptions.

In the case of unpleasant tasks, Mr. LeBoeuf notes that "all of us have important but unpleasant things to do from time to time. Given the choice of doing anything pleasant rather than something unpleasant, we'll usually choose the former."

Drive for perfection. Without realizing it, many people who procrastinate are perfectionists at heart.

"In an attempt to prove that they are good enough, they strive to do the impossible, thinking they should have no problem at all reaching their lofty goals," says Lenora M. Yuen, a psychologist who practices in Palo Alto and San Francisco, California, and conducts procrastination workshops on the West

Coast. "They usually put unrealistic demands on themselves and then are unable to meet them. Discouraged, they then retreat from the demands by procrastinating."

For example, an executive with little public-speaking experience may expect to become a spellbinder with her first few talks. A newly appointed manager, asked to prepare a report, may expect his effort to be approved without suggestions or revisions. Or a director, asked to prepare a plan for committee review, may expect that plan to be adopted without any revisions.

The gender difference. Do women procrastinate more than men? If so, why? The questions have intrigued several experts in this field.

William Knaus believes that "women not uncommonly put off things because they fear what they do will be viewed negatively." An example might be the newly appointed female manager who hesitates to take up a male manager's invitation to discuss business over lunch.

Psychologist Lenora M. Yuen agrees that women may procrastinate more than men. Citing studies indicating that women fear their achievements may be regarded as "unfeminine," she observes: "Despite shifts in contemporary attitudes, many women are still influenced by traditional prohibitions against their success.

"For a woman who feels conflict about crossing beyond the threshold of tradition, procrastination may offer some relief," Yuen says. "As long as she continues to delay, she never fully achieves success and thus never really challenges the tradition."

A fatalistic view. Some people have such a low opinion of themselves that they can't incorporate success into the picture of themselves and their lives. Feeling inadequate, they really don't expect to succeed at anything, so they simply don't try in the first place.

For example, a young professional who handled press relations for a state banking association never allowed himself to dream of stepping into the job of the public relations director. He feared that if he did aspire to the top job and got it, the success might only be temporary—and crushing.

So he found it safer to detach himself from any remote possibility of such disillusionment; he assumed that success was "just not in the cards" for him. Many procrastinators are like that.

NEW WAYS TO CURE THE HANDICAP

For those who believe they have a serious problem with procrastination, there is good news. In recent years, specialists in this field have developed new approaches and new techniques to help even the most hopeless cases.

The first and most important step toward curing the handicap, however, is the procrastinator's firm commitment to making a change. That's not as easy as it may sound. Procrastinators rather enjoy making resolutions to reform. They enjoy the process of making a list of goals, planning the step-by-step stages to reach those goals, and making up schedules and deadlines.

The problem is, the true procrastinator seldom takes the step of actually doing something. A serious commitment to change, therefore, is essential.

If procrastinators consider their problem to be relatively mild—not threatening to a career, health or family life—they might deal successfully with the problem by reading a book on the subject. Virtually all set out step-by-step programs for conquering specific types of procrastination.

If the problem is more serious, it may be worthwhile to consult a psychologist or attend one of the procrastination workshops that are now available in many cities.

The course of treatment in these approaches is roughly similar: The person is helped to identify the major areas in which he or she procrastinates and to isolate the reasons for the behavior. Then specific, measurable goals are set. For example, the goal might be: "This month I will complete my report by September 30th." Or: "I will telephone five prospects next week."

Many procrastinators also need to develop skills to help them work toward goals more efficiently. The top executive of a major corporation, for example, habitually spent an average of five minutes on each telephone call without realizing it. He suffered from what psychologist William Knaus calls "the black cord disease." Step by step, the executive was trained to cut his calls to 2.5 minutes, and the total saving in time was significant.

HOW TO STOP PUTTING IT OFF

Assuming that the procrastinator has made a commitment to change, here are eight tips and techniques widely used to put a stop to putting it off:

Recognize that procrastination is not the way to handle your affairs. Procrastinators put themselves under senseless emotional strain. Their life is filled with frustration and boredom. Recognizing and acknowledging the fact helps the procrastinator regard a chore in a new and different light.

Is a project unpleasant? In therapy, the procrastinator acquires a more mature view of life—that some tasks simply are unpleasant, and unpleasant or not, they simply must get done, or problems will develop.

Break up large problems into manageable sizes. Edwin C. Bliss, a management expert in Mountain Ranch, California, who frequently speaks on the subject of procrastination, calls this the "salami technique."

"When a task seems overwhelming," says Bliss, "pause for a moment and do a little thinking on paper. List chronologically every step that must be taken to complete the job. The smaller the steps, the better. Even the little mini-tasks that will take only a minute should be listed separately."

The thin slices of the job will be inviting, with each small chore leading into another. "Instead of looking at a gargantuan project, you're looking at a series of tiny tasks, each of which, considered separately, is manageable," says Bliss.

Plan and complete a start-up task. Simply getting started is a major problem for procrastinators. A chronic procrastinator will undertake endless nonessential small chores to avoid beginning the project. So this technique involves devising a brief, simple start-up chore—and doing it immediately.

For example, if a manager is scheduled to give a speech, he or she can start by listing four major points to make. If a report must be submitted, he or she can write the cover memo.

Make a wager. When working with procrastinators, psychologists sometimes ask the patient to make out a check as a donation to some cause he or she despises. The psychologist keeps the check in a safe place until a mutually acceptable deadline. If the procrastinator fails to meet the deadline for his or her goal, the psychologist sends out the check.

In a variation of this idea, two professionals at an association regularly bet each other on meeting deadlines. When a report is late, the payoff is a dinner at a fine restaurant.

Making wagers won't cure procrastination, but it does help to establish a pattern of success in meeting deadlines.

Devise a system of rewards. This is an effective way for procrastinators to motivate themselves, say psychologists, because it provides positive reinforcement. Before setting out to achieve a goal, the procrastinator sets a reward, one that is commensurate with the size of the task.

"But be honest with yourself," cautions LeBoeuf. "If you do the task, be sure to give yourself the reward, and if you don't complete the task, don't give yourself the reward."

Try a five-minute plan. Experts sometimes propose that procrastinators adopt a five-minute plan, committing themselves to spending just five minutes on a project they have been avoiding. At the end of the time, procrastinators are free to turn to something else if they wish, or they may continue for another five minutes.

"No matter how distasteful the task," says Edwin Bliss, "you can usually talk yourself into committing a mere five minutes to it."

Try the hardest part first. The technique of using the start-up project works well for many people, but for others an entirely opposite tack may be more effective: choosing the most difficult part of the project first. With the hardest or most distasteful part of the chore out of the way, the rest of the job will look easy.

For example, if the most difficult part of a project is gathering information, then the procrastinator should tackle this part first. Later, the step of analyzing the information will seem simple.

Tailor your environment for work. Psychologist William Knaus points out that "the business environment is full of traps that waste our time and keep us from starting or finishing important projects." Water coolers, in-boxes, coffee stations, meeting rooms, magazine racks—all make it easy for the procrastinator to fritter away time time and put off tasks.

A cluttered desk and disorganized files also contribute to procrastination. It's easy to get sidetracked by some irrelevant piece of paper. The antidote is to organize your work environment for action. That calls for using a filing system that really works; throwing away documents and other papers that have become outdated; and making sure that only materials related to the project at hand are on the desk.

IF ALL ELSE FAILS...

But what if, after trying these techniques, attending workshops, and visiting psychologists, procrastinators still cling to their old ways?

They should probably consider joining the Procrastinators' Club of America, Philadelphia, Pennsylvania, which boasts 4,500 members who never do anything on time. Les Wass, the president, enjoys meeting new members at the annual Christmas party, which the group never gets around to holding until June.

46.
WHAT TO DO ABOUT EXECUTIVES WHO CAN'T DELEGATE AND WON'T DECIDE

Robert N. McMurry

A typical problem is lack of accurate insight coupled with false self-assessment.

Know thyself, urged Aristotle, but accurate and complete self-insight, especially among senior executives, is a rare quality. Consider the case of Ronald Jennings, head of a division of a big manufacturing company in New York City, as he hears the results of a recent assessment of his performance.

"Our findings, Mr. Jennings, indicate that you have superior intelligence, are technically very competent in your job, and overall a dedicated, compulsively hardworking executive," said the evaluator.

"On the other hand, you seem to experience some difficulty in delegating authority to your subordinates. You not only take a very active role in defining their goals and objectives, but also you make it clear precisely how, when and where your people are to achieve these objectives.

"Furthermore, anything that represents even a slight deviation from established practice must first be cleared with you. You tend to overstructure and constrain the autonomy and freedom to act of those who report to you. You permit them very little independence, flexibility and decision-making. This stifles their creativity and inhibits their growth."

Mr. Jennings' response was immediate: He exploded. He agreed entirely with the first part of the assessment but declared: "I regard my skills as a delegator as one of my greatest strengths as a leader. I am the laziest man in my entire enterprise. I have always surrounded myself with strong, competent subordinates to whom I delegate a maximum amount of authority, consistent, of course, with their capabilities."

"Why then," queried the evaluator, "do you require that Les Richards, your plant manager in Minneapolis, confer with you weekly to clear all of his activities on a routine basis?"

Mr. Jennings replied: "This regular review is absolutely essential. In my estimation, Richards is little more than a novice. He needs weekly guidance and support from me. He has been in this position for only seven years."

This hypothetical scenario demonstrates a typical problem of many business executives, their almost complete lack of accurate insight into their own makeup, need and motivations.

This flaw is amplified by the fact that each is convinced he has comprehensive and completely valid insights into his strengths and weaknesses. When questioned, the typical executive will reply: "One of my greatest strengths is that I know myself. Because of these insights, I reach my goals effectively, and my major decisions are completely rational and logical. This is why I see myself as a *homo sapiens*, the reasoning man."

In reality, nothing could be further from the truth. No one can be wholly honest and objective about himself. Everyone has a self-image, and most self-images are flattering.

In many instances, as with Mr. Jennings, the characteristics that a person regards as his greatest strengths are really his greatest weaknesses. They are typical of the person who doth protest too much, who tells everyone how honest or great he is. The fallacy of such self-assessment is apparent to everyone but him.

An important influence in shaping these self-images is role expectation. For example, the popular stereotype of the executive is strong, decisive and self-confident. Many managers assume that because they occupy a supervisory role they must be correspondingly strong, decisive, and self-confident. But recent studies indicate that 75 percent of the population is notably passive, dependent and submissive. Included among those people are many victims of the Peter Principle: They have reached their first level of incompetence.

To conceal their limitations from others as well as from themselves, these executives often develop various neurotic defense mechanisms. In many cases, they seek to avoid situations where they will be called upon to make decisions, take risks or exhibit self-confidence. Typically, these executives will:

- Take flight into detail. If the executive is much too busy to consider the problem, perhaps it will dry up and blow away after a while.
- Counsel indefinite delay of action. By saying "we must crawl before we walk and walk before we run" and "haste makes waste," the executive hopes that conditions may change and eliminate the problem.
- Delegate the problem to a committee. The executive knows that committees usually take a long time to make a report and can be blamed if anything goes wrong.
- Delegate the problem to a subordinate. The executive practices democratic, participatory management and hopes the subordinate can come up with a workable solution. If he cannot, he provides a convenient scapegoat.

- Call in the experts. If the recommendations from the consultant, the accountant, or lawyer prove wrong, he can be made the scapegoat.
- Have a study made to get the facts. Most such studies require at least six months to complete and also provide convenient scapegoats.
- Look for the answers in the book. If there is no answer according to the book, no action can be taken.
- Induce the boss to handle the problem. A variation is to push the problem into someone else's jurisdiction. If kicked around long enough, the problem will either be solved or disappear. If the solution is wrong, the responsibility will lie elsewhere.
- Answer in double talk. The executive says decisively: "If this is true, we do this, except that under this or that circumstance, we do the opposite." If enough obfuscation can be created, perhaps the problem will be forgotten or will solve itself.
- Concentrate on establishing priorities. The executive says: "It is not fair to give any one problem precedence." By the time the problem is reached, perhaps the whole issue will have been forgotten, or the problem will have been solved by someone else.
- Arrange to be out of town or at a meeting. Many crises will resolve themselves while the executive attends one meeting after another. Some executives are so busy with trivia that their frenetic activities resemble the mindless gyrations of a beheaded hen.
- Deny that the problem exists. Insist that the issue is unimportant or that it was settled long ago.
- Become ill. Some executives develop an incapacitating psychogenic ailment such as an ulcer, an allergy, hypertension, colitis, nervous stomach, insomnia, chronic debilitation, or lassitude. The doctor will prescribe long rest or freedom from stress or strain.
- Drink more martinis. After a few drinks, most problems become less threatening and are easier to solve, although the solutions found in the bottle are not always the best.
- Walk out on the problem. The executive simply puts on his hat and goes home. Someone will find a solution somehow.

These self-reinforcing actions can be very costly to the executive personally and to the enterprise with which he is associated. They often lead him to be misplaced in his job, to be dissatisfied with his performance, or to fail outright. Of even greater concern, these actions tend to conceal and perpetuate the inadequacies on the job. And that eventually weakens the whole enterprise. Insecure executives cannot tolerate strong subordinates. Hence, they discourage the employment and retention of competent staff.

What can be done with such supervisors, managers and executives? How can they be given more accurate pictures of themselves? Can much be accomplished by pointing out, as in the case of Mr. Jennings, that their insights are false?

Unfortunately, no. Despite all the evidence, Mr. Jennings' image of himself will not be significantly changed. To admit to himself that he cannot delegate responsibility to others will unbalance his often fragile emotional homeostasis. Such an imbalance can lead to marked anxiety and further indecisiveness.

Obviously, a long series of sessions on a psychiatrist's couch might help Mr. Jennings, but because of time, cost and patient resistance, such therapy is rarely practical in cases such as his. Counseling may help somewhat, but the most realistic approach is not to attempt to correct a person's image of himself, but to ascertain through comprehensive in-depth assessment:

1. Which of his attributes, as he is now constituted, are advantageous to him and his job where he is presently assigned?
2. Which of his attributes are actually potentially detrimental to him or to his employer in his current job or at higher levels?
3. How can his duties be restructured to maximize his manifest vocational assets and minimize his weaknesses?

If a person's duties cannot be altered to adapt his job to him, little remains but to take him or her out of the position. Demotion, even termination, can be done in easy stages, without acute loss of face by cutting back on the executive's responsibilities, shifting him from line to staff responsibilities, making him a consultant or giving him a long separation allowance and outplacement counseling.

The practical solution is to recognize that the executive is misplaced. In Mr. Jennings' case, for example, observation of him in action shows that he will never be able to delegate authority. The more this limitation is brought to his attention, the more acute the problem will become. On the other hand, he possesses a great deal of technical expertise. In his case, the solution is to relocate him by kicking him upstairs to a prestigious staff job—assistant to the chairman for research and development—where he will have little need to delegate.

Mr. Jennings may sense that he is being downgraded, but he loses no face, usually takes no reduction in earnings, and is relieved of the necessity of making decisions. He becomes more relaxed, and his expertise is salvaged. Everybody, including the company, wins.

Robert N. McMurry is the president of the McMurry Co., a Chicago consulting firm involved in market research and executive recruiting. He received his doctorate in psychology from the University of Vienna and is the author of The Maverick Executive.

47.

EFFECTIVE USE OF TIME

Robert W. Braid

All too often we are satisfied with busy work. As long as we or our subordinates are busy, we never ask if this was the most effective use of time.

There is no magic formula to making the most of time. It is a skill developed through study and practice. The learning process is an individual thing, but there are some basic tools and concepts that can help. As a supervisor you need to know about the techniques that have been successfully used by other managers to maximize their use of time.

Keep in mind as you read these suggestions that different techniques work for different people. What may be good for one person may not be good for another. Your job is to pick the ideas that fit your style and will benefit you the most. But remember, the problem is not a lack of time. Everyone has the same amount. Nobody has more than you. The important thing is how it's used.

LEARNING TO SAY NO

Perhaps one of the most effective techniques for saving time is the ability to say no graciously. Unless you concentrate on tactfully but firmly saying no, you will find that you spend most of your time on other people's priorities.

Remember that you can't please everybody. The way you spend your time is bound to make some people unhappy.

Sometimes there are tradeoffs. For example, occasionally it is less time-consuming to accommodate someone than it might be to explain why you don't consider the person's request for your time important. And of course there are always some requests that you can't turn down, such as those coming from your boss. Even with these requests, however, it may be worthwhile to identify how they conflict with what you consider higher-priority activities. Be prepared to suggest some alternative ways of handling the work. You may not win all the time, but if you have done your homework and can honestly identify your high-priority tasks, your boss may agree. Remember, your boss is not a mind reader; he or she will never know unless you speak up.

Unfortunately, many managers, especially when they are new, find it very difficult to say no. Consequently, they wind up with far more work than they can reasonably handle. They eventually find out that saying yes and not delivering is worse than being up front and saying no from the first.

PROCRASTINATION

How many times have you heard, "That's a great idea but I just can't find the time to get to it." It's often easy to identify high-priority projects. It is quite another thing accomplishing them. Procrastination is one reason.

The two primary causes of procrastination are complexity and fear. Initially, the projects seem complex because you don't have all the answers, or overwhelming because you have no idea where to begin. Projects concerned with morale or communications fall into this category. Fear can be the culprit when you are dealing with unpleasant chores such as explaining to your boss that something has gone wrong with a major project in your department, or facing up to a discipline problem. You will have difficulty getting started on any task unless you are convinced that you can finish it successfully, and self-confidence comes from having a plan.

With complex high-priority items, begin by trying to break them down into more palatable doses. The important thing is to get started rather then divert your time and energy to lower-priority items because they are easier to cope with.

Don't be lulled into a trap by convincing yourself that you need a large chunk of quiet time to develop a strategy. Chances are that you will never have a large chunk of quiet time and, consequently, that you will never get started. Small steps in the right direction are always better than standing still.

You may begin by simply gathering information or asking questions. Discussions with people who can help you can take place over lunch or in the hall. The important thing is to get involved. One thought will lead to another. Before you know it, you will be meaningfully involved in accomplishing your goal. You'll be hooked. Then, getting involved will become easier.

Be careful to keep your eyes focused on your goal and not get carried away talking about it or collecting data. There are managers who become experts on certain problems because they read every piece of literature they can get their hands on, go to seminars, read books on the topic, but never do anything about the problems. For example, there are managers who have become experts on Management by Objectives (MBO) but have never tried to implement it in their department.

Often, setting a deadline for yourself will force you to act.

Another way to force yourself to take action is to tell a friend, or better yet your boss, what you are working on. Once you go public with your plans, you are far more likely to carry them out. Sometimes planning ahead limits flexibility and freedom, but when it comes to procrastination that can be more of an asset than a liability.

You might also take a tip from Mary Poppins: "For every job that must be done, there is an element of fun. Find the fun and snap, the job's a lark, a spree. It's very clear to see that a spoon full of sugar helps the medicine go down." Look for the rewards, focus on the benefits of a job well done, generate some internal enthusiasm. Take a minute to daydream about how good you will feel when your high-priority goal is successfully completed.

As mentioned earlier, people also procrastinate because of fear. You may be afraid of biting off more than you can chew, getting in over your head, taking on too much responsibility. Getting involved in something with an unknown or uncertain outcome creates apprehension in most people. However, the fact that you haven't faced up to an unpleasant task will haunt you until you do the task.

It doesn't help to assure you that more often than not your worst fears never materialize. The best advice one can give is to confront fear head on. Ask yourself, "What is it that I am afraid of? What is the worst possible thing that can happen?" When you have answered those questions, work on a plan to minimize the impact. This approach may not eliminate the fear, because fear is an emotion and not necessarily responsive to logic. However, it should help you to develop the courage to attack the problem. Repeated successes will help you overcome fear. It is like the first time off a high diving board. At first the diver is consumed with fright. With each successful dive, his or her fear diminishes and confidence and skill grow.

PAPERWORK

Use your secretary to screen all mail. If you don't have a secretary here are some hints for sorting mail quickly. Check the postage for bulk-rate or first class. Is it addressed to you or your job? Is the address on a gummed label from a mailing list or is it personally typed? Is the letter multilithed or typewritten? Who signed it?

After all first class, typewritten, personally signed letters have been separated from the mail, check the remaining letters by reading the last paragraph of each to see if any action is required by you. Put these aside. All the rest of the mail can be thrown out. Or those pieces that may have some interest can be put in a neat little pile to be read between more important activities. But if you don't get to them within a couple of days, they, too, should be thrown out. A good rule to follow is never handle the same piece of paper more than twice.

For letters that require answers, consider writing your response in longhand on the original letter. If you find yourself writing the same response to several different people, consider developing a model or form letter.

Managers are often asked to prepare time-consuming reports on a daily, weekly or monthly basis. Very often, the value of the report diminishes with time, or the person who originated the request gets promoted, quits or dies, but the report lives on. If you have any question about the value of any time-consuming report you prepare, try ignoring one or two reporting periods. You may be surprised to find no one complains.

READING

As a manager you spend a major part of each day reading. Consider the impact on available time if you could increase your speed and comprehension. Most high schools and colleges offer speed reading courses through their continuing education department. This could prove to be a fantastic investment. If you spend four hours a day reading, and you increase your reading speed by 25 or even 50 percent, you would be saving one to two hours a day or five to ten hours every week.

VISITORS

If you are as busy as most managers, your job probably allows precious little time for creativity. And nothing is more frustrating than having the block of time you carved out for creative work constantly interrupted. Many managers are lucky to spend one hour per week in uninterrupted time during the normal work day. Some resort to coming in early. Others stay late. Many load their briefcase and try to do it at home.

A competent secretary is probably the single most valuable asset in visitor control. Ideally, the secretary's desk should be strategically positioned to screen all visitors. You should have selected hours of the day to handle appointments. When someone schedules an appointment, your secretary can check the purpose and length of time required. With this information you will be better equipped to handle the meeting in one setting.

Colleagues who are interested in socializing and ask if you are busy can be very politely fended-out with a "Yes, could I set up an appointment, or have him (her) call you?" This is usually enough to get a "No, I'll catch him (her) later" reply.

However, no matter how well you guard you time, some interruptions are bound to occur. Here are some ideas that can help you keep the lost time to a minimum. If someone gets past the secretary, and drops in for a social call, stand up to greet the person and remain standing. This usually makes it difficult for the intruder to sit down. If this is a particular problem for you, remove all the chairs from your office.

If someone comes in for an appointment and after the meeting is over stays to bring you up to date on the latest intrigues in the company, look for a way to end the conversation—perhaps a phone call. Or alert your secretary to call you when meetings run overtime.

Another effective technique is to schedule a meeting in the other person's office. It is easier for you to leave someone else's office than to throw the person out of your own. If your favorite timewaster traps you in the hall, politely tell him or her that you are busy at the moment, but would be happy to schedule an appointment. That usually does the trick.

In time you should develop a number of techniques for dealing with interruptions without being rude. One part common courtesy and one part common sense is usually more than adequate.

TELEPHONES

You would be surprised to find out how much time you actually spend on the telephone.

To keep it to a minimum, your secretary should screen all incoming calls. A competent secretary can determine the urgency and the nature of all calls, handle most himself or herself, and refer the rest to someone who can handle them as well as you. If you have to handle a call but it isn't urgent, often "I'll have him (her) return the call when he (she) is free" will be adequate.

One thing you should do is to set up a time for call-backs. Doing so cuts the average time of a call and gives you time beforehand to gather any information you may need and consider any questions you may want answered. It would also be helpful to practice a few cut-off techniques, for example, "I know you're busy, and I have a meeting to attend."

The telephone is an invaluable asset for saving time but only if it is used properly.

SOME FINAL THOUGHTS

Benjamin Franklin said, "Time is money." Certainly, there are similarities. Time, like money, can be spent foolishly or invested wisely. It is not a question of lack of time; everyone gets exactly the same amount. The problem is how one uses or invests the time available. Time must be spent effectively, not just efficiently. A person can be busy from the moment he or she comes to work; that is efficient use of time. The question is, was that time spent on those tasks with the highest potential payoff? That's effective use of time.

All too often we are satisfied with busywork. As long as we or our subordinates are busy, we never ask if that was the most effective use of time.

If you adopt some of the techniques described here, you'll probably find yourself thinking more about how you really want to use your time, working less hard, and doing more of the things you have always wanted to do.

Robert W. Braid is professor of management, Atlantic Community College, and president of Robert Braid Associates.

48.
THE ART OF PROCRASTINATION

Bruce A. Baldwin

In almost all serious cases of procrastination, there is an unresolved emotional conflict that is triggered when key tasks are confronted. The conflict that produces your particular type of procrastination must be understood and worked out before your avoidance reaction can be completely overcome.

Did you hear about the harried executive who was asked to name the best labor-saving device known today? "The answer," he quipped, "is simple. It's tomorrow!" Procrastination is that rather unique human proclivity to find ingenious ways to justify doing tomorrow what you should be doing today. We can all relate to procrastination because we all do it to some extent.

Procrastination accounts for a plethora of organizational and professional problems. Decreased productivity, inefficiency and mismanagement stem from it. It is the root cause of unkept appointments, late projects, uncompleted reports, low grades, disordered files and missed deadlines. For the professional, procrastination produces worry, guilt, sleepless nights, depression and anxiety, just to mention a few of the emotional consequences.

In almost all serious cases of procrastination, there is an unresolved emotional conflict that is triggered when key tasks are confronted. The conflict that produces your particular type of procrastination must be understood and worked out before your avoidance reaction can be completely overcome. Here are a few of the most common psychological conflicts that produce symptomatic procrastination.

THE PLEASURE PRIORITY

Diagnostic Cue: Whenever there is a choice between a pleasurable experience now and self-sacrifice to work toward longer-range goals, you inevitably choose fun times, with a hollow promise to get your work done later.

J.D. had high hopes for his future. He envisioned himself fulfilling a lifelong dream of becoming the head of the merchandising department in a prestigious department store. Since college, his dream has been slowly fading. There is a basic disparity between his behavior and his expectations. He loves to socialize and party and does so at every chance. The result of J.D.'s choices has been mediocre grades, slow career advancement, and dimming hopes of ever realizing his dream. Whenever a good time is near, he's there regardless of other commitments and responsibilities, and he enjoys his playboy image. His work typically gets done hurriedly at the last minute, without the thought and attention to detail required to do it well.

J.D.'s problem, along with many of his colleagues, is one of priorities. Despite intellectual commitments to a career, his behavior reveals a very pleasure-prone individual who has never learned to delay gratification. His responses are much like those of a small child who pursues fun now and acts as if the future doesn't exist. J.D. has never learned to work for more distant rewards. He is basically undisciplined.

There are two workable tactics to handle this kind of procrastination. If your real priority is to have good times, then give up your high expectations and live with the consequences of your Pleasure Priority. This will reduce the conflict between your behavior and your expectations of achievement. The second tactic is more difficult: to learn to work for payoffs that will come at some point in the future rather than immediately. This requires gritting your teeth and giving up some fun times to work instead. Doing this is the only way to learn the self-discipline that is the antithesis of the Pleasure Priority. When your self-discipline develops, you will be more in control of your time and can work toward long-term career goals and have some good times along the way.

OVERWHELMED AND CONFUSED

Diagnostic Cue: You become emotionally paralyzed because you are so overwhelmed by work that you see no clear starting point and instead worry about how it's going to get done.

Jaime was a savvy and quick junior operations officer with a busy commuter airline. She wanted to advance further, but her Achilles heel was her consistent tendency to become over-involved in work. In her eagerness to succeed in the company, she added small responsibilities here and there until she was overwhelmed. Then she became depressed, anxious and fearful that she wouldn't be able to meet her responsibilities. As she fretted, she also avoided tackling the growing mountain of work on her desk. A vicious cycle began in which her paralysis worsened as uncompleted work accumulated. This pattern was broken only by someone else intervening to help her organize what had to be done and encourage her to get started. The real problem remained—letting it happen in the first place.

Emotional paralysis resulting from too much work to be done is a most painful form of procrastination. Many professionals like Jaime set themselves up for this problem because perspective on what can reasonably be accomplished never develops. Or, the problem may be an inability to say no because of an inordinate desire to please others. Some get hooked into extra work through the skillful use of flattery by others.

Avoiding the buildup of that critical mass of work is the key to prevent becoming overwhelmed and confused. When it does occur, the best strategy is to break your work down into manageable pieces that are then tackled one by one. The feelings of accomplishment as each small task is completed build momentum to keep you going to completion. As with most forms of procrastination, the biggest step is to get started.

THE FANTASY OF COMPETENCE

Diagnostic Cue: You procrastinate and then consistently rationalize your poor performance using procrastination as an excuse while continuing to believe that you could have done much better if you had only put more effort into it.

Alex had a long history of procrastination. In college, he procrastinated until right before his examinations and then justified his mediocre grades on lack of preparation. He did the same while working on projects in the aerospace research facility where he was an engineer. His work was adequate even though he habitually procrastinated. But Alex harbored a belief that he was very bright and that if he really went that extra mile on the projects he was assigned, he would rise very quickly in his specialized field. However, he never seemed to get around to it. Deep within, he feared putting himself on the line. If he put forth his best effort and then found that his work was still little better than before, his Fantasy of Competence would be smashed. Instead he perpetuated his procrastination/rationalization habit to protect his untested self-image.

This form of procrastination poses a most distressing dilemma: to continue to procrastinate to keep alive a Fantasy of Competence or to squarely face yourself and the limits of your capabilities. To choose the procrastination alternative is to live with constant reminders of what you could have done—but didn't. Yet, to give your best shot triggers fear that you will find out you aren't as capable as you thought.

If fear of disappointing your expectations of yourself is producing procrastination, then the basic tactic is to put your abilities on the line not only once but many times. Then you can assess your true capabilities. You may have to give up unrealistic expectations of dreams of success that can't be fulfilled. On the other hand, they won't be fulfilled either if you continue to procrastinate! When you face yourself and your limits the way is cleared to set realistic career goals for yourself and succeed in attaining them.

PICK YOUR TIME AND PLACE

Procrastination is such a pervasive habit that it is often accepted as almost normal. Yet, there are some tricks of the trade that do help in overcoming this habit that is so disruptive to professional advancement and psychological well-being. You must recognize and define the emotional conflict that is the psychological root of your particular kind of procrastination and work toward resolving this conflict. Then you must create the right working conditions to get critical tasks done even when part of you is resisting.

1. Pick Your Time for a Key Task. Some professionals work best in the morning while others do better in the late afternoon or evening. When you find yourself procrastinating on a key task, tackle it when you are functioning at your absolute best.
2. Don't Waste Time Preparing. It is amazing how much time you can waste preparing to work on a key task. Getting your desk cleared, making a cup of coffee and making sure pencil and paper are handy are just part of procrastination. It is better to jump right in and get started.
3. Break Down a Big Job into Small Pieces. This technique pays off because a big job isn't so overwhelming when it is broken into smaller, manageable pieces. You also get the satisfaction of seeing your progress as each step is completed.
4. Choose Your Starting Point. Perhaps not all of your task is unpleasant or some parts of it are easier than others. Start with aspects of the job you don't mind, or perhaps even like. If you are creative and pick the easiest place to start, your momentum will carry you forward through the difficult parts to completion.
5. Reward Yourself for Getting Done. Create an incentive for doing that job you've been avoiding. A steak dinner, a new shirt or blouse, or some other extra gives you something attractive to work for. Knowing there is a bonus waiting for you makes your resistance easier to overcome.

In the final analysis, two important aspects of procrastination are immutable. First, most of the time you are going to have to do the job anyway. Many people procrastinate because they learned in childhood or in married life that if things were put off long enough, someone else (parent or spouse) would finally do it. In your profession, this is clearly not the case and avoiding your legitimate responsibilities only hurts you.

Second, recognize that the act of procrastination, no matter what the cause, creates inner turmoil and lowers your self-esteem. Why allow those feelings to rule you, especially if you are going to have to do the work anyway? It saves you a great deal of emotional unpleasantness to short-circuit procrastination and get that key job done.

Bruce A. Baldwin is a psychologist in private practice in Wilmington, North Carolina. He also heads Direction Dynamics, a consulting firm.

Part VII
A PRACTICAL APPROACH: TECHNIQUES AND TECHNOLOGY

49.
SELF-MANAGEMENT:
KEY TO MANAGING YOUR TIME
An Interview with R. Alec Mackenzie

Dale Rhodabarger

There are no easy ways or shortcuts in mastering time. Time management is a very personal thing. You must select from the suggestions offered and fit them to your needs.

Q: Most Americans have been brought up to believe that the harder they work, the more they accomplish in life. What do you think of that, Dr. Mackenzie?

A: It's a myth. The adage, "Work smarter, not harder," is the recognition of the fallacy. Care must be exercised to distinguish between activity for its own sake and activity that gets results.

Q: Do most people need more time to do what they want to do?

A: Only one in a hundred will say they have enough time. Most people say they need from ten to 50 percent more. This view is alarming when we realize a startling fact about time—there *isn't* any more of it. Each of us has all the time there is.

Q: Then what's the problem?

A: The problem lies within ourselves. It's not how much we have but, rather, how well we utilize the time we have. Time is a unique resource. It cannot be accumulated like money; we are forced to spend it, whether we choose to or not, and at a fixed rate of 60 seconds every minute. Of all resources, time appears to be the least understood and most mismanaged.

Q: How, then, does one manage time?

A: In the strict sense, one does not. The minute hand is beyond our control. So it's a question not of managing the clock but of managing ourselves with respect to the clock. Once we see this principle, we understand why the management of time brings us face to face with what seem to be a staggering number of problems.

Q: Do outside influences cause the most waste of an executive's time?

A: When asked to identify their major time-wasters, most people will first list those that can be blamed on others. With a brief analysis, however, we see that virtually every time-waster can be influenced by ourselves. For instance, we tend to blame the time we waste on telephone interruptions by those people calling us. But it is we who are choosing to answer the phone. A good secretary will handle the major part of this problem by answering questions or taking call-backs at a time convenient for the executive.

Q: Do you know the top time-wasters of executives?

A: Yes. In order of importance they're telephone interruptions, overscheduling, paperwork and a cluttered desk, drop-in visitors, meetings, incomplete information, crises, fatigue, attempting too much at once, reading, team conflict, and work addiction.

Q: How can a person know if his trouble comes from himself?

A: Realistic self-appraisal isn't easy. The less secure one feels, the less inclined he is to to pursue this analysis. First, take a time inventory or log. It can yield an amazing revelation of the great portions of time you're wasting—and provide the determination to manage yourself more effectively.

Also, set your goals for each day. Write them down. As the day progresses, record the results achieved. This is part of your log. Memory is deceptive, and it's easy to deceive yourself, so record how you spend your time as you go along. Keep the log for a week or two, and at the end of that time you'll be better able to pinpoint your time-wasters.

Q: How serious is procrastination as a time-waster?

A: It's a close relative of incompetence and a handmaiden of inefficiency. Procrastinators become interruption-prone. They actually invite interruptions. Time slippage occurs in not getting started, discussions, disorganization, paperwork, overinvolvement in details, and office trivia. The procrastinator induces crisis situations and tension. Countering these bad habits requires self-discipline and perseverance.

Q: What are your feelings about working under pressure?

A: Almost everyone thinks he works best under pressure. We wait, delay, procrastinate—until the pressure forces us into action. The problem may be really deeper—a lack of internal motivation to get the job done, especially the unpleasant job.

Q: Is learning to say "No" a problem with most people?

A: Every project is on somebody's must list. Because most people don't like to say "No" they establish priorities and then add "just a little bit" of 85 things, ending up leaving most of the work undone. The greatest time-saving word in the English language is the little two-letter word "No." The key is to say it first, then give your reasons and suggest alternatives. If you give excuses first, you feel guilty when they're answered—and you often wind up saying, "Yes."

Q: How can the office be made more time-efficient?

A: The handy location of equipment and supplies in greatest demand is essential. All personnel should have the best equipment the enterprise can afford to get the job done.

Uncomfortable seating and dim lighting can lead to physical fatigue. Replacing a secretarial chair that doesn't provide the proper back support may be one of the most valuable investments. Such a simple item as a shoulder support for the telephone becomes an extremely useful tool.

A poor filing system is a constant irritation to staff people and a monumental time-waster in terms of retrieving information. Secretaries take vacations and fall sick, and for these absences alone it's imperative that the filing system be understandable.

Q: What's the best way to handle telephone interruptions?

A: Courtesy need not extend to the point of making the telephone the master instead of the servant. An inability to terminate conversations and a fear of offending people by having calls screened are frequently at fault.

The secretary must have the authority to screen all calls. She should say the executive is busy and will return the call later, unless it's a real emergency. This step allows the executive to return calls at a time convenient for him. Also, he's better prepared to respond, since his secretary will know the purpose of the call and give him necessary information.

The secretary should also place all outgoing calls, to avoid time lost in failing to get through.

Q: Do you think your time-management suggestions will be easy for executives to follow?

A: No. There are no easy ways or shortcuts in mastering time. You have to resolve to make the most of the limited time you have. Time management is a very personal thing. You must select from the suggestions offered and fit them to your needs.

It's human nature to look to others and conditions outside ourselves as the causes of our misfortunes. It takes a painful reassessment, and a willingness to be self-critical, to see how much ineffectiveness is caused by ourselves.

BASIC TIME-SAVING DEVICES

"*Keep a pocket or desk diary with you.* This surely beats jotting notes on scraps of paper, three-by-five cards, or paper napkins from a restaurant."

"*Don't start off a call with, 'Hi, Joe. How are you?'* This is an invitation to a long conversation on current events, family life, golf, vacation and so forth. A better start might be, 'Hi, Joe. I know you're busy. I have just one question.' Learn how to terminate conversations. Consider the telephone as a message machine and get off the line promptly."

"You have to ask yourself some questions. Which of your time-wasters are generated by you? Which are generated externally, by events or by other people? Of those generated externally, which could you control or at least influence? When you have answered these questions thoughtfully, you may see that in you lie both the major causes and the major solutions of your problems with wasted time. If so, you will doubtless come to this conclusion: At the heart of time management is management of self."

Dale Rhodabarger is senior editor for Computer Decisions. *R. Alec Mackenzie heads Alec Mackenzie and Associates, Greenwich, New York. He is a lawyer and internationally known lecturer and author on time management. He is the author of* The Time Trap.

50.
SUCCESSFUL TIME-MANAGEMENT TECHNIQUES FOR SMALL BUSINESSES

Linda Jane Coleman
Virginia Cavanagh Neri

Effective management of time is important for all businesses, but to the small business person who wears many hats, it is crucial to the success of his/her organization.

Time management is a growing concern of small businesses. Approximately 50 entrepreneurs who recently attended a time-management seminar for small wholesalers (businesses doing under $3 million a year and varying in size from five employees to 30) expressed the need to learn how to manage their time more effectively.

A survey of the audience determined that the biggest time-management problems facing small businesses are:

1. constant telephone interruptions;
2. too much time spent putting out fires;
3. never having enough time to finish a project in one sitting;
4. lack of time for long range planning;
5. personal disorganization, and
6. the inability to delegate effectively.

In order to make forward progress, hard work and planning are mandatory. Being caught up in the day in and day out "fire-fighting" and "routine" activities stifles time and energy for short- and long-term planning. With a competitive environment, success is impossible without setting goals and laying out plans to reach those goals.

TIME MANAGEMENT STRATEGIES

Set Objectives

"When the goal of direction is uncertain, it is impossible to know whether what you are doing is effective, or a waste of time."[1] Set both short-term and long-term goals. Long-term goals (five years or more) are important because they enable the entrepreneur to foresee his/her future. Short-term goals (one month to five years) are necessary steps toward achieving those long-term goals.

It is important that objectives be clearly stated and prioritized so that the means of achieving those objectives become evident. This enables the entrepreneur to streamline the decision-making process, especially when a number of alternatives are possible. By comparing a projected outcome with a prioritized set of objectives, the most effective choice is often readily recognized.

An important aspect of objective setting, which is too often overlooked, is establishing emergency or crisis priorities. Crisis situations can be avoided by crisis planning. Often, circumstances that are likely to lead to a crisis can be anticipated. Having a plan of action ready will enable the entrepreneur to correct the situation immediately and save valuable time. Also, documentation of how the crisis was handled will be priceless if the situation should repeat itself.

Prioritize Tasks

Once company objectives and goals have been set, tasks can be prioritized that lead to their accomplishment. Alan Lakein, author of *How to Get Control of Your Time and Your Life*, suggests prioritizing task according to "A," "B" and "C."[2] "A" items are those that cannot wait. These tasks should be done first since they are the most important, even if it means breaking them down into manageable size(s). "B" items are important but not as important as "A" items, and should be worked in as a break from the "As." "C" items are trivial items—junk mail and things that do not have to be done right away. Lakein suggests starting a "trivial drawer" to file items like junk mail. When the small-business person has a break from the high-stress tasks of business, it's a good time to go through the trivial drawer and use the time for unwinding. It is easy to turn to the "Cs," as they are less demanding, but it is important to remember that the "As" are "progress" (i.e., planning) and the "Bs" often intermediate, steps toward that progress.

Get Organized

Personal disorganization can be disastrous to the small-business person. An organized workspace and an absence of clutter can add to productivity. The phone should be within reach so that it is possible to answer it quickly and work at the same time. Only the frequently used supplies and files should be on the desk. Keep other things back where they belong, out of the way. The less on the desk, the easier it is to concentrate on the job at hand. The files to which the entrepreneur often needs access should be within reach. The files that store infrequently used records can be located across the room or in the secretary's office and pulled when needed.

It is not necessary to open every piece of mail. Junk mail is a heavy contributor to clutter. Learning to throw out junk mail can be a good habit. Sometimes it can be circulated to someone to whom it may be of interest.

Stop Procrastinating

Procrastinating is a major time waster in small businesses as well as in large businesses. Setting deadlines reduces procrastination. If deadlines for tasks are set, they will be accomplished. Without deadlines, tasks can take double the time necessary. The entrepreneur should encourage him- or herself to do an unpleasant task for 20 minutes even if it is a hated task. The task may not be as bad as it was thought (it might even be enjoyable). Learn to work on one thing at a time by blocking out work schedules. Not all tasks can be completed in eight hours (even if one had eight continuous hours to spend on a job). Decide to spend one or two hours each day on one job and block out this time every day until the task is completed.

Block Out Time

Lakein suggests a period of undisturbed time (30 to 60 minutes) each day when there are to be no interruptions. Let the people in the work environment know that this time is to be respected. It may be beneficial to encourage others in the office to do it as well. During the daily undisturbed period do those things which require concentration and quiet. Complete tasks that are behind schedule or plan for tomorrow or next year. Many small-business people find that by setting aside the same hour every day they have time to plan and accomplish the tasks that are key to the success of their organizations.

Learn to Delegate

When one wears many hats, there exists a tendency to want to "do it all." Even planning does not change the fact that there are only 24 hours in a day. In order to accomplish the goals for the organization, it is imperative to delegate responsibilities.

Delegate decisions that occur often. With clear objectives and plans, recurring decisions need not take up time. Activities that the entrepreneur is not qualified to handle should also be delegated. There is no sense in spending time on tasks that cannot be done successfully. Just because one person does not like certain activities does not mean others will not. Delegate these responsibilities to others. The entrepreneur should delegate the tasks that over specialize and under specialize him/her.

The entrepreneur's greatest duty is managing. Activities for which there is no defined goal should not be delegated. Duplicated responsibilities should be examined and clarified. Disciplinary activities should not be delegated. These tasks should be handled by the owner/operator. Also, decisions which involve the major objectives of the organization should not be delegated nor complete responsibility given to anyone, no matter how competent.

Plan Every Day

In order to be a successful business person and run a successful business, planning is an all-important factor. Every day must be planned, and the plan should be followed. Set aside time at the beginning to determine which tasks are necessary to achieve the company's goals. Have a checklist and mark the daily activities according to urgency. Mark them off upon completion. Stick to the plan as much as possible.

CONCLUSION

Setting objectives, prioritizing tasks and working effectively are more productive uses of time. Becoming adept at time management does not occur overnight. Old habits are not easy to change!

If managing time effectively is an "A" priority, sit down and follow the techniques listed in this article. Following these techniques is being more strategic about success and "time well spent!"

References

1. Mackenzie, R. Alec. *The Time Trap: How to Get More Done in Less Time* (New York: McGraw-Hill, 1975).

2. Lakein, A. *How to Get Control of Your Time and Your Life* (New York: Wyden, 1974).

Linda Jane Coleman and Virginia Cavanagh Neri are both associated with the University of Baltimore.

51.
TIME MANAGEMENT—
BUT WHAT ABOUT YOUR PEOPLE?

Jeanette W. Gilsdorf
Martha H. Rader

Time management is oriented to individual efficiency, not efficiency of the group and it does not promote teamwork. Don't lose sight of the fact that your primary job is to supervise the team.

Wilson knew when he saw Mr. Clark's closed door that he was on his own. Today Wilson had to decide whether or not to extend credit to a shaky but potentially profitable credit applicant. Last week when the matter came to a head, Clark had not been available. Clark had not returned his phone calls, and Wilson simply didn't have enough facts to be sure which way to go. Unable to tap his supervisor's greater experience, Wilson went back to his office with the demoralizing feeling that his best decision might very well lose money for the company.

Ever since Clark had attended a time management seminar, he had been fencing out his subordinates. He didn't intend this. But an excessive commitment to scheduling and to pre-set priorities interfered with necessary flexibility and human relations. Time management—which is a good servant but a bad master—was starting to cost.

Too Much Time Management Can Hurt. Time management can be helpful to someone who is well-intentioned but disorganized. However, it is important to realize that time management is task-oriented, not people-oriented. Whenever a supervisor needs to choose between accomplishing a task and interacting with another person on the job, time management would advise him or her to get the task done and schedule the human being in at some other time. In time management, people get put off, put away, put out. Its techniques must be used with care.

321

The phrase "time is money," indicates the extent to which time is valued in our culture. Time management is currently in vogue, and time management consultants have trained thousands of managers and other professionals in the effective use of time.

Let's look at some of the recommendations that form the foundations of time management, and at some of the problems that a too-earnest commitment to time management can cause.

Keep track of where your time is going. Keeping a time log can be helpful, but a supervisor should also realize and accept the idea that some time blocks on his log will say things like "chatted with Cal about his daughter's operation." Some aspects of home life influence people's outlook on their work life, and often work-related topics need some conversational preliminaries. Supervisors manage people, not just tasks, and a supervisor who has a reputation for being too task-oriented may be disliked by his or her subordinates. An effective supervisor must be sensitive to the needs of people in order to develop good working relationships with them. Time spent in developing good relationships with others is not merely wasted time, as time management consultants imply. Although you should periodically "audit" your use of time to make sure it is spent productively, do not be disturbed if some blocks appear to have been spent on personal topics and small talk.

Have a closed-door policy for certain hours every day. Recall the story at the beginning of this article. Wilson, despite several tries, could not reach Clark. Their schedules conflicted, and Clark's inaccessibility was likely to cost the company both money and morale. Although supervisors who follow this dictum may gain efficiency for themselves, they may be making efficiency impossible for the employee who needs some information in order to complete a task. If you close the avenues by which subordinates can seek information, you will be increasing the likelihood that employees will make mistakes.

Have phone calls and mail screened. This procedure presupposes that the secretary's judgment is as good as the supervisor's. Sometimes a secretary will inadvertently fence out an important call. The results will be cold fury on the part of the caller, who might be a client or potential customer. The resultant bad feeling can be costly in terms of dollars, public relations and/or employee morale.

Observe the 80-20 rule. Eighty percent of the value comes from only 20 percent of the sources. Focus on the 20 percent; ignore the 80 percent if you can. If this precept is applied to your employees, four out of five subordinates will be snubbed frequently and their needs ignored. This system is not only undemocratic, but also advocates blatant favoritism. And if the 80-20 rule is applied system-wide, then entire departments with staff functions (accounting, personnel, public relations, office management, word processing, etc.) would be classified as non-productive and would be ignored. This rule is practically guaranteed to cause 80 percent of your people to be unhappy with you and also to be dissatisfied with their jobs.

Reserve your most productive time for your most important activities. The idea is that if you are a morning person, for example, then you should schedule your most important and demanding tasks in the morning while you are at your best and arrange less demanding tasks in the afternoon. Again, this system is splendid for the person who makes the rules. He becomes unavailable to others during his most productive hours, and he schedules meetings, conferences, training sessions and so forth at his own convenience. Again, the rub is that others who need to meet with him may be giving up their prime time to do so. The supervisor can practice time management, but nobody else can.

Set your priorities: A for high-value priority, B for medium priority and C for low priority. Devote your time to the As and some Bs. Delegate or ignore the Cs. Like many of the other dicta of time management, this one also promotes a selfish disregard for the priorities of other people. A supervisor's Cs, if delegated to a subordinate, are probably going to override any As and Bs which the subordinate may have established for his or her other tasks. Also, the subordinate may not warm to the idea that his importance in the company is limited to taking care of someone else's Cs. A different potential problem arises when a subordinate requests input from the supervisor on what he considers an A item, and the supervisor doesn't accord it any higher priority than C.

Don't meet with subordinates without a specific purpose. Stringently following this advice rules out meetings held to encourage upward communication, to air grievances, and to suggest creative ideas. Lack of upward communication extinguishes initiative in subordinates, retards innovation and fosters in the supervisor the conviction that he or she has all the right answers. Time management says employees should tell the supervisor only what he or she asks them for. But a supervisor who is less rigid, and more open and accepting will not only gain productive ideas, but also enjoy the good effects of high morale among his or her subordinates.

In a meeting, stick to an agenda. To do so discourages any free interplay among minds. Countless times, the solution to a problem has been a thought, suggested by someone else's remark, made in response to someone else's idea. Minds stimulate other minds. Certainly a meeting cannot be let run rampant, but slavish adherence to an agenda can kill creativity. It also creates boredom.

Make decisions immediately. Do not procrastinate. Part of what time management enthusiasts are fond of calling procrastination involves letting a matter simmer in the decision-maker's mind. Some times deliberation is essential. Another kind of "procrastination" involves getting all the relevant information, including others' opinions, before making the decision. If the decision has much importance, it is well to recall that participatory management ensures greater commitment to making a decision work than does old-style autocratic decision making. People who have input to a decision want to help make that decision work out well.

Communicate once, clearly. Time management recommends sharp cuts in the amount of communication both sent and received. Yet communication audits indicate again and again that there is too little communication; employees say they are not getting enough information to do their jobs. Of course clarity is necessary for good communication. But just because a message seems clear to the sender doesn't necessarily ensure that it will be received, interpreted correctly or acted upon by the other person. Communication theory makes note of numerous problems that can interfere with understanding. Listeners and readers are only human. Distractions, perceptual and cultural differences, varying educational and technical backgrounds, poor memory, information overload and many other things can interfere with interpretation and follow-through. In fact, the only way to ensure that a message has been received, understood correctly and acted upon is to seek feedback from the receiver. Supervisors need to be aware that they might have to clarify or repeat the message. To a new employee—or any employee learning a new task—repetition can also be a positive reinforcement rather than just redundancy.

USE TIME MANAGEMENT JUDICIOUSLY

By no means should the concept of time management be discarded. Used judiciously, it can be the salvation of the overloaded supervisor. But though its proponents from time to time mention flexibility, the whole direction of time management can lead a user in the opposite direction, toward presetting schedules, cutting away communication and fencing out people.

Time management, especially in discussions of interruptions, speaks of keeping to "the tasks." Rarely, however, is there only one task—and tasks proceed concurrently. Most interruptions, though stopping the task temporarily, actually facilitate completion of some other tasks. The essence of a supervisor's job is to supervise people, not just tasks. And people are interdependent on one another.

Don't let time management generate a work atmosphere in which the overall efficiency of the department suffers while your own work is churned out on schedule. A supervisor who has worked to create a positive work climate in his or her unit will not wish to jeopardize morale by carrying time management too far. How extensively to use time management techniques can't really be predetermined. Each situation varies, depending on such factors as the type of organization and type of work, the workload (which usually fluctuates from time to time), the needs of the individual employee and the personality of the supervisor. Be aware, too, that it's easy to let yourself become overly enthusiastic about time management. It seems to work well for your time. However, it is oriented to individual efficiency, not efficiency of the group, and it does not promote teamwork. Don't lose sight of the fact that your primary job is to supervise the team.

A good test is to ask yourself the time management question: "What is the best use of my time right now...," then finish the question three ways:
...for myself and my goals?"
...for my subordinates and their goals?"
...for the organization and its goals?"
This test should get you thinking about the overall picture, not just the immediate task at hand, when making time management decisions.

52.
TEN STEPS TOWARD SUCCESSFUL WORK MEASUREMENT

Karl D. Hellwig

To install an effective work measurement program, supervisor and employee fear must be neutralized. This can be best accomplished by following ten basic steps.

At the outset any work measurement program is likely to encounter resistance from three groups: executives, supervisors and employees. Their opposition is a result of simple apprehension, and for a program to be successful their fears must be overcome.

Executive fear is fed from two directions. The executive is fearful that the program may expose ineffectiveness within his area of responsibility. Recriminations only aggravate the problem and increase his resistance to the program. The uncomfortable executive is pressured by subordinates who, in self-defense, speak of inaccurate measurement, the failure of the reporting vehicle, or discrimination because the program did not reach all measurable tasks and departments. Eventually his resistance turns into an outright attack upon the program.

This kind of opposition is best overcome by senior management. As long as the program is presented in a favorable light with the full support of senior management, resistance will be limited to a "wait and see" attitude. Controlling the upward pressure is also necessary to avoid a flare-up of resistance or attack.

Supervisory fear can be fed from three directions. The executive who resists the program promotes insecurity in the supervisor. Internal discomfort begins because of unknown accountability factors. Add to this the pressure from the employees reporting to the supervisor, and you have a sensitive situation. Because of the influence the supervisory level may have on the attitudes and actions of the other levels, acceptance and support are necessary at this level more than at any other for a program to be successful.

Employee fear is caused by misunderstanding, change, feelings of discrimination because others are not subject to the program, and concern whether they can measure up to the program standards. To overcome these obstacles, an open and frank attitude must be maintained by the analyst group. Employees recognize a phony attitude so it is essential that the analyst group project real concern.

To install an effective work measurement program, supervisor and employee fear must be neutralized. This can best be accomplished by following ten basic steps.

THOROUGHLY INFORM EMPLOYEES AND SUPERVISORS

Hold a general meeting with the employees and supervisor of the department to be studied. The principal objective is to quiet the fear of the unknown by explaining the program well enough to give them an understanding of what is taking place and how they will participate. It is important to show them how the program can highlight their own good performance. Explain the benefits that the program will provide for them, as well as for the company. Explain the steps to be used to establish standards. Use slides and role-playing techniques to explain the forms to be used and the activities the analyst will perform.

Tell them that their suggestions for improvements to systems and procedures will be welcomed by their supervisor and the analyst team. Encourage them to contribute all of their ideas, even if they have been submitted before. The best time to coordinate and adopt suggestions is when you are concentrating on improvement. Demonstrate how a standard will be set. Explain "leveling," and whether or not your method of setting standards is pre-leveled. Explain that standards have allowances built in which are attainable with normal effort.

Discuss the benefits with the employee. They may be loyal to the company, but unless they also receive personal benefits they will find it difficult to become enthused about the program.

Examples of the benefits they can expect are:

• reduced effort and fatigue;
• improved work stations;
• work load redistribution because of imbalance, unimportance or work below the employee's skills;
• job stability;
• performance recognition.

Open the meeting to questions and answer them as fully and honestly as possible. Resolve any doubts each individual might have concerning the program.

REVIEW AND ANALYZE OPERATIONS

Make a comprehensive review and analysis of all office operations in the department. Although often skipped, this is the most important phase of any program. Here you isolate the operations or structure in which significant cost reductions can be achieved, and determine the economic feasibility of measuring each operation.

When beginning an interview put the employee at ease and establish an easy rapport. Always present a friendly attitude, listen attentively and avoid unnecessary interruptions. Save questions until the employee has completed his immediate train of thought. Encourage the employee to offer suggestions for simplifying operations. The analysts' ideas should be discussed with the employee for their possible benefits, and to determine whether further investigation is warranted.

Make an operation list which will detail every clerical operation performed by the employee. Endeavor to get all the facts, but never question the accuracy of the information given. This can be verified at a later time and from some other source. Listen carefully and record any exceptions. Refuse to let the employee ramble; and keep the discussion on the main track. At the conclusion of the interview, make it a point to thank him for his time and help. Simple courtesies go a long way. After compiling the operations list, review and check its accuracy with the supervisor.

DEVELOP AND DISCUSS WORK SIMPLIFICATION

Review the accumulated data to determine where inconsistencies, duplication, delays and unnecessary work might be found. The analyst team should discuss the operations and all simplification suggestions to find further ideas. The ideas must be discussed with the supervisor to obtain his support, and those that are worth further investigation should be selected.

Compile the best suggestions. Organizing a presentation consists of the written description with all necessary supporting material, such as the description of operations flow charts, forms, layouts, diagrams, and cost data.

The simplified methods adopted must be designed to reduce time, effort and fatigue. Many procedures will become standardized once methods and satisfactory performance levels are known. Satisfactory performance levels, of course, will still depend upon intelligent and responsible workers.

Do your work simplification before setting standards. Avoid the duplication of effort necessary to revise a standard. When standards are based on old ways, impetus for change is relaxed and improvements can be delayed or never determined. To maximize benefits, do improvements before setting standards.

Ideas to be implemented are presented to the management level that has the authority to approve the change. It is best to begin with the suggestions received from the employees and supervisor. This will establish the proper frame of mind for the acceptance of the suggestions of the analyst team. Credit should be given to the supervisor and employees and their contribution should be emphasized. Compromises on the suggestions are acceptable, and do not destroy their value. Suggestions should be taken to a higher management level only when the returns are significant and other alternatives are exhausted.

Two classes of suggestions will usually evolve. The short-range changes can be made quickly as elimination of a basic work element. Long-range recommendations will require thorough and detailed economic justification. In some cases, a long-range recommendation may mean the discontinuance of an entire operation.

INSTRUCT THE EMPLOYEE AND INSTALL THE IMPROVED METHODS

The adopted improvements within a supervisor's own area are installed immediately. Changes which affect the work of other functional areas must be coordinated with the appropriate supervisor or manager. The analyst team is responsible for procuring all equipment and materials necessary for low-cost changes. The team, working in conjunction with the supervisor, instructs each worker in performing the operation the new way. This phase should be continued until the supervisor and the employee are satisfied that the changes are understood and functioning smoothly.

COMPILE AND CODE THE OPERATIONS LIST

Revise the preliminary operations list to reflect the changes accomplished by simplification. Arrange the final list according to the major functions of the department and then numerically code it for future reporting purposes. Review the revised list with the supervisor and manager, and answer all questions concerning the operations before beginning the next step.

STUDY AND MEASURE OPERATIONS

This is the step during which standards are established. The standard must represent an average employee working at a normal pace under normal conditions. The standard must include the time required to complete all necessary elements of the operation, including allowances for personal time, normal fatigue, rest periods and activity reporting.

The four best known techniques for work measurement are:

- Time study: employing an ordinary stopwatch. This method was used widely in 1960 but quickly fell out of use due to white-collar resistance to a blue-collar tool.
- Work sampling: a method for determining the known ratio of the development of work to the total working time by random observations carried on through a specific time period. This method is very exacting, and demands much of the analyst.
- Rated actual time: developing a standard by multiplying the output during a specified study period and applying an observed performance leveling factor.
- Predetermined time values: a method for determining standard body member movements, sometimes called *standard data*. The values may have been obtained through generally sequential movements or activities. This technique is the most widely used today.

Whatever technique is used, it is important that the employee under study have sufficient training and experience to perform the operation satisfactorily and within the prescribed system. The analysts must also be well-trained in the use of the technique to be employed. Analysts who are ill-trained or who have attitude problems will seriously impair your program.

During the course of the study, the frequency with which an element occurs within the overall standard must be determined. A separate sampling is sometimes necessary to ascertain the frequency of occurrence. This is important because the employee must receive the full time for completed items at a value for which they might normally occur. The standard must include an allowance, presented as a percentage, which reflects personal time, normal fatigue, formal rest periods and activity reporting. The usual allowance is 15 percent with amounts to about 60 minutes of a 7.5 hour work day.

Keep employee reporting as simple as possible. Determine the operations that an employee always performs on the same unit of work, and combine these into a single standard. Don't let a function by another employee or a lapse of a day or two stop you. Further, consider combining all standards into a group standard that counts only the units completed by a department or work team. Much can be done in this area to keep a measurement program alive. The sheer weight of a large number of standards can erode the acceptance that a program might otherwise enjoy.

Another cause of failure is outdated standards. A program should be maintained, otherwise lack of validity and the cost of revision will kill it. Employees will complain about programs that put them at a disadvantage. Management, on the other hand, will complain if changes have made the standards attainable even by the newest recruit. Finally, the program will cease when the cost to bring it up-to-date equals the original cost of implementation. This alone is a main cause for the discontinuance of plans two to three years old.

INSTALL ACTIVITY AND ATTENDANCE REPORTING

Installing activity reporting is not difficult. Most plans have formal reporting structures. It is necessary that an employee receive a full explanation concerning the method of reporting and as much illustration as possible. Reports submitted during the first two weeks are usually meaningless. Review the report with the employee to clear up misunderstandings and get him on the road to accurate and meaningful reporting. The individual report provides the supervisor with the performance level of each employee in a measurable job.

REPORT AND COUNSEL MANAGEMENT

A team analyst should calculate and compile reports for departmental performance levels. Some plans offer a computer package which relieves the analyst of this clerical chore. The report will tell the supervisor and manager how effective the department is, and the supervisor can determine an employee's contribution by reviewing his individual activities.

An interesting aspect of any program is the effect it has on turnover rate. The turnover rate generally falls off dramatically following the installation of a measurable plan. This is attributable to the fact that employees receive more attention than they have been used to, and begin to consider themselves important members of the firm.

It should be remembered that reports can be powerful tools. A supervisor must use them so that employees can see not only the reward for their good work but also that nonproductive employees go unrewarded—or are terminated. Otherwise, the turnover rate will climb back to its previous level. Why does the latter happen? Because you only went through the motions of establishing standards and performance reporting. Lazy employees continue to be lazy and get away with it, while the ambitious and industrious get little attention for their efforts.

Deviation should be investigated immediately to assure that standards remain fair and accurate. Since standards are statistical averages, they will point out variations which may be caused by improper reporting, unauthorized shifts of tasks, procedural changes or improper performance of the job itself. The progress of a new employee can be monitored, following a learning curve.

PLAN AND IMPROVE PERFORMANCE

In this step, the analyst team assists the supervisor in planning improvements of performance. Be fully informed of the department's operations so that reductions can be identified, while valid supporting evidence can be provided.

Use all the tools available to analyze your manpower needs. Realistic volume expectations can be used for projections of future needs, qualified by current requirements. Use a manpower analysis that records the performance level of functional areas. Adjust the performance to the desired objective of 90 or 100 percent. The difference between personnel required and the performance objective will identify the over-staffing that can be eliminated. Do this over a four week period and use the results to negotiate the manpower budget with the supervisor. Be certain that the trial period and volume statistics developed are representative.

After negotiating the budget, it is imperative that a schedule for making reductions be established. Never tell the supervisor who must be transferred or must go; allow him to make the decisions. Low performers should be moved to jobs in which they can reasonably be expected to achieve an acceptable performance. Use outright release only as a last resort. Remember, the program began by promising that no one would lose his job as a result. Within six months most low achievers will have left of their own accord and those remaining can be released without establishing uncertainty among the remaining high achievers.

IMPROVE AND CONTROL OPERATIONAL ACTIVITIES

Seek the continuing improvement and control of operations, including recommendations for long-range changes in organizations or in systems and procedures. The analyst team can help in initiating higher cost, long-range systems changes. Such changes generally require studies to determine new or revised standards. Furthermore, the analyst team must be available to a supervisor or manager for advice and counsel; their helpful attitude encourages management to seek assistance.

Your program can be a success, but will continue to be successful only by constantly reviewing and updating standards, selling and reselling the managers and supervisors on the tools and their uses, and by allowing employees to see that merit earns reward.

Karl D. Hellwig is development manager-administration, Foremost Insurance Company, Grand Rapids, Michigan.

53.
THE COMPUTER AS TIME MANAGER

Henry Weiss

Like a constantly renewable resource, time needs to be used, managed and planned to maximum benefit. Time management can be an important function of your personal computer.

It's 3:45 p.m. and you're frantically sifting through the clutter on your desk for a report due at 4 p.m. An associate hovers in your doorway, anxiously trying to get your attention. You sense that a project is on the verge of slipping away from you, washed off in a flood of telephone calls, emergency meetings and interruptions.

Is it one of those days when everything seems to go wrong? To the contrary, this is a typical day for most managers. It is what time management consultants see whenever they visit a new client. "Ask any group of managers to describe their most pressing work problem,a says New York City-based consultant Stephanie Winston, "and you're bound to hear, 'not enough hours in the day,' or 'too much to do and not enough time to do it.' The symptoms are clear: an edgy feeling that quickly becomes rage as projects fall behind schedule, multiplying stacks of paper and constant distractions."

Time cannot be created. There will never be more than a 60-minute hour, a 24-hour day or a seven-day week. For anyone who has been holding out for a change to salvage their chaotic business life, that is the bad news. On the brighter side is the infrequently pondered fact that everyone starts out with absolute, total and unrestricted access to all the time that there is. It is what happens to that access that makes the difference. Like a constantly renewable resource, time needs to be used, managed and planned to maximum benefit.

The personal computer can help. Its ability to rapidly sift, store and retrieve information in organized bundles and its interactive nature, is ideal for time management. Software publishers have obliged for years by bringing to market dozens of off-the-shelf packages with scheduling and calendar features. Recent products go a lot further: They automate and integrate the Rolodex, notepad and calculator; remind managers of impending appointments and place phone calls—some can even spot management faults. But you may not need a dedicated software package to put your computer to work on time management. Popular spreadsheet and data base management software can be pressed into service to analyze time use, and abuse, or to help implement time management principles.

Many executives are unaware of how poorly they manage their time. Winston says that the managers she sees lose, at a minimum, *an hour a day in squandered time.* "And that's a conservative estimate." Yet they are usually surprised at this assessment of their productivity. If a manager earns $50,000 a year, the company loses more than $5,000. Multiply that loss by 50 or 100 and the annual total for a large company becomes startling. The individual manager pays the price in stress, frustration and diminished accomplishment.

Even more startling are the findings of the productivity management department of Century Insurance in Stevens Point, Wisconsin. The department consults on productivity issues to Century agencies and outside companies. According to Roberto Cordero, one of the project consultants, most white-collar units operate at an efficiency level of 50 percent—that is, four hours of work for every eight-hour day. The department has been involved in hundreds of cases since its formation in 1982, and so pervasive is this finding, that the staff has dubbed it the: "4/8 Theory." Cordero also says that most managers are unaware of the extent of the time management problem.

The 4/8 phenomenon can be traced back to a nexus of problems involving planning and control. Cordero talks about empty waiting time between tasks in a project, uneven work loads and lack of delegation. Winston points to interruptions becoming a focus of activity, lack of priorities, inefficient procedures and self-sabotage, such as procrastination and perfectionism.

But the specific causes for poor time management need to be discovered in each environment and with each individual. One recently released software package, Managing Time Effectively, from Thoughtware, Inc., of Coconut Grove, Florida, attempts to do this through interactive diagnosis of a time log. This technique is used in one form or another by virtually every organizer or time consultant.

"Using a time log helps you confront yourself," says Frank Mahoney, vice president of management and organization development programs at Thoughtware, and the man responsible for the program's content. The company's approach to the time log, he explains, is to have users record every activity during the day, for at least one day, posting the time the activity began and ended, the participants, object, priority level (H-high, M-medium, L-low) and whether or not there were interruptions. Once the time log is filled in, it is analyzed, giving the users a much clearer idea of how they use time.

"There are ten areas in which the program lets you see your deficiencies," says a user of Managing Time Effectively, Vijay Mohan, manager of corporate manuals at J.C. Penney in New York. "These include priorities, interruptions, amount of control, initiative, planning, etc." Mohan purchased the program for his staff, as well as for himself. "I am hoping time management in my department will be improved by identifying the real time wasters: interruptions, distractions, procrastination. Most people don't know what the distractions are. They don't think about them, they just expect them to happen as part of the normal course of things.

When the analysis is completed, the Thoughtware tutorial suggests alternate behavior and has worksheets to help users plan ways of incorporating this behavior into their work lives. Ironically, Mohan hasn't been able to "make the time" to work with the program extensively—too many interruptions, he claims. "I now have a 'to-do list,' which I keep every day, and I handle my mail differently. It is stacked in priority order, rather than just as it came in. I also ask my secretary to screen calls."

There are other approaches to the time log. Winston, for example, the author of two books on time management and organization, believes in using this technique only to check progress after changes in organization have been made. Her method is explained in her latest book, *The Organized Executive*. She breaks the day into 15 minute intervals. For each time slot the user lists the task performed, what it applied to, who was involved, its priority (1 to 3) and a note as to whether the task was planned or involved an interruption. After a week the log is analyzed in eight ways: percentage of ad hoc get-togethers, calculation of the priority/payoff ratio, consolidation vs. fragmentation, and so on.

Winston's method is paper-based but there is no reason it can't be done with a personal computer. The log is a simple table that can be constructed with a spreadsheet, a data base management system, or a word processing program that offers basic capabilities. The advantage of creating a time log with these generic software types is that it can have any other measure the user wants to add, such as a performance rating and a ratio between priority and performance, or the number of people involved and their position.

"A basic one [log] would look like this: On the left side of the spreadsheet, running down the rows, you could list all the activities you have to perform," Cordero says. "For example, if you are a salesman, you would list such activities as visiting clients, reading reports, giving quotations, and so on. In the columns on the right you would record the estimated minutes it will take to perform each type of activity—say you figure an hour to visit a client or 30 minutes to read a report; the number of times during the day you plan to carry out each activity; the actual number of activities you perform, by category; the percentage of the actual to the plan, as well as total hours spent."

By constantly evaluating such a spreadsheet, users could see how they were performing, monitor trends and get indication on ways to increase efficiency. Cordero says the point is not to measure performance, but to see if expectations are accurate and improve planning if they aren't. "If the actual-to-plan figure is within ten percent that's pretty good; if it measures 50 percent you're really off." The productivity management team at Century uses this same diagnostic approach. It reflects the department's view that planning and scheduling are the core of the time management problem. By simply narrowing the spread between planned to actual time spent, managers can go from a 4/8 working state to a 6/8 state, Cordero claims.

Scheduling is the *raison d'etre* of programs like Time Manager, from Datamension of Northbrook, Ilinois; Shoebox, from Techland Systems, Inc., in New York City; and The Scheduler from Micro Information Systems, Inc., in Montgomeryville, Pennsylvania. As part of the scheduling process these packages let users designate the priority level of events or tasks.

The grandaddy of these packages is Time Manager. It was first released in 1979, and its checkered history since then points up both the benefits and limitations of this type of program. Initial sales were good because personal computer users wanted to do more than word processing, and an electronic calendar seemed like a natural winner. But most users soon leaned it requires a high degree of discipline to maintain the currency and accuracy of the program—and then abandoned it. Last year, Microsoft Corp., in Bellevue, Washington, stopped distributing the Apple Computer version of the program.

Marty Winston, president of Winston & Winston, Inc., a marketing, communications and consulting firm in Fort Worth, Texas, represents Time Manager's producer. He was a user of the product long before he acquired the account. "A lot of people think it's only valuable when it's up on the screen, but the last thing you need is a $3,000 calendar," he is fond of saying. If a user avoids this prejudice, "His ability to use the product can be ignited." Winston uses the computer to input schedule data and works from a printout for a selected period of time. He keeps the printout on his desk or takes it with him when he travels. "If I'm going to do a round of scheduling phone calls, I would keep Time Manager up on the screen. I'm what you call context sensitive, my tools vary with my needs."

Time Manager's key work search feature is especially appealing to Winston. "If I have to phone Wilson Jones on any given day, I can call up every previous entry with Wilson Jones on it," he says. "The tab key takes you through the retrieved entries."

Winston also uses Shoebox, which is a multiuser system with a "pre-reminder" capability. "Let's say I have a presentation to make at a conference. The system will remind me in advance by placing the conference on my calendar two to five days before it is scheduled and leaving it there until the date arrives." Shoebox can also automatically schedule repetitive appointments, like a user group meeting that might occur the first Tuesday of every month or every 10th day. This feature can be used in conjunction with the reminder feature for even better control.

The reminder or "tickler" feature is something Anita Mendez, office manager for the law firm of Mendelsohn, Heidelberg & Berr, Inc., in San Antonio, Texas, is anxious to use. At present she uses her scheduling package, The Scheduler, "to print out the docket (legal proceedings) for the month and give assignments to the attorneys." Her law firm uses another Micro Information package, ESQ-1, for time and billing functions. By having all the attorneys and paralegals log their work into ESQ throughout the day the firm's partners can tell what types of cases are the most profitable. Another benefit of the system, according to Mendez, is that "Mr. Mendelsohn can tell if an attorney is spending too much time on a project and help him to use his time more efficiently." Of course the system is used to bill clients. The two packages interface with each other, so The Scheduler can get its clients information from ESQ.

Mendez represents a vanishing breed of user. She is the last client of Counselor Systems, Inc., the Austin, Texas, firm that installed the system, to still use it. "I can sell them every time," says Counselor Systems' president Rick Cloud, "but people weren't using them. Quite frankly I felt guilty; I even took some back." Cloud now offers to loan the package until his turnkey users see if they want to buy it, but he hasn't had any takers to date. In spite of this negative sales history, Cloud insists the fault is not with the package, but with the users. "The system is only as good as the data you put into it," he says. "Most people just don't have the discipline. Used properly it can be very helpful."

Some disillusioned users of scheduling packages have moved on to the greater promise of more comprehensive systems. Their motives are supported by experts like Winston and Cordero who insist that time is only one element in the productivity problem white-collar workers face. One such package is The Desk Organizer (recently upgraded) from Conceptual Instruments Co., of Philadelphia, Pennsylvania. While it also provides scheduling capabilities, it does quite a bit more. It automates a user's Rolodex and it will even place calls if a modem is attached. It has extensive note taking capability, allowing up to 2,500 characters, or about two pages of business test; it also has electronic stamps, an alarm and calculator. There also is an embedded program-switching capability, called Meta. "It organizes your whole life without interfering with the other uses of a $4,000 to $5,000 machine," says Fred Collopy, president of Conceptual Instruments.

Benjamin Cowgill, a litigation attorney at Ashland Oil, Inc., in Lexington, Kentucky, became intrigued with the Desk Organizer after seeing it listed in a software guide. "From the sound of it I thought to myself, 'this is exactly what I need.'" But to use the package Cowgill had to wait months until Conceptual Instruments brought out a hard disk version—he uses an IBM XT with 320k of memory.

"Desk Organizer is ideally suited for calendar keeping and time recording functions," he says. "And the capacity of the program to run with other programs laying in the background is very nice. For example, I do a lot of word processing at my desk, drafting lengthy documents. If not for the Meta function I would have to go through a series of steps to get from one to the other. But with it, I can jump to my calendar and then jump right back to the precise place in the document where I had left off." Cowgill uses his computer continuously throughout the day, so the time saved in not having to switch disks and enter search commands is important to him. Other programs that are similar to Desk Organizer include Asher, from Wilcom, Inc., in Roswell, Georgia, and Get Organized, from Electronic Arts in San Mateo, California (both of which were only recently introduced); Sidekick, from Borland International in Scotts Valley, California; and Spotlight, from Software Arts in Wellesley, Massachusetts.

Packages such as Time Manager and Shoebox can also be used with other programs by adding a switching package. Winston uses Multijob from D&L Consultants, which allows him to keep Time Manager in one of three partitions in memory.

Cowgill uses the R:base data base management system to maintain his case information; before he turned to Desk Organizer he also used it for time management organization of his case information. He had set up a simple scheduling data base in which each record consisted of five fields: the case name, case number, date of the court appearance or filing deadline, a brief description of the pending action and a reminder date. "I could come in each morning and call up that data base by the date, pulling up my schedule and all the ticklers (reminder dates) just as I would if I were using three-by-five cards and a reminder box."

Because R:base is a relational system he can connect the information in his scheduling data base with his main case reference data base and come up with some interesting analytical possibilities. The link between the data bases is the case number. "Once you have a lot of data in both you can develop reports on how you use time. For example, I could see how many appointments I had on projects that involve more than $100,000 against projects that involve less than $100,000."

If a user were to maintain additional data bases, perhaps a time log and a performance appraisal log, even more revealing reports could be produced. Users would be able to tell if unscheduled events regularly intrude on their plans, if they try to manage too many high priority tasks at once, if there is too much lag time between the start of a project and its completion, if too much time is spent on activities unrelated to the user's primary responsibilities, etc. This analytic ability is more sophisticated than what is available in packages like Thoughtware because the user can develop new ad hoc queries all the time and create his own approach to keeping data.

According to Cowgill, it isn't difficult to create such an interwoven data base system. "Setting up a data base with a good data base management system would take no more than five to ten minutes at the keyboard, and maybe a half-hour beforehand deciding exactly how it was to be designed," he says. "It's important to consider how you might want the data retrieved so that enough links are built in. R:base is simple because it uses a very grammatical search terminology and because it allows for a contained term search instead of only allowing exact match searching (picking out any field of information that contains a term, even if there is other information in that field, as opposed to picking fields that match a term exactly and contain nothing else)."

In moving to Desk Organizer for his basic scheduling needs, Cowgill has sacrificed some of the analytical capability he had, but he found it too laborious to type in a full search request with R:base when someone was on the phone trying to arrange an appointment. "For the continuous way I use the computer it became too cumbersome. But I am no longer able to review my time in the way I like." This sacrifice is partly ameliorated by the fact that Cowgill can get some analyses from the company's mainframe. His secretary enters his basic time information into the system for billing purposes. Cowgill still uses R:base to maintain his case information.

One other type of software has some time management functionality: project managers. These products include MicroGnatt, from Westico, Inc., in Norwalk, Connecticut, Microsoft Project from Microsoft; Harvard Project Manager, from Harvard Software, Inc., in Harvard, Massachusetts, or Pertmaster, from Westminster Software, Inc., in Menlo Park, California. These products are generally intended for large projects with a great many tasks, some serial in nature, others parallel. But they can be used for simpler projects.

Since time is a fundamental resource in any project, planning for time use is a primary function of project management software. However, most packages will not split time up into smaller units than an hour. In spite of this limitation, project managers can be very useful in organizing a project so time is used efficiently.

Regardless of whether you use a project management or organizing package, a spreadsheet or a data base management program, time management can be an important function of your personal computer. For, as the father of modern business theory, Peter F. Drucker, says in his book, *The Effective Executive*, "Time is the scarcest resource and unless it is managed, nothing else can be."

Henry Weiss is an associate editor for Personal Computing.

54.
VIDEO TELECONFERENCING
CUTS COSTS, BOOSTS PRODUCTIVITY

John Tyson

Video meetings not only can mean more people involved in the process, but also less time needed by a production team to do the job.

For an increasing number of companies video teleconferencing is reducing travel costs, boosting productivity and improving the quality of management decision making. According to Quantum Science, more than 210 video teleconferencing systems currently are in active use in the U.S. by some 75 companies, of which 30 are among the *Fortune* 1,000. Though many corporate giants have reaped its rewards, smaller companies such as Hambrecht & Quist, the San Franciso-based investment banking firm, have made a major commitment to video teleconferencing.

San Franciso-to-New York video transmission costs have dropped to $750 an hour compared to a round-trip airline ticket, during peak business hours, of around $900. Transmission rates as low as $100 per hour between these two key points are being predicted by industry observers.

"A long-distance meeting between two of our offices lasting about one hour costs us between $600 and $1,200 for the transmission," explains Tim Schade, assistant vice president and director of communications services for American General Life Insurance Company, Houston. "With an average of six participants, we save $6,000 in travel costs, as well as reduce wear and tear on our people considerably."

Often video teleconferencing can do away with the necessity to travel altogether. In a move undertaken by American General to centralize all data processing in one location, DP managers were able to replace their decentralized system with one main computer through a series of video teleconferences over a period of three months. As many as 20 people at different American General offices participated in the elaborate data processing switch. At no time in the process was a nontelevised meeting held.

ADDITIONAL BENEFITS

Video meetings are better structured, agendas are more carefully prepared and adhered to, and, in fact, video teleconferences, measured minute by minute, are invariably shorter in length than are traditional meetings.

Video teleconferencing of space shuttle flight readiness reviews at NASA have reduced meeting time from two days to five hours. The end result of better prepared, better executed and shorter meetings is not only time saved but also noticeably higher-quality decisions being arrived at faster.

"We've seen that decisions and solutions to problems happen during the teleconferences, not afterward at a second or third meeting, as was the case before video," says Joe Sobala, NASA's communications program manager.

Video teleconferences at NASA sometimes involve hundreds of people at scores of locations in meetings that often last up to six hours. "We simply did not have the input of so many of our engineers and other professionals when we had to pick and choose who would fly to distant meetings as we do when using a video format," explains Sobala.

NASA's video teleconferencing experience demonstrates the value of bringing together in video meetings people who might not otherwise become involved in the decision-making process. Video meetings can mean not only more people involved in the process, but also less time needed by a production team to do the job.

VIDEO PROBLEM-SOLVING, TRAINING

A group of engineers at Rockwell International Corporation's Commercial Electronic Operations (CEO) used the company's video teleconferencing system to help shorten design time.

Jim Kerr, director of material and business systems for CEO, says one product was introduced 30 days ahead of schedule—partially as a result of video teleconferencing between engineers at Rockwell facilities in Texas and California.

"Once the engineers at the two locations started meeting face to face in video teleconferencing, rather than simply talking by phone, work on the design started progressing much more smoothly," Kerr says.

Often, problems can be minimized when people are well prepared. Video teleconferencing plays a role in readying staff for peak efficiency.

An American General subsidiary, Maryland Casualty Company, previously flew trainers from headquarters in Baltimore to various branch locations for intensive two-week instruction of company underwriters and claims adjusters—at a typical monthly cost exceeding $14,000.

The company found that it could enhance its training program by introducing new material incrementally in quantities that could be assimilated more readily. Training programs are now teleconferenced from Baltimore to branch offices in four-hour sessions every other day.

Results from American General indicate that trainees absorb more information with higher retention than participants in video training. Under the current televised arrangement, trainers are able to present programs to all four regional offices in the same amount of time previously allocated for training at only one location.

John Tyson is president and chief executive officer of Compression Labs Inc., San Jose, California.

55.
PLANNING FOR INTERRUPTIONS: THE SCIENCE OF MANAGING THEIR EFFECT

JoAnne S. Growney

We see clearly the cost in time we must invest in organization to avoid the time costs of our interruptions. The trade-offs between organization time and interruption time should not be ignored.

How often have you been in the following situation? You have an important project to complete, but day after day ends with you muttering, "I didn't get anything done today." Usually this muttered complaint can be translated more accurately as, "I didn't make any progress today on my important project because of the frequency of also important, and even necessary, interruptions."

This article brings to light the amazing delaying power of too-frequent interruptions, and shows that their effect can be much more devastating than intuition alone would allow us to conjecture. A model is presented for use in assessing the time lost when certain interruption patterns prevail; simple remedies to increase effective use of time are suggested.

One purpose of our model is to confirm the obvious, the fact that we pay a high price in wasted time if we attempt projects that require an uninterrupted time span longer than the average length of time between interruptions. The other, more ambitious, purpose is to provide convincing evidence that the effect of interruptions can be controlled through organization. Busy people who set aside time for planning, who organize their lengthy projects into a sequence of shorter subtasks, are amply rewarded for their investment in "interruption planning."

THE PARABLE OF THE WATCHMAKERS

The cost of interruptions is perhaps most dramatically illustrated in a tale of two watchmakers attributed to Herbert A. Simon. These two, aptly named

Hora and Tempus, both produced very fine watches that came to be in great demand. Their workshop phones began to ring frequently, bringing orders from new customers. Hora prospered while Tempus became poorer and poorer and finally lost his shop.

Both men made watches that consisted of about 1,000 parts. Each time an interruption occurred—for, example, to answer the phone—the pieces currently being assembled fell apart and had to be reassembled from scratch. Hora's secret of success was that he had designed his watches so that he could put together components of about ten parts. These ten-part components, once completed, were stable and could be set aside for later use as a unit. Ten of these components were then assembled into a larger, stable sub-system. Later the assembly of the ten larger sub-systems constituted the whole watch. Tempus, on the other hand, had no stable sub-systems and lost much more than Hora in response to each interrupting phone call.

If, for either watchmaker, the probability of interruption, while any part is being added to the assembly, is $p = .01$, then, using the model that we develop below, we can estimate that the cost of interruptions to Tempus is about 39,000 times their cost to Hora.

FORMALIZATION OF THE INTERRUPTION PROBLEM

Let us suppose we have a project or task whose completion requires a sequence of A (uninterrupted time units). In the watchmaker tale, we can identify a time unit as the length of time required to add an additional part to an assembly. Thus, for Hora $A = 10$, and for Tempus $A = 1,000$. Other tasks, such as the writing of a report, may require time intervals such as three uninterrupted hours. Three uninterrupted hours may be designated also as 180 uninterrupted minutes or 18 uninterrupted 10-minute blocks. The problem context may dictate one unit as preferable.

In this analysis, we assume that interruptions are devastating in their effect. That is, we must return to the beginning of our project—no matter how much progress has been made—and start again from scratch after an interruption has occurred. Thus, if our project is a report which we have already thought of in terms of distinct chapters which can be worked on independently, then the length of time required for a chapter (not the whole report) determines our value of A. Although this assumption of the devastating effect of interruptions is a bit more rigid than what may occur in practice, it is frequently a reasonable one. It is in exactly those cases where interruptions are approximately devastating that their effect causes a problem.

To calculate the expected effect of interruptions requires a probability estimate. We let p denote the probability of an interruption, occurring at random, during any specific time interval. Alternately, $1/p$ denotes the average number of time units between interruptions. Ability to estimate p may affect our choice of units in describing A. For example, if we wish to get a three-hour task completed without interruption and we can estimate the average time between interruptions as 20 minutes, then we might think of A as a sequence of 18 ten-minute intervals, $A = 18$, with $1/p = 2$ and $p = .5$. Numerous other pairs of related A and p values are also possible.

In this model we also assume that the interruptions are independent. Where independence does not hold—i.e., in situations in which one has control over interruptions—they cause much less of a problem. They can simply be scheduled so as to allow for the needed uninterrupted time.

In summary, then, at this point we have a model in which:

A is the number of noninterruped time units required for a task.

p is the probability of an interruption during any single one of the A time units.

$1/p$ is the average number of time units between interruptions.

Furthermore, we have stipulated that interruptions are both *devastating* and *independent*.

The *cost* of an interruption is the number of time units that become wasted time because of the interruption. In the watchmaker parable, Hora pays an average cost of five time units per interruption. For Hora the interruptions can occur at any time during his assembly of ten parts and these uniformly distributed values have a mean of 5. For Tempus, on the other hand, the average number of parts assembled without interruption is $1/p = 100$, and this figure gives the cost, to him, of an interruption. In general, if $A/2 \leq 1/p$, the average interruption cost is $A/2$. In cases where $A/2 > 1/p$, the average interruption cost is $1/p$ time units. Summarizing these two cases, with C denoting the expected cost of an interruption, we have:

$$C = \text{Min } [A/2, 1/p].$$

The probability that an interruption will not occur during any specified time interval is given by $(1-p)$. Using the assumption of independence, we may calculate the probability of *no* interruptions during A consecutive time intervals to be $(1-p)^A$. This quantity may also be interpreted as the ratio of the number of completed tasks to the number of starts. For Hora, $(1-p)^A = (.99)^{10} \approx .9$. In other words, as our intuition also suggests, Hora will complete, without interruption, an average of 9 out of each 10 assemblies that he starts. For Tempus, $(1-p)^A = (.99)^{1000} \approx .000043$. Tempus will complete, without interruption, only 43 parts in 1 million, or about 1 in 23,000. The reciprocal of the ratio of the number of complete tasks to the number of starts is also of interest. This value, which we denote by N, gives an estimate of the number of starts per completed task. We have:

$$N = \frac{1}{(1-p)^A}$$

For Hora, NH $\approx$ 1.1 starts per completed assembly, and for Tempus, NT $\approx$ 23,000 starts per completed assembly.

The probability that an interruption will occur during one of the A consecutive time intervals is $1-(1-p)^A$. Multiplying this by the average cost C of each interruption gives the expected time lost per start, which we denote by S. We thus have

$$S = C (1-(1-p)^A).$$

For Hora, the average time lost for each assembly started is SH $\approx$ .48 time units. For Tempus, ST $\approx$ 100 time units.

All of the preceding has been developed to set the stage for estimating the total time that we can expect to lose in the course of a project because of interruptions. The total time lost per assembly is the product of the time lost per start and the number of starts per completed assembly. If this total interruption time is denoted by I, then we have:

$$I = SN.$$

Substituting the formulas for S and for N yields

$$I = C (1-(1-p)^A \frac{1}{(1-p)^A}$$

Finally, substitution for C, from above, gives

$$I = \frac{(\text{Min}\,[A/2,\, 1/p])\ (1-(1-p)^A)}{(1-p)^A}$$

Applying this last formula we can calculate the total time lost per assembly for our watchmakers Hora and Tempus and obtain:

$$I_H = \frac{5 \times (1-(.99)^{10})}{(.99)^{10}} \approx .53 \text{ time units;}$$

$$I_T = \frac{100 \times (1-(.99)^{1000})}{(.99)^{1000}} \approx 2,300,000 \text{ time units.}$$

(For our calculations for Tempus and Hora to be comparable we must recall that for Hora the cost is .53 time units for each of 111 subassemblies of ten parts each, and thus Hora's actual time loss due to interruptions is 111 X (.53) $\approx$ 59 time units.) Thus Tempus pays about 39,000 (2,300,000/59) times as much time in interruption cost as Hora.

The total time, which we will denote by TT, required to complete a project is the sum of the uninterrupted time required and the time lost to interruptions.

For Hora, this sum is $TT = 1110 + 59 = 1169$. In general, if there are n subtasks, each requiring A units of uninterrupted time, and if there is an interruption pattern which costs I units of time for each subtask, the formula is

$$TT - n \times (AI) = (nXA) + (nXI).$$

AN EXAMPLE ILLUSTRATING USE OF THE MODEL

In developing our model we have indicated its application to the Tempus-Hora situation; perhaps a realistic example will be more convincing.

Let us suppose that Assistant Vice President X is trying to find time to write a first draft of a report that she estimates will take her three uninterrupted hours. Because this report requires a tight logical development and intense concentration, she feels that any interruption will be devastating; that is, after an interruption, three *more* uninterrupted hours will be required to complete the draft. Although she has never kept track of the frequency of her interruptions she is, after a few moments' reflection, able to estimate that the average time between interruptions is 30 minutes. If we measure time in ten-minute blocks, then the expected number of time intervals between interruptions is $3 = 1/p$, and $p = 1/3 \approx .33$. The project thus requires $A = 18$ consecutive uninterrupted intervals (supposing the interruptions to be independent).

Using our model, Since $A/2 > 1/p$, we have $C = 3$. Then:

$$S = 3\,(1-(2/3)^{18}) \approx 3 \text{ time intervals lost per start,}$$

$$N = \frac{1}{(2/3)^{18}} \approx 1478 \text{ starts,}$$

and the time wasted on interruptions is

$$I = SN \approx 4434 \text{ 10-minute intervals.}$$

Of course, this cost figure is a ridiculous one and confirms what we might have believed at the start, that is, that Vice President X will probably *never*, under the stated circumstances, find time to get her report written.

Let's consider some variations on the problem of Vice President X. Suppose the average time between interruptions is 60 minutes; then $p = 1/6 \approx .167$.

In this case,

$$S = 6(1-(5/6)^{18}) \approx 5.77 \text{ time intervals lost per start,}$$

$$N = \frac{1}{(5/6)^{18}} \approx 26.62 \text{ starts,}$$

$$I \approx 153.60 \text{ 10-minute intervals,}$$

which is still much too high a price to pay.

Consider a different approach. (Here we return to $p - 1/3$.) Vice President X estimates that if she can find one uninterrupted hour she can organize her thoughts sufficiently so that the report can be written in six additional half-hour segments. She arrives at work one hour early to do this. After she has invested the hour of organizational time, she has reduced A from 18 to 3. For each of the six subtasks, the interruption costs may be calculated:

$$S = (3/2)(1-(2/3)^3) \approx 1.06 \text{ time intervals lost per start,}$$

$$N = \frac{1}{(2/3)^3} \approx 3.4 \text{ starts per half-hour segment,}$$

$$I \approx 1.07 \text{ time intervals lost per half-hour segment.}$$

Total interruption costs are thus $6I \approx 21.48$ 10-minute intervals (just over 3.5 case hours). This figure is still not good but represents a significant improvement.

On the other hand, if $p = 1/6$, we have:

$$S = (3/2)(1-(5/6)^3) \approx .63 \text{ time intervals lost per start,}$$

$$N = \frac{1}{(5/6)^3} \approx 1.7 \text{ starts per half-hour segment,}$$

$$I = 1.07 \text{ time intervals lost per half-hour segment.}$$

Total interruption costs are thus $6I \approx 6.42$ 10-minute intervals (just over one hour). Of course, the extra organizing hour must not be neglected in calculating total time costs.

The strategy of working early or late to cut interruption costs is frequently used by busy people in responsible positions who must juggle their time to meet two types of requirement: time for uninterruptible reflective types of activity and time for the unscheduled interruptions from which the essential fabric of dealing with people and process is woven.

While in many cases interruptions themselves cannot be controlled, some planning can enable us to gain control of their *effect*. It is not necessary for busy people to extend their working days excessively, as some do, to *avoid* interruptions. What is required, however, is that a limited amount of time be set aside for organizing lengthy projects into subtasks, so that the time available between interruptions can be well utilized, and the effect of interruptions thus controlled. Below we present some figures and formulas that can be useful in planning and in restructuring lengthy tasks to avoid paying too high a price for our interruptions.

AVERAGE TIME LOST TO INTERRUPTIONS

It is difficult to gather good data on the actual time lost on a lengthy project because of interruptions that required a return to the start. Since the interruptions were necessary, individuals have tended to view whatever effects they have observed as also necessary and have tried to cope with such a situation rather than analyze and manage it.

CONTROLLING THE EFFECT OF INTERRUPTIONS

When $1/p \approx A$ and $p < 0.5$, the interruption costs are approximately A. It is reasonable to use this to establish a practical limit on the amount of time we will ever allow ourselves to lose to interruptions. That is, a task should never be attempted without adjustment of A and/or p so that $A < 1/p$.

If we require that interruption costs shall not exceed a fixed percentage of A, then we can derive a relationship between A and p. In particular, if we wish total interruption costs not to exceed $k \times A$ (where $0 < k \leq 1$), then from the equation $I \leq k A$ we can obtain the following constraint on p and A:

$$p \leq 1 - \frac{1}{(1 + 2k)^{1/A}}$$

If a task requiring A time units is subdivided into n subtasks, each requiring A_n ($= A/n$) time units, the number of time intervals, In, then lost on interruptions is given by:

$$I_n = \frac{n(\text{Min}\,[A_n/2,\, 1/p])\,(1-(1-p)^{A}{}_N)}{(1-p)A_n}$$

Using the formula provided as a basis for calculations, tables may be simply prepared to read off:

1. Average time lost to interruptions for ranges of A and p
2. Maximum interruption probabilities for ranges of A and k
3. Expected interruption time losses (for range of p) which result from breaking down a large task into varying size subtasks

In general, the following rule of thumb (rather than calculations) may prove most useful: if the time wasted because of interruptions is not to exceed the total noninterrupted time a project will require, then A and p must be related by A < 1.p. Any situation in which A > 1/p causes excessive waste of time and, when A < 1/p, the greater the difference the better.

ASSESSING TRADE-OFFS

Ability to organize tasks to keep interruption costs to a minimum is an art rather than a science. Since organization time will be required to reduce to subtasks, the trade-off between organization time and interruption time should not be ignored. For example, when $p = 0.2$, if one hour of organizational time is required to subdivide a 20-time-unit project into 10 subtasks of duration 2 time units each, and if significantly more organizational time would be required to subdivide the project into 20 subtasks, this latter subdivision may not be worthwhile.

CONCLUSION

There is no such thing as a project that requires A uninterrupted time units—where A is large. The truth is more like this: Without an initial investment of time to organize the project, it will require A uninterrupted time units. Unstated, when we estimate the requirement of A uninterrupted time units, is an unwillingness to invest organizational time to restructure the project into a number of subtasks of shorter duration. We see clearly the cost in time we must invest in organization and the cost of not facing the time costs of our interruptions. Generally speaking, in such cases, we are trading a molehill for a mountain. We are trusting our project completion to luck, and the probabilities are not on our side.

The Tempus-Hora parable did not tell the whole story. The beginning was omitted. Sometime, long before we entered the picture, Hora invested some organizational time in which he designed his assembly process for watches in terms of small stable substructures. His investment, perhaps great, in organization time, paid off because it provided him with low interruption costs.

Go thou and do likewise!

Reference

Simon, Herbert A., *The Science of the Artificial* (Cambridge, Mass: MIT Press, 1969).

JoAnne S. Growney is with the mathematics department, Bloomsburg State College, Bloomsburg, Pennsylvania.

56.
TELECONFERENCING SYSTEMS IN ACTION

Office Administration and Automation

Teleconferencing replaces face-to-face meetings, reducing travel expenses substantially and allowing executives to make better use of their time.

Although still in its early stages as an alternative to face-to-face meetings, Honeywell Inc.'s teleconferencing system—the Honeywell Connections—is saving the company $150,000 a month in travel expenses, and is boosting productivity.

In fact, the teleconferencing concept has caught on so well since its initial implementation in early 1981 that the Minneapolis-based corporation now has ten dedicated teleconferencing rooms at various division sites, and expects to have 15 or more at sites around the country by 1986.

"The cost of transporting Honeywell people from one place to another for some routine meetings was increasing at the rate of 20 percent a year in the late 1970s," explains Dave Perm, who was instrumental in the development of the Honeywell system, "and it looked like the escalation would continue."

Although various groups within the company had been using teleconferencing for several years, until 1980 there was no formal program within the organization.

Honeywell constructed six new conference rooms designed exclusively for audio conferencing and also graphics. An interactive graphics systems called "Electronic Blackboard," from AT&T, consists of a blackboard with an embedded wire mesh that, when written on, transfers the writing over telephone lines onto a TV monitor at the other end. The conference rooms were built in early 1981 at five division headquarters sites and at corporate headquarters.

The rooms are equipped with 3M EMT 9140 digital facsimile transceivers. The EMT facsimile equipment, when used with 3M transparency makers, makes it possible for users to transmit visual images between sites for overhead projection.

The 9140, as a stand-alone device, scans the original document, converting the image to transmittable impulses, which are then sent over telephone lines. The copy is imaged completely and accurately moments later at the other end of the telephone connection. Because the information doesn't have to be typed prior to transmission, errors are virtually eliminated.

At the present time, the audio, facsimiles, and captured frame video (a slow scan TV system whereby still photos are sent live, over a normal voice grade line, and received on a monitor) are transmitted over Honeywell's private voice network. Transmission is currently analog, but will be upgraded to all-digital when the conversion to Action/Honeywell Roadrunner switches is completed.

Audio teleconferencing is used by personnel from all divisions, particularly by professionals and first- and second-level managers.

The three largest user groups in the company are in the information systems and the process control divisions, and in the purchasing department. Information systems personnel use teleconferencing primarily between Phoenix and Boston for the development of computer software, and for meetings between field engineers and factory personnel.

For process control, the system ties together hardware and software engineering groups that work together as a result of Honeywell's acquisitions. The group has a lot of multipoint meetings involving sales and sales support personnel at sales offices and prime customer locations.

Marketing personnel have also started using teleconferencing for periodic meetings to supplement the face-to-face meetings held twice a year to review bookings and sales with regard to the annual plan.

Since early 1982, Honeywell has seen a sustained increase in the number of teleconferences held that are multipoint—three or more sites. The increase was 65 percent for 1982. But by the end of the first quarter of 1983, the number had grown by another 35 percent. After using an outside service for multiple conferences initially, growing demand dictated the purchase of a teleconference bridge that can interconnect as many as 20 sites at one time. The average number of sites now participating in such teleconferences is seven.

Many of the sites use individual offices rather than dedicated conference rooms. Occasionally, non-Honeywell locations are involved, such as key vendors or customers.

Teleconference organizers are encouraged to distribute needed materials in advance. However, the ability to supply documentation at the last minute, using the facsimile transceivers as well as overhead transparencies, gives attendees that much more backup support.

"Teleconferencing has been demonstrated to be a convenient tool for getting people together to discuss common problems and activities," Prem says. "We generally meet face-to-face with our suppliers at least every six months. In preparation for these meetings, teleconferencing serves us when defining the agendas.

"There have been many occasions when we have been able to get the right people together far more cost-effectively than we could ever have arranged without teleconferencing."

Honeywell spent approximately $25,000 to $30,000 to build each of the teleconferencing rooms. Each of the dedicated rooms has recovered the initial investment through travel cost savings, in six to nine months.

"The use of captured frame video is more likely to increase as additional applications are identified," Prem explains. "At the same time, users indicate they have found audio to be quite suitable in most applications."

"Our people are pleased that they are being kept so well informed about so many things, without having to leave home," Prem says. "They don't miss the wear and tear of traveling 2,000 miles for a two-hour meeting. Also, as a result, they are able to accomplish much more in a shorter period of time. The teleconferences tend to get to the point much sooner."

57.
A GUIDE FOR MANAGING TIME

Tony Alessandra
Jim Cathcart

In time management, it's much better to aim your sights at the results than to worry about the process. Too often we get bogged down in the means and lose sight of the end.

In discussing time management, some people argue that, "What we need to be is more efficient with our time!" Other people claim, "Let's not worry so much about efficiency, let's be more effective!"

Efficiency means doing things right. Effectiveness means doing the right things. Working efficiently is doing things with least amount of wasted effort. Efficiency gets you from point A to point B via a straight line. Inefficiency goes in circles. Effectiveness means doing the things that yield results.

Many people, when learning about time management, ask the question, "Which should I work on first, efficiency or effectiveness?" In theory and practice, the best answer is to improve your effectiveness first. It's much better to aim your sights at the results than to worry about the process. Too often we get bogged down in the means and lose sight of the end.

ELIMINATING TIME WASTERS

Time wasters come from the people around you as well as from within yourself. Some time wasters are unavoidable, but reducible nonetheless. Identify the most frequent sources of time wasters in your day. As a means of comparison, we've included a list of time wasters. Many researchers find the same handful at the top of their lists, which indicates that they are problems common to all of us.

1. Scheduling less important work before more important work
2. Overpreparing for calls

3. Starting a job before thinking it through
4. Leaving jobs before they are completed
5. Doing things that can be delegated to another person
6. Doing things that can be delegated to modern equipment
7. Doing things that actually aren't a part of your real job
8. Keeping too many, too complicated, or overlapping records
9. Pursuing unqualified or low-yield prospects
10. Handling too wide a variety of duties

SETTING PRIORITIES

When setting your priorities, there are two famous laws to remember. The first is Parkinson's Law. It states that work tends to expand to fill the time allotted for its completion. Parkinson's Law makes setting priorities twice as important. If you don't know what your priorities are, your other work will expand to fill in the extra time. It will take longer for you to accomplish less.

The second law of note is Pareto's Principle. Pareto's Principle, in this situation, states that 80 percent of your results come from 20 percent of your efforts. Another way to look at it is that 80 percent of your business comes from 20 percent of your clients.

USING "TO DO" LIST

A list of "things to do" for each day and week is a valuable aid to managing your time. A "to do" list organizes your thinking and planning onto one form in the least amount of time with the maximum amount of efficiency. Such a list is especially helpful if it coincides with the recordkeeping you already do for your company. After a short time you will find yourself handling a greater volume of work without increasing your stress. You'll simply become more efficient.

As we mentioned before, Parkinson's Law states that work expands to fill the time allotted for it. Your "to do" list should, therefore, define a specific amount of time (if possible) for each activity. This will keep work from expanding.

Your activities should be listed in order of priority. Work on high priorities first. In listing the activities, it is helpful to spell out the results as well as the process. For example, you might list, "Between 12:00 and 1:00 p.m., go to manufacturers' rep luncheon and get at least three business cards from prospects." Stating when, where and what you're going to do increases your chances of doing it successfully.

As the day goes by, check off completed activities and make any notes that seem relevant. In the evening, make out a new "to do" list for the next day and include any activities you couldn't complete.

PROCRASTINATION

Procrastination is like a virus. It creeps up on you slowly, drains you of energy, and is difficult to get rid of if your resistance is low. Procrastination is a close relative of incompetence and a first cousin to inefficiency, which is why their marriage is taboo. These suggestions will help you conquer the virus.

Give yourself deadlines. In moderation, pressure motivates. Extreme pressure debilitates. Set appointments, make commitments, write out your goals, and otherwise develop the determination to succeed.

Don't duck the difficult problems. Every day we are faced with both difficult and easy tasks. Tackle the difficult ones first so that you can look forward to the easy ones. If you work on the easy ones first, you might expand the time that they take in order to avoid the difficult ones waiting for you.

Don't let perfectionism paralyze you. This is a problem which many people have when writing proposals. They sit with pad and pen in hand waiting for the right words to come out. What they are doing is avoiding the process of writing. Be prolific in your activities. You can always go back later and polish those things you're unhappy with. Better yet, you can delegate the polishing to someone else.

Because humans are so susceptible to procrastination, you must work at building up your immunity to it. Effective action is the best medicine.

HANDLING PAPERWORK

Try to answer any correspondence immediately.

If you receive a magazine, peruse it and clip out articles you intend to read. Try categorizing your reading material into three groups: articles you must read soon, articles you should read, and articles that would be nice to read.

Naturally there will be more than mail accumulating on your desk. Adopt a policy of picking up paperwork only once. This means you should not look at something and put it back down where you found it. It's much wiser to take some form of action on the item. Decide what to do with it and move it along to the next step toward completion.

YOUR USE OF DOWN TIME

Your down time includes unstructured minutes and hours during the day when you can't get anything significant accomplished. These periods arise during traffic jams, in waiting rooms, when people fail to show up for appointments, and so on. You can fill this time instead of wasting it.

You can sit and relax, meditate or levitate. You can look at your "to do" list and change it if necessary. You can think about your goals or the obstacles that you face and determine how you're going to overcome them.

Remember those articles you clipped and saved? If you carry them with you they can be read while you're waiting for someone. It's amazing how many little tasks can be done in ten-minute time slots. Down time is also useful for making phone calls, unless, of course, you're in traffic.

TELEPHONE CALLS

The telephone is, of course, one of life's greatest time savers. It saves time over writing letters, making trips, and meeting with people. It can also be a great time waster. To avoid spending more time than necessary in calling people back, follow these suggestions.

1. Determine the best time of day for you to return calls.
2. Prepare information in advance when you call back. You can pull files and gather documents which you'll need to answer the client's questions. This is obviously a time saver to you.
3. Curtail the length of your calls, when and where appropriate.
4. Be organized. List the questions or topics you wish to discuss and have them in front of you.
5. Group your calls by type. If you are making sales calls, make then all at once. This will give you the advantage of the momentum of a mind set. You'll be in a certain thinking mode and won't have to "change gears" for every call.

RELAXATION AND STRESS REDUCTION

In our goal-oriented, hyper-motivated, money-making workday we often deny ourselves the much needed periods of relaxation. Like a high-powered sports car, we can be very impressive at high speeds but sacrifice distance, efficiency and physical integrity in the process. Our bodies and minds are designed to work well if they are not overtaxed. Frequent periods of relaxation and stress reduction are important to the longevity of our bodies and minds.

All too often the sacred coffee break is abused rather than maximized. People become focused on the process rather than the desired results of the break. A coffee or lunch break should be used as a time to relax so that you are more effective when you return to work. The relaxation you seek during a break should achieve three things:

1. It should provide distraction and get your mind off the job.
2. It should alleviate tension.
3. It should be short enough not to severely interfere with your work-day but long enough to provide you with some benefits.

There is no denying the importance of relaxation, despite its appearing unproductive.

CHANGE YOUR BAD HABITS

Managing your time efficiently and effectively will require some changes in your behavior and thinking. Those changes require practice.

Giant studies, when looked at closely, are made up of many small steps. In overhauling your management of time, you, too, need to take small steps. Start today doing those things that will make you a better manager of your time. After you've improved in one area, choose another and so on.

How about taking a moment, right now, to list the ideas you'd like to implement? Review this article and circle or highlight the items of most immediate value to you. Then put them on tomorrow's "to do" list for action. Remember this: If it is not affecting your actions, it is doubtful you believe it.

Tony Alessandra and Jim Cathcart are partners of Cathcart, Alessandra & Associates, a sales training company in La Jolla, California. Both are professional speakers and authors.

58.
HAVE YOU GOT THE TIME?

Forrest H. Kirkpatrick

The proper use of time often spells the difference between accomplishment or failure. Here is an interesting assortment of what the author calls "fallacies" about time.

Of all the resources available to people, time is perhaps the most discussed and least understood. Of the 24 hours in each day, only a limited number is available for the pursuit of business. Thus, time is not the problem, but, rather, what we do with the limited supply we have.

The use of time, therefore, becomes a personal management problem and proper use of it often spells the difference between accomplishment or failure.

Here is an interesting assortment of "fallacies" about time uncovered during years of studying management deportment (both inside and outside the management situation).

The fallacy of activity. In viewing the work of subordinates, managers tend to confuse activity with results. Insecure workers often work at energy levels inversely proportional to their certainty of direction and confidence of results. Activity, initially designed to achieve predetermined ends, so often becomes the end itself.

The fallacy of decision level. There is much to be said for the management principle that decisions should be made at the lowest possible level consistent with good judgment and availability of relevant facts. This principle is supported by the fact that higher-level decisions usually cost more, while lower-level decisions are based on greater familiarity with the circumstances involved.

The fallacy of delayed decisions. Arriving at the point of decision, many managers instinctively delay or procrastinate to avoid the commitment which follows. This syndrome has sometimes been termed "paralysis of analysis." Usually, the longer a difficult decision is delayed, the more difficult it becomes to make. Then, too, each delay lessens the time available for taking corrective action if it is wrong.

The fallacy of delegation. In the end, delegation saves time, but initially it takes time for planning what should be delegated: selecting and training staff to accept responsibility, communicating expectations, coaching and counseling for improved performance, involving the team in decisions affecting their work, and measuring and rewarding results accomplished. Ultimately, delegation saves time if done effectively.

The fallacy of the overworked manager. Many management men acquire illusions of indispensability. Their refusal to let others accept some responsibility brings mountains of paperwork to their desks; preoccupation with detail adds further clutter. Concluding that the enterprise could not survive without their continuous attention, they forego vacations, work long days and weekends and wonder why they are not properly appreciated.

The fallacy of hard work. The time-management principle of planning has proven that every hour spent in effective planning saves three to four in execution and ensures better results. The key to the hard work syndrome: Work smarter, not harder—get more done in less time.

To be efficient on the wrong task, or on the right task but at the wrong time, may he highly ineffective.

The fallacy of the "open door." Too often, the "open door" policy has come to mean open at all times. But being always available may make it impossible for a manager to get his own work done, to think through his own objectives and priorities, to concentrate on getting his own tasks accomplished. Effective managers agree on the need for planned unavailability.

The fallacy of time-saving. Prematurely terminating an important conversation in the interests of meeting another deadline may leave a problem unresolved, only to erupt in a later crisis. Hastening a decision without the critical facts has often returned to plague a hasty decision-maker. Initiating action prematurely on a project without thorough analysis of alternative courses may later be revealed as the cause for taking the least desirable path—ultimately wasting much time, effort and money.

David Sarnoff once admonished: "If you don't have time to do it right, when will you have time to do it over?"

The fallacy of time shortage. Time shortage is an illusion resulting generally from such forms of mismanagement as attempting too much in too little time, inability to say "no" to outside distractions, setting or accepting unrealistic time estimates, and confusing priorities by working on second things first.

To say that time flies is to say that we are managing things in such a way that it seems to fly. Through inadequate planning and other comparable managerial mistakes, we are leaving ourselves with too much to do in too little time.

The fallacy that time is against us. The time-harried manager who is never caught up, who is busy fighting fires and missing deadlines, will always view time as an enemy. Pogo put it well: "We has met the enemy, and they is us." Time is on our side, the moment we organize it.

Forrest H. Kirkpatrick is visiting professor of management at West Virginia University, Wheeling, West Virginia.

59.
PARKINSON'S LAW REVISITED

Jean-Baptiste Leon Say

Work expands to fill the space provided for its recording.

In the early morning mist, the industrial engineer carefully guided his gray sedan through the gate in the chain link fence, wheeled it into a parking spot hidden between two large delivery vans, and got out, quietly closing the door behind him. As he slipped in a side entrance, he thought, "A service industry...this should be easy...they don't know me here!"

The industrial engineer (IE) was going to carry out a work study in a company that provided services to the transportation industry. When a vehicle requested one or another of the services that the company provided, a small team of employees went into action, each providing some part of the requested work. To some extent the employees were interchangeable, and often chance or the pressure of work would lead to some exchange of tasks among workers. If a number of vehicles appeared and requested service, some queueing might occur, although, in general, work went on simultaneously on all vehicles, with some degradation in the speed of the service. In slack periods the employees completed records, adjusted their equipment, read the service manuals, and...rumor had it that sometimes they were idle.

The company was happy with its employees, but expected an increase in business over the next few years, and wanted to know the extent to which this would require an increase in personnel. The IE proposed a simple group timing technique in which the elementary tasks usually undertaken by one or another of the employees are listed on a form. An observer is then posted in the work area and every 60 seconds he notes which elementary task is being undertaken by each worker. The proportion of each hour taken up by one or another of the elementary tasks is taken to be that proportion of the total number of tallies marked off for that task.

In this particular application, the number and type of vehicles requiring service in each working hour would then be recorded. Next, a series of linear regressions would relate the activity levels (the tallies) to the demand for service, and thus allow estimation of the number of employees required by a given level of business.

First worker: "Hey, Ralph, who's that dude in the corner with the clipboard and the rack of pencils in the plumbing-supply plastic holder in his breast pocket?"

Second worker: "I couldn't figure him out at first, Waldo, but now I remember the face from when I worked over at the widget plant. He's doing something called a time study. Here's what we've got to do …buzz, buzz, buzz…"

The IE (thinks): "Oh, durn! I've been spotted!"

What the workers were looking for, of course, was a way to inflate the busy periods, and diminish the idle time that the IE would observe. Their problem was that they couldn't create work, because they couldn't generate the vehicle traffic. Their only degree of freedom lay in the area of the off-line tasks. While they were being observed they must have had the most complete records, the best-adjusted equipment, and the deepest knowledge of the service manuals in the land. Recording these tasks really kept the IE busy filling in his tallies.

Gentle readers, human nature is traitorous. It allows us to fall in love with those we meant to despise (and inversely), to eat what we meant to avoid, to fall into traps we have laid for others. Human nature allowed the workers to use busy-work to fill in periods that normally would have been idle. It *also* allowed them to forget to maintain the level of busy-work when any degree of real work related to the client-vehicles arose. The result was that when the regressions were done, they showed that *the amount of activity required dropped as the demand for services rose.* Forecasts based on such a model would have shown that the firm could reduce its workforce to zero if only it could double its sales!

The IE, of course, knew how to save the situation. Using a handraulic analysis of the recorded data, he found which work elements were being used to fatten the tallies, eliminated them from the analysis, and ran the regression again. He then formulated:

The Work-Study Manifestation of Parkinson's Law:

Work expands to fill the space provided for its recording.

BIBLIOGRAPHY

Anderson, R.C. and L.R. Dobyns. *Time: The Irretrievable Asset* (Los Gatos, Calif.: Correlan Publications, 1973).

Barkas, J.L. *Creative Time Management* (Englewood Cliffs, N.J.: Prentice-Hall, 1984).

Bliss, E.C. *Getting Things Done* (New York: Scribner, 1983).

Bliss, E.C. *Getting Things Done: The ABC's of Time Management* (New York: Scribner, 1976).

Bolton, J.H. *Flexible Working Hours* (New York: International Publication Service, 1971).

Burka, J. and L. Yuen. *Procrastination! Why You Do It, What to Do About It* (Reading, Mass.: Addison-Wesley, 1983).

Davenport, R. *Making Time, Making Money: A Step-By-Step Program to Set Your Goals & Achieve Success* (New York: St. Martin's, 1982).

Davidson, J. *Effective Time Management: A Practical Workbook* (New York: Human Science Press, 1978).

Douglass, M.E. and D.N. Douglass. *Manage Your Time, Manage Your Work, Manage Yourself* (New York: American Management Association, 1980).

Drucker, P. *Effective Executive* (New York: Harper & Row, 1967).

Drucker, P. *Management: Tasks, Practices, Responsibilities* (New York: Harper & Row, 1974).

Drucker, P. *People & Performance: The Best of Peter Drucker on Management* (New York: Harper & Row, 1980).

Fanning, T. and R. Fanning. *Get It All Done & Still Be Human* (Philadelphia: Chilton, 1979).

Groves, D.L. and S.L. Groves. *Developing a Time Budget* (Bowling Green, Ohio: Appalach Associates, 1978).

Hirsch, G. *Womanhours: A 21-Day Time Management Plan That Works* (New York: St. Martin's Press, 1983).

Hurley, M. *In Today, Out Today: How to Do Your Job Faster* (Englewood Cliffs, N.J.: Prentice-Hall, 1982).

Hyland, J. *The Trainer's Guide to Time Effectiveness: A Workshop* (Reading, Mass.: Addison-Wesley, 1981).

Januz, L.R. and S.K. Jones. *Time Management for Executives* (New York: Scribner, 1982).

Knaus, W. *Do It Now: How to Stop Procrastinating* (Englewood Cliffs, N.J.: Prentice-Hall, 1979).

Knaus, W. and A. Ellis. *Overcoming Procrastination* (New York: Institute for Rational Living, 1977).

Korbet, N. *Managing Time* (New York: Boardroom Books, 1980).

Laird, E. *Technique of Delegating* (New York: McGraw-Hill, 1957).

Lakein, A. *How to Get Control of Your Time & Your Life* (New York: Peter Wyden, 1973).

LeBoeuf, M. *Work Smart! How to Accomplish More in Half the Time* (New York: Warner Books, 1979).

LeBoeuf, M. *Practical Tools & Techniques of Managing Time* (Englewood Cliffs, N.J.: Prentice-Hall, 1982).

Lee, J.W. and M. Pierce. *Hour Power* (Homewood, Ill.: Dow Jones-Irwin, 1981).

Lieberman, H. and E. Rausch. *Managing & Allocating Time: Industrial* (Cranford, New Jersey: Didactic Systems, 1976).

Love, S.F. *Mastery and Management of Time* (Englewood Cliffs, N.J.: Prentice-Hall, 1978).

Mackenzie, A. and K.C. Waldo. *About Time! A Woman's Guide to Time Management* (New York: McGraw-Hill, 1981).

Mackenzie, R.A. *The Time Trap* (New York: McGraw-Hill, 1975).

Marvin, P.R. *Executive Time Management* (New York: AMACOM, 1980).

McRae, B. *Time Management* (Woodbury, N.Y.: Barron's Educational Series, to be published).

Neal, P.E. *Winning Workdays* (Washington, D.C.: Penchron Productivity Services, 1984).

Neal, R.G. *Managing Time: An Administrator's Guide* (Manassas: Neal Associates, 1982).

Nerlove, M. and D.M. Grether. *Analysis of Economic Time Series: A Synthesis* (Orlando, Fla.: Academic Press, 1979).

Niebel, B.W. *Motion & Time Study* (Homewood, Ill.: Richard D. Irwin, 1982).

Odiorne, G. *Management and the Activity Trap* (New York: Harper & Row, 1974).

Oncken, W. *Managing Management Time* (Englewood Cliffs, N.J.: Prentice-Hall, 1984).

Otnes, R.K. and L. Enochson. *Applied Time Series Analysis; Vol. 1, Basic Techniques* (New York: John Wiley, 1978).

Porat, F. *Creative Procrastination* (New York: Harper & Row, 1980).

Reynolds, H. and M.E. Tramel. *Executive Time Management* (Englewood Cliffs, N.J.: Prentice-Hall, 1979).

Rutherford, R.D. *Administrative Time Power* (Boulder, Colo.: Keneric Publishing Co., 1978).

Rutherford, R.D. *Just in Time: The Inner Game of Time Management* (New York: John Wiley, 1981).

Scollard, J.R. *No-Nonsense Management Tips for Women* (New York: Simon & Schuster, 1983).

Sharp, C. *The Economics of Time* (New York: Halsted Press, a division of John Wiley, 1981).

Simper, R. *A Practical Guide to Timetabling* (New York: State Mutual Books, 1979).

Sloan, R. *No-Nonsense Management* (New York: Macmillan, 1977).

Stokes, S.L., Jr. *It's About Time: A Practical Guide to Managing Your Most Important Resource* (New York: CBI Press, a subsidiary of Van Nostrand Reinhold, 1982).

Taylor, H. *Making Time Work for You: A Guidebook to Effective & Productive Time Management* (New York: Beaufort Books, 1982).

Webber, R. *Time & Money* (New York: Van Nostrand Reinhold, 1972).

Webber, R.A. *A Guide to Getting Things Done* (New York: Free Press, a division of Macmillan, 1984).

Webber, R.A. *Time Is Money! Tested Tactics That Conserve Time for Top Executives* (New York: Free Press, a division of Macmillan, 1980).

White, T.K. *The Technical Connection* (New York: John Wiley, 1981).

Winston, S. *Getting Organized* (New York: Warner Books, 1983).

INDEX